REFLECTIONS OF A PHYSICIST

REFLECTIONS OF A PHYSICIST

BY
P. W. BRIDGMAN

PHILOSOPHICAL LIBRARY
NEW YORK

Copyright, 1955, by the
PHILOSOPHICAL LIBRARY, INC.
15 East 40th Street, New York 16, N. Y.

PRINTED IN THE UNITED STATES OF AMERICA

PREFACE TO THE SECOND EDITION

THE FOLLOWING ten papers are here added to those in the first, 1950, edition: namely those in chapters 5, 6, 7, 8, 9, 16, 17, 24, 25, and 26. The subject matter of these new papers adapted itself to the scheme of classification adopted in the first edition, making it possible to intersperse the new papers with the old ones by merely adding the new papers at the end of the appropriate subdivisions of the preceeding arrangement, the arrangement in each subdivision being chronological.

As with the first edition, I think that none of the new papers would have been possible without the operational point of view, and these papers may likewise be regarded as examples of what that point of view may lead to. But these new papers show, I believe, another aspect, reflecting my growing concern with questions raised by the Ames "demonstrations" at Hanover and by Cybernetics and recent inquiries into the possibility of reproducing brains by machines. The pressing question is: what are the inherent limitations imposed by our thinking mechanism? What is the significance of the fact that "abstractions" and "generalizations" and the very concepts of "time" and "space" occur only in conjunction with a human nervous system? I believe that the answer to these questions, or perhaps merely a just appreciation of the significance of the questions, will lead us across a threshhold into something new and revolutionary.

SEPTEMBER, 1955

PREFACE

THIS COLLECTION of most of my non-technical writings has, I believe, a certain inner unity which might not be guessed from the titles themselves. None of these papers was written earlier than three years after the writing of my book The Logic of Modern Physics in 1926. In this book I was primarily concerned with an analysis of the new attitude toward physical concepts with which the physicist was meeting the crisis brought about by the discovery of new facts in the domains of relativity and quantum phenomena. This new attitude I characterized as "operational". The essence of the attitude is that the meanings of one's terms are to be found by an analysis of the operations which one performs in applying the term in concrete situations or in verifying the truth of statements or in finding the answers to questions. It was apparent that the operational approach was pertinent in a much wider setting than the physical phenomena to which I applied it in the book. In fact, clarification might be expected in all situations in which obscurity of meanings is one of the factors with which we have to contend, and what situations are there which do not have at least a modicum of this component?

PREFACE

The papers of this collection are the result of applying this method in a wider setting. The operational approach will be found explicitly and consciously applied in a number of the papers, but I think that it is implicit in all of them, and that none of them could have been written before I became operationally self-conscious. I am conscious of a new way of handling my mind—my thinking has a different "feel" from what it had before. Perhaps this collection will serve the purpose of enabling the reader, as he could not from the isolated papers as they appeared over a span of years, to get a little of the "feel" for himself, and to attempt to apply it to his own questionings.

The best grouping of such a variegated collection was not easily determined. I have finally classified them in five groups, although the relations within any one group are not always as close as could be wished, and arranged them chronologically within the group. The first group includes a couple of papers discussing more specifically some of the characteristics of the operational method, and a couple in which is examined in detail what I believe to be perhaps the single most drastic revision in point of view brought about by the operational approach, namely an altered appraisal of the role of the individual. The second group includes six papers in which are discussed, without mathematics or other technical apparatus, various specific applications to scientific situations outside the scope of my Logic. There might also have been included

PREFACE

here the General Principles of Operational Analysis of the first group since the burden of that paper was the application to psychology. I was much tempted to include here a paper on Mengenlehre published in Scripta Mathematica in 1934, since in this paper a different conception than the conventional one of the nature of numbers is used to give conclusions about infinite numbers which one camp of mathematicians regards as heretical. However, I resolved not to include this paper anywhere in this collection because it is on the whole rather too technical for what I conceive to be the present audience. My regret at omitting it is assuaged by the fact that in a forthcoming article scheduled for publication in the Revue Internationale de Philosophie in the fall of 1949 I take up again the question of the nature of numbers. The third group includes six papers in which the social environment of the scientist appears more or less prominently. These papers may be regarded as an amplification of various topics treated in my Intelligent Individual and Society Macmillan, 1938. The fourth section contains four papers dealing with one or another specific situation brought about by recent political changes on either the national or the international stage. These papers are not so obviously influenced by the operational approach, although I am convinced that without it I could not have written even these. Finally the last section contains two papers of a semi-prophetic character in which I examine some of the possibilities in store for the human race if it ever succeeds in developing its intelligence up to its full potentiality. I have been made keenly conscious of the need for such a development of intelligence by my own attempts to apply the operational method. For a consistent and uninhibited application of the method is not easy, and the attainment of the full potentialities of the method is only too obviously limited by inadequate intellectual power. Along the same lines as these two papers may be mentioned The Potential Intelligent Society of the Future, which has appeared as a chapter in the book published in 1949 edited by F. S. C. Northrup entitled Ideological Differences and World Order.

Perhaps the most important result of the application of the method in the social field is the emergence of a vitalized vision of the fundamental and necessary role of the individual, for the operations in terms of which all our thinking finds its meanings are operations by the individual. This results in a conception of the relation of the individual to society and of the society to the individual which affords that complete refutation of the totalitarian ideology for which we are so earnestly groping in this era. In the papers of this collection perhaps the extreme practical expression of this view of the role of the individual is contained in the "Manifesto" (page 314). Although this received some support at the time in the popular press, the consensus among my professional and academic colleagues was overwhelmingly one of disapproval. There were

PREFACE

various reasons for this disapproval. One, which appealed to my friends of a legal turn of mind, was that in a democracy it is not appropriate that any individual should arrogate to himself the privilege of acting in this way. Such action was felt not to be in accord with the "democratic process", to which I further pay my respects in Scientific Freedom and National Planning (page 320), and it was claimed that it would have been more effective and more suitable if such a statement, if it was issued at all, had been issued as the joint opinion of a representative group of physicists. It seems to me that this legalistic conception of what may be done by the individual with propriety in our political framework betrays a conception of both the state and the individual which to say the least is not operational.

I am indebted to the editors and the publishers of the various sources in which these papers were first published for their kind permission to republish. Three of the papers are here published for the first time: *The Strategy of the Social Sciences, Scientific Freedom and National Planning,* and *Sentimental Democracy and the Forgotten Physicist.*

July 1949.

TABLE OF CONTENTS

Preface v

GENERAL POINTS OF VIEW

1. Operational Analysis 1
2. Some General Principles of Operational Analysis 27
3. Science: Public or Private? 43
4. Freedom and the Individual 62
5. On "Scientific Method" 81
6. Some Implications of Recent Points of View in Physics 84
7. The Operational Aspect of Meaning ... 119
8. Science and Common Sense 134
9. Remarks on the Present State of Operationalism 160

APPLICATIONS TO SCIENTIFIC SITUATIONS

10. The New Vision of Science 167
11. Permanent Elements in the Flux of Present-Day Physics 190
12. The Recent Change of Attitude Toward the Law of Cause and Effect 206
13. Statistical Mechanics and the Second Law of Thermodynamics 236
14. The Time Scale 269
15. On the Nature and the Limitations of Cosmical Inquiries 278

CONTENTS

16. Einstein's Theories and the Operational Point of View 309
17. Impertinent Reflections on History of Science 338

Primarily Social

18. The Struggle for Intellectual Integrity .. 361
19. Society and the Intelligent Physicist ... 380
20. Science, and Its Changing Social Environment 403
21. Scientists and Social Responsibility 415
22. Science and Freedom—Reflections of a Physicist 431
23. The Strategy of the Social Sciences 441
24. Science, Materialism and the Human Spirit 452
25. The Discovery of Science 463
26. The Task Before Us 473

Specific Situations

27. "Manifesto" by a Physicist 498
28. A Challenge to Physicists 501
29. Scientific Freedom and National Planning 504
30. Sentimental Democracy and the Forgotten Physicist 516

Prophetic

31. The Prospect for Intelligence 526
32. New Vistas for Intelligence 553
    Note 569
    Acknowledgment 571
    Index 575

REFLECTIONS OF A PHYSICIST

1

OPERATIONAL ANALYSIS*

IN THE OCTOBER 1937 NUMBER of *Philosophy of Science* Lindsay has made certain criticism of the adequacy of the "operational method" of analyzing and giving meaning to the concepts of physics, documenting his criticisms chiefly from my own writings. In these criticisms he has made statements as to the method which I would by no means accept. This is not characteristic of his paper only, for I have seldom indeed seen a printed discussion of the method which I would accept as being an adequate or sometimes even fair representation of what I understand by it. It will perhaps pay therefore if I attempt to state what I conceive it to be all about, particularly since I have never attempted such a comprehensive statement and since my own ideas on the subject have been developing since I first wrote in the Logic of Modern Physics. For one reason I have hesitated to do this, for fear of seeming to subscribe to the not uncommon idea that we are dealing with some elaborate and profound new theory of the nature of knowledge or of meaning. I

*Reprinted from Philosophy of Science, 5, 114, 1938.

believe that I myself have never talked of "operationalism" or "operationism", but I have a distaste for these grandiloquent words which imply something more philosophic and esoteric than the simple thing that I see. What we are here concerned with is an observation and description of methods which at least some physicists had already, perhaps unconsciously, adopted and found successful—the practise of the methods already existed. What I have attempted is to analyze these successful methods, not to set up a philosophical system and a theory of the properties that any method *must* have if it hopes to be successful. Since I was concerned with a technique already extant, my principal method of getting others to see what the technique involved has been to exhibit examples of the technique in action, rather than to attempt any exhaustive characterization of the technique itself.

It is probably pertinent to mention the personal background of my own work. My discussion of the operational technique came only after at least ten years of more or less continuous pondering in the effort to see what was really happening in branches of physics that puzzled me. In this way I had thought through the situation in dimensional analysis, a comparatively simple field, but in which nevertheless there was a great deal of mysticism, and afterwards I had tried to see what is really involved in electromagnetic field theory, relativity theory, and those parts of quantum theory which had been developed by 1926. It was only then, after this background of my own attempts at analysis and of reading the analyses of others, that I began to see what successful analysis consists in, so that my ideas about the operational technique resulted from observation and practise of analysis. The analysis which was the object of my observation was an analysis made by physicists at a certain epoch in history, with the background of assumption and presupposition prevalent at that epoch, and with the unexpressed purposes inherent in the scientific activities of the epoch.

The analysis that was the object of observation was made for the general purpose of getting better understanding, and this in turn was seen to demand the maximum awareness of every conceivable thing that could be found in the situation. In analyzing one seeks to become aware of all the details of the physical manipulations or other happenings, and also of the details of his own thinking about these happenings in attempting to reduce them to understandability. It is a simple result of observation that the subject matter of all these attempts at understanding is activity of one sort or another, either in the perception and recognition by us of sense impressions, or in the performance by us of deliberate physical manipulation or of deliberate thought. In any event the subject of analysis is activity, and one object of analysis is to discover activities of which we had not previously been aware, and to find relationships between activities. The fact that we are concerned only with activities is reflected in a broad sense in which this matter of operations can be understood, as opposed to a more important narrow sense to be discussed presently. In this broad sense any analysis of activity is an analysis of operations. This is tautological; operations and activity here mean the same thing. The word "operation" accents the fact that the activity is usually directed activity. I report as a matter of observation that I have never come across a situation in physics, or in other fields either for that matter, in which a complete analysis of activity would not have satisfied me. We need not discuss whether there may possibly be other things to analyze, but if there are, they have not proved necessary for my purpose. Consider in particular the question of meanings, which are evidently of the greatest concern for any analytical enterprise. To know the meaning of a term used by me it is evident, I think, that I must know the conditions under which I would use the term, and conversely, to know the meaning of a term which my fellow uses, I must be able to reconstruct the conditions which compelled the use of the term by him. Analysis of the conditions attendant on the use of the term is an analysis of operations. From this point of view, *meanings are operational*.

Notice that we are not attempting to set up any theory of meaning, and do not maintain that meaning involves nothing more than operations. We are dealing with a necessary as distinguished from a sufficient characterization, in the sense of the mathematician. We are saying that unless one knows the operations one does not know the meaning. It is perhaps possible to see other elements in the complex covered by "meaning". One may perhaps be concerned with trying to account for why it is that in a given situation one should want to separate out certain particular aspects to accent by meaning. Again experience and observation determine our course. In the sorts of situation that have been of interest to me, and I judge to other physicists also, it is not necessary to be concerned with other than operational aspects of meaning. From this point of view the statement "meanings are operational" comes to be used carelessly as a *sufficient* description of the whole situation. In fact, I myself have doubtless gone further in some of my printed statements than would be justified when the statement is taken out of context. For instance, my statement on page 5 of the Logic of Modern Physics that meanings are *synonymous with operations,* was obviously going too far when taken out of context; it was in any event going farther than necessary. My own dictum is applicable to this statement of mine, namely that what a man means by a term is to be found by observing what he does with it, not by what he says about it.

The statement "meanings are operational" is so broad and general as to be tautological, and furthermore to be of little value. Operational analysis does not begin to be important until we impose certain restrictions. The situations that we analyze are practically always situations in which we are interested in accomplishing certain purposes; at the very least it is our purpose to understand. Experience has shown that certain sorts of operation are no good for accomplishing certain purposes, but that we can hope to encompass our end only by the use of restricted operations. Some of the necessary restrictions on the operations are so obvious and intuitive that we unconsciously limit the operations which we will permit ourselves in definite situations, so that if analysis discloses that the operations which we actually use in giving our meanings are drawn from outside the permitted repertory, we describe the situation by saying that the term is meaningless "because the operations do not exist". Obviously this is a narrow and a technical use of "meaningless", because from the broad point of view every term has some sort of meaning and the performance of some sort of operation was antecedent to its use. It is profitable nevertheless to permit ourselves to talk about "meaningless" terms in the narrow sense if the preconditions to which all profitable operations are subject are so intuitive and so universally accepted as to form an almost unconscious part of the background of the public using the term. Physicists of the present day do constitute a homogeneous public of this character; it is in the air that certain sorts of operation are valueless for achieving certain sorts of result. If one wants to know how many planets there are one counts them but does not ask a philosopher what is the perfect number.

OPERATIONAL ANALYSIS

It is obvious that a great deal of experience is back of the conviction that certain sorts of operation are not good operations and that others are probably safe, and as one's experience changes one's repertory of permissible operations changes also. The Greek philosophers esteemed highly certain operations which today are beneath contempt. I suppose the intellectual attitude of the present time differs most from that of the time of the Greeks in its position toward experiment and experience. Hundreds of years of attempting to find inside our own heads the necessary pattern of the external world has proved a dismal failure; we have come to feel that we can only take experience as it comes and must try to get our thinking into conformity with it.

Since experience follows no prescribable pattern, an indispensable part of the task of attempting to reduce experience to understandability is to find how to describe or reproduce that experience as accurately as possible. No detail is to be neglected as trivial until the proof has been given that it is trivial, and the only acceptable proof of triviality is an appeal to experience. In describing a "physical" experience (we all have a sufficiently common background so that the meaning of "physical" is sharp enough), observation shows that we recognize certain sorts of activity on our part as being much more definite and getting closer to what we may call the primary experience than other sorts of activity. There are certain sorts of operation that seem to us simple in the sense that when we are told to perform the operation we can go and do it unequivocally, whereas there are other operations which have perhaps just as simple a verbal expression but which nevertheless, the moment that it comes to the actual doing of them, are found to involve imprecisions and ambiguities. Thus if we are told to determine the time at which some event occurs, we can do it without ambiguity if the event occurs here beside a clock. But if the event occurs on Mars we have complications arising from corrections for the velocity of light and the distance of Mars, if we elect to determine the time on our own clock, and also ambiguities when we ask whether the time is more properly determined from our own clock or from a clock on Mars, whose rate and setting we will have to check by some sophisticated procedure. Observation shows that ambiguity is latent in any operation defined in terms of its properties, because of the inherent experimental error with which properties can be established. It seems evident enough that we should seek to reduce our descriptions of experience to unambiguous kinds of operation, and that the terms or concepts in which we frame our descriptions should be specified by such operations. Otherwise we cannot uniquely reproduce the original situation, and our attempt at description has failed. Hence arises the demand that the concepts or terms used in the description of experience be framed in terms of operations which can be unequivocally performed.

OPERATIONAL ANALYSIS

We have here no esoteric theory of the ultimate nature of concepts, nor a philosophical championing of the primacy of the "operation". We have merely a pragmatic matter, namely that we have observed after much experience that if we want to do certain kinds of things with our concepts, our concepts had better be constructed in certain ways. In fact one can see that the situation here is no different from what we always find when we push our analysis to the limit; operations are not ultimately sharp or irreducible any more than any other sort of creature. We always run into a haze eventually, and all our concepts are describable only in spiraling approximation. We can, if we want, analyze the operation which our physical experience allows us to accept for certain purposes as unanalyzable. We find that no operation is ultimately simple. We can always ask ourselves how we are sure that we are correctly performing the operation that we assume, or how we shall describe the operation to our fellow who has not had our experience. We shall probably find that in attempting to get our fellow to acquire intuitive command of our operation we have described our operation in terms of its properties, something that we must avoid wherever possible. Experience shows that the things we do can be arranged in hierarchies of complication and certainty. We analyze as far back as necessary for our purposes, and frame our concepts in terms of operations which experience suggests are simple enough for our purposes. Modern physics finds that certain operations are simple enough for its purposes while others are too complex. For the geometrical description of the objects of ordinary experience and for all the geometrical descriptions of relativity theory, the operation of determining a *coincidence* is accepted as an operation intuitively performable, which it is not necessary to analyze further. We endeavor as far as possible to build up other operations from this simple operation. Some day the discovery of new physical facts may force us to analyze the coincidence operation, but at present we do not see the necessity for it, and in fact do not see how the analysis can be made, and feel a certain security in any analysis which is reduced to this fundamental operation. In particular, we define the length of a body in terms of operations involving making coincidences of the ends of a meter stick moved successively along a body. At first every step of the procedure by which the length is measured must be uniquely specified if we are to be sure that our result is unique. We may not leave out as unessential a single detail of procedure until experience has shown that that detail makes no difference. For example, a length specified by moving the meter stick from one position to the next maintaining itself always parallel to itself must at first be distinguished from a length determined by rotating the stick through 180° for each successive position. Our present day attitude is that it is not *safe* to assume that the results of the two procedures are the same until we have proved them the same by experience.

OPERATIONAL ANALYSIS

The Greek perhaps could convince himself in his head that the two procedures *must* give the same result; we have lost his confidence in our ability to foresee the results of experience, and find it almost impossible to recapture the feeling of the Greek that he had a right to expect that he could do this sort of thing. Of course again we ultimately encounter haze; for no operation can be uniquely specified in all its details. We ultimately have to assume from sheer weariness, if nothing else, that it is not necessary to carry our specifications beyond a certain degree of refinement; the place where we draw the line is again dictated by experience. But experience has sufficiently shown that refinements which at one time were unthinkingly assumed to be without importance are actually important when the range of our experience is extended or the accuracy of our measurements is improved. Thus at one time no one thought of the necessity of distinguishing between a tactual length or an optical length. Relativity theory now shows the necessity for distinction.

This matter of different operations which give very nearly or perhaps the identical result brings up one of the strongest objections that have been made to the view of the relation of operations and concepts just described. Thus at the end of the last paragraph we spoke of a "tactual length" and an "optical length". Many people would say that these expressions are merely paraphrases for *"length measured by a tactual procedure"* and *"length measured by an optical procedure"*, and would understand by the concept "length" whatever it is that is denoted by the common word "length" in the two expressions. This is a perfectly possible point of view, but is to a large extent verbal, for every one must agree that experience shows that there are a great many cases in which obviously different operations yield the same result, and that in practise we call by a single name the common result of all the different equivalent operations. Furthermore, I think everyone would agree that for a great many practical purposes this is a most useful thing to do, and that one would be merely going out of his way to invent and use different names for different equivalent operations. But on the other hand, when one's purposes are not immediate practical applications, but when one is trying to analyze and to understand, one must seek to recover the complexity of the primitive situation. If one has shown that "optical length" and "tactual length" are equivalent, then for the purposes of analysis this is something to be remembered, perhaps by the invention of a special nomenclature like $length_1$ and $length_2$, rather than something to be deliberately forgotten by the adoption of a single term. The reason that this is something to be remembered rather than to be forgotten is that it is not *safe* to forget. The equivalence of two operations is established by experiment, and we must always adopt the attitude that the results of such an experimental proof may be subject to revision when the range or accuracy of our experience is increased.

OPERATIONAL ANALYSIS

The feeling that is is not *safe* to forget distinguishably different procedures is in the atmosphere of present day physics; it is the result of a wide experience and is not shared by anyone like the Greek whose experience is so narrow that he can still think that all experience must conform to the pattern of something that he finds in his head. All that anyone can maintain here is that for purposes of analysis and understanding it is *better* at first to employ concepts deliberately framed so as to keep in view recognizable differences of procedure. Of course later, perhaps for the purposes of some special theory, one may find it convenient to fuse the results of recognizably different operations under a single name, but it is never safe to *completely* forget what one has done.

Some people are made uncomfortable by insistence on the operational aspect of concepts because they want to make "concept" cover somehow the fact that the results of the operations have been found useful, and also the precise way in which they prove useful. This again is largely a verbal matter and a matter of taste. Perhaps "concept" can be given this extended connotation, but one certainly enormously complicates the situation by trying to do so and furthermore does not escape uncertainties arising from experimental error, for the precise use which one will make of a concept in dealing with experience may be expected to change as the range of experience changes.

We have not as yet made any explicit limitations

on the sort of operations that we should employ except that they should be unambiguous, but it has happened that our examples have involved simple "physical" manipulations such as can be performed in the laboratory, as, for example, in our description of the meaning of length. This has led to what I regard as the most wide-spread misconception with regard to the operational technique. It is often stated that the operational point of view demands that all the concepts of physics, for example, find their meaning in terms only of physical operations performed in the laboratory. Thus Lindsay states in the second paragraph of his paper: "The essential meaning of operationalism in physics is that physical concepts should be defined in terms of actual physical operations". It is true that he later qualifies this slightly, but he evidently regards the qualification as unimportant. Nothing could be further from my own attitude, in fact I think examination of my writings will show that "mental" operations have been often mentioned. It seems to me that the most superficial examination of what we do in any situation, even a situation which we might perhaps describe as predominantly "physical", shows at once that "mental" operations are involved, and further that no sharp distinction is possible between "physical" and "mental" operations. For instance, we measure the length of an object by counting the number of times that a meter stick can be brought into coincidence in a special way with the object. Is the operation of counting a "mental" or a "physical" operation? My own use of language would make the counting operation "mental", yet this is an integral part of many "physical" procedures.

By an extension of this same point of view it is often maintained (Lindsay does it) that the operational point of view demands that the physicist use no constructs in his theorizing, or in general in his efforts to understand, which do not find their meaning in exclusively physical operations. This seems to me to be a restriction for which the only justification could be that experience had shown it to be a useful restriction. But the most superficial examination of what physicists do when they theorize shows that as a matter of fact they do find it very useful to employ all sorts of constructs not defined by purely physical operations. Most of these nonphysical operations are the operations of mathematics or logic; it is particularly obvious in the case of modern wave mechanics that many of the constructs are of this sort. "Paper and pencil" operations is perhaps a suggestive name for many such operations. The variety of such possible "paper and pencil" operations is doubtless greater than the variety of conventional operations of the laboratory; the enormous wealth of such operations makes them a most fertile field for the invention of intermediate constructs. Many of the "paper and pencil" models constructed in this way are of great value. For example, my analysis of the concept of probability showed that it was to a very large extent a "paper and pencil" concept. Lindsay seems to feel that I implied that therefore it was not a useful or permissible concept, but such was by no means my intention. Of course when the ultimate object of the theory is the description of a concrete physical situation, we must demand that the ultimate outcome of the theory be expressible in terms of operations applicable in the concrete physical situation, but I can see no reason why one should not allow himself any latitude whatever in his intermediate constructions.

Whatever the nature of the concept, whether it involves the "physical" operations of the laboratory or the "paper and pencil" operations of one or another kind of construct, we must demand that the operations be such that they can be unambiguously and straightforwardly performed. This is a practical matter; no operation can be specified with complete sharpness "unambiguously and straightforwardly", but observation of what we do in meeting the situations of experience shows that as a matter of fact there are certain operations about whose performance we have no hesitation. This is true of the operations of mathematics no less than of the operations of the laboratory. One such operation, for example, is that of increasing any given integer by unity. I believe that no mathematician has the slightest question but that this operation can always be performed. There are other operations in mathematics which cannot be performed so unambiguously, such as operations involving infinity; these operations are often specified by their properties.

OPERATIONAL ANALYSIS

In mathematics much the same situation arises that arises in physics; in foundation studies, in which one wants to secure the maximum awareness of what one is doing and the maximum security that he is not involving himself in contradiction, one would do well to use only concepts whose meaning is found in such unambiguously performable operations. For in this way, just as in physics, the description of a situation in mathematics reduces to the description of an actual experience, namely the performed operations, and actual experience is not self-contradictory. Even this procedure cannot give absolute security, for there is no method of guaranteeing the future of the operations we now accept. In particular one can never be sure that at some time in the future he will not think of something which had not previously occurred to him which will make operations unsatisfactory in which no flaw is at present suspected. Even the operation of adding unity to an integer is subject to this limitation. It is merely that this technique is the best which we have.

I think there are at least two reasons why an operational analysis is important. The first is that we usually have preconceived ideas about the operational situation, picked up perhaps by imitating the assumptions which our fellows make in their use of concepts, and the analysis often shows these preconceptions to be incorrect, so that we discover that we had been trying to do things that we had not realized. The second reason is that having found what the situation is we are then in a position to utilize our experience. Experience shows that certain kinds of operation are good for certain purposes, and if our concepts do not involve the kind of operation that we had supposed, then we revise our opinion of what the concept is good for, and the use which we accordingly make of it.

Verbalizing plays an important part in the thinking of most people and, correspondingly, verbal operations are very extensively employed in thinking. Apparently most of our verbalizing arises from the endeavor to make adequate connection with experience, and accordingly, many of our verbal operations are of the greatest value in dealing with experience. In particular, practise has shown us how to use various blank verbal forms with effectiveness, as, for example: "What shall I do next?", or "Who said that?" etc., etc. Substituting in verbal forms constitutes one sort of verbal operation. The use of such verbal forms may be of great value in analyzing the operational make-up of our concepts, for in this way we can make ourselves aware of the conditions under which we would use a term. We may, for example, ask ourselves, "Would you say this or that about such and such a term?" By asking ourselves this sort of question not only do we uncover bits of "objective" knowledge of the situation which we may have in the back of our heads, but I think we also discover that we often unthinkingly try to force a concept into such a mold that we *can* say certain things about it. That is, we often make unsuspected verbal demands of our concepts. Suppose, for example, we are trying to make more precise to ourselves what we mean by "life" and "death". Various criteria that might be applied in the laboratory are proposed, but then someone says "Would you say that an organism was dead if it could be brought back to admitted life by the administration of any drug, known or unknown?" I think a great many people have a strong impulse to answer this question in the negative. By making this verbal experiment we discover that we unthinkingly use the concept of "life and death" as if it admitted certain verbal operations. But we also demand that the concept be defined in terms of "objective" operations. Common usage of language seems to show that many people have the primitive feeling that some "objective" criterion of life and death can eventually be found corresponding to the verbal demand, but I think as we grow in experience we lose the feeling that there *must* be some laboratory operation corresponding to the verbal demand. Such a feeling can have only vicious results when we want to achieve the maximum security.

It is thus evident that there may be "good" or "bad" verbal operations. Here, as always, there is no evidence that a *sharp* distinction can be drawn between "good" and "bad". It is, I think, the tacit understanding back of the usage of most terms that the meanings can eventually be reduced to non-verbal operations. In describing the situation, "verbal" may be used in the broad sense, including all sorts of verbalization, or in the narrower sense of "bad" verbalization, that is, a verbalization not adapted to its tacit purpose. A concept which is predominantly verbal only in the "bad" sense is often described as a "verbal" concept without qualification, and the sense in which "verbal" is used often has to be judged from the context.

A great many of our common inherited concepts turn out to be predominantly verbal in the narrow or bad sense, such as all the old absolutes of physics. "Absolute" length, for example, has actually been defined as "length perceived in the mind of God". Analysis will show I think that "perceived in the mind of God" is almost entirely verbal—the operations which determine its meaning are mainly the operations of saying certain things about it. To the modern physicist it is so obvious that concepts defined only in terms of verbal operations are unsuitable for meeting "objective" situations that he automatically does not consider such operations, so that he would describe the concept of "absolute" length as one for which "no operations exist", and therefore "meaningless". This leads to a certain ambiguity or even self-contradiction in talking about the operational technique. From the broad point of view all meanings are operational, and the meaning of "absolute" length is to be found in the corresponding operations, which here turn out to be verbal, whereas from the narrower point of view of the present day physicist the operations corresponding to the concept "do not exist". I think if isolated parts of my writings are juxtaposed, it would be possible to find such contradictions. Thus I have talked about the contrast between what one says about what one does and what one actually does, with the implication that what one says is not a form of doing, whereas in other places it is very definitely recognized that talking or verbalizing is certainly an activity. I think, however, that if one is on the lookout it should always be easy to judge from the context whether the broad or narrow meaning of operation is to be understood.

We have seen that as long as one is concerned only with physical or similar applications the profitable application of the operational technique is so obviously restricted to its narrower aspect that in practise one is inclined to forget the broader aspects. But when one comes to make applications to less precise situations, as to economics or law or in general to situations of predominantly social complexion, one encounters more importantly the verbal aspects and the necessity for adopting the broader point of view. In a book just issued I have discussed social matters with this technique, and I have sometimes felt my hands somewhat tied by the narrower usage of "operations" to which consistency with my earlier writings would sometimes seem to commit me. However, I do not think that there can be a serious source of misunderstanding, and that the context always makes it plain whether operation is to be understood in the broader sense of anything, mental, manual, or verbal, that can be recognized as activity, or in the narrower sense of activity that is obviously adapted to the tacit purpose.

I think that trial will convince one that no less important results are to be obtained by the application of the operational technique to social questions than to physical questions. For we nearly always have preconceptions as to what our social concepts are good for and the character of the underlying operations, and we use the concepts subject to those preconceptions, whereas analysis will often disclose that the operations which build up the concept are such that we have no right to our expectations. Analysis will often disclose that the only operations which can be found in a concept are verbal operations. There are many cases of open verbal chains; the meaning of a term is to be found in the fact that it can be combined verbally in a certain way with another term, and the meaning of the new term in its verbal combinations with still another, and so on endlessly, with never an exit into something "objective", that we do with our hands or see with our eyes or feel. [Notice that "objective" is not being used in the sense of contrasted to "subjective", but may include certain aspects of the "subjective".] The implication in the usage of a great many of our terms, however, is that ultimately there is emergence into something "objective". I think there can be no question but that we use such words as "justice" or "truth" with the implication of such ultimate objective emergence of meaning. The discovery that such emergence often does not occur, but the only operations are verbal, will I think profoundly modify our practical attitude toward the social situations to which we have been accustomed to apply the concept.

It must not be at once assumed that any concept which is almost completely verbal in this way can be of no value and must be discarded. I think there are many concepts of this character, most useful as intermediate terms in our thinking, and not to be discarded because of their verbal character, any more than the ψ function of wave mechanics is to be discarded because its value cannot be assigned at every point of space and time with the instruments of the laboratory. Clean-cut classification of terms into those which are purely verbal is not to be expected here any more than anything clean-cut is to be expected anywhere. In particular there is obviously no sharp distinction between "paper and pencil" operations and verbal operations. But there are certainly terms in which the verbal element is much more important than we would have guessed without analysis, and some of these may be of the greatest utility in every day usage. For example, if we analyze what we mean by "the past" we discover that a large part of the meaning is verbal. Most people would say that the past is such a thing that there are "facts" with respect to the past, as for example, it is a "fact" that the sun rose this morning. But if someone says to us "There is no way of proving that the entire universe was not created five minutes ago, every part of it being created in the condition that you think it had reached five minutes ago as the result of age-long evolution" we can find no method of controverting him and are made to see that the operations defining "the past" are more largely verbal than we had supposed. Although we have a concept that is to a certain extent verbal, it is nevertheless useful. This shows incidentally that our verbalisms have no automatic method of ensuring self-consistency, and that we do well to be cautious in our handling of predominantly verbal concepts.

One can envisage here a new discipline, as yet hardly begun, of the detailed analysis of the operations involved in every-day concepts. Such a discipline will involve in the first place the selection of those operations which are to be recognized as fundamental—probably the selection of the best operations for this purpose will involve a good deal of trial, and there will be delicate decisions to make. For instance, in giving meaning to the future I think the operations of making plans or drawing up programs or forming expectations for the future must be recognized. It will be easy to fritter away a good deal of analytical energy in discussing to what extent this operation of planning is verbal, a question which it seems to me is unimportant.

Not only may there be verbal terms useful as intermediates in our thinking, but in society as at present constituted a great many terms about which we are mistaken in feeling that the operations are "objective", whereas examination shows that they are verbal, are nevertheless of the greatest social use because by the use of them with their mistaken implications we can procure the action from our fellows which we desire. However, in spite of their usefulness, I think that the common tacit ideals with respect to language are such that most people would feel that such terms are illegitimate, and that they should be discarded, once their operational makeup had been recognized. Most usage of such terms may perhaps eventually disappear if the race ever achieves a higher intellectual plane, but that it will be a slow process one may see by imagining with what enthusiasm demagogues would welcome the abolition of such terms.

In summary, it appears that we are not dealing with anything new or definite enough to be dignified by being called any kind of an "ism". It would be difficult to exhaustively characterize the operational technique of analysis; it is more of the nature of an art to be learned by the practise of it and by observation of its practise by others. It certainly does not attempt to set up a theory of meaning or to be an epistemology. In so far as it is concerned with meanings it is concerned with necessary as distinguished from sufficient conditions. So far as it is anything definite at all, it is a technique of analysis which endeavors to attain the greatest possible awareness of everything involved in a situation by bringing out into the light of day all our activity or operations when confronted with the situation, whether the operations are manual in the laboratory or verbal or otherwise "mental". It is an art to make the analysis emphasize the significant operations. The conviction that such an analysis of operations is important is to a certain extent characteristic of the scientists of the present epoch—the old Greek philosophers would not have felt this way. The value of an operational analysis is often to be found in the fact that it allows us to profit more easily by our general experience—our experience has shown us that certain sorts of operation are good for certain purposes. If the analysis shows that we have been mistaken in the operations which we had supposed were involved in certain concepts, as it often does, then our experience enables us to revise our estimate of the adequacy of the concept to accomplish what we wanted. Operational analysis is valueless without a background of experience, and the conclusions from such an analysis can have no validity which is not already conditioned by the experience. The situation here on a larger stage is much the same as on a smaller stage with regard to dimensional analysis, for this too enables us to capitalize certain sorts of experience, but without the experience it is impotent.

2

SOME GENERAL PRINCIPLES OF OPERATIONAL ANALYSIS*

THE READER NEED hardly be warned that as regards specific applications of any of the following to psychology I have only the competence of an outsider.

I shall not attempt to answer the questions in order but shall rather give a more or less general exposition in which many of the topics touched in the questions naturally present themselves, but in a different order. Questions 9, 10 and 11 touch on fundamental matters which may be answered incidentally in a general discussion.

It will, I think, not be unduly restrictive to consider definitions as applied to terms. A term is defined when the conditions are stated under which I may use the term and when I may infer from the use of the term by my neighbor that the same conditions prevailed. Any method of describing the conditions is permissible which leads to a characterization precise enough for the purpose in hand, making possible the recovery of the conditions to the necessary degree of approximation. Terms used in

---

*See Note at end of text, p. 385.

a scientific context must be subject to the presuppositions of scientific enterprise. One of the most important of these is the possibility of checking or verifying the correctness of any statement; in fact, this may be taken as characteristic of *any* serious enterprise. Checking that the conditions are satisfied is done by performing certain operations, so that for all essential purposes the definition may be specified in terms of the checking operations. These operations usually involve some element of deliberate direction by the checker; this deliberate direction may not be any more articulate than placing oneself in such a position that one's sense organs may be acted on and in paying attention to the resulting sensations. In any event the process of checking involves activity of some sort, so that from the point of view of utmost generality, in which the operation is understood in the sense of any conscious activity, definitions *must* be operational and it is tautological to speak of operational definitions. However, such great generality is of little use. In order to be of practical value, the operations must, at the very minimum, be such that they are repeatable and performable on demand; in fact, this would seem implied in the idea of checking. Whether there are such operations or not can be found only by experiment, and, as in every experimental situation, absolute precision is not attainable. No operation can be specified with absolute precision, and no attempt to repeat an operation can be proved to have been completely successful. But in practise there are operations which can be repeated by the same person or different persons under the same or different conditions without hesitation and with the accompaniment of no phenomena which demand the assertion that there has been failure to repeat. Definitions should be framed in terms of operations of this sort. It is not necessary that such operations be especially simple, or that they be analyzed into all discernible components—merely that they be repeatable with assurance.

One of the greatest advantages of an operational breakdown of a situation is that it reduces it to a description of an actual happening—of something that has actually been done or that has actually occurred—and therefore it has the validity of actual experience. In particular, there is no room for concealed contradictions. "Hypothetical operations" (Question 3) may be of doubtless value, but the full operational meaning of 'hypothetical' is complex. A hypothetical operation must have its meaning in terms of a program of actual operations, into which it can be broken down. It is to be regarded as a shorthand statement indicating that if certain operations are performed and certain results obtained, then certain other activities will be engaged in, but the program, if valid or even meaningful, must be capable of being broken down into operations which we now know how to perform. The meaning of "the other side of the moon" (Question 3, [a]) is complex and indirect, but expressible in terms of presently performable operations, such as observing the change in illumination of Mars when the other side of the moon shines on it.

It is my personal opinion that the paradoxes of the infinite in mathematics (Question 3, [c]) arise precisely because in mathematics infinity is sometimes defined in terms of impossible operations, and that in all cases where the concept of infinity is legitimately handled its definition can be reframed in terms of actual operations.

One of the chief advantages of making definitions operational is that it increases precision (Question 1). I find that I myself use terms without either precisely formulating the conditions which demand their use, or without, in certain cases, having more than a vague feeling that the conditions are now such that the term may be appropriately used. When my neighbor uses the term, I observe only too frequently that I cannot deduce from his use of it the occurrence of certain antecedent or subsequent occurrences which I believe are implied in his use of it. In such cases reduction of definitions to operational terms increases precision, so that operational definitions are called for when increased precision is called for. Furthermore, by exposing the nature of the underlying operations, we discover whether our terms are really good for what we thought they were good for. To do this we capitalize any experience we may have had. In this way we often find that we have been mistaken in our uncritical opinion of what went into the term. This procedure is especially valuable in exposing verbalisms.

A strict application of these ideas means that one never has the 'same' construct defined by two independent operations (Question 2), but in this case there are properly two constructs which may be proved by experiment to give results indistinguishable within certain margins of experimental error and within certain ranges of phenomena. But it is never safe to assume that they will continue to be equivalent in a new range as yet unexplored. In fact, this is one of the advantages of the operational method; it ensures against a repetition of the situation in physics which led to the adoption of the theory of relativity. This situation arose from the uncritical assumption of the equivalence of operations at high velocities which had been shown to be equivalent within experimental error at low velocities.

Whether 'experience' is a proper construct for operational definition (Question 4) is a question for experiment. One has to ask in the first place whether a definition is necessary in the sense that misunderstandings arise because of its usage in different ways by different people. One then has to ask whether an operational breakdown into simpler components is possible, and this question has to be answered by experiment, which in general will involve actually producing the simpler components.

Operational definition certainly may and often does form a regress (Question 1 [b]), but I can see no reason for thinking that it may be an infinite regress. It seems to me that the situation may be more like the situation presented in mathematics by semi-convergent series, in which the goodness of the approximation can be improved up to a certain point, but beyond that divergence begins. The specification of operations within operations I believe may presently pass beyond the range of verbal language and reach a situation where one can only point at an operation and imitate it. The attainment of further precision on this level must be difficult to say the least, and we may find ourselves stymied in trying to make indefinite progress.

Since operations are usually used in a context of purpose of some sort, one may if one likes speak of good or bad operations (Question 5), but I personally would usually prefer to speak of useful or non-useful operations. It certainly must be recognized that some operations are more useful than others.

Operational analysis is mostly restricted to questions of meaning and as such can have only partial congruence with the universe of experimental method (Question 6).

I can see no reason why the operational method should have any inhibiting effect on any legitimate theorizing (Question 7), and in so far as it has any effect at all, it can be only beneficial because it increases precision. Pratt's objection that all theoretical explanation is circular amounts to an argument that induction is circular, which I believe to be true and to be particularly obvious in the light of an operational analysis of what is involved in an induction. The fact of circularity need in no wise detract from usefulness.

Part of Question 11, "Can a phenomenon be identified or its properties be defined in terms of the events (operations) which are effective to produce it?" is closely related to the dictum of Question 8 that "intelligence is what the intelligence test tests". Without doubt it is possible to apply the procedure suggested here, but I believe that the situation seldom arises which one would be content to treat finally by any such method as this. Such procedures should be used only in the preliminary stages while the phenomena are still incompletely explored and many correlations remain to be found. In fact, it seems to me at least debatable whether even in the preliminary stages other procedures might not sometimes be better. "To define a phenomenon by the operations which produced it" involves unproved assumptions. It implies that performance of the same operations will always be followed by the occurrence of the same phenomenon, and this statement is operationally meaningless unless there is some method of checking the truth of the statement. This again implies that it means something to say 'same' phenomenon, which implies, unless we are here dealing with a pure convention, that there is some other method of recognizing the phenomenon when it recurs than through the operations of the definition. Operational definitions, in spite of their precision, are in application without significance unless the situations to which they are applied are sufficiently developed so that at least two methods are known of getting to the terminus. In the situation above, definition of a phenomenon by the operations which produced it, taken naked and without further qualification, has an entirely specious precision, because it is a description of a single isolated event, without even the existence of a criterion to determine when it recurs or whether the description of the event is complete.

With regard to the intelligence test, the assertion as it stands begs the question. The question-begging word is the humble 'what'. The assertion that the intelligence test tests a 'what' implies the repeated application of the test and the discovery that the results of the test have the properties of a 'what'. It seems to me that the actual situation here is one of spiral approximation, as it so often is. We use the word intelligence to describe certain aspects of the behavior of ourselves or our fellows, but with undesirable vagueness and subject to conditions which we do not fully realize ourselves, and which we discover only by experimenting with ourselves by asking whether we would call such and such concrete behaviors examples of intelligence or not. On the other hand, we have the practical problem of discovering some simple procedure or test which, when it is applied and gives certain results, will give the same answer as the more vague procedure which we often cannot formulate in advance. Our attempts to do this are at first unsuccessful. We discover modifications in the test which give greater success, but at the same time, by checking in a large number of instances we refine our original conception of what we will be willing to call intelligence, or may even discover that what we were trying to do cannot be carried through. But if it can be carried through we have come out with at least two different methods of getting to the same place, one of which is presumably so much easier to apply than the other that we shall use it when feasible.

With regard to the analysis of experience into discriminatory responses, it seems to me that this must be only a preliminary stage which must eventually be split into simpler components. The complete operational specification of the antecedents of the response includes an operational description of the subject of the test, and since the directions for the test at present have to be given linguistically, all the questions of language and complete cultural background of the subject are involved. We should eventually be able to answer such questions as to what extent the discriminatory response is conditioned by the cultural background of the subject, and this cannot be done, or at any rate has not been done, with present methods of procedure. The question becomes especially pressing in connection with such discoveries as, for instance, the ability to discriminate a 'volume' characteristic of sound distinct from its physical intensity.

REJOINDERS

THE VARIOUS DISCUSSIONS have forced again on my attention the curious and almost universal reluctance to accept what seems to me one of the most immediate consequences of the operational point of view. Several of the contributors have referred to science as of necessity being public in character; I believe on the other hand that a simple inspection of what one does in any scientific enterprise will show that the most important part of science is private. I have elaborated this position at some length in a paper and will not repeat here the considerations presented there.

The question with regard to the public or private character of science is only part of the larger question of public versus private in general, which has also been a subject of some discussion in this symposium. An analysis of what I do discloses that in situations in which I am concerned with distinctions between mine and thine my operations are patently dual in character. The operations which justify me in saying, "My tooth aches", are different from those which justify me in saying, "Your tooth aches". The operations which justify me in saying "the toothache which I now have feels like the one which I had last week" are recognizably not the same as those which might justify me in making a similar statement about your tooth-aches. Going further, any operations which give whatever meaning they may have to statements like "my toothache feels like your toothache" are obviously compounded of the operations which separately give meaning to my toothache and your toothache. In fact, this situation is so obviously a compound of heterogeneous elements that it is coming to be a rather common point of view that the best way to treat such questions as "does your toothache feel like my toothache?" is to call them pseudo questions. In general, the operations by which I know what I am thinking about are different from the operations by which I convince myself of what you are thinking about. The question never arises, "Am I deliberately deceiving myself with regard to what I am thinking about?" but the question often arises as to whether you are deliberately deceiving me with regard to what you are thinking about.

The whole linguistic history of the human race is a history of a deliberate suppression of the patent operational differences between my feelings and your feelings, between my thought and your thought. A language which reproduced the dualistic character of what happens would have different words for your thought and my thought. The reason for the suppression of the distinction and the use of a single word is doubtless social. We understand and manage to get along with our fellows by the device of saying "my neighbor has feelings exactly like mine". It is easy to imagine that the possession of this linguistic device may have been of universally decisive survival value. It by no means follows, however, that a linguistic usage which has arisen under the stimulus of an immediate social necessity is the most advantageous or is even adequate to meet the complete scientific requirements. There is little connection between survival value and truth.

The topic to which Professor Skinner devotes the major part of his discussion is obviously intimately related to what we are considering here, but it is recognizably not the same. Professor Skinner is concerned with how to treat the reactions of my neighbor to stimuli which we would all describe as private to him. I think it must be conceded that Professor Skinner is right in his contention, if I understand him correctly, that the only possible way of dealing with this problem is to convert "private for my neighbor" into "public for me". I think, however, that there is danger that his scheme of procedure may involve the tacit thesis that it is possible to go further and establish the full operational equivalence of "public for me" and "private for me". This equivalence may conceivably ultimately be established, perhaps by an elaboration of methods suggested by Professor Skinner, but it is at any rate plain that the equivalence has not yet been established. The most superficial observation is sufficient to show that the operations by which I now deal with the "public for me" are qualitatively different from the operations by which I now deal with the "private for me". To ignore this difference, or to set up the thesis that the difference is unimportant until it is proved, is opposed to the entire spirit of the operational approach. It may be objected that it would lead to impossible complication to insist on the differences between public and private—that a strict application of this point of view would mean that there are as many "sciences" as there are people engaged in "sciencing". This may indeed be the case, but if it is we can do nothing about it but accept it. The first consideration must be "what is true?" not "what is simple?" I believe that nearly always the first results of a careful operational analysis will be to bring complication rather than simplification. The conceptual structure which we have inherited is a conventionalized and simplified structure, in which we usually do not know what the simplifications are or what are their consequences. The first task of the operational approach is usually to recover the full complexity of the primitive situation.

I suspect that most persons with a 'practical' frame of mind will have little patience with these considerations, because they believe they already know the answer, and that considerations of this sort can in the end make little or no difference with any of our procedures. This attitude is of course an exceedingly dangerous attitude and has often led to disaster in the past. It is my own considered opinion that the matter is of transcendent importance. The entire human race, ever since the appearance of articulate speech, has been so conditioning itself to suppress the difference between me and thee that most members of the race have lost any capacity they may ever have had to recognize even the existence of the issue. Simple observation shows that I act in two modes. In my public mode I have an image of myself in the community of my neighbors, all similar to myself and all of us equivalent parts of a single all-embracing whole. In the private mode I feel my inviolable isolation from my fellows and may say, "My thoughts are my own, and I will be damned if I let you know what I am thinking about".

All government, whether the crassest totalitarianism or the uncritical and naive form of democracy toward which we are at present tending in this country, endeavors to suppress the private mode as illegitimate, as do also most institutionalized religions and nearly all systems of philosophy or ethics. Yet the private mode is an integral part of each one of us, ready to flare into action under the stimulus of any new exploitation of the individual. I believe that no satisfactory solution will be found for our present social and political difficulties until we find how to handle together as of equal importance the social and the private modes of each of us. Each of us, in moments of clarity or stress, reverts to the private mode in spite of millennia of exhortation and instruction. In these moments of clarity we know that the private mode is as justifiable as the social mode and even more inescapable. It seems to me that only when I deal with both modes do I become capable of achieving complete rationality. No government or social order can be ultimately successful, if its members are intelligent and allowed to follow their own intellectual processes to their logical conclusions, until a reconciliation has been achieved between these two modes. In fact, it seems to me that this is the supreme justification for the sort of democracy toward which we ought to be heading but unfortunately are not, namely, that it alone makes sense from the point of view of the completely rational behavior of the individuals who compose it.

The extent to which any discipline suffers by its failure to recognize and insist on the social and the private modes of individual behavior depends on the subject matter. In physics the question hardly presents itself. But in psychology it seems to me that we do want to deal with topics which demand a clear recognition of the operational duality with which at present we are constrained to deal with all questions of me and thee. To assume that this operational duality may be ignored assumes the result of what is at present only a program for the future. In the light of present accomplishment this assumption seems to me exceedingly hazardous. Until it has been shown that the program has reasonable prospects of being carried through the operational approach demands that we make our reports and do our thinking in the freshest terms of which we are capable, in which we strip off the sophistications of millennia of culture and report as directly as we can what happens. Among other things this demands that I make my reports always in the first person and in a language which reproduces the structure of my universe. Since one aspect of the structure of my universe is the operational difference between mine and thine, I must make my report in a language which recognizes this operational duality. Since such a language does not at present exist, one must be devised. For the present it will probably be sufficient never to use such words as thought or feeling without qualification, but always to qualify, as "my thought", "your thought", or "my feeling", "your feeling". It may be that eventually we shall be able to take account of the operational dichotomy in the universes of each one of us in some simpler way. But until that time, it seems to me that by ignoring the dichotomy psychology is engaging in an unnecessary gamble, and is probably riding for a fall.

3

SCIENCE: PUBLIC OR PRIVATE?*

ONE THING WHICH has struck me most as I have read the articles of the Encyclopedia of Unified Science is the complexity that can be discerned in many of the operations which for the purpose of the article are treated as elementary. It is apparent that Unity of Science, like every other discipline, has its own stock of "atoms of discourse", suited to its own purposes. Experience in physics would prepare one to expect that for certain purposes it may be profitable to attempt to analyze these atoms further. The atom of discourse, or presupposition commonly made by most adherents of the Unity of Science movement, with which I shall be chiefly concerned, is with regard to the nature of "science". My present concern with this matter has arisen from my extreme difficulty in communicating my meaning to other people. The difficulty has been a genuine puzzle to me, until quite recently a discussion with one of my colleagues disclosed a difference of attitude on fundamental matters so revelatory that I am encouraged to return again to the attack.

*From Philosophy of Science, 7, 36, 1940. Paper read at the Fifth International Congress for the Unity of Science in Cambridge, Mass. on Sept. 4, 1939.

My point of view is that science is essentially private, whereas the almost universal counter point of view, explicitly stated in many of the articles of the Encyclopedia, is that it *must* be public. I purposely do not stop at the beginning to attempt a precise definition of the terms, although it is obvious enough that there is a certain amount of haziness in the ordinary usage of "science", and "public" and "private", and although it is perhaps also obvious that if we defined these words exactly at the beginning there would then be no disagreement. For I think everyone does as a matter of fact use these words with enough definiteness so that he unhesitatingly says either "science is public" or "science is private", and it is primarily the implications back of this usage that I want to bring out. I hope that after this analysis it will appear that the usual point of view gives greater weight to certain features than one perhaps might after more detailed consideration.

It is to be remarked that the view that science is essentially public is in perfect accord with the intellectual fashion of the times of emphasizing that all our activities are fundamentally social in nature. In support of this view it is evident enough that not only all our institutions, but also all the tools of thought of any of us have developed in social surroundings, and in the construction of any of them, such as language in general, or logic or arithmetic or other forms of mathematics in particular, many people have made mutually dependent contributions. There is therefore no doubt that in arriving at their present form the social factor has as a matter of fact been decisive. This is by many felt to be so important that the public nature of science is often made a matter of definition.

The subject may be approached by noting the answers we give when we ask what we would do in various situations, for the thing that we say science is has got to be consistent with all the things we can say about it. I begin by reporting the answer of my colleague which started this discussion and which I found so revelatory. He is a psychologist, and I asked him how he would react if his report of some observational fact of psychology was in direct contradiction to that of his qualified fellows. His immediate and unhesitating answer was that he would have to accept the report of his fellows as correct. For, said he, what is "correct" except the consensus of qualified observers? thus accepting by implication the usual definition of science as public. This answer of his was to me so unexpected that something like a cry of dismay escaped me. We then discussed the matter, and presently my colleague was saying that he hadn't thought about this sort of thing very much, that what he had said was his natural and instinctive answer, and that he supposed that in the business of psychology one had to be particularly suspicious of his own judgment and rely to an especial degree on the report of his neighbors.

This experience suggests the question of whether

it is a fact that the instinctive attitude of most people is that the overwhelming majority of their fellows *must* be right because of the very nature of right, so that confirmation or verification by their individual selves is superfluous. Such an attitude would certainly fit in with the present fashion of emphasizing the social nature of everything that a man does; it is as natural an attitude in a society committed to the virtue of democracy as in one committed to totalitarianism. If this attitude is typical of competent scientists, then it is easy for me to understand why I find such great difficulty in making my point that science is essentially private. I believe, however, that in so far as this attitude is typical, it has been adopted without due consideration.

Since the situation in psychology is rather complicated, let us in further examination of what is involved take elementary arithmetic or logic as representative of science. What do I do when I announce a certain result on adding a column of figures, but my neighbor, looking over my shoulder, assures me that I am wrong? I am sure that I, and I believe most of my audience also, am not content to accept this simple statement, but check my neighbor's claim by any of a variety of methods, and do not in the end accept his claim unless I can check it for myself independently of him. My experience is that in almost all cases I have in the end been able to reach agreement with my neighbor. There are, however, exceptional cases; in some of these my neighbor may turn out to have made an escape from an asylum. However, I always get agreement with my neighbor if he is what I call "normal". It follows, of course, that if I and any one normal neighbor agree, all my normal neighbors must agree with each other. It is a natural consequence of this situation that I often reverse the relations; if ten of my normal neighbors independently assure me that the sum of a column of figures is 137, it is highly probable that I will accept 137 as the "correct" result, without making the addition myself.

Emphasis on the importance of these facts of observation and this aspect of the situation I think influences most people to describe science as public. But in what spirit and with what purpose do I accept the report of my fellows that the correct result is 137? Examination of what I do shows me that I accept the verdict of my neighbors only as an easier method of getting the result to which my own activity would have led me, or as a means of checking against my own mistakes, which I can guard against otherwise, if I choose, by more troublesome procedures. That is, there are other criteria which I can apply than the criterion of publicity, and I am sure that I would retain these criteria even if the criterion of publicity should fail. My arithmetic must enable me to deal with my own experience with consistency and success in certain respects; for example, I must be able to buy and sell and not run into bankruptcy. Or, passing beyond the field of simple arithmetic, the requirement that I impose on myself in general is that I be able to adapt myself with success to my environment, and the decision as to whether I have made the adaptation is one which I make and which no other can possibly make for me. If my neighbor says "Go to, you have not successfully met your environment because you are now dead", it moves me only to derision. If my neighbor tells me that he himself is successfully adapting himself to his environment at the moment that I see him fall into the water, I can only retort by quoting my own experience, that is, what I have seen and heard.

A necessary but not a sufficient characterization of what I want to call science is that it is an activity which satisfies certain criteria with regard to success in meeting the environment. The important thing is not the precise form of the criterion, but that the criterion is applied by me. This I take to be a simple matter of observation. It is further a matter of observation that the science at which I arrive in this way is in agreement with what my fellows say and do, but this is an additional fact, and is not vital to the situation. If I define science as that which satisfies my criteria and at the same time as that which is public, I am guilty of an over-definition. The feeling that this wide-spread agreement between my fellows and myself requires explanation, and that by saying that science is public we have in some way explained this fact is, I think, partly responsible for the wide-spread insistence that science is necessarily public. If one carefully examines what is involved in such an explanation, I venture to suggest that he will uncover a streak of verbalism or of metaphysics.

Another reason that I call the publicity aspect of science less vital is that if I maintain the publicity requirement I cannot say certain things that I would like to say. If, for example, I had always lived alone on a desert island, and had found how to anticipate the seasons or the phases of the moon, I would want to call certain aspects of my activity scientific. Or if I and my neighbors could not agree on arithmetic, and they were continually falling into bankruptcy while I prosecuted my own business successfully, I would want to call my arithmetic scientific in distinction from theirs.

There are aspects of my private science which are tinged with publicity. If, in order to save myself time, I accept what you tell me without detailed examination, as I often must, then I naturally will try to safeguard myself in every way as to your reliability. Experience has shown me that one of the best possible safeguards is that other people should agree with you. That is, although my science is private, I am very likely to demand that your science be public. If one wants to define science as "your science", then it must be admitted that in almost all cases it is public, in this sense.

It has been implicit in all that we have done hitherto that we have treated science as an activity. This does indeed seem to be essential and should be emphasized. Science considered as a "body of knowledge" as it often is when its rôle of publicity is emphasized, seems to be an abstraction on a level which is predominantly verbal. But I should not, for example, want to say that science is contained in libraries or in any sort of written document. The printed page consists of marks which are capable of guiding activities in me which under the proper conditions may be scientific activities. Science does not begin until my activities begin. A recent writer in Philosophy of Science has said "science is sciencing". With this I would heartily agree. The reason that I often find it convenient to describe the contents of a book as science is that I am convinced that if I allowed the marks in the book to guide my activity I would then find that these activities of mine satisfied my criteria for being scientific. This conviction may arise from a long and complex experience.

The process that I want to call scientific is a process that involves the continual apprehension of meaning, the constant appraisal of significance, accompanied by a running act of checking to be sure that I am doing what I want to do, and of judging correctness or incorrectness. This checking and judging and accepting, that together constitute understanding, are done by me and can be done for me by no one else. They are as private as my toothache, and without them science is dead.

Perhaps after all this to-do some of my audience will be willing to grant my original contention, namely my conviction that if the situation were sufficiently considered and the terms suitably defined my fellows would grant that it goes deeper to describe science as private rather than public. But even granted this modicum of success, what shall I say to the reproach of triviality? After the point has been seen and made, is it important? As a matter of fact I do frequently use the report of my neighbors in deciding what my own action shall be, and in the overwhelming majority of cases I do impose the criterion of publicity on my own logical processes in order that I may privately accept them, as is shown by my desire to make this paper convincing. Why insist then on such a purely academic distinction, one which is almost never applied in practise?

To this reproach I would return a general and a particular reply. In particular reply I could attempt to point out places where it seems to me that a recognition of the ultimately private nature of science is important. For example, it seems to me important with regard to our whole point of view respecting the nature of logic and mathematics. It is customary to think of these disciplines as purely "formal" in character, in distinction to such "applied" disciplines as physics or the geometry of actual space. Consider, for example, what is involved in the syllogism in its simplest form "All a is b. All b is c. Therefore all a is c". It is obvious enough that this is not just a static array of marks on paper, which might be photographed, but with which one can do nothing else. That these marks guide me in a process is evident enough when I reflect that the thing involves an order. But there is more to it than following the marks in the right sequence; the marks have *significance*, and the fact of significance involves a background that is not contained in what I see on the paper. There are various aspects to the significance of these marks. At the very minimum I recognize it as the essence of the pattern, regarded as purely "formal" in the conventional sense, that certain marks recur: "a", "b", and "c" occur twice. That is, I think of the second "a" as the "same" as the first "a". Without this recognition and understanding the marks on paper would indeed be something merely to be photographed. But what do I mean by this "same"? How do I recognize "sameness"? Does it ever actually occur, and if it does where do I find it? It is obvious that the "sameness" does not reside in what I see on paper, because microscopic differences could certainly be found in the two "a's".

Furthermore, the "a", "b", and "c" are restricted in other ways; they are symbols for things which may be substituted for them, and there are restrictions which would be very difficult to formulate precisely on the sort of substitution permissible.

It appears then that the reduction of the syllogism to a formalism is a very incomplete reduction; beyond the formalism there is an enormous amount of complexity, and this complexity cannot be expressed in what is written on paper or even said. I think it is suggestive to apply the same word to this complex of tacit restrictions and conditions which I have previously used in discussing the equations of theoretical physics, and say that every syllogism involves implicitly a "text" or body of comments as to meaning and use. As with the equations of physics, because this text is practically never made explicit, one has to make his own text, perhaps at first by watching how other people use the syllogism, but eventually by observing what conditions must be fulfilled in order that the syllogism must serve his purposes.

The text imposes conditions. I have to be aware of these conditions as I perform the process in which I am guided by the marks on paper, and I have to be continually checking myself to be sure that the conditions are being met. This checking and awareness is private; no one can do it for me. Nevertheless I can do it with confidence, and I may accept it for my purposes as "atomic". Although performable with confidence, it is, it seems to me, something in which the attribute of certainty in no wise inheres, but it is sicklied o'er with the pale cast of human fallibility. The syllogism as a whole, formal part plus text, is something which by no means has the certainty that is commonly associated with the purely formal. Since the text has such a preponderating part in any logical enterprise, the practical value of emphasizing the formal aspects of logic cannot reside in any resulting certainty, but must be sought in directions connected with methodology.

If the activity which is logic involves a text, then

it is a consequence that when the text changes the logic changes, although the guiding marks on paper may remain constant. This is consistent with my own experience. I have no adequate acquaintance with conventional symbolic logic, and I could not read the simplest technical paper without extensive preparation, but I think that nevertheless I have done enough mathematics and have looked into enough papers on symbolic logic to have some general conception of what it is all about. I observe that as I get older my attitude changes in a way which I think is significant. When I was younger I had a certain facility in reading a formal logical analysis, which I could do with satisfaction and with conviction that everything was in order. But as I get older I lose my sense of *ease* in the operations of logic. I do not think this loss is due to senile decay, but I believe that it is rather because I now see more than I did before. I am continually bogging down at the beginning, even with so admirably written an exposition as Tarski's Mathematische Logik. I can't let myself go as I am obviously expected to; too many questions keep intruding themselves. Take the simplest theorem in the calculus of propositions. Some universal statement is made about propositions p, q, r etc. I look at the statement to see whether it seems right and checks with my own experience. Have all propositions p, q, and r which I have made had the relation stated? Before I can answer I have to know what this thing is that is called a "proposition". Are there concealed conditions which I have not thought of? Does it by any chance happen that all the "propositions" which I may have used up till now have certain common properties which may not be possessed by the propositions I may make tomorrow? It is not easy to think through exhaustively all the propositions one has ever made and see their common characteristics. Then what is this tacit quality of "sameness" in a proposition? for the theorem to which I am trying to give my assent uses "p" in more than one place and thereby implicitly ascribes a meaning to the sameness of a proposition made with identical or even different words at different times and places.

My process of giving assent to a theorem of logic may be described as finding a text which I can accept as complete. That this text is complicated is evident when one considers the matter of paradox. Paradox is evidence of inadequacy in the text. The game of logic may be played only with certain kinds of counters; if one uses the wrong sort of counter paradox may arise. The specifications for the counters are made in the text so that an inadequate text means possible paradox. Now there is never any defense against paradox. I have no way of being sure that tomorrow I may not think of something that had not occurred to me before, even though the text I am using today has the sanction of immemorial public acceptance. Furthermore, as a matter of fact, paradoxes are unearthed every now and then; the inadequacy of texts hitherto thought adequate is thereby made evident and by implication the complexity of the text. Any particular paradox is in the first instance discovered by some individual, who thereby discovers the inadequacy of his private text, which may of course also have been in part publicly accepted. It is, I think, particularly evident that advances into new territory are the result of private activity and therefore of private science.

So far, I have been concerned with various ramifications of my particular reply to the reproach of triviality. I now consider what reply may be made in general. In general I do not believe it is safe to discard as trivial any feature of a situation until it has been proved to be trivial. It is certainly highly dangerous to comfortably assume that a consideration is trivial until one has seen what the issue is here. The issue is not just whether it is more profitable to emphasize the private or the public aspect of science. The issue is the deeper one of the unavoidable dual character of many of the words that we use in describing what happens to us and our fellows. The words denoting sensation obviously have this character: "my pain" and "your pain", or "my consciousness" and "your consciousness" are evidently different because the experiences are different, and the things that we do in order to decide whether to say "my pain" or "your pain" are different. The same duality extends to many words dealing with our activities: "I think" is different from "you think", and "I desire" from "you desire". In so far as science is an activity we have to recognize the same duality: "my science" is different from "your science". If we were willing to deal with this situation by completely reforming our language so as to emphasize the dual character of all these words, then we would not be concerned very much with whether science is private or public, for the situation would be dealt with well enough by the existence of two words, one for "my-science", and another for "your-science". But language has not been so reformed, and we are constrained to get along with a single word. It is my point that the differences between "my science" and "your science" are peculiarly important and necessary to emphasize. It is only "my science" that is alive. Until "your science" becomes "my science" it is as dead and sterile as substitution of numbers into a formula by a high school student. I have preferred, therefore, as long as language has not developed the machinery for dealing with this duality, to say that science is "ultimately" or "essentially" private. Perhaps there are other verbal methods of dealing with the situation that would have been more happy.

A linguistic problem that must sometime be solved is to develop a machinery for dealing with these dualities. It is in the general scientific tradition, and in particular, I think, it is one of the presuppositions of the Unity of Science movement, to ignore these dualities. The ideal appears to be a non-personal language, in which such expressions as "I think", "I feel", "I know" never occur. We need not go in detail into the reasons for this, but the possibility of getting along with such a non-personal language has become an assumption at the bottom of most of our scientific activity. The validity of this assumption has never, I believe, been adequately examined. In suppressing these personal expressions I am doing an unnatural thing, that sometimes demands obvious circumlocutions and always involves an element of convention and construction. If I want to express what obviously occurs, I have got to use the first person. Has it ever been adequately proved, or has ever the assumption been adequately examined, that in forcing myself to speak non-personally I have not thrown away something vital? The point of view that emphasizes the public character of science is closely allied to the point of view that postulates that I have not, but I very much question whether this postulate can be maintained over a wide enough field of activity to be sufficiently profitable. There are certainly things which I can say to myself that do not come within the scope of such a postulate, but which I can nevertheless say with all the certainty with which I can say that there is a chair over yonder or that two times two is four or any other statement of science. The thesis that science is adequately treated as public is the thesis that such private statements can be dispensed with in scientific activity. But I think I have shown above that this is almost certainly not true. When I follow the marks on paper that constitute a treatise on symbolic logic, I am not willing to call my activity scientific unless I can say at each stage of the process "I understand", a statement which is just as private as when I say "my tooth aches".

It seems to me that we are doing things in the wrong order. The contention that if I want to reproduce what happens I have to use the first person seems to me so obvious that it needs only to be said. All our experience emphasizes the importance of reproducing what happens; any scientific enterprise must begin with adequate description. The development of a linguistic technique for the exclusive use of the first person not only has been shirked, but it appears to be regarded as an unworthy object of endeavor. This is in accord with the scientific tradition of the last 300 years. I do not know to what extent this is deliberate.

The thesis of at least a part of the Unity of Science movement that everything can be expressed in the physical language apparently involves, to judge by what is done, the assumption that the physical language is itself necessarily non-personal, with never the use of the first person. On the contrary, I can see no reason why one should despair of a physical language which is also a language of the first person. A language of the first person, in which one does not hesitate when necessary to talk about his own purposes and judgments, need not be a "mentalistic" language, and may have all the definiteness, certainty, and reproducibility that one demands in a language suited to scientific use. One has just as much certainty in stating his *conviction* that two plus two makes four is a correct statement as he has in stating the *fact* that two plus two makes four. This shows that the dividing line between statements about facts and statements about feelings may get pretty nebulous. Is one not going out of his way to attempt to maintain a sharp dividing line? In a subject like physics it is perhaps easy not to cross the line, but even here I have found as I push my analysis of what is involved in the accepted operations of physics that I do continually want to cross the line. But in other disciplines it may become highly artificial to maintain the distinction. I believe an example is Professor Dewey's article on the Theory of Valuation which has just appeared in the *Encyclopedia*. A guiding motif of this exposition is obviously to discuss all aspects of valuation in the physical, public and also non-personal language. This attempt may be conceded to have been successful, but as I read it I could not help feeling how much better it would have gone if Professor Dewey had permitted himself the use of the simple perpendicular I. In general I think that the thesis of Unity of Science cannot be overthrown if this thesis is merely that one will never get into contradiction by using only a non-personal physical language. In fact I would expect that this thesis certainly could be maintained by the exercise of sufficient virtuosity simply because the dividing line between the public and private cannot be made sharp, but at what cost in complication, artificiality and clumsiness in the practise dictated by the thesis!

It appears to me that a linguistic technique of

the first person not only has got to be attempted, but it has also got to be successful, merely because such a technique would reproduce what palpably happens in our scientific activity, and this is admittedly already largely successful. There are obvious difficulties to be overcome in developing such a technique. Over against the difficulties there are certain immediate felicities in the use of the first person. For example, exposition written in the first person becomes more patently merely a collection of marks on paper to guide me in my own activities. One thing in the development of such a technique is certain, and this may allay some of the natural misgiving at turning our backs on the line of development of 300 years, namely that a distinction has got to be made between my-feeling and your-feeling, something which at present is almost never done, and which has enormous social implications. I think Professor Dewey would not have hesitated to write his article in the first person if he had had at his command a linguistic device for making this distinction.

4

FREEDOM AND THE INDIVIDUAL*

THE LAST THING that the average human being wants to be made to see is that as a matter of fact he is already inescapably free. This obviously does not mean free economically or politically, for these forms of freedom have not yet been generally attained and are still the object of passionate endeavor. What is meant is that inner freedom in virtue of which every individual leads his own life eternally free from his fellows within the walls of his own consciousness. So obstinate is man's refusal to admit this elemental fact that his social institutions and even his language, the tool of his thought, have from time immemorial assumed such a structure as to obscure recognition of the fact and to make even utterance of the fact well-nigh impossible. All the intellectual machinery which an individual receives as his heritage and with which he strives as best he can to adapt himself to his environment is a tissue of rationalization inspired by fear lest he see that he is really free. The oldest and the grimmest jest that man has perpetrated against him-

*From *Freedom: Its Meaning,* edited by Ruth Nanda Anshen, Harcourt Brace and Co., Inc., 1940.

self is the jest that Adam and Eve in the Garden of Eden really *wanted* to eat the fruit of the tree of knowledge.

Everyone soon comes to realize and accept certain special aspects of freedom. Everyone who ever gets anywhere knows that he has to make his own decisions for himself. Everyone finds that no one is so much concerned with his own problems as himself, and that if he wants to be sure of getting a thing right he has to do it for himself. He finds that he has no *right* to the interest or even the sympathy or understanding of others. He finds that whether or not he is free from other people, other people are free from him, and that the various devices he employs to control the actions of others are not necessarily successful. He is not *certain* of getting safely to the other side if he walks blindly across when the traffic light is in his favor, and if he does not arrive safely it is really on him not on the man who has illegally run him down.

But although adaptation to certain of the aspects of freedom has got into the unconscious practise of most people, an adequate intellectual and emotional realization of the implications is most rare. We may attempt to obtain such a realization by reflecting on some of the commonest features of experience. No one would attempt to make a blind man experience one's sensations when confronted with a sunset. In a situation like this it is easy to say that there is something incommunicable about a sensation when the corresponding organ does not exist. But when the organ does exist, is the sensation then communicable? Does the red of the sunset sky appear to my seeing neighbor the same as to me? What shall I do to find out? Examination discloses that I can only analyze his behavior in certain situations, including in his behavior his spoken words. There is never a comparison of his *sensation* with mine. My sensation is private, forever incommunicable. This is sometimes, but not often, recognized, as in a recent Readers' Digest one of the examples of "a more picturesque speech" was "private as pain". Because my sensation is private, "my-sensation" cannot have the same meaning as "your-sensation", so that it is meaningless to ask whether your sensation is the *same* as mine.

Here we encounter one of the obstinate infelicities of language. "Sensation" is usually used without qualification by a "my" or a "your", as if there were a unique meaning, making qualification unnecessary. But analysis shows that the situation is irreducibly two-fold. I know what I mean by "my-sensation"; for my present purpose it is not necessary to analyze further. But what shall I mean by "your-sensation"? When it comes right down to it, how do I know that you have sensations anyway? Certainly what I do to establish that you have sensations is different from what I do to establish that I have sensations, and since what I do is different, the meaning is different. What I do to establish that you have sensations is indirect and complicated and involves argument of one sort or another with myself. I see that you have organs similar to mine, and I observe that you behave similarly in similar situations. Would I not then be merely going out of my way to assume that you do not have sensations like me? The answer is that for certain purposes I *would* be going out of my way to assume a difference between you and me, and because these purposes control so many of the situations of ordinary life the convenience of a single word is accepted. For a very important concern in most of my contacts with my fellows is to anticipate how my fellow is going to act, and the best way I have been able to invent for predicting the actions of my fellow is to say to myself "How would *I* act in a similar situation?", of course modifying my action to take account of such considerations as "if I were as sick as he" or "if I were as stupid as he". My answer as to how I would act depends on what I imagine my sensations would be. Hence it comes that what I mean by my fellow's sensations is what I imagine my own would be in the same situation. This act of imagining myself in the other fellow's place is done so easily that I forget what I am doing and presently find myself using a single word, "sensation", covering both my- and your-, and still a little later materializing my dualistic linguistic creation by attaching meaning to "sensation" as such, unqualified by "my" or "your". Hence we finally come to handle "sensation" in a largely verbal way, to gratify impulses of verbalization. This uncritical use of the word "sensation" is not something that you and I have come to by ourselves, but it is something that we have inherited. But however we came by it, there is no question but that we do use the word in this way. If we did not, we would not in the first place have tried to force into our question "is my fellow's sensation of red the same as mine?" a meaning different from that which analysis disclosed.

Language, then, presents sensation as something in common between my fellow and myself, a bond of union, whereas my sensation is inexorably private, and eternally separates me from my fellow.

"Sensation" has been used in a broad sense; it includes not only what is correlated with the conventional sense organs, but embraces all that I understand by "conscious activity", including all conscious thought. There is grave danger here of being misunderstood; "conscious" and "consciousness" have such a history of metaphysical abuse, particularly by professional psychologists, that implications are almost certain to be read that I do not intend, or of which I am not even aware. My use of the word is without these professional and conventional implications. "I am conscious" is only another way of saying "I-think", "I-feel", "I-am-aware". I do not say that I *have* consciousness; neither can I say without extension and alteration of meaning that you are conscious. In the primitive meaning there is as little sense in saying that you are conscious as in saying that your sensation of red is the same as mine. For what do I do to establish that you are conscious?

Most of the words with which I describe the actions of my fellows are as irreducibly dual in meaning as is "sensation" or "conscious". These words have an altered and derived meaning in addition to their primitive meaning, which is obtained by imagining what I would be doing in the same situation. For instance, what do I mean when I ask "I wonder what you are *really* thinking about?" Here, as in so many cases, we have to distinguish between what the analysis, when we actually carry it out, discloses must be the meaning, and the nebulous anticipation that we usually have as to what the analysis will disclose. It is often the latter that we have in mind when we talk about "meaning". I think an analysis will show that all that I can mean by asking what you are really thinking about is what I imagine I myself would be thinking about if I were in the same situation as you, including in "same situation" all the enormously complicated things covered by what I can see, or hear other people say, or can get you to say by questioning or other methods, including taking account of such things as your imagined inferior or different intelligence. But when I have finished, I see that I have merely projected myself. I think this result does not agree with what most people would say their vague anticipations are as to what the meaning will turn out to be; they probably anticipate that the analysis can be made to disclose something in which there is no mention of "me". We can express the fact that the analysis does not come out as we had anticipated by saying that it is impossible to give the *desired* meaning to "your real thoughts"; we are trying to impart a meaning that is impossible.

Common usage is infested with situations in which we want to have certain meanings and in which we verbalize on the assumption that these are the meanings, but in which analysis shows that the desired meanings are impossible. This is particularly true of almost all the "me-your" situations. For instance, what is the meaning of "we"? We love to say "we" and "our"; it gives a cozy and all-together feeling that is most comforting. Evidently what I mean by "we" is "you *and* I"; this is to be said slowly so that one can appreciate that the "and" in this expression is the "and" of merely formal conjunction only. It is a symbol that one is to do two different kinds of thing, one to the "you" part and another to the "I" part. Thus, "we feel happy" is a contraction for "You feel happy and I feel happy", with a different meaning for "feel" and "happy" in the two parts of the sentence.

There is one curious situation in which the usual relations are reversed, in which I experience what is yours and never what is my own. This is with respect to death. I know what the death of animals and other people means. I have definitions that tell me what to do to determine whether another is dead or not. But this never applies to my own death, although I always talk of my own death as if it were something on the same footing as the death of another. We are careless of this distinction, and perhaps partly because of it, although doubtless for other reasons also, we think of our death as a form of our experience. This attitude toward our own death is I believe back of the many utter irrationalities of society in everything that pertains to death, and is therefore of enormous social significance.

The dichotomy of meaning of all these words has been so obscured by social and linguistic usage that many people find it almost impossible to see what is behind the verbalism. And because our language makes it difficult to see the dichotomy of meaning, we find it almost impossible to realize the dichotomy of the actual situation—the essential difference between me and thee—the essential isolation of each of us from our fellows. Right here is an example of the inaccuracy into which our linguistic habits are continually leading us. Of course all that I can say is that *I* am inexorably isolated from my fellows; to say that my fellows are isolated from me or from each other involves an extension and alteration of meaning like that we have already analyzed.

There are at least two reasons why it is so difficult to realize the underlying dichotomy of meaning in all these social words. In the first place the technique of using words in this dual fashion has been drummed into us by all our social training. It was an invention of the very first magnitude when man first learned how to anticipate the actions of his neighbor by saying to himself "How would I feel and act if I were in the same situation?" We, at this epoch, find it difficult to appreciate the magnitude of this invention; the very meaning of the subjunctive mood in which we express what to do; our "if I were", involves the invention itself. The invention was at first a complex thing, demanding as part of it the simultaneous development of a suitable language. But the invention having flowered, it proved most congenial to the genius of the race; it was no trick at all for one to imitate another as he saw him use this invention. It has grown to enormous usefulness, and is the universal and practically the only method by which each of us adapts himself to the action of his fellows; it is used in every act of social adjustment. No wonder that the short-hand expression for what we do, namely "my neighbor has feelings just like mine", should get accepted at its face value. In fact, acceptance of it has got made into a social virtue, and the point of view becomes a primary motivation for acceptable social conduct, as for example, in the golden rule.

The second reason we find it so difficult to realize the dichotomy of our language is that it is so very pleasant to ignore it. The picture which fits in so easily with our language, namely of our fellows and ourselves all being similar pieces in one large pattern, all having similar feelings and thinking similar thoughts and appealed to by the same motives, is one which is very pleasant for other than reasons of linguistic convenience, for it harmonizes with our nature as social animals. We like to be surrounded by our fellow beings, and to feel that we are all harmoniously striving for the same ends and affording each other mutual support. This feeling must go far back into the history of the race, and have been bred into the race by the survival value of cooperative effort. The fact, then, that linguistic convenience fits in so patly with the primitive social urge makes it all the more inevitable that the linguistic urge, with all its consequences, will be followed without critical analysis, for most people are incorrigible rationalizers.

It is very much the fashion at present to emphasize the potency of the social motive in molding human institutions. But I think the thesis can be and is carried too far, when it is claimed, as so often it is, that the *only* important molding factor has been the social. It is, however, natural that the thesis should be over-emphasized, because in so doing we satisfy the fundamental craving for support from without. The sciences have been contaminated by this over-emphasis on the social factor no less than have the other disciplines; it is very much the fashion at present to say that science is essentially "public". In fact, the name of science is often applied by definition only to that which is publicly demonstrated and accepted. But what does one find when he examines what he actually does? In making this examination it will be sufficient to typify science by logical reasoning, since logical reasoning is part of all scientific activity. The value of logical reasoning lies in the assurance of the correctness of the conclusion that one has when he has properly gone through the logical processes. Now everyone knows that the conviction of the correctness of a proof or an argument can be obtained only by oneself, after he has made and understood the proper analysis. No one else can make me see or understand, no matter what pressure he may exert on me. I may *say* that I understand when I do not, in order to silence too vociferous an instructor, but "he who consents against his will is of the same opinion still". The feeling of understanding is as private as the feeling of pain. The act of understanding is at the heart of all scientific activity; without it any ostensibly scientific activity is as sterile as that of a high school student substituting numbers into a formula. For this reason, science, when I push the analysis back as far as I can, must be private.

In spite of our stricture, it is evident enough that there is an enormous public aspect to all scientific activity. I usually accept what my qualified neighbor assures me is a scientific fact, and I more often than not defer to my qualified neighbor's scientific judgment. Particularly do I defer to the consensus of the scientific judgment of a large number of my fellows whose scientific attainments I respect. There are at least two reasons for this. In the first place I know that I am likely to make mistakes, so that a necessary part of any scientific activity of my own in which I can feel confidence is to check what I have done to see that I have not made a mistake. I often enough do discover mistakes of my own, and I can also discover mistakes in what my fellows have done. Conversely, when my fellow tells me that I have made a mistake I frequently find, by checking again myself, that he is right. Particularly when a number of my fellows independently say that I have made a mistake I almost always find that they are right. It comes, then, that I use the consensus of opinion of my fellows as a method of checking against my own mistakes. In the second place, my time is limited. I have time to think through for myself only a limited number of conclusions, and particularly I have time to collect and verify for myself only a limited amount of scientific data. I therefore accept the statement of my fellow with regard to an enormous number of scientific facts and an enormous number of conclusions drawn by him by logical processes. These results of my fellows are collected in libraries and classified, where I may get at them when I need them. But I accept this work of my fellows only because it is my potential experience; if I were not convinced that if I repeated his observations and measurements and his logical processes I would check his results, the record of his activity would be of little interest to me. Hence I demand as a condition in any valid scientific publication that it be recorded in such a form that I can repeat it and verify it. The spirit in which I demand that the scientific activity of my fellows be public is therefore paradoxically that in this way I ensure that what they have done may become my private possession, and it is only in so far as it has the potentiality of becoming my private possession that it is of interest to me. The essence of science is private; science as a living thing is my science.

If I now step back a little for a comprehensive look at what I have been doing in analyzing my activities, I see that there are two levels at which I operate, the public and the private level. When I say "we", and think of myself and my fellow in the same terms, or use as meaningful such expression as "my fellow has feelings just like mine", or think of objects as eternally existing in their own right independent of any observer, or when I talk about the body of scientific "truth" as a *thing* that anyone may apprehend by the proper approach, I am on the public level. But when I say "It means nothing to ask whether the feelings of my fellows are the same as mine for all I can know is what he says and does", or when I ask under almost certain danger of being accused of solipsism "What do I mean when I say that things exist eternally independent of any act of observation?", or when I recognize that "truth" without a vitalizing act of understanding by *me* is dead, I am on the private level. The public level is tremendously important, and most of our individual and social living is done on this level. Our language is so constructed that we are almost forced to talk on this level. As we have seen, before the dawn of history the discovery of the public level constituted an invention, perhaps the very most important invention ever made; by it we achieve an economy of intellectual effort without which existence under present conditions might well be utterly impossible. But always beyond the public level, waiting for a deeper analysis, is the private level. It is on the private level that I realize my essential isolation; here is my awful freedom that I can hardly face.

It looks to me as though most people manage to spend almost all their lives exclusively on the public level. We begin life not conscious of any level at all; we presently find ourselves on the public level because of our whole scheme of education, and society does its best to keep us there for the rest of our lives. If some method could be devised by which it could be guaranteed that everyone would always live only on the public level, a possible satisfactory existence might be ensured. But of course it is impossible by fiat or education to suppress a vision that is waiting for anyone to see. Right here is, I believe, the tap root of most of our difficulties; everyone of us has the potentiality when pushed far enough of discovering for himself the private level. This discovery is almost always the result of some bitter experience. Curiously, one usually discovers his own freedom, I think, by discovering that other people are free from him. Someone else refuses to abide by a social convention which I had always treated as binding, and I make the disconcerting discovery that there is no way of compelling the other fellow to accept the assumption back of the convention and so to act of his own free will in accord with the convention. The converse consideration then reveals itself, namely that my fellows are powerless to compel me to accept their interests and purposes. If the conflict of interests is too great and other conditions are right, a gangster is born. There is something of the gangster in all of us, as we discovered during prohibition. The gangster is vividly aware of the existence of the private level; it seems to me that he thinks straighter than many of the good people who deplore his existence. Or one discovers that there are things that cannot be said and questions that cannot be asked. A child who fears that he was adopted, and who is also convinced that his ostensible parents would feel justified in falsehood in order to keep the knowledge from him, sees that he is estopped in asking them whether he is their own. The bitterness of realization of isolation in such a situation may force a premature maturity.

The discovery of the existence of the private level thus means at the same time a discovery of one's own essential isolation, and therefore of the impossibility of anyone else getting a hold on one without one's consent. But society does claim to have a hold on one through all sorts of sanctions, and language is constructed in this atmosphere. The almost inevitable first reaction when one realizes the situation is for one to think that people and society have been saying things that they don't do, that they don't intend to do, and that they can't do. Hence arises a conflict with that very deep human need for consistency between what we do and what we say. People feel abused, disillusioned, and hurt when they discover that things are different from what everyone is saying. It is the perennially pathetic will to believe that a reconciliation between what we do and say is now at last being accomplished that makes possible the propaganda of dictators. The attempt to adapt oneself to what one sees to be the actual situation is a further embittering experience, and society does not thrive on bitterness.

The most important and the ultimate problem of education is to get people to see that there is a private level beyond the public level, and to learn how to live with this realization, or in other words to learn to live with their freedom. The solution of the educational problem demands fundamental revisions. Language, now adapted almost exclusively to the public level, will have to be modified and adapted to permit expression of what one sees on the private level. Deep-seated social instincts and taboos will have to be recognized for what they are, and their field of meaning and application delimited. For instance, one of the very obstinate things to overcome will be the impulse to carry over to the private level all the associations of the "selfishness" complex. So strongly are many people conditioned to the necessity for unselfishness that their intellectual exploration automatically stops when they sniff the faintest whiff of the odor of selfishness. I cannot say to my conventional neighbor "On the private level everything *must* be self-centered" without his retorting automatically "But isn't that terribly selfish?", and the discussion has closed before I can reply. But every sophomore in his bull sessions knows and delights to say this so obvious thing; it is only later when he begins selling bonds that he realizes that this is one of the things that he then cannot say.

The education of the future will meet the situation by making us conscious of the two levels of use of language. On the public level selfishness refers to a reprehensible code of conduct; on the private level it expresses a simple fact, no more to be argued with than any other fact of observation. Probably in order to deal with this matter it will be necessary to invent two different words, but there is far more to it than anything so simple.

Future education will have to show the individual how to live in the midst of his social isolation, but perhaps it will be even more difficult to awaken a realization of all the implications of *intellectual* isolation and to devise a method of adaptation. All the supernatural paraphernalia, which for many people is all that makes life tolerable, will simply have to go. There is no possibility of continuing to feel that one is in a *sympathetic* world, which is evolving according to some purpose with which one may feel oneself congenial, after one has seen that it does not make sense to say of even his fellow human being "He has feelings like mine". It is not that the world is really neither beneficent or malign but instead neutral; it is that it is meaningless to think of the world in terms of beneficence. We are trying to apply an intellectual category that is inapplicable; we are trying to do something with our minds that cannot be done. Much of the machinery of thought on the public level has to be ruthlessly discarded. On the level on which one is asking "What do I mean when I say that objects exist?" one has neither principles or truths, for these are inhabitants of the public level. But nearly everyone derives intellectual support from a feeling of the existence of everlasting principles in the background. It is hard to see that these are *my* devices and to give them up and accept that it is impossible to do what I was trying to do when I invented them. It is hard to admit that there are no certainties, and that the probabilities with which I would fain replace them cannot have the meaning I would desire. Intellectual activity is ultimately as isolated as are my feelings, and all these things have got to be done.

I stand alone in the universe with only the intellectual tools I have with me. I often try to do things with these tools of which they are incapable, and I have often been misinformed and have delusions as to what they are capable of, but nevertheless it is my concern and mine only that I get an answer. An individual trying to wrench himself free from the comfortable support of all the ages into an adequate realization of what his freedom means will probably feel that the only virtue applicable to the situation is fortitude. But fortitude is necessary only as long as he stands on the traditional public level. A generation properly educated from the beginning to recognize the private level will not have to gird itself with fortitude, for never having had the feeling of intellectual support, it will have to indulge in no heroics in giving it up, but will be as objective with its freedom as the most correct scientist is today in his limited field. The uncertainty and the difficulty is in the transition. Will you and I be strong enough and wise enough to get across?

5

ON "SCIENTIFIC METHOD"*

IT SEEMS TO ME that there is a good deal of ballyhoo about scientific method. I venture to think that the people who talk most about it are the people who do least about it. Scientific method is what working scientists do, not what other people or even they themselves may say about it. No working scientist, when he plans an experiment in the laboratory, asks himself whether he is being properly scientific, nor is he interested in whatever method he may be using *as method*. When the scientist ventures to criticize the work of his fellow scientist, as is not uncommon, he does not base his criticism on such glittering generalities as failure to follow the "scientific method," but his criticism is specific, based on some feature characteristic of the particular situation. The working scientist is always too much concerned with getting down to brass tacks to be willing to spend his time on generalities.

Scientific method is something talked about by people standing on the outside and wondering how the scientist manages to do it. These people have been able to uncover various generalities applicable to at least most of what the scientist does, but it seems to me that these generalities are not very pro-

*From The Teaching Scientist, December 1949, written at the request of the editor.

found, and could have been anticipated by anyone who knew enough about scientists to know what is their primary objective. I think that the objectives of all scientists have this in common—that they are all trying to get the correct answer to the particular problem in hand. This may be expressed in more pretentious language as the pursuit of truth. Now if the answer to the problem is correct there must be some way of knowing and proving that it is correct —the very meaning of truth implies the possibility of checking or verification. Hence the necessity for checking his results always inheres in what the scientist does. Furthermore, this checking must be exhaustive, for the truth of a general proposition may be disproved by a single exceptional case. A long experience has shown the scientist that various things are inimical to getting the correct answer. He has found that it is not sufficient to trust the word of his neighbor, but that if he wants to be sure, he must be able to check a result for himself. Hence the scientist is the enemy of all authoritarianism. Furthermore, he finds that he often makes mistakes himself and he must learn how to guard against them. He cannot permit himself any preconception as to what sort of results he will get, nor must he allow himself to be influenced by wishful thinking or any personal bias. All these things together give that "objectivity" to science which is often thought to be the essence of the scientific method.

But to the working scientist himself all this appears obvious and trite. What appears to him as the essence of the situation is that he is not consciously following any prescribed course of action, but feels complete freedom to utilize any method or device whatever which in the particular situation before him seems likely to yield the correct answer. In his attack on his specific problem he suffers no inhibitions of precedent or authority, but is completely free to adopt any course that his ingenuity is capable of suggesting to him. No one standing on the outside can predict what the individual scientist will do or what method he will follow. In short, science is what scientists do, and there are as many scientific methods as there are individual scientists.

6

SOME IMPLICATIONS OF RECENT POINTS OF VIEW IN PHYSICS*

PROFESSOR C. I. LEWIS SUGGESTED to Professor Lameere that there might be a certain interest for European readers of the *Revue Internationale de Philosophie* if I prepared a statement of some of the points of view which I have already discussed in various American writings. The invitation of Professor Lameere to do this I am happy to accept.

These points of view had their origin in the attempt to understand and to generalize the methods by which physicists had successfully met the conceptual crisis brought about by the discovery in the early years of this century of new experimental facts in the domains of relativity and quantum phenomena. The crisis was met only by the adoption of an attitude so radically novel that for many years the older generation of physicists could see in it only paradox and self-contradiction. The essence of the new attitude reveals itself most plainly from an analysis of what Einstein did in his special theory of relativity. Although it is not by any means the whole story, a vital part of the foundation of the special theory of relativity is to be found in the realization by Einstein that a part of the appearance

*From Revue Internationale de Philosophie, October, 1949, No. 10.

of paradox is a consequence of an uncritical attitude toward the meaning of the terms which we had used in describing the experimental results. Our meanings had been naive, whereas the experimental situation proved, when instrumental refinement was carried beyond a certain point, too complex to be described in such naive terms. Familiar concepts like length and time proved complex when a careful analysis was made. The method which disclosed the complexity was an analysis of what we do when we measure the length of discrete objects or the time of concrete events. It turned out that there were recognizably different procedures for measuring the length or the times of events which we had previously assumed uncritically were measured by a single unique procedure, and that it made a vital difference which of these procedures was used in describing the phenomena as simply as possible in the new domain of high velocities.

That is, Einstein recognized that such apparently simple concepts as length and time have multiple meanings, so that there are different kinds of length, for example optical length and tactual length, and that the precise meaning involves the procedure used in obtaining lengths or times in concrete instances. This attitude toward meanings is what I have called "operational." I first expounded it at considerable length in a book published in 1927 and have expanded or modified it in various writings[1]

---

[1] *The Logic of Modern Physics,* Macmillan, New York, 1927; *The Nature of Physical Theory,* Princeton University Press, 1936; *The Intel-*

since. The thesis is that I do not know the meaning of a term unless I can give an "operational" account of it. This means, if the term is one with concrete application, that I be able to tell what I do in determining in any concrete situation that the term is applicable, or that I be able to reconstruct what it was that my neighbor did in selecting the term to describe the concrete situation to me. Although this operational aspect of meanings is only a partial aspect, it is in many situations perhaps the most important aspect, and in a society with a sufficiently homogeneous background it is often all that we need concern ourselves with. This remark applies to meaning in its two modes. If I alone am concerned, experience shows that an operational analysis gives the precision, articulateness and stability to my concepts that I need in discussing situations with myself. On the other hand, if it is a question of communication, it is obvious that if two members of society agree on their operational description of the meaning of a term there will be no confusion in their communication of meaning. In a given setting, the operational analysis of meanings plays a potent part in ensuring clarity and may be made an important tool. In physics it is proving most useful, and I think few physicists would now be satisfied unless their terms were defined in a way that is essentially operational, whether or not they would

---

ligent Individual and Society, Macmillan, New York, 1938; *Operational Analysis* (Phil. of Sci., 5, 114-131, 1938); *Some General Principles of Operational Analysis* (Psych. Rev., 52, 246-249 and 281-284, 1945).

apply this word in characterizing the definition. It is my belief that an analysis of the meanings of concepts in terms of operations can be made equally fruitful in other fields also.

Certain general comments may be made on operational analysis. Initially, the analysis into operations must be made as articulately and completely as possible. The operations back of a concept must at first be uniquely specified and only such operations must be used as can be unequivocally performed in the situations in question. A concept defined by two sets of operations, although the experimental evidence may be that these two sets of operations lead to identical results, must at first be classified as two concepts. The reason for insisting on meticulous attention to distinctions of this sort is that experience has shown that it is not safe to neglect them. All experimental procedure is fringed with error; two procedures can never be shown to be equivalent except within a certain margin of error; when the range of experience widens two different procedures which were hitherto equivalent within error may become recognizably different. It was this that happened in the domain of relativity phenomena at high velocities. By a meticulous insistence on uniqueness of formulation a repetition of the relativity crisis may be avoided. Not only has experience in physics yielded the conviction that a unique specification is the only safe specification, but it has gone further in yielding the active expectation that when old ranges are greatly exceeded it is the rule that formerly equivalent procedures will yield divergent results.

The presence of an operational component in any analysis of concepts seems to me to be a simple result of observation and not to be a matter for argument. It is doubtless more usual to attempt an analysis in terms of objects of the external world or in terms of fixed and static elements of other sorts. But when I ask myself what I mean when I say that objects exist, or that there is an external world, the only answer that I can give is in terms of activities of one sort or another.

Any analysis of meanings into specific operations or activities is obviously not an ultimate analysis, as indeed no analysis is or can be. We require of any analysis that it be one which for the purpose in hand and in the particular context is adequate. Whether any specific analysis will be adequate or profitable can usually be decided only on the basis of a considerable experience. Any specific analysis cannot attempt to penetrate beyond a certain point; that is, in a certain context, certain operations are to be accepted as unanalyzed. For instance, in special relativity theory the operation of judging the coincidence of an event with the position of the hand of a clock, that is, the operation of determining the "local" time of an event, is assumed to be an operation that all observers can perform intuitively, unequivocally, and with the same result, and is therefore unanalyzed. It is obvious enough that no finality or rigor or certainty can inhere in any breakdown of operations into those which are "intuitively" performable. I have no method of ensuring the "same" operation as my neighbor except imitation or observation or description, and none of these can have any assurance of definitiveness. It must be sufficient for us that in many situations it proves that there are simple operations intuitively performable adequately adapted to our purposes. There is no way of predicting what these operations are, and no way of knowing when we have found them except the check offered by an extensive experience. Operational analysis, without a vitalizing experience, is formal and empty. It makes no pretense to go to the "bottom" of things.

It may seem to many that it is unsatisfactory to leave the fundamental operations unanalyzed and intuitive, but that some definition of the operations which are accepted as fundamental should be attempted. It seems to me that there are dangers in this. For how shall an operation be defined? Either in terms of other operations, in which case we have sidestepped the issue, or else in terms of its properties. The latter brings back all the difficulties that we are trying to avoid, because the proof that a certain operation has certain properties can never be given except with a margin of experimental uncertainty, so that we can never be sure that when precision is pushed to new limits it will not appear that operations with such properties do not exist. This was exactly the situation that arose with regard to the Newtonian definitions of absolute space and time that touched off the whole relativity development. I believe that the indefiniteness involved in accepting intuitive operations as our unanalyzed is unavoidable.

It is by no means necessary that the operations chosen as fundamental for the analysis be physical operations with physical instruments, as is sometimes mistakenly stated. For obviously the activity of the experimenter in dealing with a physical situation, or more generally with other situations in which concepts are used with definable meanings, is not an activity which can be exhaustively described in physical terms, but there is necessarily a "mental" component. It is only necessary that the components of mental activity be described in such terms that the subject or his fellow can uniquely reproduce them on demand. It is not profitable to attempt an exhaustive classification of the non-instrumental or "mental" operations. One very broad group of these may, however, be specially considered, namely those which are used by the theoretical physicist in putting his theories in mathematical form. A large part of the mathematical activity of the theoretical physicist is concerned with the manipulation of his mathematical symbols on paper, and we shall accordingly speak of "paper and pencil" operations as suggestive of this whole class of non-instrumental operations. Now at one time or another some physicists have expressed the idea that all paper and pencil operations are eventually reducible to instrumental operations. It seems to me that there is no acceptable argument as to why this should be necessary or desirable, and I believe that observation shows that theoretical physicists do profitably employ concepts which can in no way be reduced to instrumental operations. Quantum mechanics is full of examples; the psi function is one of the simplest.

It is perhaps not at first evident why an operational analysis of meanings is of value or what its value is. The value is, I think, to be found in the fact that it enables us to see more clearly whether we are likely to attain the purposes we have in view. Our experience has shown that certain procedures are useful for attaining certain purposes and that other procedures are not useful or are actually harmful. If the "good" procedures are used in forming our concepts, then we may anticipate success, whereas if we find that "bad" procedures are involved we will do well to modify our concepts. Furthermore, actual analysis discloses that in many instances we had made unconscious assumptions about the nature of the procedures we were using; we had assumed that they were "good" procedures without taking the trouble to find what the procedures actually were; whereas when we make the analysis we find that they were "bad" procedures. This was the situation with regard to the concepts of length and time before Einstein made his analysis. Here again there is no getting away from the appeal to experience, which alone is capable of telling whether in the context of a given purpose any specific procedure is "good" or "bad."

With this brief exposition of what is involved in the operational method I now turn to a consideration of some of the results of its application in actual situations. In any actual applications the first task is to find what are the operations which in the given context are treated as unanalyzed. In the context of the ordinary situations of daily life it will be found, I think, that these unanalyzed operations are to a surprisingly large extent purely verbal. Usually, of course, any simple term is used in a given situation with confidence, with no attempt at justification of the propriety of using the term, and with no consciousness that justification is required. If the necessity for justification appears, so that some form of analysis is forced on one, it will be found I think that often one makes a very simple sort of verbal experiment to assure himself that the term was correctly used. Execution of the verbal experiment constitutes the operation that in this case gives the meaning. This verbal experiment consists simply in saying to oneself: "would I say thus and thus in such and such a situation?" The asking of the question gives the pause for a somewhat higher degree of self consciousness in appraising the situation, and the answer is usually given with confidence without any attempt at exhaustive analysis of what the precise character of the situation may be. Furthermore, one usually feels assurance that one's neighbor would give the same answer to the verbal experiment, and when one has the consciousness of potential corroboration by one's neighbor the issue of the meaning of the term is regarded as disposed of and not thought of further. The underlying situation is obviously exceedingly complex here. Consciousness of potential corroboration by one's neighbor involves a background of common culture and language which it would be hopeless to attempt to analyze exhaustively, but there is no doubt that in practice human beings can and do act in this way.

One may attempt to push the analysis a step further by asking what are the meanings of the terms used in characterizing the situation as "such and such" in our verbal experiment. This situation may often be "objectively" characterized in some way or another, but it may also be a situation which is itself characterized only in verbal terms, for instance, a situation created by a statement or a question from my neighbor. The analysis can obviously be pushed indefinitely, step by step. I think our experience shows, in the case of those concepts which ostensibly deal with the external world, that we require that our analysis of meaning must eventually emerge into contact with the external world, so that we can free ourselves from the verbal encumbrance. We demand of our terms in physics, for example, that this eventual objective emergence be possible. Whether such emergence actually occurs cannot in general be told until the analysis has been made. Thus the concepts of absolute space and absolute time of Newton proved not capable of emergence beyond the verbal, whereas the local time and optical length of Einstein do thus emerge.

Analysis discloses, I believe, that many of the terms of daily life are incapable of being made to emerge into the "objective," but that they are part of open verbal chains. It is our naive expectation that objective emergence is possible in many cases where analysis shows that it is not. One value of an operational analysis consists in the discovery of our mistaken expectation. This holds preeminently for many of the terms of conventional philosophy and religion, such as "being" and "reality" and "God."

Man, in the course of his intellectual development, has erected verbal structures of almost inconceivable complexity, and these structures have come to be just as truly a part of the human environment as the physical environment. In the verbal environment man exhibits patterns of behavior which have a definiteness, uniformity, and stability sufficient to give them social value. Man can adapt himself to his fellow man by the use of concepts whose unanalyzed operations are exclusively verbal. It does not seem surprising that this should be possible in view of man's long verbal history. Neither is it impossible that the character of the verbal background should be such that concepts which can be analyzed only into verbal operations should nevertheless be applicable to the objective external environment. This doubtless occurs, and furthermore a verbal analysis of an objective situation may often be suggestive, but we can feel no security in a situation such as this, and we usually do demand, when we stop to think about it, that we be able to get away from open verbal chains when dealing with the external world. We certainly make this demand in our science.

In spite of the inconceivable complexity of our verbal structures, all our language and also our thinking operates under a universal restriction, namely we strive to employ in our thinking only terms with fixed and static meanings, analogous to the objects of the external world. Yet to the most untutored observation talking and thinking are continually evolving activities; tomorrow we talk about what we were talking about yesterday and the objects of our discourse are continually creating themselves. With our blunt intellectual tools the everlasting wonder is not that we have as much trouble with language and thought as we do, but that we can get along as well as we do.

The first result of an operational analysis is usually not to bring simplification, but complexity. We discover that most of our concepts as used in daily life are actually multiple and that different sets of defining operations are used indiscriminately. Otherwise expressed, most of our common concepts are over-defined. From the point of view of a methodology that seeks to attain the maximum precision the undesirability of this is obvious. We must insist, at first, on uniqueness in our operational definitions. But in daily life exactly the opposite point of view prevails, and those concepts survive as useful which have a number of approximately equivalent operational definitions applicable in a range of circumstances. In daily life the point of view of relativity theory that there are different kinds of length, for instance, such as tactual and optical, is often repudiated, and it is stated that the concept "length" comprises that which is common in all those situations to which the term length in any operational sense is applied. This is a possible attitude, but it may be an unprofitable attitude and it is fraught with danger, for later new knowledge may show that there is nothing common in the various situations which is worth emphasizing. Our growing appreciation of the complexity of the physical world leads to a feeling of the greater profitableness of striving for the greatest precision rather than the greatest inclusiveness in our concepts.

Since meanings are in our control, it is conceivable that we might find it desirable sometimes to give a term a multiple meaning deliberately, that is, if this can be done without leading to self contradiction in any conceivable circumstance. This possibility affords a method of dealing with some of the conventional questions of philosophy different from the usual. For instance, we may reply to the question "Do objects continue to exist in the absence of any perceiving mind?" by saying "You may say that objects continue so to exist if you find it *convenient* to say so." *But,* if we find it convenient to say so, we must recognize that we have thereby chosen to give a multiple operational meaning to "exist," one meaning which holds when there is a perceiving mind present and one when there is not. It is not at once evident, however, that it is possible to so give a multiple operational meaning to "exist" without ever getting into contradiction. The discovery of whether such contradiction is ever possible constitutes, I believe, the only profit to be found in a serious discussion of the original question.

Turning now from this general consideration of what we find when we examine meanings of the terms of daily life, let us consider more particularly what we find when we analyze our scientific concepts, especially those of the physical sciences. Perhaps the most striking result of this analysis, as already intimated, is that we never find simplicity, but as we push our analysis further we encounter ever greater complication. Any apparent simplicity turns out to be the result of human construction. The validity of all such construction must be suspect when we invade new domains. In fact, one of the chief purposes of an operational analysis is to recover the complexities of the primitive situation, and it is one of its chief virtues that it is able to. When we make this analysis we find that the character of the world gets continually hazier as we push our analysis further, and that certainty and definiteness are the illusions of a comparatively early stage of the analysis. We are capable only of a spiralling approximation, and there is no method of assurance that the process will ultimately be even convergent. The stage of the greatest illusion of certainty is the stage at which we are content with an analysis of the external world into material objects, which we think of as having a permanence in themselves and whose changing relations to each other in time determine experience. This analysis into individual and permanent objects is one which our thinking processes exploit to the greatest possible extent, and we are not comfortable in our thinking unless we have managed so to make our constructs that they can be handled like the things of ordinary experience. But the world is too complicated to permit forcing into so straight a mold, even in the situations of physics. It seems to me that physics is recognizably still attempting to operate with some concepts contaminated with a spurious reification. For instance, the energy concept is handled as though energy were a thing, whereas analysis discloses that the only operations in terms of which energy receives its meaning involve *two* states of a system plus the process by which the system is transferred from one state to the other. It is a consequence that it is improper to speak of the energy of a single state of a system as one could if energy were like a thing. This improper view of the nature of energy has obscured much of the discussion of Einstein's celebrated mass-energy relation, and has also resulted in a good deal of meaningless speculation about energy being one of the two primary constituents of the universe, the other being "matter." Other concepts of physics which I believe have not yet thrown off the shackles of a false reification are of light, or radiation in general, as being a thing travelling, or of the "field" as something independent of the operations of the definition which generated it.

The analysis of the external world into objects is one which for all purposes of common sense may be accepted as ultimate, in fact one definition of the realm of common sense might be the realm in which objects are accepted as unanalyzable. But, as always, it is possible to push the analysis further and ask what we mean when we say that this or that is truly an object. And, as always, it is possible to give an answer of sorts in this case by saying that we are dealing with an object when certain aggregates of the sense impressions of ourselves and our fellows have certain attributes of universality and permanence. This analysis which carries us beyond the object, is an analysis into activities or happenings, and in order to make this analysis we have to be able to recognize the activity or the happening as itself identifiable and endowed with the ability to recur. How we are able to do this is a further story which need not concern us now, but that we do it is shown by simple observation. The reproach of solipsism has sometimes been imputed to this point of view with regard to objects, but it seems to me that this rests on a misconception. It is not the same to say "objects do not exist except in my mind" as to ask what we mean when we say "objects exist."

Perhaps the most deeply entrenched of all the positions maintained by the cult of reification is with respect to the nature of numbers. It is almost universal to think of numbers in the Platonic sense as being in many respects like things, each with its own individuality and identity, and such that it is meaningful to say that this or that number "exists." Thus in his recent book Bertrand Russell says that it is certain that numbers "exist" which have never been thought of by any one. This almost universal Platonic way of thinking about numbers it seems to me is a very close analogue of the common sense way of thinking about objects. Just as in the case of objects it is possible to carry the analysis beyond common sense, so in the case of numbers it is possible to carry the analysis beyond Plato. From this point of view it is a deeper and truer description of the nature of a number to say it is something that we do that may be repeated rather than to say it is a thing. It seems to me that operational analysis demands this view of the nature of a number. If we adopt this point of view, certain consequences follow. Perhaps the most important are with respect to the infinite processes which form the subject matter of much of "Mengenlehre." From the point of view of operations, and this means operations actually carried out or performable, an "infinite" process can only mean a process which is specified in such a way that the process is non-self-terminating. An infinite number is a certain aspect of what one does when he embarks on carrying out a process formulated in this way, that is, an infinite number is an aspect of a *program* of action. From this point of view it does not make sense to speak of infinite numbers as "existing" in the Platonic sense, and still less does it make sense to speak of infinite numbers of different orders of infinity, as does Cantor. In developing the Cantorian point of view the "diagonal Verfahren" for proving the nondenumerability of the transcendental numbers plays a fundamental role. But is the proof by the method of the diagonal process cogent? Many mathematicians aggressively maintain that there can be no doubt of the validity of this proof, whereas others do not admit it. I personally cannot see an iota of appeal in this proof, but it appears to me to be a perfect nonsequitur— my mind will not do the things that it is obviously expected to do if this is indeed a proof. But I can see that if I had the Platonic concept of numbers and in particular of the infinite numbers as of something already existing with individuality and identifiability, that then my mind would make the steps that it is expected to and I would emerge with the conviction of proof. A somewhat similar situation occurs for me with regard to the paradoxes of Zeno. No formulation of these paradoxes has ever been able to give me the feeling of paradox, but I can see that if I literally thought of a line as consisting of an assemblage of points and of an interval of time as the sum of moments without duration, paradox would then present itself. In general, paradox can be felt only in a context of presuppositions, usually unconscious, and similarly proof is not a completely formal, mechanical, automatic affair, but it demands a background which may be as complex as the whole content of a culture. Here is conceivably a method of analysis for the unexpressed presuppositions of various systems of thought, namely by studying the conditions under which proof or paradox is felt.

This matter of the diagonal proof and the nature of numbers indicates that the extent to which we push our analysis is not entirely in our control, although we have spoken of pushing our analysis to one or another point depending on our purposes. The extent to which the analysis is pushed is also to a certain extent a matter of vision, for once having caught a vision one cannot always forget it, no matter what the purpose of the moment. The feeling of paradox or of proof which may be the accompaniment of a less extensive vision can never be recovered once the wider vision has been seen. I believe that it involves a wider vision to think of the objects of the external world in terms of groups of activities rather than in terms of common sense, or to think of numbers as something that we do rather than in Platonic terms, and that once having seen the wider vision we find that there are things which we can no longer do with our minds.

Repudiation of the diagonal process and the orders of infinity of Cantor at the same time eliminates the paradoxes conventionally associated with "Mengenlehre." Indeed, adoption of the operational view towards concepts automatically removes paradox or inner contradiction. For any conceptual situation reduced to operational terms becomes a description of an actual occurrence, and actual occurrences are not contradictory. Contradiction is always our work, and we can encounter it only when we are mistaken about what we think we are doing.

A personal note may be added to these remarks about "Mengenlehre." In 1934 I published the paper entitled *A Physicist's Second Reaction to Mengenlehre* in which I described the change in my personal attitude since my first contact with the subject 30 years before. This first contact was that of youth, in which I found the Cantorian analysis stimulating and convincing, whereas my return to the subject 30 years later, after acquiring the operational point of view from my experience in physics, had found me unable to feel any cogency in the accepted proofs or even any meaning in some of the conventional concepts. In that paper I indicated in detail how a number of the paradoxes disappear in the new conceptual atmosphere. The reception which that paper received was a surprise and a disappointment, for it produced no appreciable effect, being dismissed by one school of mathematicians as being "essentially sound but very naive" and dismissed by the other school as without appreciation of what constitutes mathematics. With this, I dropped all concern with the matter for a number of years, being occupied in the laboratory, and returned to it for a third time only a couple of years ago, stimulated by a lecture from a visiting well known mathematician who referred to the proof of the diagonal process as universally accepted and admitted to be sound beyond the peradventure of a doubt. I thereupon attempted to reexamine the whole matter, and in this enlisted the help of discussions with a colleague who is a professional logician of high standing and who also thought the diagonal proof sound. After the exchange of several long letters we reached agreement at least to the extent of both seeing that the diagonal proof is a proof only in the context of the Platonic concept of the nature of number. I think my colleague still does not accept the idea of numbers as something we do rather than as things. At the same time I was able to understand a little better why the ordinary mathematician clings to his Platonic concept of numbers. He does this because he is not interested primarily in rigor, but rather in fruitfulness. He is interested in doing things and in getting results, and the Platonic concept, leading to infinities of different orders, has proved stimulating and fruitful. The fact that paradox also occurs is indeed unpleasant, but is regarded as probably not too great a price to pay for the richness of the results. This is a perfectly understandable situation, but I think that the mathematician who has once seen a number as something that we do will not be able to go back to the Platonic concept, and will eventually find how to reformulate in the new framework those of the old results which have validity, and at the same time avoid the old paradox.

One other aspect of the mathematics which we use in our physical theories may be mentioned in addition through the nature of numbers. This is that in mathematics there is nothing corresponding to the margin of error which fringes all our knowledge and description of the external world. No physical measurements can be made with a precision beyond a few decimal places, whereas in mathematics there is no bound to the decimals that may be heaped up or to the largeness or the smallness of the numbers that we manipulate. This is enough to reveal mathematics as palpably our tool and construction, not reproducing with complete success the obvious structure of the world to which we wish to apply it. With this recognition it is fatuous to think of the role of mathematics in such terms as did Jeans, for example, who could exclaim "God is a Mathematician."

Mathematics is often reduced to logic; does the operational view have anything to say about the nature of logic? I believe that not only it does, but that it essentially alters our entire attitude toward logic, particularly our feeling that we have here something completely precise and sharp, perhaps because it is purely "formal." To see what is involved, consider the syllogism in its conventional form: "If all a is b, and all b is c, then all a is c." It springs to the eye that the syllogism has a strong operational component, for these are not just static marks on paper, but they have an order, without which the syllogism is meaningless. The conclusion *follows* from the premises. The marks on paper direct us in a succession of operations which have to be performed in time. Furthermore, the symbols of the syllogism have a context of meaning, and unless they have this context the syllogism is indeed an empty array of marks on paper. In particular, the symbols each occur twice in the syllogism; this implies that at the very minimum the context must be such that the symbol "a," for instance, stands for the same thing the second time that it occurs as the first. This implies the existence of some method by which it may be determined that it does indeed stand for the "same" thing on both occurrences. Furthermore, the implication is that this is not an empty requirement, but that there are indeed things of which it makes sense to say that they remain the same during the discourse. But what sort of a thing is it of which this may be said? Is it the objects of every day life? These do indeed appear to casual inspection to have an identity and to remain the "same," but physics tells us that every material object is continually emitting and receiving radiation, and that its energy content continually fluctuates, even in the idealized state at absolute zero of temperature. Since the energy content must be reckoned as part of the object, it appears when we push our analysis far enough that objects with identity are not encountered in experience. Or is it the things that we do that have identity and permanence? Can we do the same thing twice? We have assumed that we can, and this assumption has played a fundamental role in our formulation of the operational method. But when we push our analysis far enough, we see that we never do the same thing twice, for time has passed between performances, and my clock reads differently on the second doing. When we speak of doing the same thing twice we are isolating a piece of experience from the rest, and there is no procedure for making the isolation sharp.

It would appear, then, that the requirement of "sameness" implied in the syllogism is a requirement that cannot be met sharply, but with only a degree of approximation. How good must the approximation be to permit use in the syllogism? The answer is not obvious, for many a paradox has occurred because the approximation which at first was assumed good enough in actuality was not. Is there any other answer than that the approximation is good enough if the syllogism gives a correct result when used according to the assumption? In any event, whether or not an answer can be found, what has become in such a setting of the "certainty" which was thought to inhere in the operations of logic?

If the syllogism is to have content, then in every concrete application there must be some method of verifying the correctness of the conclusion. With this necessary background of potential operations of verification it seems to me that it is a misrepresentation to speak of the syllogism, or of logic in general, as having only formal content. The possibility of verification would seem to imply the possibility of getting to the same terminus by two different paths; the syllogism provides one method of getting to the terminus, and the process of verification implies a second path. The second path implies some factual element and is not purely "formal." The larger context in which the syllogism has meaning and significance is not purely formal.

There is another aspect of the conclusion of the syllogism which I think is important. We *assent* to the conclusion. The syllogism is something to be *understood,* as well as a piece of mental machinery by which we can grind out correct answers. Understanding the syllogism means that we recognize that the conclusion "must" follow from the premises. This recognition of inevitability it seems to me always occurs whenever we have the experience of *proof.* Logic enables us to formulate some of the necessary conditions which must be satisfied before proof is recognized, but the conditions so formulated are by no means sufficient, as one can discover by watching some ten-year-old reading the *Principia Mathematica.* It would probably not be possible at present to formulate a sufficient set of conditions for the acceptance of proof, but one general characterization is obvious, namely that proof is a private matter. A proof presented to me with the authority of the greatest logician in the world is not a proof for me unless I can "see" it. Any use I may make of such a proof is mechanical, leading it is true to correct results in a limited domain, but sterile when I try to carry it into new fields.

There is thus a private component in the enterprise of logic. There is another private component not only to logic but universal to any intellectual enterprise, or at least any such enterprise to which the attribute of correctness may be imputed. How shall I guard against my own mistakes, or how shall I assure myself that I am really doing what I think I am doing? How do I know that I am not dreaming? I think there is no intellectual enterprise in which the possibility of self-doubt does not lurk in the background, and no intellectual enterprise in which we have confidence in which there is not some method by which we may at least partially remove such self-doubt. The methods by which we give ourselves such assurance are complicated and seldom formulated, but I think they contain recognizably an introspective component which must be private and furthermore cannot possibly be made sharp. Herein is a justification for the contention that we never achieve perfect sharpness, for we can obviously always push our analysis to the point of self-doubt. The apparent sharpnesses of logic and mathematics are at a different and earlier level, where we have deliberately conspired not to push our analysis to embarrassing lengths.

If every intellectual enterprise contains a private component then science as a special case also contains a private component. It is usual to ignore this private component and to think of science as an essentially "public" enterprise; in fact the possibility of publicity is sometimes made a part of the definition of science. It is obvious that under this sort of a definition the much prized "objectivity" of science is ensured. Although this public component in science doubtless exists and is important, I believe that the private component is even more important. For any scientist worthy of the name does not accept the public body of scientific knowledge simply because it is public or has the authority of the consensus of his colleagues. He does not accept any scientific result of others unless he is convinced that he too could obtain the same result if he took the time and the trouble, and he demands that any scientific investigation published in a technical journal be described in such terms that he can see how to go to work to verify the result for himself. No argument presented to him by his colleague is accepted as valid unless it bears the impress of *proof*. Now both these matters, the potentiality of repetition by himself and the presence of proof, are private. No creative science can exist without them. Indeed if one means creative science in the narrower sense of advance into new territory, then from the very definition creative science must be private, for always the advance into new territory is made by some individual. But even in the broader sense of a creative science which for every scientist is at least *recreative,* the private component seems to me incomparably more important; without this component science is formal and dead.

There is another aspect of science closely related to this matter of public versus private. If the meanings of science are to be found in operations, then there must be a performer of the operations, and this is of necessity a human performer. A complete formulation of what is involved in any scientific enterprise must have somewhere in the background the performer of the operations. Now it seems to be the instinct of the conventional scientist to try to suppress this performer in the background, and in fact he makes an ideal and a virtue out of such suppression. This is sometimes expressed by saying that any scientific formulation must be freed from its anthropomorphic elements. Perhaps this urge to get rid of all human reference and the conviction of the necessity for it has been pushed to its extreme form in the general theory of relativity of Einstein. In this theory the fundamental equations of physics are formulated in generalized coordinates from which all mention of any particular reference system has disappeared, and from the form of this generalized formulation certain conclusions are purportedly extracted as to the nature of the general laws. It is obvious that the frame of mind of Einstein, who expects that a formulation like this is possible and capable of giving information, is entirely different from the frame of mind engendered by the operational approach which recognizes that an operation demands an operator, so that the nature of meaning itself makes it impossible to get away from a reference system (the operator). In Einstein's yearning for absolute information and meaning it seems to me that the ghosts of Newton's absolute space and time are walking again, ghosts which Einstein himself had apparently exorcised in his special theory of relativity. Of course, if one is to indulge in a criticism like this of Einstein's general theory, it is incumbent to show how it was that he got his results. I have attempted to do this in detail in my *Nature of Physical Theory* and again in a chapter in the book edited by Schilpp on the Philosophy of Einstein scheduled to appear in the fall of 1949. In brief, it appears to me that the results have followed, not from the form of the equations as one might infer, but from the requirement of simplicity, which is something quite different. This is not the place, however, to pursue this matter further.

One meets the same endeavor to get away from the human reference point and to find absolute meanings in a very much broader setting than that of the physical sciences. This has been the theme of much of philosophy and is involved in the asking of such questions as "Do objects continue to exist in the absence of a perceiving mind?" It seems to me that the very nature of meaning itself makes it impossible to get away from the human reference point, and that to attempt it or to set it up as a goal betrays a fundamental misconception.

Let us now revert briefly to some of the further consequences of the operational point of view in the situations of daily life. Perhaps the most immediate is, as already stated, an enhanced realization of the complexity of our conceptual structures. Nearly all our concepts have multiple meanings, usually not explicitly stated, and one or the other of these meanings is predominantly used on one or another level of activity where the operations have a certain degree of homogeneity. One is not usually conscious of this, however, and uses the same word on different levels with the implication of a unique meaning. It is, for example, just as important to recognize that "theological truth" is not the same as "scientific truth," because the operations by which the truth of a theological statement is verified are not the same as the operations by which the truth of a scientific statement is verified, as it was in relativity theory to recognize that "optical length" was not the same as "tactual length" because the corresponding operations were different. In fact, I think that one may anticipate that the consequences of failure to recognize that there are two or more kinds of truth may be even more disastrous than failure to recognize two kinds of length, because the situations in which the concept of truth are applied are so much more complicated than those in which we apply the concept of length. In these complicated situations we have the potentiality for vastly greater unsuspected detail than we ever did in the comparatively simple physical situations of relativity. Failure to recognize the presence of multiple meanings is, I believe, one of the most prevalent sources of misunderstandings. A thoroughgoing application of the operational analysis of meanings puts in our hands, I believe, the possibility of eventually eliminating failure of agreement on meanings as a source of friction in human affairs. No more potent instrument of good will can be imagined.

The operational clarification of the meaning of certain specific terms may be anticipated to have important repercussions. For instance, a metaphysical conception of the nature of the State cannot survive the analysis of the nature of the operations which in any concrete situation give meaning to statements about the State. The situation is very similar with respect to Society, which is often thought of as a sort of superpersonality, with rights and a value superior to those of the individuals who compose it. Any operational analysis of social situations leads inevitably back to the component individuals. *The individual is the unit in terms of which all our social concepts ultimately find their meanings.* No totalitarian philosophy of the state or society can survive a realization of this. It seems to me that here is a sound basis for combatting the totalitarian ideology, a basis which we had lost in our loss of the conviction of the worth of the individual human soul in the sight of God, which was the justification for democratic ideology accepted by our fathers.

The appearance of the individual at the bottom of any social analysis now leads me finally to attempt to state what seems to me the most drastic revision of our outlook forced by an uninhibited operational analysis. Not only does the individual intrude himself unmistakably when we push our analysis as far as we can see, but that individual is I. All the operations in terms of which I make my analyses are operations by me. Any description which I can give of what happens must be made in the first person. When I make a statement "objectively" in terms of a public science I am involving myself in an obvious construction to the effect that you and I are equivalent. But the chasm of meaning between you and me is unbridgeable because the operations are different. The operations which justify me in saying that I am conscious are different from the operations which justify me in saying that you are conscious, as are the operations for saying that my tooth aches from those for saying that your tooth aches. Whenever I treat thine and mine on the same basis I am deliberately using words with a dual operational meaning, and my reason for doing this is one of convenience. The enormous convenience in social situations requires no argument. For example, we are enabled to say: "Other minds exist beside mine, and they are like it." Now it seems to me there is no absolute answer to the question "Do other minds exist beside my mind?" The answer is: "You may say yes if you find it convenient to do so." But if we choose to say yes, we must recognize that we have thereby dualized the concepts of mind and existence. We have not necessarily involved ourselves in a fatal dilemma by choosing to dualize our concepts, for it is conceivable that there may be no overlapping of situations. It might be that always we shall either be able to apply the operations which define "exist when you are concerned" or the operations which define "exist when I am concerned," so that we would have merely the sum of two situations. Whether this is actually the case or not can be told by examination. My belief is that this will not turn out to be the case, but that it often happens that we apply the "you" operations in "me" situations, as when we think of our sensations in terms of our bodily organs apprehended in the same way as we apprehend the organs of our fellows. We can expect confusion when we do not recognize cases of overlapping usage of the "you" and the "me" operations, or perhaps we can say better public and private operations, and it seems to me that this is indeed the source of most of the confusion in philosophical discussions of the perennial you-me problems. For example, failure to distinguish between public and private operations is I believe at the bottom of the difficulties usually felt in connection with the "problem" of the freedom of the will. "Freedom" here has meaning only for private operations, while the determinism which introduces the dilemma has its meaning in terms of public operations.

It is conceivable that the situation could be dealt with by renouncing the "me" operations altogether and by dealing with all "me" situations by "you" operations exclusively. But to do this would require a self-renunciation which is apparently beyond human self-control, and even if done, it would be at the crippling expense of discarding something that we know we can always do. It seems to me that the only realistic way of dealing with the situation is to recognize that we have here a fundamental dichotomy which pervades every aspect of our relations with our fellows. We will never achieve freedom from possible dilemma and paradox until we devise a method of thinking and a language in which this dichotomy is incorporated. From the point of view of the conventional "objective" language of "reality" it may appear that this involves such great complexities as to be hopeless. In fact, our failure ordinarily to even recognize the existence of the situation may be explained by its obvious complexity. For instance, if the science of every one is private, do we not have as many sciences as there are individual scientists? We automatically shy away from a situation as complex as this. But although we may appear to have complexity here, it is from the old point of view of a hybrid reality in which all the other I's are comprehended under the same reality as I myself. If the actual operational construction of the world, as revealed by observation, is accepted at its face value, this dilemma will never arise, nor will we use a hybrid reality concept in our thinking, and at most there can be only "my science" and "your science" or "my pain" and "your pain." In most of the purely physical sciences recognition of this dichotomy will make little actual difference. But in such subjects as psychology it will make a great difference, and we may expect that in social situations in general an adequate apprehension of it will demand a complete reformulation of social philosophy.

In concluding, I think it must be evident that hardly more than a beginning has been made on the task of remaking the world from the operational point of view. In physics, much remains to be done, particularly, I think, in making a more articulate analysis of the concepts of physics into their instrumental and "paper and pencil" aspects. In philosophy, a greater consciousness of the complexity of our verbal structures will result in a shift of emphasis and interest. Most philosophical discussions of metaphysics, for example, will appear to be fundamentally discussions of the properties of our verbal structures and of their adequacy to deal with various verbal situations. In religion, the realization that it is impossible and meaningless to transcend the human reference point will bring the vision that the history of religion since the birth of the race has been the history of an attempt to evade the fundamental problem of humanity, namely to find its springs of action within itself. In the social and political domain it will appear that all social and political philosophy has failed to recognize the dichotomy which to a fresh and unspoiled vision is the most striking feature of the experience of each of us, and in failing to recognize the dichotomy has inextricably confused public and private operations. Adequate recognition of the dichotomy will force a revision of the philosophy at the basis of our legal and social structures.

7

THE OPERATIONAL ASPECT OF MEANING*

THE PHYSICAL SCIENTISTS who were present at the first meeting and heard the talk of Professor Jakobson must have been struck by the difference of attitude toward meanings between the linguist and the physical scientist. If I understood Professor Jakobson correctly, for the linguist the meaning of a term is to be found in whatever it is that is common in all its usages. Now the various usages of a term originated with different people, who look at things in different ways, and who are constantly faced with new situations, for which they find no exact word in their language as they have it, and who, in order to communicate the new thing as best they can, seize on some analogy between the present and old situations, and extend the use of an old word, which thereupon becomes altered in meaning. At any epoch, therefore, the meaning of a word for the linguist is an aspect of human behavior as it has been altered by a complex past history. The meaning of a word at any epoch is to a certain extent fortuitous, significant of the special features in past usage of the word which happens to have stuck in the memory of the users. This, I think, is correct

*From Synthese, 8, 251-259, 1950-51.

as a factual description of the meanings of words as used in everyday life, and as such is proper subject for detailed study by the linguist. Whether the state of affairs thus disclosed is desirable or not is another matter. For some of the purposes of daily life it is desirable, because it gives a certain flexibility to communication which makes it possible to meet novel situations. Furthermore, for the speaker it has the advantage that it diminishes the mental effort of finding the proper verbal form in which to communicate, because the listener, by the use of good will, can tolerate a certain degree of vagueness. In fact, Professor Zipf might want to formulate a mathematical theorem here to the effect that maximum economy for the whole social effort demands that the listener spends as much mental effort in understanding a speaker as the speaker spends in finding his verbal formulation. But for other of the purposes of daily life the vagueness and imprecision of such usage of words is undesirable, as everyone knows who has waited an hour for an appointment because of misunderstanding.

The physical scientist is perhaps the one person who finds the vagueness and imprecision of the conversation of daily life most intolerable, and who has been driven, as a precondition to the plying of his trade of science, to using his terms with a much greater degree of precision. This implies that his meanings have to be precise. The subject of meaning has many aspects, many of which need not concern us. The aspect with which we shall be mostly concerned deals with communication, provided that communication is understood in a sense broad enough to include communication with oneself. For if I write a memorandum to do something tomorrow or write out a mathematical analysis to which I expect to return at some later time, or just plain talk to myself, I am in a sense communicating with myself through the symbols that I use. In order that the communication be effective, whether with myself or with another, it is required that the meanings be clear, and it is with this aspect of meaning in its relation to communication that we shall be mostly concerned.

What is the criterion of effective communication, especially in scientific situations? Whatever the criterion, I think it will always be found to involve action of one sort or another. If I am trying to describe a situation, the criterion that I have successfully communicated it, is that my fellow be able to *reconstruct* the situation. Or if I am trying to influence his behavior, the criterion of success in my communication is that he acts in the desired way or even the communication may be successful *as communication* if he refuses to act in the desired way. The action resulting from the communication of meaning need not be a strikingly overt action—it may be nothing more than the creation of a frame of mind. The success of the communication *as a whole,* that is, the meaningfulness of the communication, is therefore to be found in the actions which accompany it. Now for many purposes the communication as a whole may be analyzed into parts, usually words, and one of the functions of language is to ensure that the meaning of the whole be determined by the parts. This may be expressed by saying that the parts have meaning. There are at least two aspects of the meaning of the parts; there is in the first place the absolute requirement that the parts in juxtaposition have meaning, since the communication as a whole has meaning, and, in addition, in a great many cases the parts in isolation have sufficient individuality, so that they have meaning in isolation. This is shown by the fact that in most cases it is possible to find a fairly adequate translation of the individual words from one language into another. In the following we shall be mostly concerned with the meaning of terms in isolation. We shall assume that language may be so constructed and the common background of usage in any homogeneous culture may be such that when the meaning of the terms in isolation is known their meaning in combination is also fixed. We are obviously omitting very large questions here, in particular, the whole question of syntax.

What now is the criterion that the meaning of a term in isolation is known? Here again the criterion can be formulated in terms of action. If I know what it was that my fellow did to decide to use the term, or if my fellow can reconstruct for himself what it was that I did in deciding to use the term, then, I think we must say that the meaning of the term in that particular usage is fixed. Meaning thus specified may be vague or precise, unique or multiple, reflecting the character of the communicants and their background. But in any event the situation must be dealt with articulately enough so that the correctness of the decision to use the given term can be subject to some kind of check. This check may be relatively superficial, as when I re-examine my decision by merely asking myself. "Would I use such and such a word in such and such a situation?" The answer can often be given confidently and reproducibly without any vivid consciousness of what it is that gives confidence. What gives the confidence may be a most complex thing, and involve the entire unconscious background of education and culture, but this is immaterial provided only that my fellow can sense what sort of a situation made me choose my word, and he usually can do this if the common cultural background is sufficiently homogeneous.

We see, therefore, that a specification of meanings, both of isolated terms and of communication in toto, involves a specification of action of some sort. This I have expressed by saying that "meanings are operational." In its generality this statement is tautological. But in the context of scientific usage, because the purposes of science are restricted, the sorts of operation that can be used in giving meanings must be restricted so as to give the sort of meanings that are demanded in scientific activity. The most important requirement here is precision, and we have to ask what sort of operations are compatible with precision. But precision is itself an unprecise word; we may, for example, have logical precision or we may have precision in physical measurement. We need both sorts of precision in science, and they are different. Even with regard to a physical measurement, different sorts of precision may be distinguished, precision of method and precision of result.

To make the matter concrete, let us examine the meaning of one of the simplest terms of physics, length. We use length with the ordinary connotations of physics, namely that objects "have" length in the sense that a certain class of operations of measurement may be applied to any object, and the result of this operation is a number. This number, so determined, is found to satisfy certain relations and may be used for certain purposes; for example, it may be used in the description of the geometry of objects, which will be found as a matter of experiment to be sensibly the geometry of Euclid. We might, therefore, say that the meaning of length is determined by the requirement that any number, determined by any sort of operation, may be called a length if it is one of the elements in a Euclidian geometry associated with the physical system. That is, we are here trying to define length in terms of something common to many situations in the same way as the linguist treats meaning. But how about precision and uniqueness? It is obvious that this definition is far from unique, because for one thing, we have not the scale of magnitude, but could measure length in centimeters or parasangs. This, however, is more or less trivial and can be met by a simple addition to the definition. Let us rather define the length of objects as numbers associated with bodies which satisfy a Euclidian system of geometry, and such that the number associated with some specified concrete object shall be unity. Have we now attained precision and uniqueness? It is evident that the complete physical picture, which includes both the definitions and the applications of the definitions to concrete instances, has neither precision nor uniqueness. Because whether a geometry is Euclidian or not can be verified only within a certain margin of error. It is conceivable that no method of assigning numbers to objects would result in a Euclidian geometry if accuracy of measurement could be very much increased beyond that possible today. Furthermore, within the precision of measurement now attainable, it is obvious that we do not have uniqueness at all with regard to the procedures for obtaining the lengths of objects. We may have approximate uniqueness in the length numbers, but these length numbers may be obtained indifferently by a variety of entirely different procedures, for instance, measurement with a meter stick or by triangulation with a theodolite. We have to recognize, however, that since all physical measurement is subject to error, the proof that the length numbers, obtained by different procedures, are the same can be given only within a certain margin of error, set by the possible precision of physical measurement at this epoch.

Into this situation a new note was injected by Einstein with his special theory of relativity. This theory was created to meet the new experimental situation brought about by an increase in experimental accuracy, the effective result of which might be described by saying that it was found that the geometry of material objects was not Euclidian. I am here using Euclidian in an extended sense to cover both the old classical geometry and mechanics, Euclidian and Newtonian together, forming a single picture. The new experimental discoveries of the properties of objects traveling with high velocity therefore knocked out the foundation of the old definition of length. The weakness of the old procedure was now apparent. We had been using experimentally established properties in our definitions, which were therefore subject to possible revision whenever increased experimental accuracy forced a revision of our description of these properties.

One method of partially meeting the hazards of the situation is obvious, namely, we can eliminate the hazard arising from a multiple operational definition for length, which subjects us to the constant danger that we may get different numbers by these different operations when experimental accuracy is improved. We may do this by defining length in terms of a unique procedure. This, at the same stroke, removes a most serious logical defect from the former procedure, for when we defined length as numbers associated with objects obtained by certain procedures which satisfied a Euclidian geometry, we were guilty of an over-definition. In other words, definition, or the assigning of meanings, in terms of unique operations is the only *safe* procedure in physical situations. Furthermore, in other situations, such as those of logic where the equivalence of two operations may be logically proved, definition in terms of more than one operation is not necessary. If the implications back of the common usage of a term are such that it is not amenable to specification in terms of a unique operational procedure then the presumption is that this term is not suitable for scientific use. It was by an analysis of this sort that Einstein showed that the term "simultaneity" is not a suitable term for scientific use.

In seeking the precision demanded by scientific use we have thus been led to discard the common sense method of handling our environment in terms of objects with properties, and have substituted for it a point of view that regards a reduction to activities or operations as a safer and better method of analysis. (Perhaps the philosophers will see here a resemblance to the "transactional" point of view, basic to the recent book of Dewey and Bentley, *Knowing and the Known*.)

Something is implied here with regard to the sort of operation that can be employed in this safer and better analysis. In the first place, a rather widespread misapprehension may be corrected as to the nature of the permissible operations. It is not infrequent to hear it stated that the operational point of view with regard to meanings demands that all the operations be physical operations, like the manipulations of the laboratory. It is obvious that for many of the terms the operations must be primarily of this character, as for example, length. But even here, the operation of measuring length, as ordinarily specified, involves a non-instrumental component, in this case, counting the number of times the meter stick is applied to the object. This counting is usually done in the head of the operator, so that in general we recognize mental operations as well as the instrumental ones. Most of the operations of theoretical physics, which is so largely composed of mathematics, are of this mental sort, or, as I have called them in this setting, "paper-and-pencil" operations. It is a requirement of any valid physical theory, in so far as it is physical in distinction from mathematical, that eventually the paper and pencil operations emerge into a level where connection can be established with instrumental operations. But for the intermediate constructions no such requirement need be exacted, or is exacted in the practice of successful theoretical physicists, as indeed there seems no reason why it should. I think that in many of the situations of theoretical physics the precise way in which instrumental operations are intermingled with paper and pencil operations is not adequately realized, and the untangling of them is a profitable topic for analysis.

We return to the operation. How firm a foundation do operations give for our analysis? How precisely may operations be specified and performed? Do we ever really perform the same operation twice? Is a unique specification in terms of operations possible anymore than a unique specification in terms of properties is possible? I think there is no a priori answer to these questions and that the only answer possible to us is in terms of observation. Perhaps the only possible answer here is in personal terms. I can report that for me activity, or happenings, or operations, are at a deeper level of analysis than objects or their properties. For example, I know how to go work to analyze what I mean when I say "Objects exist independently of a perceiving mind," and my analysis is into terms of happenings or activities. I do not find it so easy to go to work to analyze what I mean by saying that I am now doing the same thing that I did yesterday, and any analysis that I attempt seems to be into terms of other happenings. There are certain operations which I can perform with such a degree of security that for all purposes of my scientific use I do not feel the need to attempt an analysis of them. The operation of adding unity to an integer or of counting is such an operation on the mental level; the operation of noting the coincidence of the end of a meter stick with a point of the object being measured is such an operation on the physical level.

What we are in effect doing in thus preferring the operational attack is to say what we *do* in meeting new physical situations has a greater stability than the situations themselves and that we can go further without revising our operations than we can without revising our picture of the properties of objects. Or, expressed somewhat differently, our methods of handling the external world have a greater stability than the external world itself. Is there any justification for this except the spectacular success that this point of view has had in relativity and quantum theory? I think we can find such justification in our present expectation of how we would handle any alteration in the character of our physical experience. If the world suddenly went strange on us, stones starting to fall upward or the moon to revolve backward, we know that we would, at first at least, continue to try to cope with the new situations in the way we do with the present ones. We would continue to count the objects about us, or to measure their lengths with meter sticks, or to observe the time of events by coincidences with the hands of a clock, in our effort to try to discover some sort of correlation in the new situations. To say that we would deal with novel experience in this way is merely another way of saying that we regard our operations as having a greater permanence and stability than the things on which we operate. Ultimately, of course, we can have no assurance that we shall not discover ambiguities in operations which at present seem so simple that we do not think it profitable to attempt to analyze them, or indeed that we shall not have a completely new vision which shall supersede the operational approach completely. It is merely that the operational approach at present is the best that has been done in trying to get into touch with our environment, and indeed it seems to have a certain inevitability and necessity as viewed from this epoch.

Finally, I would like to briefly mention another implication of the operational approach to meaning which has impressed itself on me only lately, and which I have not yet had time to think through in any detail. We have seen that our meanings are to be found on the level of activities. The meaning of a proposition in symbolic logic, for example, is found in the activities which are guided by the symbols. Now activities are performed in time and have duration. The meaning associated with the activity must have certain of the attributes of its origin. For most purposes, in particular for the purposes of this exposition thus far, it is adequate to think of a meaning as a static completed thing, from the point of view of the finished operation. But what about the meaning while the operation was being performed, while it was no longer complete? At what stage in the operations did the meaning appear? I think it is obvious that meaning is not just something that either is or isn't, but that meanings are generated in time and they *become*. An example may make clearer what I mean, an experience of mine this summer. I was reading an article by Tarski in the collection of Feigl and Sellars,[1] and found this sentence: "The sentence printed in this paper on page 58 line 19 is not true." This is what actually

---
[1] H. Feigl and W. Sellars, *Readings on Analytical Philosophy*.

happened as I read it, that is, as my thoughts were guided by following in time the sequence of marks on paper. When I got as far in my reading as the words "line 19" I stopped and looked for page 58, which proved to be the page I was then reading, and then counted down to line 19, which proved to be the line I was then reading. Whereupon I said to myself, "Doesn't Tarski know that he can't talk about a sentence before it has yet become a sentence?" That is, he had used the word sentence before there was any sentence, and which did not exist until the completion of the line. Here was a meaning in process of becoming, and it was treated as though it were already there. The result of this was paradox. The paradox is here resolved by noting the impropriety of thus neglecting what here is the key to the situation, but which in most situations may be entirely disregarded. In fact, it is difficult to see how language could function at all if we did not allow ourselves the privilege of looking ahead and treating what we intend to do as already done.

It seems to me that there is concealed here a whole new domain, the domain within which meanings are in process of generation. It is the domain within which the meaning of the individual terms gets compounded into the meaning of the integrated whole; it is thus the domain of grammar and syntax and most of language. There must also be a host of other phenomena associated with the becoming of meaning of which we are usually entirely unaware, and which only occasionally force themselves on our attention, as in the paradox above. In analogy with the fine structure of spectroscopic phenomena in physics, we might refer to phenomena of this kind as phenomena of the fine structure of meaning. The invention of a method of coping with all the phenomena of the becoming of meaning would be analogous to the invention of fluxions by Newton, and perhaps may require even greater intellectual capacity.

8

SCIENCE AND COMMON SENSE*

I SHALL HAVE TO BEGIN by recalling some matters that have been said so many times that I can expect only to bore you, but this is a risk that I can see no way to avoid if I am to make my main point. You all know that, since the turn of the century, discoveries have been made in physics, culminating in the unlocking of nuclear energy in the atomic bomb, which have entirely revolutionized our outlook, not only our outlook with regard to the construction of the world around us, but our philosophical ideas as well with regard to our relationship to the world. It is the latter to which I would like to direct your attention.

The new discoveries that have forced the revolution were in the realms of relativity and quantum phenomena. We shall see later that the quantum phenomena were more revolutionary in their implications than the relativity phenomena, but historically it is probable that the relativity phenomena played the more important role at first. The new relativity phenomena were highly paradoxical and included such effects as meter sticks whose length changed when they were set in motion, clocks that ran slow when moving, and weights that be-

*From Scientific Monthly, 79, 32-39, 1954.

came heavier when moving. In fact, these effects were so paradoxical and contrary to common sense that some physicists and most men in the street refused to accept them and even sought to throw them out of court by ridicule.

But the facts refused to be thrown out of court, and the paradoxes were resolved by Einstein's theory of restricted relativity. This theory embraced, in the first place, the mathematical machinery by which all the experimental facts were correlated into a single mathematical structure. But no less notable as an intellectual achievement and equally essential to the removal of paradox was Einstein's handling of the physical concepts that entered the mathematical edifice. It is this latter that is our concern.

There are two aspects of Einstein's handling of the physical concepts. There is, in the first place, a realization that the paradoxes involved primarily questions of meaning and that the common-sense meanings of such terms as *length* and *time* were not sharp enough to serve in the situations presented by the new facts. In the second place, there was the method by which the necessary increased sharpness was imparted to the meanings. This method was to specify the operations that were involved in concrete instances in applying the term whose meaning was in question. For example, what do we mean when we say that two events are simultaneous? Einstein insisted that we do not know what we mean unless we can give some concrete procedure by which we may determine whether or not any two specific events are simultaneous. Analysis of the concrete procedures that we might use brings out the fact, not noticed before, that what we do to determine whether or not two events are simultaneous depends to a certain extent on the events themselves and is different and more complicated if the two events take place at different places than if they take place here. Furthermore, this analysis disclosed that what an observer does to determine whether two distant events are simultaneous is different from what another observer does who is in motion with respect to him. Simultaneity of two distant events is, therefore, not an absolute property of the events, the same for all observers, but is relative to the observers.

It is the same with length. What do we mean when we ask what the length of a moving object is? Applying the operational criterion of meaning, the meaning is to be sought in what we do when we measure the length of the moving object. When we analyze what we might do, we discover that there are several different possible procedures, equally acceptable to common sense. Thus, if we are asked to measure the length of a moving streetcar, we might take an instantaneous photograph of it and measure the length of the photograph, or we might board the car, meter stick in hand, and proceed to measure it as we would any ordinary stationary object. If we get the same answer by the two procedures, we shall doubtless be satisfied and think that our catechizer was unnecessarily fussy in insisting that we tell exactly what we do to measure the length.

But here is where the new experimental facts come in that were not suspected before relativity theory. For it turns out that when we make our measurements with extreme precision, or when the streetcar is moving with very great velocity, the results of the two methods are not the same, so that the precise method must be specified if we want to talk exactly about the length of the moving car. In other words, it is ambiguous to talk about the "length" of a moving object until we have specified exactly how the length is to be measured; and when we have specified the exact procedure, the results we get are generally different, depending on what the exact procedure is. In particular, by one of the two procedures just indicated, the length of the moving car would be the same as when it is stationary; and, by the other, it would be less. We see at once that we cannot treat this situation by the methods of common sense and say that it is absurd that the length should change when the car moves, because it *must* change according to at least one of our possible definitions. Realization of this at once removes the atmosphere of paradox from the statement that the length changes when the object is set in motion.

The precise way that we define length when the body moves is a matter of choice, and we will make our choice in the way most convenient for us in the light of all the experimental facts. It would take us much too deeply into relativity theory to attempt to see why the method that Einstein chose for defining the length of a moving object is, all things considered, the most convenient for the physicist. Suffice it to say that the method chosen was not the method that leaves the length unchanged by the motion, although such a method is possible and, for certain restricted purposes, might be considered more convenient.

Relativity theory has thus shown the importance of precision of meanings. It has disclosed that some of the apparently simple terms of common sense are actually complex when we attempt to apply them in situations beyond the bounds of ordinary experience. In these new situations, we are forced to make a choice between procedures that are equivalent in the ordinary range. The account we give of the new situation depends on the procedure that we choose —that is, on the meaning we give our terms. In discovering that in fact we do need to make distinctions of which we have never thought and which to a naive first impression appear a matter of indifference, we are discovering that in fact the world is not constructed according to the preconceptions of common sense.

The sort of phenomena with which quantum theory is concerned teach the same lesson as relativity theory, namely, that the world is not constructed according to the principles of common sense. However, the way in which common sense fails is somewhat different in the case of quantum phenomena. The unfamiliar world of relativity theory was the world of high velocities; the new world of quantum theory is the world of the very small.

Quantum theory began modestly enough with the discovery that some of the most familiar facts of daily life cannot be understood on the basis of the common-sense views of matter prevalent at the end of the last century. For example, it was impossible to understand why we cannot see a kettle full of boiling water in the dark. Common sense, when translated into mathematics, said that we should see it, but every burned child knows that we cannot. The paradox has now been removed from this and other related effects, so that we now understand, in a way that would have been incredible 25 years ago, most of the phenomena displayed by ordinary matter. This understanding has been provided by quantum theory. The theory is highly mathematical and it is well-nigh impossible to give an adequate outline of it in nontechnical language, but the one simple crude idea back of it all is that when we deal with very small things, such as atoms or electrons, the ordinary common-sense conception of *things* is no longer valid. The renunciation of common sense thus demanded by quantum theory is more drastic than that demanded by relativity theory. For now we get ourselves into *logical inconsistencies* if we try to think of things in the microscopic domain in the same way that we think of the objects of ordinary experience.

Suppose, for example, that I have a box with a partition in the middle and one electron on each side of the partition. I remove the partition for a moment, so that the electrons have an opportunity to exchange positions. I now find when I replace the partition that I again have one electron on each side of the partition. It now involves me in logical contradiction to ask whether the electron that is on the right side of the partition is the same electron that in the beginning was on the right side, or vice versa. Neither can I ask exactly how fast is the right-hand electron moving. Knowing that the electron is on the right of the partition makes it logically contradictory to know how fast it is moving. These are indeed revolutionary restrictions. Not to be able to ask which electron is which means that the electron does not have identity, and not being able to ask how fast it is moving means that the common-sense categories of space and time do not completely apply to it.

Consider another example. It is possible to make a so-called electron gun with which a stream of electrons may be fired at a target. If we start with a comparatively crude gun firing a coarse stream of electrons, we find that the stream of electrons behaves much like a stream of water from a hose, so that we cannot hit with it a single sharp point of the target, but there is more or less scattering. Now common sense might lead us to expect that our marksmanship would become better as we refined the apparatus by making it more and more delicate and capable of dealing with a finer and finer stream of electrons. Experiment shows, however, that our common-sense expectations are entirely wrong, and that matters get worse instead of better as we refine the apparatus. In the end, when we have, at great pains, constructed a gun capable of firing single electrons, we find that we have almost completely lost control of the situation. No two shots ever come alike despite the best we can do, and we might as well spin a roulette wheel to find what part of the target any electron will hit.

The electron gun illustrates the general principle that, in the microscopic domain, events cannot be made to repeat. The situation thus disclosed is bad enough from the practical point of view, but I believe that it is even more upsetting from the conceptual point of view. For the one intellectual lesson that science has perhaps most insistently underlined is that our mental machinery is capable of making mistakes and that we continually have to verify and check what we are doing. The fundamental method of verification is repetition; the repeatable experiment has come to occupy such a position that the very definition of truth is often framed in terms of verification by repetition. It looks as though it does not mean anything in the quantum domain to ask for the truth about any specific event, yet how can I get along without the concept of truth? You may try to extricate yourself from the dilemma by saying that, although *I* may not verify the occurrence of some event by repeating the experiment, I *can* verify it by getting confirmation from some other observer who has also witnessed it. But this, unfortunately, is not a way out, because here we encounter another of those baffling properties of the microscopic world, namely, that an elementary event may be observed by only one observer. Confirmation by public report thus becomes impossible. To many, it might seem that thereby science is made impossible, science sometimes being defined in terms of publicity. However, if you are willing to grant that quantum theory is part of science, you see that matters are at least not quite as bad as this. Whatever the method by which eventually we get intellectual order into this situation, I think you can see that the observer must play a quite different role in the quantum domain than in the world of everyday life.

All these considerations mean that the conventional forms of thought are no longer applicable in the realm of the very small. I think you will agree that my foregoing statement is justified, namely, that the failure of common sense disclosed by quantum theory is more drastic than that disclosed by relativity theory. For, when in relativity theory we go to very high velocities, we merely encounter properties of matter that are strange to common experience, whereas when we go far enough in the direction of the very small, quantum theory says that our forms of thought fail, so that it is questionable whether we can properly think at all. One can imagine the consternation of our old philosophical friend Immanuel Kant who declared that space and time are *necessary* forms of thought.

What is the answer to the dilemma with which quantum theory confronts us, and where do the roots of the difficulty lie? Are we faced with the necessity of devising new ways of thinking? It does seem to me that eventually we shall have to find better ways of thinking, but I suspect that any improved method of thinking that we are capable of devising will eventually come up against essential limitations of some sort that will prevent its unlimited application. In the meantime, no agreement can be discerned at present among the experts with regard to the details of any way in which we might reform our thinking. As an example, there is the irreconcilable schism between the views of Einstein and Bohr on quantum phenomena. Whatever the eventual solution, I think we can at least be sure that it will be outside the realm of common sense. Furthermore, I believe the experts would at present agree that whatever new way we devise to think about the microscopic universe, the meaning of our new concepts will have to be found back at the level of the large-scale events of daily life, because this is the scale on which we live our lives, and it is we who are formulating the new concepts. This recognition and agreement entails, I believe, a consequence that is not commonly appreciated, namely, that the seeds and sources of the ineptness of our thinking in the microscopic range are already contained in our present thinking in the large-scale region and should have been capable of discovery by sufficiently acute analysis of our ordinary commonsense thinking.

I would now like to direct your attention to some qualities of our ordinary everyday thinking that are commonly overlooked but seem to be beginning to attract more attention and, I believe, may eventually give us truer understanding of the nature of our thinking process and its limitations. What I shall now say must be taken as strictly my own opinions. I have no professional philosophical competence to speak on these matters, and it is even probable that many of my fellow-physicists would not agree with me, if indeed they have any opinion on these matters at all.

You have all doubtless had some acquaintance with cybernetics, a subject named and largely created by Professor Norbert Wiener at Massachusetts Institute of Technology and you know how much attention this subject is attracting and how many people are working at it. Apart from any specific results that may come out of all this activity, such for example as discovering how to make bigger and better robots that will continually usurp more and more of the functions of human intelligence, it seems to me that the mere fact that so many people are concerning themselves with this subject is going to have important repercussions. For when so many people try so hard to make a machine that functions like the human brain, the point of view will gradually spread that the human brain is itself a machine of sorts. It will also be recognized that this machine must have limitations inherent in its structure, and that the things which the machine can do, including in particular thinking, is in consequence also subject to limitations. Thinking is done by the brain, and the presumption is that thought has characteristics imposed by the character of the brain. At any rate, we will come to see that we may not expect to understand the nature of thought at least until we understand the nature of the brain. If you ask why we should be concerned with the nature of thought, I would reply: the realization that the nature of thought is something which cannot be merely taken for granted is a realization that seems to be gradually dawning on us as we ponder the significance of our failures in the fields of relativity and quantum theory.

You will not, I think, ponder for long what limitations are imposed on thought by the structure of the brain until it will suddenly strike you that what is really happening here is that the brain is trying to understand itself. But is not this a brash thing for the brain to try to do, for how can the brain analyze its own action, when any conclusions at which it arrives are themselves activities of the very brain that was the original problem to understand? At the very best, the situation would seem to be somewhat strained and artificial, and you may perhaps anticipate that any conclusions at which we may arrive cannot have as simple and straightforward a significance as we had perhaps hoped. This does indeed seem to be the case. What we are encountering here is a special case of a system trying to deal with itself. Such situations occur not infrequently, and it seems to be the general rule that such situations present special difficulties and infelicities.

Many of the well-known paradoxes of logic arise when a system tries to deal with itself. A stock example is the ostensibly complete map of the city in which the map itself is located. If the map is complete, it must contain a map of itself; that is, the map must have a map of the map, and this in turn demands a map of the map of the map, and you are off on a chase that has no end. Within the last few years, a theorem with regard to such a system has been proved, a theorem that has been hailed among logicians as a truly epoch-making discovery in logic. This theorem was enunciated by Gödel, now in the Institute for Advanced Study at Princeton. In very crude language, the theorem states that no logical system can ever prove that it itself is a perfect system in the sense that it may not contain concealed self-contradictions. This theorem, at one stroke, stultified the endeavors of some of the ablest mathematicians, just as earlier the discovery of new mathematical theorems had stultified the efforts of the circle-squarers and the angle-trisectors. Mathematicians had long been trying to prove by the principles of mathematics that mathematics contains no hidden inconsistencies, inconsistencies that some day might be discovered and bring down the whole imposing mathematical edifice in ruins. But Gödel's theorem showed that this is an impossible sort of thing to prove. The conclusion is that, if one wants to prove that mathematics is free from concealed self-contradictions, one has to use principles outside mathematics to prove it. If one then wants to prove that the new principles are free from contradiction, one must use other principles beyond and over those in question. We here encounter a regress that has no logical end and, humanly, ends in human weariness and the finite length of human life. This means that the human intelligence can never be sure of itself; it is not a tool capable of unlimited perfectibility, as is so often fondly imagined. All we can ever say is that, up to the present, we have found no inconsistencies where we have looked.

There is one other recent development that tends to make us more self-conscious of our intellectual limitations. In Hanover, New Hampshire, Adelbert Ames, Jr., with a number of collaborators, especially A. Hadley Cantril, of the department of psychology of Princeton University, has been studying in recent years how the perceptions of different people adapt themselves to situations that have been purposely devised to differ from the situations ordinarily encountered in daily life. For example, one can play tricks with perception by making lines converge or diverge which ordinarily experience leads one to expect must be parallel. By combining various kinds of motion with curiosities of perspective, one can produce sensations completely foreign to ordinary experience, which the unaccustomed brain fits into its perceptual scheme in forced and unnatural ways. A striking example is the so-called trapezoidal window. A wooden frame like an ordinary window frame, except that the top and bottom sashes are not parallel, is rotated uniformly about a vertical axis. When the narrower end of the frame approaches the observer, the converging lines, associated ordinarily with greater distance, present the observer with an unaccustomed dilemma. Most observers resolve the dilemma by seeing the window frame in oscillating motion, back and forth, rather than in uniform rotation. In general, the way in which the observer perceives this and other strange situations varies with different persons and even varies with the same person, depending on what has been happening to him in the immediate past. This means that what a person sees in a given situation may, to a certain extent, be manipulated and controlled by another person.

Of course, there is nothing new in illusions. At Hanover, however, the study of such effects is being elaborated into a systematic technique for finding out about the nature of our perpetual processes. I think that most people, once they have seen the demonstrations, would be convinced that such studies cannot help being of great value in revealing details of the ways in which our perceptual machinery works.

Personally, however, I find these studies tremendously suggestive and stimulating from a point of view of greater generality, namely, in emphasizing the significance of the mere fact that we perceive at all. This is one of those things that are so universal we never think of them unless our attention is forced by some dramatic situation. Perception we have always had with us and we take it completely for granted. We *see things* out there in space moving about, and that is all there is to it. We accept these perceptions at their face value and, on them as a foundation, we build the pattern of our "reality." To this reality, we ascribe an absolute existence transcending its origin and ask ourselves how it is that the human brain can be capable of apprehending the absolute. By asking this question, we disclose our hazy feeling that what a brain can do is probably limited in some way. But except for this hazy feeling, it seems to me that the question is improperly put, and the fact that we ask it discloses an improper attitude on our part. Instead of asking how human brains can apprehend "reality," we should ask what sort of thing it is that the human brain can fashion to call reality. It was, I believe, Suzanne Langer who remarked that philosophy advances, not by finding the answers to the questions of preceding generations, but by finding that those questions were improperly put. Here it seems to me is obviously a question that has been improperly put. The perceptions of time and space have been furnished to us by the machinery of our nervous systems. This machinery is a terribly complicated thing, which in spite of its complication does not give rise to perception until it has received a long course of preparation and education. Anyone who has watched a small infant trying to coordinate its visual and tactual sensations recognizes that we acquire our perceptual abilities only by arduous practice. Yet we take our space and time with a deadly seriousness. Even so great a scientist as Sir Isaac Newton could say that space is the sensorium of God, and nearly every philosopher treats thought as in some way transcending the machine that thinks. It will doubtless be disturbing to many to give up our transcendentally fundamental time and space, but I think there is perhaps something to be gained also. Perhaps when we learn to take them less seriously we will not be so bedeviled by the logical contradictions in which they sometimes now involve us, as when we ask questions about the beginning or end of time or the boundaries of space.

There is another respect in which I have found the experiments of Ames most stimulating, namely, in disclosing details of our mental processes of which we are ordinarily completely unaware. For example, as one watches the rotating trapezoidal window, one's perceptions are in a continual state of flux, melting and forming and metamorphosing into one another in a way quite unfamiliar. How can one find words to describe such unfamiliar happenings, or how can one catch and hold such things? How can one even store in memory what he has experienced so that he may be sure that the manner of fusion of two perceptions which he has just experienced is the same as the manner of fusion which he experienced yesterday?

Of course, ever since psychoanalysis started, we have known that there are processes occurring in the brain that never get to the level of consciousness, but here it seems to me that we have something different, because here we are encountering new sorts of conscious experience. Among these, there are *transient* mental phenomena, accessible to sufficiently acute introspection. For example, as we listen to our fellow, the meaning that he is trying to convey grows before it is complete. Meanings do not spring full grown into our minds but pass through a stage of development that is seldom, if ever, the subject of analysis. It seems to be a general characteristic of our mental processes that we like to operate with static and complete things—we want our words to have fixed meanings and we analyze space into points and time into instants. But to sufficiently acute analysis, the fixed and static does not occur—it is something that we have constructed, and in so doing we have constructed away a whole world of mental phenomena.

It would seem not impossible that this world of transient phenomena and fine structure could be recovered and opened to us by deliberate cultivation and invention. What is needed is the invention of an introspectional microscope. Not until we have amassed a considerable experience of this world will we be able to talk about it or even remember our experiences. Gaining mastery of the microscopic world of introspection will involve much the same sort of thing that happens to a baby or to a kitten when its eyes are opened. Study of the process of gaining mastery of the new introspectional world may help us to reconstruct imaginatively what happened to us in our own babyhood.

It does not yet appear what the final method will be for dealing with all these considerations. I believe that the final solution will have to carry further the consequences of the insight that quantum theory has partially glimpsed, namely, that the observer must somehow be included in the system. The point of view of classical physics, and I believe also of all orthodox human thinking up to the present, was that the observer is a passive spectator, expressed sometimes by saying that what he observes would be the same whether he were watching or not. Quantum theory points out that this is only an approximation valid in the realm of large objects. The very act of observing a small object involves a reaction between the object and the observer, a reaction that must be allowed for in reconstructing the system from observation. To which we now add the insight that the relationship between the observed and the observer is a much more intimate relationship than these quantum considerations would suggest, and that it is in fact meaningless to try to separate observer and observed, or to speak of an object independent of an observer or, for that matter, of an observer in the absence of objects of observation.

It seems to me that our eyes are gradually opening. We are coming to recognize that it is a simple matter of observation that the observer is part of what he observes and that the thinker is part of what he thinks. We do not passively observe the universe from the outside, but we are all in it up to our necks, and there is no escape. It would be difficult to imagine anything more contrary to the tenets of common sense or to the attitude of the human race since it has begun to think. The common-sense way of handling our minds has, without doubt, been of decisive importance, and the discovery of the common-sense way of thinking was, doubtless, in the beginning a bit of an invention, perhaps the most important invention ever made. One of the things that we are in fact doing in accepting the common-sense way of thinking is to declare that, for our purposes, we do not need to complicate our thinking by continually holding ourselves to an awareness that the thinker cannot be divorced from what he thinks. We have thus brought about a tremendous simplification in our intellectual processes, and in the history of the human race the common-sense attitude has been more than justified. It seems to me, however, that we are approaching a position where we can recognize the limit of usefulness of this way of thinking. Common sense evolved in the comparatively simple situations of the primitive experiences of the human race, and although it may have been an invention, we may be sure that it was an unconscious invention, adopted with no due consideration of its limitations or possible alternatives.

The world with which common sense was evolved to cope was simple with respect to the range of physical phenomena that it embraced, and simple also with respect to the social organization of the communities in which common sense was practiced. In the last 50 years, we have drastically extended our physical range toward high velocities and toward the microscopic and have been able to retain our command of the situation only by discarding those common-sense methods of thinking about physical things which had served the human race from the beginning. We may well ask ourselves whether something analogous may not be expected to occur, or is not in fact already occurring, when we pass from the simple to the complex in phenomena other than those of the physical world, using *physical* in its narrower sense. There are at least two other classes of nonphysical situations. These are social situations and the situations presented by the creation of abstractions or by abstract thinking. Consider first the social situations.

There will be, I suppose, no disagreement with contention that, in the last few generations, the complexity of our social environment has tremendously increased. With modern methods of communication with the speed of light and of transportation with more than the speed of sound, the social environment of each person is becoming effectively the whole world. Plain analogy with what has happened in physics suggests the question of whether we are not here encountering an extension of range in our social experience that will demand an analogous abandonment of common-sense methods of social thinking. By common-sense methods of social thinking, I mean those methods that developed in small communities and are fitted to deal with nothing more complex than the social situations presented by small communities. From this point of view, most of our social thinking would seem to be of the common-sense variety. One characteristic social attitude springing from such an origin is the conviction that there is one and only one "correct" or "right" social philosophy or world-view, or one line of conduct that one "ought" to follow. Such a point of view could be pretty well maintained in a community small enough to offer a background of uniform social experience to all its members and able to enforce conformity on all dissenters. But the impossibility of any such view has become amply apparent when the community has become the whole world, and we are forced to revise the very meanings that we attach to *truth* or *right* or *ought*. It would appear that there is a moral perception analogous to our physical perception of objects in space and time and, like our physical perceptions, dependent on our past experience. We may suppose that the savage, who has never seen a civilized window frame, when confronted for the first time with the rotating trapezoidal window, will see it, not in oscillating motion as we do, but in uniform rotation. Analogously, the Hindu, brought up in the religious traditions of his group, perceives as a moral imperative that he must not kill the mosquito that annoys him. The realization of this is not new; the anthropologist has been dinning it into our ears for some time. The anthropologist, however, could point his moral only in somewhat academic terms and mostly from the record of the past by presenting us with the divergent practices of different peoples in different epochs. The lesson is now pointed with incomparably more dramatic force in our endeavors to find a basis for the harmonious living together of the entire world, a problem that demands the simultaneous reconciliation of so many divergent outlooks. At the very least, we shall have to evolve a new social philosophy and discover some method of getting rid of the provincialism that seems so right to common sense.

In addition to the social situations, a second nonphysical factor in our lives is afforded by our abstract thinking. How long the human race has been thinking and talking abstractly I suppose even the anthropologist cannot tell us, but it appeals to me as a good guess that we developed our common-sense method of handling the situations of daily life before we began abstracting. It is known that there are primitive peoples that have not yet formed as simple abstractions as "tree." The extension of thinking from concrete objects to abstractions constituted an extension of range sufficiently great to suggest the question, inspired by our experience with relativity and quantum theory, of whether the methods adequate to deal with the world of concrete objects continue to be adequate to deal with abstractions. To put the question is to suggest the answer. In the answer, I believe we can glimpse the solution to a riddle that has long baffled us. There is a class of people whose profession is to deal with abstractions—that is, the philosophers. By long tradition, philosophical thinking has come to be regarded by most people as the most exalted of all thinking, and the philosopher is often regarded with an approach to veneration. But along with this veneration most people are disillusioned and feel the futility of the whole philosophical enterprise, because after 2000 years of argument philosophy has settled no questions and no two philosophers agree. This situation can be understood in a measure when we recognize that the philosopher essentially is applying to abstractions the same common-sense methods that are applicable in the realm of concrete objects. I think simple observation of any conventional philosophical system will justify this statement, or, if one wishes, one can find a formal argument by Philipp Frank to show that the theses of philosophy are essentially the theses of common sense extended into the realm of abstractions. For example, Plato ascribes to ideas a reality like the reality of the objects of common sense. But ideas are not like things, and to treat them like things is only a kind of poetry. The cure for the common-sense attitude toward abstractions is to seek the meaning of our abstract terms by an analysis at least as searching as the analysis that we have been forced to apply to such simple physical terms as *length* or *time*. Such an analysis is seldom applied to abstractions, but the common-sense implications in our verbal habits are uncritically accepted. For example, one of the great abstractions is truth. In talking about truth, one uses such expressions as *the* truth, or thinks of truth as eternal in the heavens, which all may know and on which all can agree. But just as in physics we have been forced to recognize that there is not the one length of common sense but different kinds of length, such as optical length or tactual length, depending on our choice of method of measurement, so analysis will disclose that there is not just the one truth of common sense but different kinds of truth, depending on the method used for establishing "truth." For example, scientific truth is not the same as theological truth, and we must not talk about them as if they were and as common sense wants us to. Since truth is such a frequent topic for discussion in philosophy, this one example will suggest the modifications in conventional philosophical thought that might follow the abandonment of the common-sense attitude toward truth. Perhaps the philosophers might even agree. Even if the philosophers prove unregenerate, outside the realm of philosophy abandonment of the common-sense attitude toward truth will go far toward eliminating bigotry and intolerance.

In conclusion, the problem of devising successful substitutes for common sense has not yet been solved, and we are standing only on the threshold of a new era in human thought. Although the final solution is not in sight, there are certain lessons that we can take to heart at present in the expectation that we shall not have to retreat. It seems to me that, as a minimum, we henceforth cannot regard a man as well educated who does not intuitively recognize that common sense is not to be taken for granted, or who does not handle his thinking as a tool in the awareness that every tool has limitations built into it. Such a man, looking to the past, can only be amazed that the human brain has, by cut-and-try methods, evolved procedures as effective as it has for dealing with the world around us; looking to the present, sees perhaps the most important reason for the present internal social difficulties of the human race in its uncritical use of traditional habits of thought; and looking to the future, can feel only optimism for the time when we shall have learned how to substitute consciously directed control of our thinking for the blind procedures of common sense.

9

REMARKS ON THE PRESENT
STATE OF OPERATIONALISM*

THERE WOULD SEEM TO BE no reason why I am better fitted than anyone else to open this discussion. As I listened to the papers I felt that I have only a historical connection with this thing called "operationalism." In short, I feel that I have created a Frankenstein, which has certainly got away from me. I abhor the word *operationalism* or *operationism*, which seems to imply a dogma, or at least a thesis of some kind. The thing I have envisaged is too simple to be dignified by so pretentious a name; rather, it is an attitude or point of view generated by continued practice of operational analysis. So far as any dogma is involved here at all, it is merely the conviction that it is better, because it takes us further, to analyze into doings or happenings rather than into objects or entities.

What I conceive to be involved here may be a little clearer if the historical background is understood, and I hope you will pardon me if I interject some personal remarks. The date usually associated with this is 1927, the year of the publication of my book *The Logic of Modern Physics,* but prepara-

*From Scientific Monthly, 79, 224-226, 1954, remarks made at the symposium of the AAAS on Operationalism at the Christmas meeting, 1953.

tion for this in my own thinking went back at least to 1914, when the task of giving two advanced courses in electrodynamics was suddenly thrust upon me. Included in these courses was material from the restricted theory of relativity. The underlying conceptual situation in this whole area seemed very obscure to me and caused me much intellectual distress, which I tried to alleviate as best I could. Another cause of distress was the situation in dimensional analysis, which at that time was often so expounded as to raise doubt whether experimental work was really necessary at all. The dimensional situation proved comparatively simple, and I was able to think the situation through to my own satisfaction—an experience that perceptibly increased my intellectual morale. The analysis, which was essentially operational, although the word was not used, was published in 1922 (*Dimensional Analysis,* Yale Univ. Press). I think the word *operation* was first explicitly used in a discussion that I gave at the Boston meeting of the AAAS in 1923 at a symposium on relativity theory participated in by George Birkhoff, Harlow Shapley, and myself.

The Logic of Modern Physics was written during a half sabbatical in 1926 under a stringent time limit, for I knew that at the end of September my laboratory would reabsorb me. In view of this time limit, I had to map out the questions that to me appeared most pressing and to be satisfied with discussions of which I could say "at least this much must be true and be part of the final picture," and not attempt the more ambitious program of a complete analysis. In short, I was compelled to be satisfied with a "necessary" as opposed to a "sufficient" analysis. A great many interesting and important leads had to be left unexplored: for example, an analysis of what it is that makes an operation suitable for the formulation of a scientific concept; again, in what terms can operations be specified. It has, in fact, been a surprise to me that, since the publication of my book, so much of the concern of others has been with abstract methodological questions suggested by the endeavor to erect some sort of a philosophic system rather than with attempts to follow the more concrete and obvious leads.

Since writing the book, I have never again been able to devote as sustained attention to this field but have had to content myself with shorter excursions, resulting in a number of articles and a couple of thin books. But at the same time, with the continued practice of operational analysis, my ideas have been changing and growing and gaining in generality. If I were to start today to expound my attitude systematically, the order of presentation would be different. The general points of view would be presented earlier in the treatment, with, I think, avoidance of much confusion. It is often thought that there is a normative aspect to "operationalism," which is understood as the dogma that definitions *should* be formulated in terms of operations. As I see it, there is in the *general* point of view nothing normative whatever. An operational analysis is always possible, that is, an analysis into what was done or what happened. An operational analysis can be given of the most obscurely metaphysical definition, such as Newton's definition of absolute time as that which flows by itself uniformly and equably. What is more, any person can make an operational analysis, whether or not he accepts what he supposes to be the thesis of "operationalism," and whether or not he thinks he is wasting his time in so doing. So far as the "operationalist" is to be distinguished from the "nonoperationalist," it is in the conviction of the former that it is often profitable and clarifying to make an operational analysis, and also, I suspect, in his private feeling that often the "nonoperationalist" does not want to make an operational analysis through fear that it might result in a change in his attitude.

If one has consistently used operational analysis, I think one's general point of view comes to acquire a certain flavor and certain considerations come to be emphasized in his thinking; these I shall endeavor to characterize briefly. In the first place, one is impressed by the observation that operational analysis can always be pushed to the point where sharpness disappears. The "yes or no" signal of recent information theory, the "all or none" firing of a neurone of the physiologist, and so on, lose their sharpness when considered as processes occurring in time, and the operations of logic lose their sharpness when the analysis is pushed to the point of self-doubt. Again, one is impressed by the complexity of the verbal structure that mankind has erected through the ages. Here is an autonomous world in which a man can, and frequently does, live a more or less self-contained and independent existence. On the other hand, despite the complexity of the verbal world, the external world of objects and happenings is inconceivably more complex—so complex that all aspects of it can never be reproduced by any verbal structure. Even in physics this is not sufficiently appreciated, as is shown, for example, by the reification of energy. The totality of situations covered by various aspects of the energy concept is too complex to be reproduced by any simple verbal device. As a corollary of the continued interplay of the verbal and the "objective" worlds, I personally have come to feel the value of analyzing our operations as far as possible into their "instrumental" and "paper-and-pencil" components and think there is much here that is still unexplored. I think there is much to be done in nonscientific fields along these lines. For instance, I anticipate that many of the operations of philosophy will be found to be essentially verbal and incapable of being made to emerge into the instrumental world. I believe that revolutionary results will follow a full realization of the inescapability and immanence of the element of human enterprise.

Turning now to a consideration of a couple of

the points raised by the preceding papers, I am not particularly disturbed by the fact that it is sometimes difficult to fit the apparent demands of "operationalism" into a logically complete and satisfactory scheme. Part of this failure I think arises from misconception of what is involved; but in any event, as I have already intimated, I would expect that the analysis could be pushed so far that it would become unsatisfactory logically. That this should be possible appears to me to be fully as much a commentary on the nature of logic as on the nature of "operationalism." At the same time, I fully agree with Hempel that there is much unnecessary vagueness in such matters, as for example, in the answer to the question of what it is that makes an operation "good" for the purposes of the scientist. There is certainly much room for improvement here, and I think the improvement will be naturally forthcoming when the operational point of view has reached a higher state of development than at present.

With regard to Lindsay's question concerning my meaning in saying that it is desirable that the paper-and-pencil operations of the theorist be capable of eventual contact, *although perhaps indirectly,* with instrumental operations, I shall answer by giving two examples. The first is concerned with the stress at any interior point of a solid body exposed to external forces. This stress is a complex of six components, constructed by the theoretical physicist and incapable of measurement by any instrument, if for no other reason than that the interior points of a solid body are inaccessible. However, the stress is connected through the equations of elasticity theory with the forces acting upon the free forces, and these forces have immediate instrumental significance. Here, what I meant by an "indirect" connection is the connection through the equations of elasticity. Again, the psi function of wave mechanics, defined as a probability amplitude, is at first a pure construction of the theoretical physicist, but again it makes connection through mathematical operations, in this case operations of integration, with the mean density of electric charge, which does have instrumental significance.

With regard to my concern to show that there can be no instrumental distinction between action at a distance and action through a field, I did not feel badly about the discovery, as Lindsay inferred from my, I fear, obscure exposition. On the contrary, I felt much pleased with myself, because my reading of scientific literature had led me to suppose that most physicists assume that there is some essential "physical" difference between these two points of view. In showing that this distinction is on the "paper-and-pencil" level, I thought that I was really saying something. In general, I think that there need be no qualms that the operational point of view will ever place the slightest restriction on the freedom of the theoretical physicist to explore the consequences of any free mental construction that he is ingenious enough to make. It must be remembered that the operational point of view suggested itself from observation of physicists in action.

10

THE NEW VISION OF SCIENCE*

I

THE ATTITUDE which the man in the street unconsciously adopts toward science is capricious and varied. At one moment he scorns the scientist for a highbrow, at another anathematizes him for blasphemously undermining his religion; but at the mention of a name like Edison he falls into a coma of veneration. When he stops to think, he does recognize, however, that the whole atmosphere of the world in which he lives is tinged by science, as is shown most immediately and strikingly by our modern conveniences and material resources. A little deeper thinking shows him that the influence of science goes much farther and colors the entire mental outlook of modern civilized man on the world about him. Perhaps one of the most telling evidences of this is his growing freedom from superstition. Freedom from superstition is the result of the conviction that the world is not governed by caprice, but that it is a world of order and can be understood by man if he will only try hard enough and be clever enough. This conviction that the

*From Harper's Magazine, March, 1929.

world is understandable is, doubtless, the most important single gift of science to civilization. The widespread acceptance of this view can be dated to the discovery by Newton of the universal sway of the law of gravitation; and for this reason Newton may be justly regarded as the most important single contributor to modern life.

The point of view for which Newton is responsible is well exemplified by the remark often made that every particle of matter in the universe attracts to some extent every other particle, even though the attraction is almost inconceivably minute. There is thus presented to the mind a sublime picture of the interrelatedness of all things; all things are subject to law, and the universe is in this respect a unit. As a corollary to this conviction about the structure of the universe, an equally important conviction as to man's place in the universe has been growing up; man feels more and more that he is in a congenial universe, that he is part and parcel of everything around him, that the same laws that make things outside him go make him go; therefore, he can, by taking pains, understand these laws. These two theses so closely related—that the world is a world of order and that man can find the guiding motif of this order—have come to be the tacit cardinal articles of faith of the man of science, and from him have diffused through the entire social structure, so that now some such conviction essentially colors the thinking of every educated person. It is to be emphasized that the justification for this conviction is entirely in experience; it is true that, as man has grown older and acquired more extensive acquaintance with nature and pondered more deeply, he has been increasingly successful in reducing the world about him to order and understandability. It has been most natural to generalize this experience into the conviction that this sort of thing will always be possible, and to believe that as we delve constantly deeper we shall always be able to give a rational account of what we find, although very probably the difficulties will become continually greater.

The thesis of this article is that the age of Newton is now coming to a close, and that recent scientific discoveries have in store an even greater revolution in our entire outlook than the revolution effected by the discovery of universal gravitation by Newton. The revolution that now confronts us arises from the recent discovery of new facts, the only interpretation of which is that our conviction that nature is understandable and subject to law arose from the narrowness of our horizons, and that if we sufficiently extend our range we shall find that nature is intrinsically and in its elements neither understandable nor subject to law.

The task of the rest of this article is twofold. In the first place I shall try to give some suggestion of the nature of the physical evidence and of the reasoning that has forced the physicist to the conclusion that nature is constituted in this way. This task is by no means easy; for not only is it impossible to indicate more than very partially the physical evidence, but it is often necessary to compress into a few sentences steps in the reasoning that can be completely justified only by long and difficult mathematical or logical analysis. The second part of the task is to envisage a few of the far-reaching consequences on the whole outlook of mankind of the acceptance of the view that this is actually the structure of nature. This aspect of the situation can be appreciated without a detailed grasp of the preliminary analysis.

II

The new experimental facts are in the realm of quantum phenomena. Comparatively little has been written for popular consumption about this new realm which has opened in the last fifteen years. The man in the street has been much more interested in relativity, which to him has seemed extremely interesting and revolutionary. Occasionally, however, there has filtered down to him the news that nearly all the theoretical physicists are occupied with a new order of phenomena which they find very much more exciting and revolutionary than any in the realm of relativity. For after all is said and done, the practical effects of relativity, measured in dollars and cents or in centimeters and grams, are exceedingly small, and require specially designed experiments executed by men of the highest skill to show their existence at all. The phenomena with which quantum theory deals, on the other hand, are of the greatest practical importance and involve the simplest aspects of everyday life. For example, before the advent of quantum theory no one could explain why a tea kettle of water boiling on the stove should not give out enough light in virtue of its temperature to be visible in the dark; the accepted theories of optics demanded that it should be visible, but every burned child knew that it was not.

One reason that the man in the street has not sensed this new domain is that it is much more difficult to explain than relativity; this is partly due to the nature of the subject, and partly also to the fact that the physicist himself does not understand the subject as well. I shall not in this article rush in where the angels have not ventured, but it is, nevertheless, necessary to try to give a glimmering of an idea of what it is all about.

Although all the phenomena of ordinary life are really quantum phenomena, they do not begin to stand out unequivocally in their quantum aspect and admit of no other interpretation until we have penetrated very far down into the realm of small things and have arrived at the atoms and electrons themselves. It must not be pretended that the nature of the quantum phenomena met in this realm of small things is by any means completely understood; but a suggestive characterization of the general situation is that atomicity or discontinuity is an even more pervading characteristic of the structure of the universe than had been previously supposed. In fact the name, "quantum", was suggested by the atomicity.

We were a long time in convincing ourselves of the atomic structure of ordinary matter; although this was guessed by the poets as early as the beginning of the Christian era, it was not generally accepted as proved, even by physicists, until the beginning of this century. The next step was the discovery of the atomic structure of electricity; there are indivisible units of positive and negative electricity, and the atoms of matter are constructed of atoms of electricity. This situation was not even guessed until about 1890; the proof and acceptance of the doctrine have taken place within the memory of the majority of the readers of this article. Finally comes the discovery that, not only is matter doubly atomic in its structure, but that there is an atomicity in the way in which one piece of matter acts on another. This is perhaps best understood in the case of optical phenomena. It used to be thought that light was infinitely subdivisible—that I could, for example, receive at pleasure on the film of my camera either the full intensity of the sun's radiation, or, by interposing a sufficiently small stop, that I could cut the intensity of the light down to anything this side of nothing at all. This is now known not to be true; but the light which we receive from the sun is atomic in structure, like an almost inconceivably fine rain composed of indivisible individual drops, rather than like the continuous flood of infinitely subdivisible radiation that we had supposed. If I close the stop of my camera too much I may receive nothing at all on the film, or I may receive a single one of the drops in the rain of radiation, but there is no step between one drop and nothing. The recognition that radiation has this property means that in some respects we have come back very close to Newton's ideas about light.

The proof that this is the structure of light can be given in many ways. Perhaps the most illuminating for our purpose is that discovered by Arthur Compton, for which he received the Nobel prize. Compton's discovery consisted in finding that the drops of radiation behave in certain ways like the material drops of ordinary rain; they have energy and mass and momentum, which means that when they collide with matter they behave in some respects very much as ordinary bodies do. The laws which govern the interaction or collision of ordinary bodies are known to any graduate of a high-school course in physics; he could calculate what would happen after two billiard balls had collided provided we would tell him exactly how each of the balls was moving before the collision, and what were the elastic properties of the materials of which the balls are composed. In making the calculation he would use, among other things, the two fundamental principles of the conservation of energy and the conservation of momentum. Now Compton showed that what happens when a drop, or better a bullet, of radiation collides with an electron is also governed by the same two fundamental principles. The proof consisted in showing that the way in which the electron rebounds is connected with the way in which the bullet rebounds by equations deduced from these principles; this is one of the features which makes Compton's discovery of such a fundamental importance.

But Compton's experiment contains another feature, and it is this which seems destined to revolutionize the thinking of civilization. Go back to the billiard-ball analogy: An expert billiard player can, by proper manipulation of the cue ball, make the two balls rebound from the collision as he wishes; this involves the ability to predict how the balls will move after collision from their behavior before collision. We should expect by analogy to be able to do the same thing for a collision between a bullet of radiation and an electron; but the fact is that it never has been done and, if our present theories are correct, in the nature of things never can be done. It is true that, if someone will tell me how the electron bounces away, I can tell, on the basis of the equations given by Compton's theory, how the bullet of radiation bounces away, or conversely; but no one has ever been able to tell how both will bounce away. Billiards, played with balls like this, even by a player of infinite skill, would degenerate into a game of pure chance.

This unpredictable feature has been seized and incorporated as one of the corner stones in the new theory of quantum mechanics, which has so stirred the world of physicists in the last three years. It has received implicit formulation in the "Principle of Uncertainty" of Heisenberg, a principle which I believe is fraught with the possibility of greater change in mental outlook than was ever packed into an equal number of words. The exact formulation of the principle, which is very brief, is framed in too technical language to reproduce here, but I shall try to give the spirit of the principle. The essence of it is that there are certain inherent limitations to the accuracy with which a physical situation can be described. Of course we have always recognized that all our physical measurements are necessarily subject to error; but it has always been thought that, if we took pains enough and were sufficiently clever, no bounds could be set to the accuracy which we might some day achieve. Heisenberg's principle states, on the other hand, that the ultimately possible accuracy of our measurements is limited in a curious and unsuspected way. There is no limit to the accuracy with which we can describe (or measure) any one quality in a physical situation, but if we elect to measure one thing accurately we pay a price in our inability to measure some other thing accurately. Specifically, in Compton's experiment, the principle states that we can measure the position of the electron as accurately as we choose, but in so doing we must sacrifice by a compensating amount the possibility of accurately measuring its velocity. In particular, if we measure with perfect accuracy the position of the electron, we have thereby denied ourselves the possibility of making any measurement at all of its velocity.

The meaning of the fact that it is impossible to measure exactly both the position and velocity of the electron may be paradoxically stated to be that an electron cannot have both position and velocity. The justification of this is to be found in the logical analysis of the meaning of our physical concepts which has been stimulated by the relativity theory of Einstein. On careful examination the physicist finds that in the sense in which he uses language no meaning at all can be attached to a physical concept which cannot ultimately be described in terms of some sort of measurement. A body has position only in so far as its position can be measured; if its position cannot in principle be measured, the concept of position applied to the body is meaningless, or in other words, a position of the body does not exist. Hence if both the position and velocity of the electron cannot in principle be measured, the electron cannot have both position and velocity; position and velocity as expressions of properties which an electron can simultaneously have are meaningless. To carry the paradox one step farther, by choosing whether I shall measure the position or velocity of the electron I thereby determine whether the electron has position or velocity. The physical properties of the electron are not absolutely inherent in it, but involve also the choice of the observer.

Return to the analogy of the billiard ball. If we

ask our high-school physicist what he must be told before he can predict how the billiard balls will rebound after collision, he will say that, unless he is told both how fast the balls are traveling when they collide, and also what their relative positions are at the moment of collision he can do very little. But this is exactly the sort of thing that the Heisenberg principle says no one can ever tell; so that our high-school computer would never be able to predict how a bullet of radiation and an electron behave after collision, and no more could we. This means that in general when we get down to fine-scale phenomena the detailed results of interaction between the individual elements of which our physical world are composed are essentially unpredictable.

This principle has been built into a theory, and the theory has been checked in many ways against experiment, and always with complete success. One of the consequences of which the man in the street has heard a good deal is that an electron has some of the properties of waves, as shown so strikingly in the experiments of Davisson and Germer. Of course no one can say that some day a fact may not be discovered contrary to the principle, but up to the present there is no evidence of it; and it is certain that something very much like this principle, if not this principle exactly, covers an enormously wide range of phenomena. In fact the principle probably governs every known type of action between different parts of our physical universe. One reason that this principle has not been formulated before is that the error which it tells us is inherent in all measurement is so small that only recently have methods become accurate enough to detect it. The error is unimportant, and indeed immeasurably small when we are dealing with the things of ordinary life. The extreme minuteness of the effect can be illustrated again with the billiard balls. Suppose that at the instant of collision the position of the balls is known with an uncertainty no greater than the diameter of a single atom, a precision very much higher than has ever been attained. Then the principle says that it is impossible to measure the velocity of the balls without a related uncertainty; but on figuring it out we find that this uncertainty is so small that after the lapse of one hundred thousand years, assuming a billiard table large enough for the balls to continue rolling for one hundred thousand years, the additional uncertainty in the position of the balls arising from the uncertainty in the velocity would again be only the diameter of a single atom. The error becomes important only when we are concerned with the ultimately small constituents of things, such as the action between an atom of radiation and an electron.

III

It is easy to see why the discovery that nature is constituted in this way, and in particular is essentially unpredictable, has been so enormously upsetting. For the ability to predict a happening is tied up with our ideas of cause and effect. When we say that the future is causally determined by the present we mean that if we are given a complete description of the present the future is completely determined, or in other words, the future is the effect of the present, which is the cause. This causal relation is a bilateral relation; given the cause, the effect is determined, or given the effect, the cause may be deduced. But this means, in the particular case that we have been considering of collision between a bullet of radiation and an electron, that the causal connection does not exist, for if it did the way in which the electron rebounds after the collision would be determined, that is, it could be predicted, in terms of what happens before the collision. Conversely, it is of course impossible to reconstruct from the way in which the electron and the radiation rebound the way in which they were moving before collision. Hence the rebound of the electron is not causally connected with what goes before.

The same situation confronts the physicist everywhere; whenever he penetrates to the atomic or electronic level in his analysis, he finds things acting in a way for which he can assign no cause, for which he never can assign a cause, and for which the concept of cause has no meaning, if Heisenberg's principle is right. This means nothing more nor less than that the law of cause and effect must be given up. The precise reason that the law of cause and effect fails can be paradoxically stated; it is not that the future is not determined in terms of a complete description of the present, but that in the nature of things the present cannot be completely described.

The failure of the law of cause and effect has been exploited by a number of German physicists, who have emphasized the conclusion that we are thus driven to recognize that the universe is governed by pure chance; this conclusion does not, I believe, mean quite what appears on the surface, but in any event we need not trouble ourselves with the further implications of this statement, in spite of their evident interest.

One may be sure that a principle as revolutionary in its implications as this, which demands the sacrifice of what had become the cardinal article of faith of the physicist, has not been accepted easily, but there has been a great deal of pondering and searching of fundamentals.

The result of all this pondering has been to discover in the principle an inevitableness, which when once understood, is so convincing that we have already almost ceased to kick against the pricks. This inevitableness is rooted in the structure of knowledge. It is a commonplace that we can never know anything about anything without getting into some sort of connection with it, either direct or indirect. We, or someone else, must smell the object, or taste it, or touch it, or hear it, or see it, or it must affect some other object which can affect our senses either directly or indirectly, before we can know anything about it, even its existence. This means that no knowledge of any physical property or even mere existence is possible without interaction; in fact these terms have no meaning apart from interaction. Formerly, if this aspect of the situation was thought of at all, it would have been dismissed as merely of academic interest, of no pertinence at all, and the justification of this would have been found in the supposed possibility of making the inevitable interaction as small as we pleased. The defender of the old point of view might have flippantly remarked that a cat may look at a king, by which he would have meant that the act of observation has no effect on the object. But even in the old days a captious critic might have objected to this easy self-satisfaction by pointing out that light exerts a pressure, so that light cannot pass from the king to the cat without the exercise of a certain amount of mechanical repulsion between them. This remark of the captious critic now ceases to be merely academic because of the discovery that light itself is atomic in structure, so that at least one bullet of radiation must pass if any light at all passes, and the king cannot be observed at all without the exertion of that minimum amount of mechanical repulsion which corresponds to a single bullet.

This evidently alters the entire situation. The mere act of giving meaning through observation to any physical property of a thing involves a certain minimum amount of interaction. Now if there are definite characteristics associated with the minimum interaction, it is conceivable that no observation of anything whatever can be made without entraining certain universal consequences, and this turns out to be the case. Let us return again to the useful billiard-ball analogy. What must our high-school calculator know in order completely to calculate the behavior of the balls after collision? Evidently, if he is to give a complete description of the motion, that is, give in addition to direction and velocity of motion the exact time at which the balls are in any particular location, he must know how long the collision lasts. This means that the act of collision itself must be analyzed. This analysis is actually possible, and in fact rapid-moving pictures have been taken, showing in detail how the balls are deformed during their contact together.

Returning now to the collision between a bullet of radiation and an electron, in order to determine completely the behavior after collision we must similarly analyze the details of the process of collision. In particular, if we want to predict where the electron is after collision we must analyze the collision sufficiently to be able to say how fast the electron is moving at each instant of the collision. But how shall this analysis be made? If the analysis means anything, it must involve the possibility of observation; and observation involves interaction; and interaction cannot be reduced below a minimum. But the collision, or interaction, between the electron and radiation that we are analyzing is itself the minimum interaction. It is obvious that we cannot discover fine details with an instrument as coarse as the thing that we are trying to analyze, so that the necessary analysis of the minimum interaction can never be made, and hence has no meaning, because of our fundamental dictum that things which cannot in principle be measured have no meaning. Therefore, the act of collision cannot be analyzed, the electron and radiation during collision have no measurable properties, and the ordinary concepts, which depend on these properties, do not apply during collision, and have no meaning. In particular, the ordinary concept of velocity does not apply to the act of collision, and we are prepared to expect something curious as the result of the collision. In fact, the detailed working out of the theory shows that the meaninglessness of velocity during the act of collision carries with it the consequence that the electron emerges from the collision with a certain nebulosity or indefiniteness in properties such as position, which according to the old point of view depend on the velocity, and it is precisely this nebulosity which is described in Heisenberg's principle.

The infinitesimal world thus takes on a completely new aspect, and it will doubtless be a long while before the average human mind finds a way of dealing satisfactorily with a situation so foreign to ordinary experience. Almost the first necessity is a renunciation of our present verbal habits and of their implications. It is extraordinarily difficult to deal with this new situation with our present forms of expression, and the exposition of this paper is no exception. The temptation is almost irresistible to say and to think that the electron *really* has *both* position and velocity, only the trouble is that our methods of measurement are subject to some limitation which prevents us from measuring both simultaneously. An attitude like this is justified by all the experience of the past, because we have always been able hitherto to continue to refine our methods of measurement after we had apparently reached the end. But here we are confronted by a situation which in principle contains something entirely novel, and the old expectations are no longer valid. The new situation cannot be adequately dealt with until long-continued familiarity with the new facts produces in our subconsciousness as instinctive a grasp as that which we now have of the familiar relations of everyday experience.

IV

The implications of this discovery are evidently most far-reaching. Let us first consider the scientific implications and, in particular, the implications for physics. The physicist is here brought to the end of his domain. The record of physics up to the present has been one of continued expansion, ever penetrating deeper and deeper, and always finding structure on a finer and finer scale beyond previous achievement. Several times in the past even eminent physicists have permitted themselves the complacent announcement that we were in sight of the end, and that the explanation of all things was in our hands. But such predictions have always been set at naught by the discovery of finer details, until the average physicist feels an instinctive horror of the folly of prediction. But here is a situation new and unthought of. We have reached the point where knowledge must stop because of the nature of knowledge itself: beyond this point meaning ceases. It may seem that we are getting back pretty close to the good Bishop Berkeley, but I think that actually nothing could be wider of the mark. We are not saying that nothing exists where there is no consciousness to perceive it; we are saying that existence has meaning only when there is interaction with other existence, but direct contact with consciousness need not come until the end of a long chain. The logician will have no trouble in showing that this description of the situation is internally self-contradictory and does not make sense; but I believe that, nevertheless, the sympathetic reader will be able to see what the situation is, and will perhaps subscribe to the opinion that to describe it the development of a new language is necessary.

The physicist thus finds himself in a world from which the bottom has dropped clean out; as he penetrates deeper and deeper it eludes him and fades away by the highly unsportsmanlike device of just becoming meaningless. No refinement of measurement will avail to carry him beyond the portals of this shadowy domain which he cannot even mention without logical inconsistency. A bound is thus forever set to the curiosity of the physicist. What is more, the mere existence of this bound means that he must give up his most cherished convictions and faith. The world is not a world of reason, understandable by the intellect of man, but as we penetrate ever deeper, the very law of cause and effect, which we had thought to be a formula to which we could force God Himself to subscribe, ceases to have meaning. The world is not intrinsically reasonable or understandable; it acquires these properties in ever-increasing degree as we ascend from the realm of the very little to the realm of everyday things; here we may eventually hope for an understanding sufficiently good for all practical purposes, but no more.

The thesis that this is the structure of the world was not reached by armchair meditation, but it is the interpretation of direct experiment. Now all experiment is subject to error, and no one can say that some day new experimental facts may not be found incompatible with our present interpretation; all we can say is that at present we have no glimmering of such a situation. But whether or not the present interpretation will survive, a vision has come to the physicist in this experience which he will never forget; the possibility that the world may fade away, elude him, and become meaningless because of the nature of knowledge itself, has never been envisaged before, at least by the physicist, and this possibility must forever keep him humble.

THE NEW VISION OF SCIENCE

When this view of the structure of nature has once been accepted by physicists after a sufficiently searching experimental probe, it is evident that there will be a complete revolution in the aspect of all the other physical sciences. The mental outlook will change; the mere feeling that boundaries are set to man's inquiry will produce a subtle change of attitude no less comprehensive in its effects than the feeling, engendered by Newton's conquest of celestial mechanics, that the universe was a universe of order accessible to the mind of man. The immediate effect on scientific inquiry will be to divert effort away from the more obviously physical fields back to the fields of greater complication, which have been passed over by the physicist in his progress toward the ultimately little, especially the field of biology.

Another important result of the realization of the structure of the world is that the scientist will see that his program is finite. The scientist is perhaps only a passing phase in the evolution of man; after unguessable years it is not impossible that his work will be done, and the problems of mankind will become for each individual the problem of best ordering his own life. Or it may be that the program of the scientist, although finite, will turn out to need more time than the life of the world itself.

But doubtless by far the most important effect of this revolution will not be on the scientist, but on the man in the street. The immediate effect will be to let loose a veritable intellectual spree of licentious and debauched thinking. This will come from the refusal to take at its true value the statement that it is meaningless to penetrate much deeper than the electron, and will have the thesis that there *is really* a domain beyond, only that man with his present limitations is not fitted to enter this domain. The temptation to deal with the situation in this way is one that not many who have not been trained in careful methods of thinking will be able to resist—one reason is in the structure of language. Thought has a predisposition to certain tendencies merely because of the necessity of expressing itself in words. This has already been brought out sufficiently by the discussion above; we have seen how difficult it is to express in words the fact that the universe fades away from us by becoming meaningless without the implication that there really is something beyond the verge of meaning.

The man in the street will, therefore, twist the statement that the scientist has come to the end of meaning into the statement that the scientist has penetrated as far as he can with the tools at his command, and that there is something beyond the ken of the scientist. This imagined beyond, which the scientist has proved he cannot penetrate, will become the playground of the imagination of every mystic and dreamer. The existence of such a domain will be made the basis of an orgy of rationalizing. It will be made the substance of the soul; the spirits of the dead will populate it; God will lurk in its shadows; the principle of vital processes will have its seat here; and it will be the medium of telepathic communication. One group will find in the failure of the physical law of cause and effect the solution of the age-long problem of the freedom of the will; and on the other hand the atheist will find the justification of his contention that chance rules the universe.

Doubtless generations will be needed to adjust our thinking so that it will spontaneously and freely conform to our knowledge of the actual structure of the world. It is probable that new methods of education will have to be painfully developed and applied to very young children in order to inculcate the instinctive and successful use of habits of thought so contrary to those which have been naturally acquired in meeting the limited situations of everyday life. This does not mean at all that the new methods of thought will be less well adapted than those we now have to meet the situations of everyday life, but on the contrary, since thought will conform to reality, understanding and conquest of the world about us will proceed at an accelerated pace. I venture to think that there will also eventually be a favorable effect on man's character; the mean man will react with pessimism, but a certain courageous nobility is needed to look a situation like this in the face. And in the end, when man has fully partaken of the fruit of the tree of knowledge, there will be this difference between the first Eden and the last, that man will not become as a god, but will remain forever humble.

11

PERMANENT ELEMENTS IN THE FLUX OF PRESENT-DAY PHYSICS*

MANY OF US COULD, I believe, confess to a feeling of breathlessness at the rapid changes of our present physical progress, and some of us might even, in a moment of candor, admit a little resentment at our shortness of breath. Let us discuss together what we may perhaps best do to recover our poise.

The changing situation which is responsible for our discomfort is complex. First and foremost there is our changing experimental knowledge, reaching over the entire range from the infinitely small to the infinitely large. The upsetting feature here is not so much that we have discovered an enormous array of new facts, which in themselves are difficult enough to keep pace with, as that these facts have proved in many cases to be irreconcilable with our previous expectations of what was possible, so that we have been forced to change our entire conceptual attitude. These conceptual changes have in many cases been associated with mathematical theories, which are being continually formulated at an ever-accel-

*From Science, 71, 19, 1930. Address of the retiring vice-president and chairman of Section B — Physics — A.A.A.S., Des Moines, Iowa, Dec. 1929.

erating tempo and in a complexity and abstractness increasingly formidable. Some of the more important landmarks in this progression are: The electromagnetic theory of light, the special theory of relativity, the general theory of relativity, the quantum theory of Bohr, the matrix calculus of Heisenberg, the wave mechanics of Schrödinger, the transformation theory of Dirac and Jordan, the group theory of Weyl and now the double quantization theory of Jordan and others. These have come crowding on each other's heels with ever-increasing unmannerliness, until the average physicist, for whom I venture to speak, flounders in bewilderment.

Are there not some general principles disclosed in all this welter of mathematical reconstruction in which the average physicist may find a sense of comparative peace, of some security that his endeavors to reconstruct his conceptual attitude will not have to begin over again next week and of some assurance that his program of future activity lies along lines of real significance?

One very broad generalization from past experience is that whenever we extend the domain of experiment we must be prepared for unexpected new facts. If we whole-heartedly accept this generalization as of real significance, important conclusions follow which apply to both our experimental activity and our conceptual outlook. On the experimental side it follows that every real extension of our present experimental range is worth while and necessary. An increase of accuracy of measurement constitutes an increase of range, so that any one who can increase the precision of any sort of measurement makes an important contribution. Not every one may be interested to increase by a factor of ten the precision of weighing, for example, but there are persons to whom this sort of refinement is congenial, and who can now pursue the line in which they are most skilful, while the others of us can enthusiastically applaud their skill.

Further, in formulating to ourselves what the present situation actually is, we should cultivate a more deliberate self-consciousness of the accuracy of our present experimental knowledge. This should get into our courses of instruction, certainly into those for our graduate students if not into the elementary courses. We should all know the limits of accuracy obtainable, for example, in measuring a length or a weight or an interval of time or a temperature; we should know how accurately the inverse square law of gravitation has been established, or how accurately the gravitation constant or the velocity of light or the gas constant has been determined.

Our point of view gives added importance not only to every increase of precision but also to other sorts of increase of the experimental range, and those who take a constitutional satisfaction in pushing our experiments to higher temperatures or to higher electric or magnetic fields or to higher pressures or to higher light intensity or to higher gravitational or accelerational fields may feel a renewed sense of the importance of their contribution. But although experiments over greater ranges or with increased precision acquire an increased importance, it does not follow that all results here are equally interesting or significant, or that the prospective experimenter can expect to make his choice with his eyes shut and be awakened by the knocking of the postman bearing the Nobel prize. The postman is more likely to knock at the door of the man who in extending our range reaches qualitatively new effects, such as the wave-like structure of matter.

On the conceptual side, perhaps the most important principle disclosed by our continual discovery of strange new facts whenever we extend the domain of experiment is that the actual experimental world transcends all our efforts to get into perfect mental contact with it. We must by now feel that it is a little naive continually to hope that our last theoretical formulation will prove to have arrived at the long-sought goal, when in the past our hopes have been continually shattered by each new discovery. Acceptance of this situation carries with it the conviction that in the last analysis any adequate scheme of getting into touch with experiment can be only descriptive, for no theoretical scheme of explaining nature can be regarded as secure until verified by every possible experiment, and when every such possible experiment check has been applied, the theory degenerates into a description. The fact that every acceptable description of nature is rational might at first be thought to have some deeper significance, but I believe that analysis will show that this means simply that we refuse to accept any description which is not framed in such terms as to be adapted to our mentality, a requirement so inevitable as to be almost without significance.

Another suggestion which may be of value in our search for elements of stability in our attitude is afforded by our ever-increasing appreciation of the importance of the unavoidable subjective element in any account which we can give of our experience. We used to demand that the ultimate goal of physical theories should be nothing less than the discovery of the underlying realities. To-day our demand for reality is much less insistent, in large part because we are much less confident that the ultimate reality, which we thought to be our goal, has any meaning. The meaning to be attached to reality is to a large extent a personal matter and changes with time, but I believe it is fair to say that the sense in which every one used reality a few years ago and the sense in which the majority use it to-day has "uniqueness" as a minimum connotation. It would not have been admitted that two entirely different explanations of the universe could each be equally real, but to-day we see that uniqueness in an explanation is an impossible ideal, and the quest for reality, in so far as reality connotes uniqueness, must be abandoned as a meaningless quest. A sufficient basis for this change of attitude could be found in the proof of Poincaré that any aggregation of phenomena, no matter how complicated, is always susceptible of an infinite number of purely mechanical explanations. The reason that we are not interested in giving an explanation of quantum phenomena on a purely mechanical basis is that any such explanation would involve the assumption of a prohibitively complicated amount of detail concealed beyond the reach of any contact with experiment. It is natural, therefore, to find that the demand that our theories reproduce reality is becoming replaced by the demand of convenience and simplicity. Another requirement in a satisfactory theory has recently been much emphasized by Heisenberg and his school, namely, that our theories should contain only observable quantities. This involves so modifying the concept of reality as to make it closely associated with the possibility of direct observation. But although this alternative formulation of the reality concept has at first a most satisfying aspect, I believe that in the actual working out it is less satisfactory than in anticipation. In fact, I am inclined to think that Heisenberg's demand that only observable quantities enter the theory played only a suggestive rôle in leading to one of the many possible solutions and was as sterile in actually compelling the adoption of his form of theory as was the corresponding demand of Einstein that the law of gravitation be written in an invariant form. For if one examines how the principle works in practice, it will be seen that all that is demanded is that the raw material which is fed into the calculating machine and the final results which are taken out shall connect with direct observations. All the intermediate processes and operations, the internal pistons and gears of the theory, have as much the character of pure inventions as anything which Poincare might have proposed. However much one might have been inclined fifty years ago to see some warrant for ascribing physical reality to the internal processes of a theory because of its success in meeting the observed situation, certainly no one of the present generation will be capable of so naïve an attitude after our illuminating experience of the physical equivalence of the matrix calculus and the wave mechanics.

As a consequence of all this, the attitude of the physicist to-day is changing toward mathematical theory. As a whole, he takes it far less seriously, recognizes that it contains less of reality and more of a purely suggestive character than he had realized, and lays more emphasis on the demands of simplicity and convenience. There are puzzling questions to be answered and instinctive reactions to be overcome in adopting this point of view. It is hard to resist the conviction that there is some deep underlying significance in the fact that the mathematical operations of the matrix calculus of Heisenberg, for example, make such wonderful contact with experiment. But what the precise significance of this may be eludes formulation, and in the meantime the physicist must fortify himself with somewhat skeptical considerations like the following:

On the one hand, mathematics is a study of certain aspects of the human thinking process; on the other hand, when we make ourselves master of a physical situation, we so arrange the data as to conform to the demands of our thinking process. It would seem probable, therefore, that merely in arranging the subject in a form suitable for discussion we have already introduced the mathematics—the mathematics is unavoidably introduced by our treatment, and it is inevitable that mathematical principles appear to rule nature.

What do these general considerations have to do with our program of action? In the first place, we are going to be exceedingly cautious in ascribing any finality to the details of the present mathematical theories. There is among the younger and more enthusiastic members of the physical community a tendency to regard the present theories as final which the more sedate members must combat, even in the face of all the successes of the present theories. One of the most certain lessons of the past is that no amount of success in the youth of a theory is any guarantee of a hale and hearty old age; this is to be expected and is a consequence of the transcendence of nature. Against this view, an enthusiastic protagonist of the new theories might with considerable justification, I believe, urge that there are certain elements of genuine novelty in our present outlook which offer a basis for the belief that we may be on the point of breaking away from our often-repeated cycles of revision and reformulation. But although there may be distinctly encouraging signs of a brighter future, I believe that nevertheless there are specific elements of weakness in the present situation which justify the suspicion that our present theories still need thoroughgoing modification. Perhaps one of the most serious weaknesses of the present theory is the way in which it deals with static effects. One important consequence of the Heisenberg principle is that an electron can not stand still, yet a potential energy is substituted into the fundamental equations of the theory which retains the old fiction of an inverse square force emanating from a stationary center, and which palpably has no meaning in terms of direct experiment. Such a thing is entirely opposed to the spirit of our new outlook. We are to expect that presently the apparently static inverse square law of force will be described in statistical terms. Another suggestion that the present theory marks only a halfway stage of progress is to be found in its treatment of the universal constants, such as the gravitation constant, the velocity of light, the charge and the mass of the electron and the quantum h. No one, I suppose, is yet so pessimistic as to give up the hope that eventually we will be able to give an account of these constants, instead of always having to carry them in our equations as elements imposed from without. One may also hope to have sometime a theory of the equality of the charge on proton and electron.

Perhaps these misgivings about the permanence of our present theories seem of too vague and general a character to be of much significance, but I believe that in the past we have been many times too willing to forget any very broad general objections to which our theories may have been subject, in our satisfaction with their success in dealing with fairly wide classes of special phenomena. For example, the fact that the classical principle of equipartition of energy demanded that the atoms be mathematically rigid should in itself have been sufficient to show that any attempt to reduce all action to pure mechanics was certain to fail.

All this must not be allowed in any way to minimize our conviction of the very great importance of carrying through the analysis of all possible consequences of our many new mathematical points of view, but it does suggest that many physicists who are not professionally interested in making new contributions to new mathematical developments, but rather want to understand what there is of permanent significance in present developments, may with a clear conscience omit to work through the details of much of recent mathematics, in the conviction that it is of more or less transient character. But apart from the mathematical details, and perhaps sometimes not intimately connected with them, there are certain broad qualitative points of view characteristic of the new theories which every physicist should grasp and incorporate into his thinking. Perhaps the two most important of these points of view are (1) that the measurable properties of electrons embrace some phenomena which we find convenient to describe in terms of the wave phenomena of ordinary experience, in addition to the older and more familiar phenomena which we have satisfactorily dealt with in terms of a particle picture; and (2) that there is some essential limitation to the sorts of measurement that can be made simultaneously on elementary things, which is formulated in Heisenberg's principle of uncertainty. In speaking of these points of view as two I do not wish to imply that they are not logically connected, for they are very intimately related.

It is possible to direct just criticism at the mathematical deduction of these two principles from the logical premises. The wave mechanics is open to various objections, one of the chief of which to my mind is that it provides no way of dealing with transient phenomena; this fact constitutes to a certain extent a failure of the fundamental principle, for it is only transient phenomena which are directly observed. Further, the deduction of the Heisenberg principle as a necessary consequence of the fundamental assumptions has failed to satisfy many and does indeed seem to contain a certain feature inserted arbitrarily into the theory. But I believe that in spite of these criticisms these two points of view transcend the mathematics by which they were derived, and that, inspired and guided by the mathematics, we have come upon a point of view which is of more permanent value than the mathematics itself.

These two points of view, if I understand correctly the claims made for them, should be sufficient, in conjunction with other physical knowledge which we already have, to determine the nature of the elementary processes and entities which analysis of our physical experience discloses to us. Here we reach the actual frontiers of physical exploration, and doubtless the most fundamental problem confronting us is to acquire understanding of these things. The more complicated things, such as the chemical properties of molecules, involve processes of mathematical synthesis which we need not expect to grasp intuitively and which will not be completely worked out for some time in the future, but of the qualitative nature of the underlying elemental processes and entities all physicists should now attempt to acquire some intuitive command. Since the new theories are formulated so as to be consistent with the cardinal principle that the properties of a thing have no meaning which is not contained in some describable experience, our intuitions should be able to tell us what to expect in various experimental situations involving elementary things. This does not mean that the experience in terms of which our intuition thinks is necessarily an experience so closely connected with actuality that we could go into the laboratory and make the experiments, but the experiments must be such as are allowed in principle by the new theories. For instance, we can conceive ourselves in principle determining the frequency of a single photon by finding the location on a photographic plate of a single developed grain exposed in a spectroscope of infinite resolving power, although we may perfectly well recognize that to make such a measurement is beyond our present experimental skill. Our intuitive grasp of an elementary situation may, then, be tested by our ability to describe what to expect in terms of conceptual experiments. I believe that in the devising and discussing of such conceptual experiments there is an important field which may be cultivated, particularly at the present time, with much profit. It should be possible to build up a formal structure in which the properties of photons and electrons and other elemental things, such as quantum interactions, are described in terms of conceptual experiments, and from simple properties deduce more complicated properties in much the fashion of Euclid. In fact, the resemblance between this ideal and Euclid is a rather close one, for that part of the analysis of Euclid which consists in moving figures about and comparing them by superposition amounts to nothing more than conceptual experiments with geometrical figures. A systematic development of the conceptual experiment would be found by many, I believe, to give a more illuminating insight than a painful acquisition of the details of the present mathematical picture.

As suggestive of what may be done here, I append a list of questions which are to be answered in terms of conceptual experiments allowed by the new point of view.

(1) Are experiments on single "naked" electrons possible? How may one be sure that he has a single electron in his apparatus? Are there any methods of detecting the presence of an electron that do not demand that the electron be traveling with fairly high velocity? Can a stationary electron be detected?

(2) How may the charge of a single electron be measured? Is there any theoretical limit to the accuracy with which a single measurement of charge may be made? Or is an accurate value of e obtainable only from statistical measurement?

(3) What is the evidence that an electron has independent existence in empty space? May one electron stream receive a deflection on impinging on another?

(4) Is the equivalence of the charge on electrons and protons a statistical or an individual effect? How accurately may the charge of an individual electron and proton be proved equal?

(5) How may the magnetic moment of a single electron be found?

(6) What properties may an electron have simultaneously? We know that it can not simultaneously have position and velocity. May the charge, the mass, the momentum and the energy be simultaneously determined?

(7) Is a single electron subject to a gravitational field?

(8) To what extent does an electron have identity? May it be observed continuously, or is there a minimum time between successive observations?

(9) How do the measurable properties of an electron in those places where, according to the wave mechanics, the kinetic energy is negative differ from those of a classical electron?

(10) How may the frequency of a single photon be measured?

(11) May the frequency of a single photon be measured without at the same time compelling it to have some direction, that is, are frequency and direction independent properties?

(12) May the energy of a single photon be measured independently of its frequency?

(13) Does a single photon have a plane of polarization, that is, may the plane of polarization of a single photon be measured? (I have been able to discover no method of doing this.)

(14) Can the velocity of a single photon be measured? All experimental determinations of the velocity of light have been essentially measurements on a steady state.

(15) What experimental method is there of detecting the motion of a single photon?

(16) How many properties does an individual photon have simultaneously? For example, may the velocity, the frequency, the direction, the momentum and the energy be measured simultaneously?

(17) Does a photon have independent existence in empty space? Can two crossed streams of photons be made to disturb each other?

(18) To what extent does a photon have identity?

(19) Is there any method by which the emission of a photon from an atom may be detected which does not involve receiving the emitted photon?

(20) What sort of a constant is h? May it be determined from a single quantum process, or is it essentially statistical? The six methods for determining h listed by Birge are all essentially statistical.

(21) Is there any evidence that two quantum processes ever interfere with each other, or that one begins before the other has ended?

It will very probably be found that the answers to some of these questions can not at present be given without a rather intimate acquaintance with mathematical theory, but I believe that this is merely a temporary phase and that ultimately we shall be able to demand that our theories be so formulated that we can answer these and other questions intuitively without recourse to formal mathematics. In the meantime, I believe that any one who attempts to devise the conceptual experiments by which these questions may be answered is not only increasing his own understanding of fundamentals but is also making an important contribution to physical progress.

12

THE RECENT CHANGE OF ATTITUDE TOWARD THE LAW OF CAUSE AND EFFECT*

NEARLY EVERY EDUCATED person, brought up in present-day society and under the influence of the scientific ideas and spirit which pervade our intellectual life, prides himself in the belief that nothing happens without there being some cause for it. We may briefly characterize this attitude of ours by saying that we believe in the law of cause and effect or in the causality principle. To many of not too cynical a temperament this attitude will seem the most sweeping characteristic of the mental difference between the superstitious savage and the cultivated product of a hard-won civilization.

It is now becoming common knowledge that one of the most startling developments of the altogether surprising progress of physics in the last few years has been a weakening of the belief of the physicist, at least, in the validity of the causality principle. I want to examine with you this situation—to inquire

*From Science 73, 539, 1931. Delivered at the University of Wisconsin, April 21, 1931.

in what sense we are losing our conviction of the validity of the causality principle, and to discover some of the implications. I want especially to emphasize that I am concerned only with the objective aspects of the situation. The idea of causality which we shall discuss is as remote as possible from the subjective questions of free will or determinism which are often associated with it, both in popular discussions and in a number of recent more technical discussions by scientific men. We shall be concerned only with the domain accessible to experiment, and the causality principle, in the sense in which I use the term, is a principle dealing with the findings of actual experiments.

We shall not be able to get very far without trying to make a little more precise what we mean by the causality principle. What do we mean in any concrete situation by saying that the event A is the cause of the event B? There is at least one obvious condition to be satisfied; B must occur later than A, for no one would think of saying that something happening now was the cause of something which had already occurred in the past. But mere sequence in time is not enough. For instance, in society as at present constructed one's education is almost always completed before embarking on the sea of matrimony. But do we therefore say that the cause of our getting married is that we are educated? That is, there may be sequences in time which we recognize as due to accidental and irrelevant associations. What more then, is necessary than mere sequence in time? I believe that examination will show that we must at least have invariable sequence—the event B must always follow the event A under all sorts of conditions. But this involves being able to repeat the experiment, and it seems to me that the idea of invariable recurrence on repetition is indeed essentially involved in the notion of causality and perhaps comes closest to what is usually meant by causality. For example, suppose that I have a heavy weight attached to a support by a string; then I shall find that whenever I cut the string the weight falls, so that my definition in terms of invariable sequence would lead me to assert that the cause of the falling of the weight was the cutting of the string. But the situation is not quite as simple as this, for in the repetition of the experiment as ordinarily performed a number of the conditions are not varied, and who shall say that some one of these invariable conditions is not responsible, and therefore the true cause, of the weight falling? For instance, if I could by some heroic means remove the earth, then we are all convinced that the weight would no longer fall when the string is cut, and so we could justify the contention that the true cause of the falling of the weight was not the cutting of the string but the presence of the earth. But a still more critical analyst might contend that even the presence of the earth would not be sufficient to make the weight fall if it were not for the law of gravitation, and that therefore the true cause of the weight falling is the law of gravitation.

An impartial examination of the various arguments would convince us that there is much to be said for each of them; if we should decide that one of the claimants was correct and the others wrong, I think we should find it impossible to defend our decision against the objections of the losers. This sort of dilemma occurs very frequently. Sometimes one tries to save the day by the introduction of such ideas as that of immediate and remote or primary and secondary causes, but no such compromise ever works satisfactorily, as may be seen in our simple example by selecting some definite feature as the primary cause of the falling of the weight, to the exclusion of all others.

The conclusion to be drawn from these difficulties is, I think, that the notion of causality is not sharp and can not be made logically precise, but it is only a common-sense notion, used in describing many situations of daily life with sufficient accuracy for ordinary needs. I believe that analysis will show, however, that all situations which may be described from the common-sense point of view as those to which the law of cause and effect applies have certain more general properties. Whenever our knowledge of a situation has become sufficiently deep for us to attempt an analysis of its various events into cause and effect, we find that we have merely had sufficient experience with the situation to observe certain uniformities of behavior, certain regularities in the sequence of events, of the sort that when certain events occur other definite events follow. This characteristic of uniformity I take to be the fundamental feature in the situation. The analysis of events into sequences which are causally related is simply one of the ways of exhibiting certain uniformities and recurrences.

What now is the criterion that in a given physical system one has mastered the essential uniformities and has not merely stumbled on something accidental? I think that every one will admit that the supreme test is the ability to predict; if our neighbor is always able to accurately predict the future behavior of any physical system, I believe that we should all admit that he had completely mastered the uniformities of the system. Conversely, I think that we shall easily admit that without uniformities in the past behavior of a system no conceivable basis for predicting the future exists. The essential thing, however, is the ability to predict; granted this we have comparatively little concern with the language or system of philosophy in terms of which our neighbor may choose to describe his feelings in the matter. Furthermore, we shall all, I think, admit that in a system completely governed by the law of cause and effect the future should be predictable if we know the complete past history of the system, and conversely, if we know how to predict the future from the past, we should expect to be able to formulate some sort of statement as to the uniformities of the system which could be put into the form of a law of cause and effect.

It appears, then, that uniformity, causality and predictability all have certain common aspects, and for rough purposes may be treated as more or less equivalent. It will suit the purposes of this exposition to lay the emphasis on predictability and I shall in the future be concerned with this aspect of the situation. We may now reformulate our statement of the beginning that nearly every civilized person believes in the law of cause and effect by saying that nearly every civilized person believes that the future of a system is in principle predictable when we know all about its past behavior. To avoid argument, I am perfectly willing to make the qualification that this discussion shall be limited to the realm of purely inanimate things, leaving out altogether biological phenomena.

As a historical fact, classical physics has been committed to a much more restricted formulation of the possibilities of prediction in stating that the future could be predicted if the present position and velocity of each particle is known. This conviction arose from the belief that the laws of Newtonian mechanics, which can be formulated in terms of differential equations of the second order, completely govern the motion of the actual physical universe. This formulation, however, is much more restricted than we need to make it for our argument and in fact there are difficulties with the Newtonian conception of predictability when attention is paid to various propagation effects which are discussed in elementary expositions of relativity theory. The essence of the situation for our purposes is that we have become convinced that the behavior of nature exhibits regularities of such a kind that from observation of the events of the past we can predict those of the future.

What now is the basis of this belief of ours in the thorough-going uniformity of nature or in the essential predictablity of future events? It must at once be admitted that this belief in its wide-spread acceptance is largely an outgrowth of the last few hundred years. Savage and superstitious man sees in nature nothing but the capricious; it is only after long experience and observation that the simple uniformities begin to emerge, first the regularities in the motions of the heavenly bodies and then the same regularities in the simpler terrestrial mechanical systems. It was a tremendously stimulating discovery to find that simple uniformities in the motions of the planets which could be formulated in simple mechanical laws recurred also in the motion of terrestrial systems, and to find that as we acquired skill in analyzing systems of increasing complication these same simple uniformities continued to describe the uniformities being newly discovered. It is no wonder that after physics had experienced success after success in mastering systems of increasing complication it came to look on this success as no accident but the expression of an underlying prin-

ATTITUDE TOWARD THE LAW OF CAUSE AND EFFECT

ciple. In some such way arose the conviction of the essential uniformity and predictability of nature; it was of course recognized that in the walks of daily life, as distinguished from the artificial situations of the laboratory, the power to predict was more conspicuous by its absence than its presence, but this was ascribed merely to the enormous complication of actual physical systems, and the conviction became general that by sufficiently refining the accuracy of our measurements and increasing their scope we might some day hope to reduce the most complicated system to predictability with any desired degree of accuracy.

It is to be emphasized that although the justification for this conviction arose entirely from experience of the external world, it constituted, nevertheless, even in the simplest possible case, an idealization of that experience. For any concrete physical situation a prediction about a future event could be verified only within the limits of experimental error. The conviction that the future is predictable down to the last detail arose entirely from the experience that whenever the precision of measurements was increased the predictions which it was possible to make on the basis of the measurements always became better. But the uncertainty arising from experimental error could never be eliminated, and even in the most favorable cases the jump from the actual experiment to the ideal formulation of it involved a process which the mathematician or the physicist would describe as a long range extrapolation.

But now in the last few years all these expectations have changed, and the change has arisen primarily from the discovery of new experimental facts. Nothing previously found by experiment ceases to be true. Physics never has to retract statements about experimental facts when these statements are made with sufficient care to reproduce the physical situation with fidelity, that is, when due regard is paid to the limits of experimental error. Thus the law of gravitation should not be formulated baldly as the law of the inverse square, but rather that the attraction varies as the inverse square within certain limits of error, perhaps one part in a million, or whatever the greatest precision happens to be at present. The only genuine retractions which physics or other science has to make are in its statements about what it anticipates may in the future be found to be true about experimental realms not yet entered. So in the present situation, physics finds that it must retract a hope or expectation which it had based on previous experience, but it has not had to retract any statement about actual experiment. The expectation was that by increasing the accuracy of measurement indefinitely we would be able to make predictions about the future with indefinite precision. This turns out not to be true, for we have recently found that when we increase the refinement of our measurements beyond a certain point and enter a domain of small things not before accessible, the new domain is full of the most capricious irregularities, unlike the regularities in the domain of ordinary experience, so that in the new domain no refinement of measurement enables us to predict the future. The new domain in which this disturbing state of affairs holds is the domain in which the motions of single electrons or atoms are concerned, and is, of course, enormously remote from the domain of everyday affairs, in fact, so remote that only within the last few years have physical methods been sufficiently refined to enable us to enter this domain at all. The situation is not unlike that presented by the semi-convergent series of the mathematician. Situations are not uncommon in mathematics in which the goodness of the answer to a problem may be improved up to a certain point by increasing the labor of computation, but if labor is put into the calculation beyond this point the answer becomes poorer instead of better.

Our new understanding of the experimental situation can be made in the following bald statement: "As a matter of fact, events are not predictable in the realm of small things." This is practically equivalent to saying that in the realm of small things the law of cause and effect does not operate.

Some little experience has proved to me that this bald statement is likely to awaken in many persons the most active hostility, and this audience would indeed be unique if it did not contain an appreciable number of persons who positively bristle with animosity at such a statement. The reaction which this statement is most likely to produce is this: "You have not proved that in the realm of small things the future is not predictable, but all you are justified in saying is that you have not yet found how to predict the future. In fact, judging by past experience, there is every reason to think that if we keep on trying we shall eventually discover how to predict in this domain which at present seems so hopeless". This objection, I am sure, will appeal to many as entirely sound, but I believe that nevertheless it can not be maintained, and one of the points which I am most anxious to make this afternoon is my reason for thinking this position not to be sound. I hope that the positiveness of the assurance of the physicist in this matter will not give the unpleasant impression of mental arrogance which it easily might. I believe that every physicist recognizes that one can never say with complete assurance that his present theory is correct. There is nevertheless at least one statement which, when it can be made at all, can be made with absolute assurance, and that is that we are now taking into consideration ideas which had not previously occurred to us. All that the physicist is maintaining is that we have now at our command new experimental facts and new ideas and that in the light of them our former ideas must be modified.

It must be conceded that certain parts of the objection of our bristly critic are well taken. We have not, of course, proved that the future is not predictable, and we can say only that we are not at present able to predict and do not believe that we shall ever be able to. In fact, in the very nature of logic, it can never be proved that an entirely unexpected discovery may not be made some day which will enable us to predict the apparently unpredictable. We shall have to admit that from this point of view the tactics of the objection is very clever. From another point of view also the tactics is clever in that it puts the burden of proof on the advocate of the new point of view in effectively asking him "by what right do you expect that no one ever will find out how to do what to-day we do not know how to do?" I believe that nevertheless, in spite of the superficial strength of the objection, it is fallacious.

Let us in the first place examine what the experimental situation is which leads us to say that events in the realm of small things are unpredictable. When, in the domain of large things, we fail to predict, it is usually because of the extreme complication of the physical system, as, for example, in our endeavors to predict the weather or mob psychology. In the domain of small things, however, the element of complication is lacking and our failure arises from another reason. The reason we fail is because those regularities which are the basis on which we are able to make predictions in the simpler situations of large scale experience are entirely lacking in the domain of small things. Let us imagine the simplest possible large scale situation—a billiard ball rolling without friction or other interference on a table top. Let us imagine the table top marked with lines a foot apart. Then we all know that if we observe the ball to be at the zero mark when the second hand of our watch points to zero, and to be at the one foot mark when the second hand points to one second, when the second hand points to two seconds we shall find the ball at the two-foot mark. This is the simplest example well conceivable in which we project into the future a uniformity of behavior in the past, and, parenthetically, is doubtless the origin of the ordinary concept of velocity. But experiment shows that if we were dealing with an electron instead of a billiard ball the experiment would entirely fail, and if the electron had been observed at zero at zero seconds and at one foot at one second, at two seconds we might sometimes find it at seven feet and sometimes at five feet, or sometimes at minus one foot, and indeed sometimes at two feet, like the billiard ball. As a matter of fact this ideally simple experiment probably has not been performed, but inference from the results in less simple cases leads us to be convinced that such would be found to be the state of affairs if the experiment were made.

If capricious results like those just described for the electron happened in the experiment with the billiard ball we would almost certainly say that the initial conditions had not *all* been the same the time the ball appeared at the seven foot mark as when it appeared at five feet, and we should endeavor to find something that we had failed to take proper account of in specifying the initial conditions. Furthermore, we are convinced that this procedure would be successful in the case of the billiard ball, and that search would disclose the missing feature. We are also convinced that it would need some rather striking feature to account for the billiard ball sometimes turning up at seven feet and sometimes at five feet. But in the case of the electron, all our experience indicates that the missing feature does not exist, but that in systems in which the initial conditions are completely identical the electron will sometimes appear in one place and sometimes in another. Anything more unlike ordinary experience would be difficult to conceive, and the consequence is that there is very little basis indeed for making a successful prediction of the future position of an individual electron.

The experimental evidence, then, apparently forces us to the conclusion that if some basis for predicting the behavior of a single electron is to be found, it must be entirely different from the basis of prediction for ordinary events. Why is it that the majority of physicists at present believe that there is good reason to think that this basis for prediction will never be found, but that on the contrary we shall always have to treat the motions of single electrons as beyond the reach of prediction, that is, beyond the law of cause and effect? The reason is not that the physicist is either lazy or a quitter. Part of the reason is rather to be found in the quite surprising success achieved within the last few years by that body of physical theory variously described as "quantum theory" or "wave mechanics". The very foundations of this theory contain as an integral part the hypothesis that the individual electrons, as also the indivisible units of radiation, have the fundamental property that in any specific situation their behavior as individuals can not be predicted, but only the average behavior of large numbers. One explicit deduction from the theory which is directly concerned with predictability has been much discussed, namely the Heisenberg Principle of Uncertainty. This is usually formulated as a statement about the accuracy of measurement, the fundamental idea being that if we strive to increase the accuracy with which we make one kind of measurement we must pay a price in a necessary decrease in the accuracy of some other kind of measurement. Specifically, I can not measure the position and the simultaneous velocity of the electron with any desired accuracy, but if I increase the accuracy of my measurement of position, my measurement of velocity becomes less accurate in such a way that the probable value of the product of the two inaccuracies is of the order of magnitude of Planck's constant, h, divided by the mass of the electron. The principle applies equally well to the measurement of the position and velocity of an ordinary body. The reason why the principle is important for the electron and not for ordinary bodies is that the mass of the electron is so very much less than that of any ordinary body that when I divide

ATTITUDE TOWARD THE LAW OF CAUSE AND EFFECT

Planck's constant, h, by the mass of the electron I get a comparatively large number, that is, a comparatively large uncertainty, whereas the quotient of h by the mass of an ordinary body is so much smaller as to represent an uncertainty below ordinary methods of detection.

The Heisenberg principle, as I have just formulated it, does not seem to make statements about predictability, but that it really does may be seen by considering the significance of the velocity about which we are talking. To make the problem concrete, go back to moving electron. If I observe it at the one-foot mark at a certain time and then one second later at the two-foot mark, I know that its velocity during this second was exactly one foot per second. It is not this velocity with which the Heisenberg principle is concerned, and indeed the Heisenberg principle sets no limit to the accuracy with which this velocity may be determined. The velocity with which the Heisenberg principle is concerned is the velocity to be ascribed to the electron after, not before, the second observation. Now the only way I have of checking whether any statement about this second velocity is correct is to predict where I shall find the electron at a later instant of time. If the Heisenberg principle is correct, this prediction can not be made with precision; we thus see that the Heisenberg principle is really a statement about the impossibility of accurately predicting the course of the electron.

There is a point here which it will pay to emphasize because there has been considerable misconception about it. The *modus operandi* by which the uncertainty gets into the situation is through the act of observation—the electron can not be observed without bouncing an atom of radiation from it or doing something equivalent, and whatever the process of observation, the motion is interfered with. The essential fact is not that the act of observation interferes with the motion; if this were the only effect we could allow for the amount of interference by calculation. The essential fact is that the act of observation interferes with the motion by an unpredictable and incalculable amount. The fact that the amount of interference is unpredictable is an integral part of the theory.

Those persons who for one reason or another are anxious to save the face of the causality principle have often stated the conclusion from the Heisenberg principle in another way. They say that the causality principle is still valid, only it turns out that we are unable to make the measurements which are demanded in applying the causality principle, that is, in making a prediction. This contention it seems to me may easily degenerate into a mere matter of words, and become highly unprofitable. The essential fact is that it appears to be due to a law of nature and not to any temporary failure of ours that we can not make the measurements that we demand for our attempted predictions. In this situation it seems to me that we are keeping as close as possible to the actual facts in making the bald statement that experiment now makes it highly improbable that the future is predictable.

Not only is the Heisenberg principle checked by experiment, but apparently all other deductions from the wave mechanics theory are also checked with equal success. In fact, the success of theory has been so great that the statement is often made by its enthusiastic advocates that in no case where it has been correctly applied, that is, without blunders in the calculation, has it failed, and that no experimental facts are known which are in contradiction with it. The average physicist now takes the next step, and draws the conclusion that because of the success of the theory the fundamental hypotheses on which it rests must also be very probably correct. It must be admitted that this last step is rather dubious from the logical point of view, because it does not follow at all that because our conclusions are correct our reasoning or our premises must be correct, and in fact there are a number of instances in physics in which the fundamental hypotheses have been changed without changing at all the superstructure as shown, for example, by the change in attitude toward the physical reality of the ether.

I think we would have to admit that if the sole argument of the physicist were the success of the theory as at present formulated we would have some ground for scepticism as to how long the present attitude would last. But the physicist has other reasons for his attitude. Along with his experimental activity he has been active in critically examining the fundamental concepts of physics. Among other things he has examined the grounds on which rest our conviction that nature is uniform or predictable and has come to the conclusion that at least the burden of proof is now on the side of those who maintain that nature is uniform and can be described in terms of a causality principle. The reasons for this conclusion I have already intimated, but they are worth repeating. The physicist recognizes that belief in uniformity or predictability is a belief compelled by no inner necessity, but is a belief that has gradually grown up as a generalization from large scale experiences; that as long as experience was confined to the large scale things of daily life an ever increasing number of phenomena could be brought under the approximate sway of the principle, but that as soon as physical methods became sufficiently refined so that we could deal with small scale phenomena, uniformities became less and less conspicuous, until we finally arrived at electrons and photons, the ultimate structural elements of the physical world as we know it where we would expect the utmost in the way of simplicity and uniformity but where, on the contrary, experiment shows that uniformity in its original sense has entirely vanished.

The situation thus contains two elements: There is in the first place the recognition that the notion of causality, in the sense in which I am using it, was an outgrowth of experience, and that the extent to which the causality principle is valid is solely for experiment to decide. This attitude I believe must now be accepted by every one who will take the pains to examine the argument. In the second place there is the conclusion from experiment that as a matter of fact nature is very far from predictable or that the causality principle fails by large amounts to be valid for small-scale events. If the first point is accepted, then the second may be accepted as a summary of the best experimental knowledge at present, without resentment or antagonism or rebelliousness. This willingness to accept the findings of experiment must remain permanently a part of our attitude, whether or not future experiment justifies present optimism about the complete adequacy of wave mechanics. This, then, is the chief idea that I hope you will carry away from this talk; that it is purely a matter for experiment to decide whether nature is predictable in the domain of small things or not; that until some at present totally unlooked-for development turns up to prove predictability or to make it plausible, we must assume that the causality principle does not apply in this domain, and that this conclusion is to be accepted without prejudice or passion just as any other experimental result is accepted.

What difference is the recognition of this situation now going to make to us? As far as actual action in most concrete situations of daily life goes, it will make practically no difference at all. Large-scale phenomena will remain for all practical purposes just as predictable as they ever were. The reason for this is that in no case have we ever been able to predict large-scale phenomena with more than a certain degree of approximation; the goodness of the approximation has been fixed by the accuracy of the measurements. Furthermore, in nearly all cases, the inaccuracies of our measurements arise from the ordinary imperfection of our instruments, recognized and well understood long before the Heisenberg principle was formulated, and these inaccuracies are so great that the uncertainty in our predictions arising from them is much greater than the uncertainty arising from the action of the Heisenberg principle. In most practical situations the Heisenberg uncertainty is so very far beyond the reach of detection by ordinary means that from the practical point of view its effects will in nearly all situations remain forever of purely academic interest.

There is a difficult point here which we may stop to examine for a moment. At first sight it is not easy to see how it is that if large-scale phenomena are built up from small-scale phenomena and if the small-scale phenomena are essentially unpredictable, the large-scale phenomena acquire approximate predictability. The reason is that although any single small-scale phenomenon is unpredictable, experiment shows that nevertheless there is a sort of regularity in large numbers of them which permits combinations of them to be predicted, approximately. This sort of regularity is of the sort that may be described as statistical. Let us go back to the illustration of the electron moving over the marks on a table, and let us suppose that the electron has been observed at the zero mark at the zero of time and at the one-foot mark at one second. Then it is a matter of experiment that if I attempt to predict where the electron will be found at two seconds I shall make a great many mistakes, but it is also a matter of experiment, neglecting a consideration which is not important for this argument, that if I always guess that it will be at the two-foot mark, I shall in the long run make fewer mistakes and obtain a better score than if I make any other guess. There is thus a certain regularity in the aggregate results of a great many experiments, although the results of individual experiments may fluctuate widely, being now greater than the average and now less. If I could make a great many experiments simultaneously, it is evident that I could make a good prediction about the average result of all of them taken together, because in a great many experiments those individual results which are too high will cancel with those which are low, leaving outstanding merely the average. Something very much like this is involved when experiments are made on ordinary matter, for even the smallest bits of matter that can be distinctly seen in the microscope still contain a very large number of electrons, and the behavior of the whole bit of matter is merely the average behavior of all its electrons, which can therefore be predicted with much success. In fact, as already stated, the mean fluctuations of the individual electrons are less than the uncertainties arising from other and more ordinary sorts of imprecision of measurement.

It might seem, therefore, as though there could never be any practical effects arising from such small-scale uncertainties. This, however, would be too hasty a conclusion. If one makes the deliberate attempt, it is possible to magnify such small-scale events sufficiently to bring them into the range of everyday experience. An example of this sort of thing is known to every physicist in the Geiger counter. This apparatus is so constructed that the effect of the entrance of even a single electron into the sensitive part of the apparatus is amplified with vacuum tubes to such an extent as to give a crack of sound in a loud speaker, or to perform other functions, such, for example, as starting or stopping a piece of machinery. Now the electron which enters the apparatus may be the result, for example, of the radio-active disintegration of a single atom. The disintegration of such an atom is the sort of thing that experiment and theory both show is essentially unpredictable. It would therefore be possible, by utilizing an arrangement of this kind, to make all the lights of a great city flicker up and down, and it would be absolutely impossible to predict when the next eclipse would occur.

Some of you may have read a recent story by Lord Dunsany in which a crazy power magnate wards off the vengeance of the powers above by gigantic prayer wheels driven by 10,000 horse power steam turbines. We may similarly romance about the future religion of a superstitious race by imagining in the inmost shrine of their temple a speck of radio-active salt in process of disintegration, and attached to this a train of vacuum tube amplifiers, which shall ever and anon flood the temple with light, or beat a tom-tom, or perhaps sacrifice a victim. A rather good argument might be made for this sort of thing, and it really appeals to the imagination in many ways, for we have here the possibility of a spectacular projection into the realm of ordinary sense of the eternally inscrutable foundations of our physical world.

In the realm of ordinary physical objects, however, this sort of unpredictability probably seldom occurs unless it is the result of deliberate design. It is not quite so evident, however, what the true state of affairs is in biological systems. I gather the impression that at the present time a number of biologists are prepared to admit that not infrequently the adjustment of a single cell may be so delicate as to be thrown out of balance and a reaction started by the entrance of a single free electron or light corpuscle into the cell. In such cases the behavior of the individual cell must be admitted to be unpredictable. In one simple field of biological experiment the facts have already been definitely established. It has been shown that when certain unicellular organisms are radiated with alpha particles, the death of the organism results if a single alpha particle makes a direct hit on the nucleus of the cell. The death of any single organism is therefore an absolutely unpredictable event, although in a large colony of such organisms the average number of deaths may be predicted by the methods of life insurance statistics. The important question now is whether in large-scale organisms consisting of many cells the adjustment is ever so delicate as to be thrown one way or the other by the unpredictable action of only a few cells, or whether so large a number of cells must cooperate in any large-scale movement as to make all large-scale movements approximately predictable by the methods of statistics. This question can be answered only by experiment, and it is certainly one of the most important questions to which biology can address itself. At the same time it is obviously one of enormous experimental difficulty, for no experiment can be repeated under identical conditions on an organism complicated enough to have memory.

A word of warning may be interjected here. Many will be tempted to see a connection between the question of the predictability of the behavior of organic systems and those questions which have always exercised the human race, determinism and free will. It seems to me that there is no connection. The former is primarily a question of physical fact, while the latter are predominantly questions of a subjective character which involve those emotional experiences which the subject goes through when on the point of making a decision.

The concrete physical changes which are likely

to arise from our modified attitude toward the causality principle are therefore small. I believe, however, that there will be very important effects on our methods and habits of thought and our entire outlook. One of the most obvious effects of these discoveries is in prescribing the program for future scientific investigation. One such possibility I have just indicated, namely, the examination of the question as to whether the behavior of complex biological organisms is ever initiated by unpredictable small-scale events. A similar question arises with respect to other sorts of physical happenings; are there anywhere in nature mechanical systems of such a high degree of instability, as for example in the turbulent motion of a liquid, that an unpredictable small-scale event initiates a large scale event, which thereby itself becomes unpredictable? Another possible program for future scientific investigation is in devising simple experiments which shall demonstrate less indirectly than we now can some of the statistical effects of small-scale events. For example, the invention of a photographic plate such that the impact of a single photon is sufficient to make a single grain of the plate developable would be an enormous assistance.

Apart from these concrete effects on our scientific program there will be many other less tangible results of our changed mental outlook, which I have not time to elaborate in detail here, but I shall try to give a few brief indications of what may be expected. A parallel may be drawn from the theory of relativity. Although the theory of relativity deals with phenomena which are so difficult to detect as to require instruments of the highest delicacy, nevertheless it has made exceedingly important changes in our attitude toward the fundamental concepts of space and time. I believe that in the same way the clear recognition that causality can not function in detail in small things, as has been supposed, but can have only a statistical meaning, must have important repercussions on our thinking. In fact, activity is already beginning in the ranks of the philosophers which bears out this contention. Many articles and even books have already appeared in which the endeavor is made either to explain away the importance of the new findings, or else to discover how we may adjust ourselves to them. The bearings on epistemology are apparently considered especially important. A single possibility may be mentioned. At a recent discussion between philosophers I heard it argued that the principle of sufficient reason is an absolute *sine qua non* of thought, that the human reason must by its very nature refuse to accept the possibility, to go back to the well-worn example of the billiard ball and the electron, that in one experiment the electron should appear at the seven-foot mark and in another at the five-foot mark, without there being some reason for the difference. To which I am afraid that the brutal physicist would be tempted to rejoin that if the human reason is incapable of accepting the situation, so much the worse for the human reason. How-

ATTITUDE TOWARD THE LAW OF CAUSE AND EFFECT

ever, these are questions of technical philosophy which are entirely beyond my sphere, and I shall not say anything more about them for fear of making even more egregious blunders than I may have already.

Apart from philosophical questions, however, it seems to me the realization that it is possible to exemplify on a large scale such things as our capriciously disintegrating radio-active material, which may serve as the nucleus of a superstitious religion, or may equally well serve as a most excellent gambling device, can not fail to get under the skin of the man in the street. This objectifies in the most striking way the limitations of the human intellect, and I believe that the greatest changes in our mental outlook will come as a consequence of the realization of just these human limitations—we had thought the human reason capable of conquering all things, we now find it subject to very definite limitations. We can definitely conjure up physical situations in which the human reason is powerless to satisfy itself, but must passively be content to accept phenomena as they occur, which constitutes in fact a reversion to the mental attitude of primitive man, which is purely receptive. What is more, the strictly scientific attitude recognizes no escape from the situation, but it must be accepted as inherent in the nature of things, and no way out attempted by such inventions, material or conceptual, as primitive man makes.

The realization of human mental limitations will,

I believe, have the greatest effect, and the process of adjustment will be slowest, in such non-scientific activities as philosophy, religion, as already suggested, and very probably education, for some just apprehension of the possibilities of the human intellect should be imparted in any satisfactory educational program. The adjustment in scientific activity I believe will be made more rapidly, and in fact it is possible to see even now in what the adjustment will consist.

A formulation of the purpose of scientific activity which appeals to me as rather exhaustive is the understanding, prediction and control of events. It might be thought that the discovery that there are aspects of nature which are not understandable, predictable or controllable would work havoc with this scientific program. But the way out is already obvious. If it is true that there are certain aspects of nature which are neither controllable or predictable, then the obvious course is to avoid these aspects of nature. This may sound like a flippant suggestion, but the matter is really to a large extent in our own power. We have seen that although single small-scale events are unpredictable, the statistical average of large numbers of them is highly regular and predictable. The obvious course of action, then, whenever we want to be sure of the result, is to so arrange the apparatus or machine as to respond only to statistical averages, and not to function like a Geiger counter in response to single small-scale happenings. If it should prove that the large-scale behavior of biological organisms is unpredictable, then we shall take pains never to depend on the behavior of a single such organism whenever we have to be sure of our results, but this is hardly more than we do already.

The situation with regard to *understanding* small-scale events will probably take a little more adjustment, because it involves giving up an ideal which we had set ourselves. But even here the adjustment can hardly take more than one generation, and in science generations are short. Analysis will show, I believe, that what we call understanding consists in picking out from a situation elements with which we are already familiar. The difficulty in the present situation is that we are not familiar with systems in which individual events occur with no close connection with past events, so that naturally we are confused and seek for a hidden connection. But as our familiarity increases and the strangeness gradually wears off, we shall come to feel that it is natural and proper that small-scale events show only statistical regularities, and we shall come to be satisfied with our understanding of a situation when we have analyzed it sufficiently to show, if we are dealing with large numbers, the statistical regularities to be expected, or, if we are dealing with small numbers, the corresponding capricious variations. In fact, a number of the younger generation have already achieved this degree of emancipation, and the rest of us by deliberate effort may hope to attain it.

13

STATISTICAL MECHANICS AND THE SECOND LAW OF THERMODYNAMICS*

ONE THING THAT has much impressed me in recent conversations with physicists, particularly those of the younger generation, is the frequency of the conviction that it may be possible some day to construct a machine which shall violate the second law of thermodynamics on a scale large enough to be commercially profitable. This constitutes a striking reversal of the attitude of the founders of thermodynamics, Kelvin and Clausius, who postulated the impossibility of perpetual motion of the second kind as a generalization from the uniformly unsuccessful attempts of the entire human race to realize it. Paradoxically, one very important factor in bringing about this change in attitude is the feeling of better understanding of the second law which the present generation enjoys, and which is largely due to the universal acceptance of the explanation of the second law in statistical terms, for which Gibbs was in so large a degree responsible. Statistical mechanics reduces the second law from a law of

*From Bulletin of the American Mathematical Society, April, 1932. The Ninth Josiah Willard Gibbs Lecture, delivered at New Orleans, Dec. 29, 1931, at a joint meeting of the American Mathematical Society, the American Physical Society and Section A of the A.A.A.S.

ostensibly absolute validity to a statement about high probabilities, leaving open the possibility that once in a great while there may be important violations. Doubtless another most important factor in present scepticism as to the ultimate commercial validity of the second law is the discovery of the importance in many physical phenomena of those fluctuation effects which are demanded by statistical mechanics. It is very hard indeed for one who has witnessed the Brownian motion for the first time to resist the conviction that an ingenious enough engineer might get something useful out of it, and I have no doubt that many in this audience have tried their own hand at designing such a device, and I also have no doubt that their success has been discouragingly nil.

There are other aspects also of the statistical point of view which have become prominent in the last few years, as for example, the speculations of Eddington on time's arrow and on the meaning of time in general, the speculations of Lewis as to completely reversible time, all the recent concern and new notions about the destiny of the universe as a whole, in which thermodynamic arguments play a most important part, and it is of course notorious that the notions of probability, which are fundamental in statistics, are at the very bottom of wave mechanics.

It is evident, therefore, that the statistical point of view entails consequences important both conceptually and practically. In the hope of helping a little to a better understanding of the situation I propose today to examine a few of the implications and consequences of the statistical point of view. The program is a very modest one, and I hope you will have no expectation of a final solution of any of these difficult questions; my primary purpose is to awaken a more vivid self-consciousness of what the situation actually is. I shall be mostly concerned with the classical statistics, and shall have less to say about questions raised by wave mechanics; we shall find that the questions raised by the classical point of view are sufficiently fundamental. I shall throughout adopt the point of view that I have called *operational*, that is, I shall seek the meaning of our statements and concepts by trying to analyze what it is that we do when we are confronted with any concrete physical situation to which we attempt to apply the concept or about which we make the statement.

It is in the first place most important to realize that the statistical method, in which the notions of probability are fundamental, has, when applied to the understanding of physical situations, certain inherent, unique, logical characteristics, so that any account which statistics can give of physical phenomena must have an entirely different aspect from that of such a method of approach as classical mechanics, for example. The reason for this is that probability is not a notion which can be applied to concrete individual events, whereas we demand that we understand, or predict, or control, the individual event. I demand to know what will happen when I throw this particular stone in the air, or explode this particular charge in the cylinder of a gas engine. Ordinary mechanics gives an unequivocal answer, and in general the explanations of ordinary mechanics make direct contact with just such concrete individual physical events. But the notions of probability have no such application to individual events, and in fact the notion of probability is meaningless when applied to an individual event. The proof of this is given by mere observation of what we do in applying the notion of probability. Suppose that I show you a die and remark that I intend to throw it in a minute. You volunteer the information that the probability is one-sixth that the throw will be a six. I am sceptical and ask you to justify your statement by pointing out the property of the event, when it takes place, that can be described as a probability of one-sixth for a six. I then make the throw and get a six. What possible characteristics has this single event that can justify your statement? Your statement has immediate meaning only when applied to a long sequence of events, or when applied to the *construction* of the die and the method of throwing it. Even when applied to a sequence of events there is always an unbridgeable logical chasm thwarting a precise application of the notion of probability to any actual sequence. Consider, for example, the classical example of tossing a coin. In practice our first concern is to determine whether the coin is a fair coin, that is, whether it is equally likely that heads or tails appear. Suppose that we make a million throws, and find the excess of one or the other not to be more than 1,000. Then we are likely to say that the coin is fair. But, logically, we are bound to recognize that the coin may have been loaded so that heads were, perhaps, nine times as likely to appear as tails, only that we had happened on one of those excessively rare sequences in which as many tails appeared as heads. Rigorously, there can be no method by which we can be sure that all our past experience has not been one of these excessively rare sequences which logically we are bound to recognize as possible in any statistical assembly.

Passing over these logical difficulties in applying precisely the notions of probability to any actual physical situation, it is evident, I think, that when applied to individual events, probability can have only a secondary or derived meaning. I believe that an examination, as the operational point of view prescribes, of what one does, will show that the meaning to be ascribed to the probability of individual happenings is to be found in the rules of the *mental* game that one plays in thinking about and trying to understand the individual events. This has important consequences when we attempt to use the notions of probability in building physical theories. We must recognize in the first place that any physical theory demands the construction of some sort of model. Now any model involving notions of probability is of necessity more remote from the physical situation and more esoteric in character than the more usual and naive models, such as are offered by ordinary mechanics. For any statistical model involves conventionalized events to which the notions of probability are by definition applicable, although the notion of probability does not apply at all to the concrete physical events which are the counterpart of the events of the model. It is therefore not surprising that the connection between the properties of the statistical model and the corresponding physical system is somewhat different from the connection in the more ordinary sorts of model.

It would be possible to digress considerably here to discuss the properties which we demand in our models, and the uses to which we put them. The subject is fairly obvious, however, and I believe we can safely assume an understanding of the essential features. The least exacting demand that we make of a model is that it serve as a calculating device, by which we can predict actual physical happenings, and for this purpose any sort of consistent correspondence between the model and the physical happening is satisfactory. The simplest way in which the statistical model can satisfy this simplest and minimum demand is evidently that actual happenings in the physical system shall correspond to high probabilities in the statistical model. This furthermore seems to be the only possibility and all that we can do; in the model there are no certainties, only probabilities, some of which, it is true, may be very close to unity, whereas in the physical system there are invariable happenings, as for example, a cake of ice *always* melts when it is heated above the melting point, or the external atmosphere *always* rushes into an exhausted electric bulb when it is cracked. On the other hand, it is most natural to say that low probabilities in the model correspond to infrequent occurrences in the physical system. But to go further, and specify exactly how close to unity we shall demand that the probability be that is to correspond to an invariable happening, is not so easy, and there seems to be a certain unavoidable fuzziness here defeating every endeavor to make sharp connection between the model and actuality. There is a still greater difficulty in giving a precise physical significance to events in the model of low probability; we shall return to this question. For the present the important point for us is that any statistical model is in peculiar degree purely a *paper and pencil* model and peculiar limitations may be expected in the use of such a model.

If the only demand that we put on the model were that it should serve as a computing device, the situation would be comparatively simple and could be quickly dismissed. But as a matter of fact we make the more exacting demand that the model enable us to *understand* the physical situation, and to this end we demand that there be a further correspondence between the properties of the model and of the physical system. Since we do not usually make the extreme demand that the model enable us to understand *all* the physical properties of the system at once, we usually do not demand that there be an exhaustive correspondence between the properties of the physical system and those of the model, but we are satisfied with a correspondence of those properties only which are pertinent for our immediate purposes. Thus for the discussion of the thermodynamic properties of a perfect gas, a model is usually sufficient in which the molecules of the actual gas are replaced by perfectly elastic spheres or ellipsoids, although such a model gives no hint of the optical properties of the actual gas. It is curious, however, that even for thermodynamic purposes we would not be satisfied with a model in which the number of fictitious molecules is not equal to the number of actual molecules which various other sorts of physical evidence lead us to ascribe to the actual gas.

If, now, we are attempting to find a model for the thermodynamic properties of a gas, we see that the accepted models which satisfy these additional requirements go far beyond the original demands, for in such models we encounter all the phenomena of fluctuations. Strictly, such a model never comes to equilibrium, and cannot therefore possess any property which strictly corresponds to temperature as defined classically in terms of equilibrium states. The remarkable fact, of course, is that the fluctuations of the model were found to correspond to fluctuations in the physical system, as shown by the Brownian motion, and in consequence we have now come to recognize that temperature is physically only an approximate concept, instead of the exact concept originally assumed in the thermodynamics. This gives us at once one possible method of dealing with the second law and its apparent violations. If we choose to formulate the second law by the statement that dQ/T is an exact differential, then by its very form it applies only to those situations to which the temperature concept applies, and since the temperature concept never exactly applies to any physical situation, we are left with a law which may be rigorously exact in the limit, but which applies to no actual situation. This method of meeting the situation may perhaps be satisfactory to the pure logician, but to the individual interested in filling his pockets by bootlegging entropy, such considerations will appear as uninteresting and as ineffectively legalistic as the restrictions which the more ordinary sort of bootlegger fails to recognize.

It is probably not possible to set up a mechanistic model of a purely thermodynamic system, for the thermodynamic system knows no details, but only pressure and volume and temperature, whereas it is the essence of a mechanical model that it contain details which can have no counterpart in the physical system in so far as it is purely thermodynamic. This prepares us to recognize that the concepts of thermodynamics have no absolute validity, but are relative to the operations, and in particular to the scale of the operations which we use. Thus a fluid in turbulent motion may have a temperature from the point of view of a thermometer with a bulb several centimeters in diameter, but may have no temperature from the point of view of a minute thermocouple such as biologists have recently used in probing the interior of single cells. Or again, the entire body of phenomena to which the so-called third law is applicable would immediately appear in a different aspect and the third law would no longer be applicable if the operation of taking atoms apart and recombining them was added to the other permissible operations of a more conventional character. In recent papers Dr. David Watson has discussed some of the consequences of a recognition of some of the other relativistic characteristics of the entropy concept.

There seem to be two diametrically opposite and equally natural reactions to an appreciation of this situation. The first reaction is that of the younger generation, part of which, at least, expects to discover some day in the realm of microscopic operations the possibility of a profitable entropy bootlegging business, and there is, secondly, the reaction of the other school, which is convinced that the second law involves something absolutely fundamental, and that any formulation in terms involving relative magnitudes or permissible operations can be only an incomplete formulation.

In the endeavor of the second school to find a more fundamental formulation it is natural to attempt to capitalize the striking success that the statistical point of view has already had in dealing with the phenomena of fluctuations. One recent and well-known attempt in this direction is that of Eddington to appraise the second law in terms of what is essentially a shuffling process. Eddington sees in the universal tendency for entropy to increase, or for a system to pass from a less to a more probable configuration, the analogue of what happens when a pack of cards is shuffled. Now although there may be strong points of analogy between these two processes, it seems to me that there are also essential differences, and that the analogy on the whole is not a happy one. Shuffling acquires meaning only when we are able to apprehend the cards as individuals by marking them so that we can identify them as individuals, but in such a way that there shall be absolutely no effect on the shuffling process. The picture that Eddington had in mind was a pack of cards freshly received from the manufacturer, arranged in suits and by rank in the suits, and then shuffled and losing all trace of its original arrangement. But as G. N. Lewis has remarked, the arrangement of the cards in suits is one of entirely arbitrary significance; from the point of view of some other game than whist the initial arrangement was already a completely shuffled arrangement as well as all the subsequent ones. Or we may look at it in another way. Imagine an infinite sequence of deals, the cards being partially shuffled between each deal, and suppose that a complete record is kept of all the hands. Somewhere in this sequence there will be deals in which the cards are distributed among the hands by suit and the arrangement in each hand is by rank. If one examines the record it will be found that as one proceeds away from the exceptional deal, both forward and backward in the sequence, all trace of the regular arrangement becomes obliterated. That is, shuffling with respect to any configuration selected arbitrarily as of special significance is symmetrical with respect to past and future time, and the analogy with the thermodynamic situation disappears. There are other difficulties with the shuffling point of view. We have seen that shuffling has meaning only when the cards can be identified as individuals. But if the cards can be *handled* as individuals, they can be unshuffled, as any whist player will demonstrate to you within five seconds of picking up his hand. To see in the shuffling process something analogous to the inexorableness of the increase of entropy in nature involves the thesis that, although it may be possible to identify the elements in a physical situation, there is some restriction in nature which prevents us from treating these elements separately and sorting them out. This, it seems to me, is a hard doctrine. There is no suggestion of such a state of affairs in any picture offered by the classical mechanics and classical mechanics was all that Eddington had in mind. Until the reason is elucidated for this surprising inability of ours to handle what we can see, I believe that the shuffling analogy must be judged only to obscure the situation rather than to clarify it.

At first glance, the possibility of understanding the strange restriction against touching what we can see is even more remote from the wave mechanics point of view than from the classical, for seeing is now to be considered as a kind of touching, namely touching with a photon. It may well be, however, that we have here the key of the ultimate solution, for it is not sufficient merely to touch, but the touch must also control; such a kind of touch doubtless requires the cooperation of a great many photons, and thus will be less possible to attainment than the touch by a single photon which is sufficient for recognition. But this point of view we do not follow further here.

Not only does Eddington see in shuffling the complete analogy of the inexorable increase of entropy, but he sees something even more fundamental, namely an explanation of the properties of time itself, and in particular why it is that time is unsymmetrical and flows only forward. This he has expressed by saying that the increase of entropy of the universe is what it is that gives direction to time's arrow. This conception deals with such fundamental matters and has been hailed in so many quarters as being of such unique profundity, that we may be pardoned for stopping for an examination of what is involved. Eddington sees the crux of the matter in an essential difference between the equations of ordinary mechanics, including electrodynamics, and thermodynamics. The equations of ordinary mechanics and of electrodynamics, which express what Eddington calls primary law, are of such a character that the differential of time may be reversed in sign with no change in the equations, as, for example, in the equation for a falling body, $d^2s/dt^2 = -g$. It is evident enough that the equation is unaltered if the sign of dt is changed; the question is what is the significance of this observation? The significance that Eddington ascribes to it is that the equation is unaffected by a reversal of the direction of flow of time, which would mean that the corresponding physical occurrence is the same whether time flows forward or backward, and his thesis is that in general there is nothing in ordinary mechanical occurrences to indicate whether time is flowing forward or backward. In thermodynamic systems, on the other hand, in which entropy increases with time, time enters the differential equation as the first derivative, so that the direction of flow of time cannot be changed without changing the equation. This is taken to indicate that in a thermodynamic system time must flow forward, while it might flow backward in a mechanical system.

As thus expressed there seems to be considerable vagueness about some of the ideas; this vagueness I find in Eddington's original formulation. Such vagueness is natural and perhaps inevitable in a popular exposition, but if we are to understand from the operational point of view what is involved here, we must try to be more precise. Careful analysis has not yielded to me more than the following as an exact statement of what is involved. Imagine a closed system, and an assistant with a note book in which at a given instant of time he notes all the data necessary to characterize completely the configuration of the system. At a later instant of time he records the corresponding data in another note book. He then gives us the note books and we try from a study of them to determine which set of data was recorded at the earlier instant of time. If the system was a thermodynamic system we can make the decision because the entropy increases with time, but if the system was mechanical system we cannot decide which note book was used first, because examples could be set up for either one or the other. Eddington expresses this difference by saying that the direction of flow of time has no significance in the mechanical system.

It is, of course, true that the differential equation of the mechanical system is differently constructed from that of the thermodynamic system, but the significance of the difference does not need to be formulated as does Eddington. We must in the first place remember that the equation of the mechanical system, for example, $d^2s/dt^2 = -g$, applies not only to a single system, that is to a single falling body, but applies as well to a family of systems. The equation has the property that, corresponding to every specific system, with its particle at a definite point moving with a definite velocity at a definite instant of time, another system is possible with its particle in the same position at the same instant, but with a negative velocity. This is because the equation is of the second order, and gives on integration two constants, which may be so adjusted as to give any position and any velocity at any instant of time.

MECHANICS AND SECOND LAW OF THERMODYNAMICS

Imagine the second system set up; as time goes on it will trace out in reverse sequence the positions of the first system, as may be seen from the equation itself, which may be written

$$\frac{d^2s}{dt^2} = \frac{dv}{dt} = \frac{d(-v)}{d(-t)} = -g.$$

It is this fact which makes it impossible to decide, in our example above, which note book was used first, because there is no way of telling from the entries alone whether they applied to the first or the second system. But in no case is there any question of time flowing backward, and in fact the concept of a backward flow of time seems absolutely meaningless. For how would one go to work in any concrete case to decide whether time were flowing forward or backward? If it were found that the entropy of the universe were decreasing, would one say that time was flowing backward, or would one say that it was a law of nature that entropy decreases with time? It seems to me that in any operational view of the meaning of natural concepts the notion of time must be used as a primitive concept, which cannot be analyzed, and which can only be accepted, so that it is meaningless to speak of a reversal of the direction of time. I see no way of formulating the underlying operations without assuming as understood the notion of earlier or later in time.

Lewis in a recent paper *The Symmetry of Time in Physics* adopts a point of view in some respects similar to that of Eddington, although Lewis would certainly disclaim more than very partial agreement with Eddington. Lewis speculates about the fundamental significance of the symmetry of time in physics. His point of view takes its origin from the four-dimensional representation of events employed in relativity theory, and the consequent reduction of all propositions in kinematics to propositions in four-dimensional geometry, rather than from the form of the equations of mechanics, as in Eddington's theory. But both neglect what I believe to be the most important aspect of the situation. Both the equations giving the motion of the system and the four-dimensional representation of the motion are only a small part of the story. The equations are without significance unless the physical operations are also defined by which numerical values are assigned to the various symbols of the equations. For instance, in treating a falling body, we need in addition to the equation itself a set of directions for the use of the equation, in which it is set forth, among other things, that s is the number obtained by making with a meter stick certain manipulations connected with an arbitrary origin and the instantaneous position of the falling body. Similarly in the four-dimensional representation, we must know the physical operations by which the numerical values of the coordinates are obtained which go into the four-dimensional diagram. If one examines the operations by which meaning is given to the symbols which occur in the equations or to the coordinates in the geometrical representation it will be found that the time concept has to be assumed as primitive and unanalyzable, for the operations essentially assume that the operator understands the meaning of later and earlier in time. For example, in order to find the velocity of a particle, one has to observe its position at some one instant of time and combine with this in a prescribed way the result of another observation at a later instant. If one does not intuitively understand what is meant by a later instant, there is no method of formulating the operations. The same situation is involved in specifying a thermodynamic system. One of the variables is the temperature; it is not sufficient merely to read at a given instant of time an instrument called a thermometer, but there are various precautions to be observed in the use of a thermometer, the most important of which is that one must be sure that the thermometer has come to equilibrium with its surroundings and so records the true temperature. In order to establish this, one has to observe how the readings of the thermometer change as time increases.

This point of view, that the schedule of operations by which the symbols acquire meaning is as important a part of the physical situation as the relations which are found to hold between the symbols themselves, has an important bearing on a very widely spread tendency in modern physics and science in general to see nothing as significant except the relations, and so to reduce all science to a kind of topology. It is this point of view that is at the bottom of Einstein's philosophy when he says, for example, that all that is observed is a series of space-time coincidences, and which Eddington expresses by saying that nature may be reduced to a series of pointer readings. If one grants that the ultimate object of physics is to establish a certain sort of relation between us and the world of our senses, to speak with a certain monstrous naïveté, I do not see how it is possible to discard as irrelevant the fact, for example, that the fourth coordinate in the four-dimensional geometry of relativity has to be obtained by an entirely different sort of operation from the other three coordinates, or to regard the entire situation as exhaustively characterized by the relations between the numbers, irrespective of how they are obtained.

We return now to a further consideration of our statistical model and the methods by which we shall establish a correspondence between its properties and those of the physical system. Hitherto we have been gratifyingly successful; events in the model of overwhelmingly high probability correspond to invariable happenings in the physical system, and less common events in the model, such as fluctuation phenomena, are found to be prophetic of a previously unsuspected new domain of physical effects, typified by the Brownian motion. Encouraged by this success, it is natural to think that we have got hold of something real, whatever that may mean, and to push our scheme of correlation to the logical limit, and say that all the excessively rare events corresponding to low probabilities in the statistical model are correlated with corresponding rare events in the physical system. Now it is a consequence of the fundamental assumptions which have gone into the usual statistical model, namely that all elementary configurations are entirely independent of each other, so that the probability of any configuration is to be calculated by purely combinatorial methods from the relative number of ways in which the configuration can be realized, that there is some chance of the occurrence of any configuration, no matter how unusual its properties. This would mean that in the corresponding physical system any configuration whatever, compatible with the fixed conditions, would occur occasionally, as, for example, the gas in a box will occasionally automatically all collect itself into one end. This conclusion is indeed taken literally by many experts in statistical mechanics, and in the literature statements are not uncommon, such, for example, as that of Bertrand Russell in a recent magazine article that if we put a pail of water on the fire and watch it for an indefinite time, we shall eventually be rewarded by seeing it freeze. It seems to me that there are a couple of objections that can be made to the conventional treatment of rare occurrences, which I shall now examine.

The first difficulty is with the technical method of calculating the chances of observing a rare configuration, and is concerned only with the model itself, and not with the physical application of the results of the calculations. In computing the chance of any configuration, it is always assumed that the elements of the statistical model are without influence on each other, so that the chance of a given configuration is given merely by enumerating the number of complexions corresponding to the given configuration. For example, in the kinetic theory of gases it is assumed that the location of any molecule and its velocity is, except for the restriction on the total energy and the total volume, independent of the location or the velocity of any or all of the other molecules. It may be proper enough to postulate this for the model, but we know that it cannot rigorously correspond to the physical system, for the molecules of a gas do interact with each other, as shown by the mere fact that they conserve their total energy, and the transmission of energy from one molecule to another takes place only at a finite rate, so that if, for example, at one instant all the velocity were in a single molecule, we would find that immediately afterward only molecules in the immediate vicinity had any velocity. This means that the assumption of complete independence must be recognized to be only an approximation, and some way of handling this approximation must be devised. The method usually adopted is to cast the problem in the form of inquiring how many observations must be made in order that the chance of observing the desired rare configuration may be one-half, for example, choosing the time between observations so long that at each observation all appreciable trace of the previous configuration shall have been obliterated, so that the assumption of independence may apply. The point now is this: the time that one has to wait for the probable obliteration of all traces of a previous configuration becomes longer the rarer the previous configuration; obviously it takes longer for a gas to efface all trace of having been all concentrated in one-half of its available volume than to efface the traces of a small local concentration. The situation is, therefore, that not only must we make an increasingly large number of observations in order to hope to witness a rare configuration, but the interval between our observations must also get longer. It is merely the first factor which is usually considered; when both factors are considered it is not at all obvious that the process is even convergent. This point should be subjected to further examination.

There is another difficulty connected with the mere calculation of the probability of rare occurrences presented by quantum theory. All classical calculations assume that the molecules have identity. But the uncertainty principle sets a limit to the physical meaning of identity. It is not possible to observe the position and velocity of any molecule with unlimited precision, but there is a mutual restriction. After an observation has been made, the domain of uncertainty in which the molecule is located expands as time goes on. If the domains of uncertainty of two molecules overlap, then the identity of the molecules is lost, and a subsequent observation will not be competent to decide which molecule is which. The only way of maintaining the identity of the molecules is by making observations at intervals so frequent that the domains of uncertainty have not had time to overlap. But this time is obviously much shorter than the time between observations demanded by the requirement that all trace of the previous configuration shall have been wiped out. Furthermore, the act of observation, by which the concept of identity acquires meaning, alters in an uncontrollable and unpredictable manner the motion of the molecules, whereas the statistical treatment requires that the molecules be undisturbed between successive observations. It seems, therefore, that the physical properties of actual molecules as suggested by quantum theory are different from those of the molecules of the model, and this would seem to demand at least designing new methods of calculating the chances of rare occurrences.

Apart from these objections, which may be met by the discovery of new theoretical methods of attack, it seems to me that the most serious difficulty with this question of rare states is met in the process of transferring to any actual physical system conclusions based on a study of the corresponding model. Suppose, for example, that we are discussing the problem of the tossing of some particular coin. If the coin is a fair coin, that is, if the chances of heads and tails are even, then our statistical model consists merely of a sequence of one or the other of two events, each of which is as likely to occur at any time as the other, absolutely independently of what may have happened elsewhere in the sequence. The theoretical discussion of this model is very easy, and we are convinced that conclusions drawn from a discussion of the model will apply to the tossing of the coin, always provided that the coin is a fair coin. As a particular problem we may consider the chance of throwing heads ten consecutive times. The chance of this is $(1/2)^{10}$, or $1/1024$, which means that in every 1,000 consecutive throws the chances will be roughly even that there will be somewhere a sequence of 10 heads.* But 1,000 throws are a good many, and it may be that we have never made so many throws, and are content merely to make the prediction that if some one else should make so many throws it would be found to be as we say. But suppose that some one questions the fairness of the coin, and says that he has reason to think that there is a bias of 10% in favor of throwing tails, so that the chance of a head at a single throw is only 0.45 instead of 0.50. We find now on making the calculation that we shall have to make roughly 10,000 throws in order to have an even chance of getting a sequence of 10 heads; and, in general, that slight imperfections in the fairness of the coin make very large differences in the chance of rare occurrences. In view of this, we feel that it behooves us to make some objective test of the fairness of the coin before we venture to publish our prediction that we are

---

* I am much indebted to Mr. H. M. James for a rigorous solution of the interesting problem involved here. He finds that between 1422 and 1423 throws are necessary for a 0.5 chance of ten or more consecutive heads.

likely to get a sequence of 10 heads in 1,000 throws. We make the most direct test possible by appealing to the fundamental definition of fairness, which is that in a large number of throws the ratio of the number of heads to tails tends to equality. But how many throws are necessary to establish such an equality with satisfactory assurance! There is another theorem here, namely that in n throws the chances are even that we shall have an excess either of heads over tails or of tails over heads of 0.6745 $n^{1/2}$. Neglecting the numerical factor for our rough purposes, this means that if we make a hundred throws the chances are nearly even that the number of heads is somewhere between 46 and 54. To establish the fairness of the coin we would have to make a considerable number of 100 throws at a time and observe whether or not the number of heads clusters between 46 and 54. If, on the other hand, there is a 10% bias in favor of tails, the number of heads will cluster between 40 and 50. The precise number of sequences of 100 throws at a time necessary to convince us that there is no 10% bias in favor of tails obeys no definite criterion, but it is certainly of the order of ten or more, which makes 1,000 or more throws altogether. But this was the number of throws necessary to obtain one of the rare sequences of 10 heads.

The conclusion from all this is plain; in order to establish with sufficient probability that the actual physical system has those properties which are assumed in estimating the frequency of rare occurrences it is necessary to make a number of observations so great that the probability is good that the rare occurrence has already been observed. In other words, purely logical statistical considerations never can justify us in predicting events so rare that they have never yet been observed. A pail of water has never been observed to freeze on the fire; statistical considerations give us no warrant whatever for expecting that it ever will. Such predictions can be made only on the basis of considerations other than statistical. Thus in the case of the coin, an exact measurement of its dimensions and of the degree of homogeneity of its metal might convince us that the chances of heads and tails were even, because of our knowledge of the laws of mechanics. But when we come to the molecules of a gas or the elements of other physical systems to which the statistical method of treatment is usually applied, we see that there is no method of independently handling the elements, so that the statistical method of testing the validity of our assumptions is the only possible one. This is a most natural situation, because if we were capable of dealing with the elements of the physical system as individuals we could apply more powerful methods than the statistical. Incidentally we may remark how very insensitive the statistical method is in studying elemental properties; this is shown by the example of the coin above, where we had to make something of the order of 1,000 throws to establish an asymmetry of 10%. In many cases, however, the statistical method is doubtless the ultimate and the only method.

Another of the applications of statistical ideas in which there has always been much interest, and especially lately, is to the problem of the ultimate fate of the universe. It is a very common opinion that the second law, in its original classical form, demands the ultimate *heat death* of the universe, because of the inexorable increase of entropy to a final maximum, when all temperature differences shall have been wiped out. The chief mechanism in the ultimate equalization of temperature is obviously the radiation that is continually emitted by the stars. The human mind has, however, shown itself curiously unwilling to accept the prospect of a heat death, and there have been a number of attempts to avoid such an unwelcome conclusion. At least two of these, somewhat similar to each other, are based on the statistical interpretation of the second law. The first of these utilizes the theorem that in a closed mechanical system any configuration, once experienced, is bound to recur after the lapse of sufficient time. According to this view, the universe endlessly goes through cycles of repetition, the so-called Poincaré-Zermelo cycle, of prodigious but calculable duration. The obvious objection to this picture is that in order to realize a Poincaré-Zermelo cycle the laws of classical mechanics would have to be satisfied with an exactness quite fantastic, hopelessly beyond the possibility of direct or indirect verification. The second attempt to make statistics avoid the heat death rests on the theorem that a statistical assembly is never in complete equilibrium, but is always subject to fluctuations, and these fluctuations may attain any intensity if we only wait long enough. The present state of the universe is then to be regarded only as a fluctuation, with the possibility that similar fluctuations may recur in the future. The difficulty with this point of view is the excessive rareness of the sort of fluctuation corresponding to the present state of the universe compared with the approximate dead level of the *heat death*. The previous considerations apply; this is one of those configurations so rare that one has no right to predict its occurrence unless it has been previously observed. One might predict from purely statistical considerations the occurrence of such a fluctuation in the future if one were sure that one were observing such a fluctuation now. But where is the evidence for this? According to the astronomers the fluctuation has been taking the last 10^{16}, or perhaps now 10^{10}, years or so to smooth itself out to its still considerable roughness, and there is certainly no evidence that before 10^{16} years ago the entropy was decreasing instead of increasing.

There are other objections to an application of the second law to the entire universe. The original formulation of the second law was, of course, restricted to isolated systems. By what logical right can the argument be extended to the entire universe? A natural reply is that relativity theory seems to demand that the universe is finite, so that the whole universe becomes the sort of isolated system demanded by the classical formulation. But I believe that examination will nevertheless show a very important difference between the smaller and the all-embracing closed system. Statistical mechanics, if it is to avoid the difficulties already discussed when applied to any individual physical situation, must make the assumption of molecular chaos. But what in the physical situation gives rise to molecular chaos? If we imagine a gas, for example, in a perfectly reflecting enclosure, and suppose that the molecules are perfectly elastic spheres, then, according to the classical picture, every collision takes place under perfectly definite conditions, so that a mathematician of sufficient power could compute backward from the present configuration to the configuration at any past time, as, for example, when a partition might have been removed from the middle of the compartment. This sort of condition certainly cannot be described as molecular chaos. But the walls are molecular in structure, so that the reflection of the individual gas molecules follows no definite rule. If we regard the molecules in the wall as part of the external universe, and if there is no coordination between the motion of the molecules of the wall and what is taking place in the gas because of the enormous magnitude of the external universe compared with the gas inside, then a physical reason justifying the assumption of molecular chaos is at once apparent. When the entire universe is considered there can be no such justification as this for assuming molecular chaos, but the whole course of events must, from the classical point of view, run a rigorously deterministic course, to which statistical considerations do not apply. It may be objected to this argument that a gas in contact with its walls in the way described above is not an isolated system. It is, of course, not completely isolated, but it is nevertheless as far as the thermodynamic requirements go, which are concerned only with transfers of energy and of heat from the outside. Complete isolation would seem to be incompatible with molecular chaos.

It was intimated at the beginning of this discussion that the *heat death* is supposed to be a consequence of the second law, and that the continuous enormous radiation into empty space of the stars is the most striking manifestation of this tendency. This point of view sees in the emission of every photon by a star part of the inexorable increase of entropy. I believe, however, that this is fallacious, that the relations are different, and that the heat death with which we are confronted as a consequence of continued radiation is an affair of the first law, not of the second, and will take place when all the energy of the universe has been radiated away, not merely when the energy is uniformly distributed. Elementary considerations justify this contention. Consider a body radiating into empty space. It is continually dropping in temperature and losing in energy. The emission of radiation therefore decreases the entropy of the radiating body. Consider next a body in thermal equilibrium with its surroundings; since it is in equilibrium its entropy is constant, and furthermore it absorbs as much radiation as it emits. Absorption of radiation, therefore, increases the entropy of the absorbing body. This is sufficient to give a straightforward account of entropy changes in radiation problems. Consider two bodies confronting each other in a cavity at constant temperature. A photon leaves one of the bodies, decreasing the entropy of that body. During the passage of the photon across the space separating the two bodies the entropy is to be thought of as associated with the photon and residing somewhere in the intermediate space. When the second body absorbs the radiation, the photon with its entropy disappears from the empty space and increases the entropy of the absorbing body. At all stages of the process the entropy of the entire system is unchanged. But now suppose that one body radiates to another at lower temperature. This process is irreversible and is accompanied by an increase of entropy. The first two steps of the process, emission of the photon and passage across the intermediate space, are the same as before, and are therefore accompanied by no net change of entropy. It is only the last stage of the process, absorption by the body at lower temperature, that can give the uncompensated increase of entropy. The mechanism of this increase is to be found in a diffusion of the energy of the photon into the greater number of degrees of freedom corresponding to the lower temperature. Actually, this argument is over-simplified and must be modified by a consideration of the distribution of the photons through the spectrum, but the details of this point of view need not concern us further. The immediate point for us is that emission of radiation into empty space is not an entropy-changing process; the increase of entropy can occur, if it occurs at all, only during the act of absorption.

But what physical evidence have we of the absorption of the light radiated by the stars? To save the situation we must postulate absorption under completely unknown conditions. But is the assumption of such unknown conditions in regions so terribly far beyond access to us in order to save the second law any easier as an intellectual feat than the assumption of other unknown conditions which would defeat the second law? Are we not completely in the dark here, and had we not better admit it?

Finally, I briefly summarize what I believe to be the principal results of this analysis and indicate the possible lines of future progress. The most important result will be, I hope, a keen realization that in using statistics we are only using a paper and pencil model, which has logical difficulties within itself and difficulties of application to concrete physical situations which are very much greater than the corresponding difficulties with more ordinary sorts of model. Some of these difficulties I believe can never be surmounted, so that the statistical model can never be satisfactorily used by extrapolation either into remote epochs of time, to predict rare events, or into remote reaches of space, to give us an idea of the course of universal evolution. Our model has not given us a satisfactory answer to our initial question as to the possibility of commercially profitable violations of the second law. The answer to this question will probably be found when the wave mechanics point of view has been completely worked out. Some of the other logical difficulties of the classical statistics, I believe, will also be surmounted by the adoption of the wave mechanics point of view, which assumes probability to be a primitive property of the elements of the model, rather than an emergent property resulting from the cooperation of great numbers. Before, however, the wave mechanics thesis of the primitive character of the notion of probability can be accepted, much more experimental work is necessary. If the thesis is supported, as seems probable from the evidence now at hand, this will constitute to a certain extent a defeat of the purpose of the classical statistics, which was to *explain* why many physical assemblages of large numbers of elements obey the rules of probability. But even granted that the primitive character of the notions of probability acquires an experimental verification, it seems to me that some of the logical difficulties will persist, justifying a doubt as to the possibility of ever setting up a logically completely satisfying correspondence between our models and our experience.

14

THE TIME SCALE*

The Concept of Time

THE CONCEPT OF TIME which I shall talk about is not the profound and sometimes poetic concept of the philosopher, but the prosaic concept of the physicist. I hope it will not be presuming too much to assume that this is also the concept of the astronomer, for I suppose that most of us will agree that the astronomer is a sort of physicist—whether a super- or a sub-physicist I shall not attempt to discuss.

As you all know the physicist has discovered recently that he must demand as essential in all concepts which can be useful to him a certain fundamental quality which I have ventured to call "operational". That is, the meaning of any concept is to be sought in the operations, whether physical or mental, which are performed in making application of the concept. This point of view received its first and perhaps most important application by Einstein in his analysis of the concept of simulta-

*From The Scientific Monthly, August, 1932. Paper given at a symposium at the Harvard Observatory on the occasion of the dedication of the Astrophotographic Building, March 23, 1932.

neity, and has by now become fundamental in wave mechanics as expounded by Bohr, Heisenberg, and Dirac.

Applying the operational criterion to time, the meaning of the concept of time, as it is employed by physicists and astronomers, is to be sought in the operations by which the time at which events occur is determined. The methods which we adopt for assigning a time to events change when the character of the events changes, so that time may appear in various guises. The simplest events to deal with are those taking place here and now. The time which we assign to such events may be called, following the theory of relativity, the "local time". One aspect of such local time is of such irreducible simplicity that no way has yet been found which does not treat it as unanalyzable; this of course is not a reproach because unanalyzables must always terminate any logical analysis. The aspect to which I refer is that of simultaneity—we assume that we can tell intuitively when two events in our immediate vicinity occur simultaneously. The concept of the simultaneity of two events occurring at a distance from each other is much more complicated, and it was Einstein's analysis of this which was mainly responsible for the special theory of relativity. But the simultaneity concept is not enough even for local time; in addition we must have some method of measuring local time, that is, some method of assigning numbers as the time of local events. An instrument by which such numbers are assigned is called a clock, but if any one should ask me for directions for constructing a clock or for specifications by which he could determine whether an instrument which purported to be a clock was actually one or not, I could not give him a satisfactory answer. In fact, here at the very root of one of our most fundamental concepts is a surprising deficiency—no satisfactory definition has yet been given of a clock. The best that we can do is to point to actual mechanical systems which we choose to call clocks, and you are of course proudly conscious that the clocks *par excellence* are afforded by the bodies of astronomy.

Distant events, of which knowledge can be obtained only by light signals, must have time assigned to them by more complicated operations than those which suffice for the local system, and this means that in our thought the time of distant events must be distinguished from the time of local events; we may distinguish by calling the time of distant events "extended" time in contrast to the "local" time of near-by events. The astronomer is obviously dealing almost entirely with extended time. It is nevertheless true, I believe, that nearly all astronomers think of the extended time of distant events in terms of the connotations of the local time of their own personal experience. For example, it is quite usual for an astronomer to speak of the "age" of a light beam, and he sometimes seems to get a particular sort of kick from the realization that the light which he receives to-day from the most distant nebula may be of the order of 100 million years old. On reflection it is obvious enough that the "old" as applied to a light beam has entirely different connotations from the "old" which may describe a hat or even a fossil at the bottom of the Grand Canyon. We have in the first place the dictum of relativity that the beam of light itself does not grow old or that if you or I could accompany the light beam on its travels we also would not notice the passage of time, but would live throught the entire 100 million years with no change in any of our bodily functions, and without the need of even a single meal. What we mean when we say that the light beam is one hundred million years old is that it left the nebula one hundred million years ago, and what we mean by this again requires the most careful analysis. To give this meaning we must assign a distance to the nebula, and obtain the time by dividing the distance by the velocity of light. But to get the distance is not at all straightforward, and involves all sorts of assumptions and approximate reasonings by analogy, which leave an enormous possibility for error in the final result. It is popularly supposed that astronomy is a science of fabulous accuracy, but the accuracy is all of a special kind, namely, accuracy of angular position, whereas most distances are not at all well known, for even the most accurate may be uncertain by something of the order of one part in 10,-000. It is evident, therefore, that the connotations in saying that a beam of light left a nebula one hundred million years ago are so different from the connotations involved in the time back to remote events on this earth as to make it an almost different concept.

It is also not unheard of to allow oneself to wonder what may be happening on some distant star "now". To give meaning to this question there must be some way of answering it. Even in thought the only way for me to find what is happening "now" in the distant nebula is to send a wireless message to my confederate in the nebula, who will receive it after a hundred million years, and then must consult what may be his equivalent for the library of the British Museum, where he will almost certainly find only the sketchiest sort of record of what was happening one hundred million years ago. He will then wireless the message to me, who will receive the reply at the advanced age of two hundred million years, and the reply will probably be nothing more specific than the statement that during the 10,000 years centering around the day on which I made my original inquiry a certain kind of rock was being laid down. The connotation of the "now" in distant places is obviously so different from that of ordinary experience as to make this a different concept.

We have so far assumed that there is no difficulty with the concept of remotely distant time in the local frame of reference. By this I suppose we mean that some method exists by which we can satisfactorily assign dates to local events in the remote past. There is, however, a very important limitation on the meaning that can be assigned to remote time imposed by the Heisenberg uncertainty principle. Position and velocity can not both be measured with unlimited precision, but there is mutual restriction. If I make any sort of a determination of the position of an object. I thereby introduce an uncertainty into its velocity. But if the position of the body in past time is to be found. I must know its velocity, so that any uncertainty in its present velocity involves an uncertainty in its past position. It is obvious, I think, that the further back in time we go, the greater becomes the uncertainty in position. If we go back far enough the position becomes so blurred as to make our original object indistinguishable from others, and the past becomes radically different from the present in that the identity concept disappears. In the same way, the future becomes more and more blurred the further ahead we try to predict, until all details are lost. It is not hard to calculate that after a lapse of something like 10^{100} years the identity of any two originally distinct stars would be entirely confused, so that one must not try to peer as far as this into the future. It is not uncommon, however, to speculate about intervals of time in connection with a possible Poincaré-Zermelo cycle of the whole universe in comparison with which 10^{100} years is the mere drawing of a breath.

Not only does the astronomer deal with long intervals of time in the past in thinking about the time of dispatch of light signals which are now arriving at the earth, but he deals with enormously greater intervals of both past and future time in tracing backward or forward the course of stellar evolution in his search for the origin or ultimate destiny of the stellar universe as we know it. It is here, and in a degree characteristically peculiar to astronomy, that the greatest assumptions have to be made, and it seems to me that there is also the greatest need for perpetual vigilance and the most vivid consciousness of exactly what we are doing. Any reconstruction of the past or extrapolation into the future from observations of present configurations can be made only by assuming certain laws governing the motions. Thus we assume the conservation of linear momentum or the conservation of angular momentum, or the conservation of energy, or, if we seek for special refinement, we assume the generalized equations of relativity. But these laws themselves are generalizations from past experience, and are affected with all the uncertainty pertaining to any result of experience. To the untutored critic it must appear a trifle rash to venture to peer 10^{16} years back into the past or even greater distances into the future on the basis of laws verified by not more than 300 years' observation. The only justification for such hair-raising extrapolations is to be found in the tacit assumption of some system of metaphysics; we are convinced that nature obeys mathematically exact rules, and that we have found some of them. The reason we are convinced that we have found them is that our metaphysics persuades us that nature has a taste for the law of the inverse square or for some other rule which our gray matter finds it comparatively easy to formulate. The metaphysical conviction that we have penetrated the arcana of nature is particularly strong in the adherents of generalized relativity, who are so convinced of the inevitableness of their philosophy that they are persuaded that even the stars in their courses must recognize the cogency of the argument. There has been no more surprising spectacle afforded by science for many a year than that of the two leading British astronomers lying down together like the lion and the lamb, giving up their most cherished and potent arguments of a few moments before, and joyfully accepting a reduction of a million fold in the time scale of the universe on the basis of a metaphysics and three not too certain checks with experiment. Surely there are plenty of unexplained phenomena to disturb so easy a complacency—the cosmic rays, which were discovered only yesterday, are becoming less well understood with every fresh investigation, the *raison d'être* of the heavy stars is at least obscure, the whole theory of stellar structure seems alarmingly chaotic to an ignorant physicist, and to-day on the front page of the papers is the "neutron", which certainly carries the potentiality of a certain amount of reconstruction.

Destructive criticism is always easy, and I am afraid that I am even more blameworthy than the ordinary destructive critic. I have nothing else to suggest, and I am sure that I would have been overcome with pride if I had had the ability to construct any one of the important modern theories. But I hope that I should not have taken what I might have done too seriously; that I would have recognized that I was merely carrying through to their logical conclusion certain consequences of formulations which I had found it convenient to make in getting into touch with the external world, and that I would have recognized, therefore, that I was to a certain extent only playing an absorbing mental game with myself. I hope that I should have been on the everlasting lookout to recognize that all my laws were probably inexact, and that I should have certainly been trying to make new experiments and better observations to get a little closer to things as they are, as I am sure all the astronomers here are doing already.

15

ON THE NATURE AND THE LIMITATIONS OF COSMICAL INQUIRIES*

EARLY COSMOGONIES WERE almost entirely fanciful in character and were often largely of emotional or religious import. Only within the last few hundred years have we been able to produce cosmogonies with truly scientific pretensions. In the last two decades activity has increased markedly, beginning perhaps with the generalized theory of relativity of Einstein, followed by the work of Eddington, Jeans and Milne on the structure of the stars, and more recently by the theory of the expanding universe of Lemaître and the speculations of Tolman on cosmical thermodynamics. As in physics, probably the chief stimulus to recent activity is to be sought in our rapidly expanding experimental knowledge. It is obvious, however, that there are certain permanent limitations on the possible observational material provided by astronomy; we shall never be able to get into the inside of the stars, for example, or to go back a million years in time. Corresponding to

*From The Scientific Monthly, 37, 385, 1933.

these observational characteristics, there must therefore be certain essential differences between the nature of the structure that we can erect on these observations and other observational disciplines, such as physics, where the observational control is much more far reaching and intimate. In the following I shall attempt to give some analysis of the nature of the structure that can be erected on the observational material of astronomy. I shall seek to find the nature of the structure in terms of "operations"; our study will involve an examination of the nature of the observational material, of the methods used in interpreting this material, and of the methods by which we may check the validity of any solutions that we may find.

The observational material is subject to one obvious and essential limitation in that it is almost entirely optical in character. The only exception consists in the examination of actual celestial material which reaches the surface of the earth in the form of meteorites. Knowledge of this sort is at present very scanty, although it is daily becoming more important; it will always, however, be subject to obvious vital limitations due to the small size of any such meteoric material with which we can deal. The optical material consists, in the first place, of observations of the direction of the heavenly bodies; secondly, of the intensity of the total radiation from each individual object; thirdly, of the spectral characteristics of this radiation; and finally, in a few cases, of interference or other phenomena involving differences in the character of the radiation from different parts of the same object.

Measurements of direction are of high precision, down to a small fraction of a second of arc. This is sufficient, by the method of parallax, to give fairly good information about the distances of the nearer objects. No measurement of astronomical distance, however, has an accuracy of much more than 0.1 per cent. Beyond the range of parallax, observation gives merely a projection in two dimensions of position, and distance has to be estimated by indirect methods involving extrapolations of observations made in the parallax zone, where it is possible to test the legitimacy of the method. Perhaps the most important of these methods is the estimate of the distance of the Cepheid variables in terms of an empirical connection between the size and the period established in the zone of parallax. This method is used by very wide extrapolation. Any such extrapolation must be prepared to defend itself against the criticism that there may be systematic changes at great distances in the connection between period and size. Such a defense is impossible until we have more exact knowledge than at present of the mechanism responsible for the variation of the Cepheids, and in any event a defense would always be impossible against the suggestion of the existence of effects at present unknown. We have to make our extrapolation as we do because in our ignorance we are powerless to suggest any plausible way in which the observed connection between size and period might be different.

The astronomer is forced to go even further than this, however. Much observation has developed in him certain "hunches". For instance, if he sees projected on the celestial sphere a large number of stars, far beyond the parallax distance, all grouped within a small disk, such as would be the case if he were observing a globular cluster, he will reverse the argument and say that the observed stars are actually grouped together in space into a globular cluster. Further, if he is fortunate enough to find within the group Cepheid variables, he will fix the distance of the whole group by the extrapolated distance of these variables. If the distances of all the Cepheids turn out to be nearly the same, the assumption of an actual globular cluster is felt to have a high degree of "probability".

By hook or by crook, therefore, the astronomer is able to assign distances to a large part of his observed objects; the confidence which he feels in these distances decreases as the absolute value of the distance increases.

The distribution of light in the spectrum of each star gives information about the mean temperature of the effective radiating surface and the chemical composition of this surface. Inference as to these quantities is made in large part on the basis of laboratory measurements, but also, especially as to the effective temperatures, on the basis of theory by which the effects of temperature and pressure on the dissociation of the elements may be extrapolated to temperatures and pressures beyond experimental reach. The theory involves quantum mechanics and thermodynamics, and we are fairly well satisfied with it, for the extrapolations are not particularly large as such things go. The inferences about the chemical composition are also satisfactory; in fact I think any astronomer or physicist would regard this as perhaps the most satisfactory part of our information. But even here, the assumption has to be made that the laws which we find in our laboratory experiments are not essentially modified under the extremely different stellar conditions, and I suppose it would be impossible to give a thoroughly logical answer to a carping critic who wanted to insist that this is really only an assumption and might not be legitimate. The carping critic will, however, find it impossible to convince a physicist that 5,000 spectrum lines, all in approximately the same position, do not mean the same element, iron, in the star that they do on the earth. The argument again here rests on considerations of probability, which appeal to every one with scientific experience, but which nevertheless involve vague and imperfectly understood ideas which have so far eluded precise formulation.

The optical data sometimes permit estimates of the angular diameter of the star by interference methods, but the estimate of size is usually more indirect, involving the assumption of the universality of various empirical relations which are capable of direct verification in only a few favorable cases. At any rate, whatever the details of the method, the astronomer has estimates of the size of a large number of the stars, of precision much less than the precision of the best distances.

The mass of a star may be determined if we are fortunate enough to be dealing with a star which constitutes one member of a binary, the period and the separation of which may be observed. The mass of a large number of stars has been determined in this way. In calculating the mass from these data the inverse square law of gravitation has to be assumed, with the same constants as observed in the solar system, and again there is no defense against the criticism of possible changes in the law of gravitation at great distances or in remote epochs of time.

Finally, observations of position at different times are accurate enough to give the apparent motions of a number of celestial objects; these combined with distance give the velocity in space perpendicular to the line of sight. Spectroscopic observations of the Doppler effect give the radial components of velocity, assuming that we know how to separate the Doppler effect from other effects giving rise to spectral shifts. Altogether, there is a rather large amount of material permitting us to give motions in space of varying degrees of accuracy.

Besides the characteristics of the data of astronomy already discussed, there is one other very essential characteristic, in that it is all "observational" in the narrower sense. We have to take what we find, without the possibility of studying what happens when we vary the conditions, which constitutes such a powerful method in physics and chemistry. Astronomy is the observational science *par excellence*; geology is much like it but with growing possibilities of experimental control afforded by geophysics, and perhaps we may next place biology, until recently an observational science, but becoming rapidly completely experimental.

Such is the nature of the observational material and the inferences it allows as to distances, sizes, motions, compositions and physical state. Our problem is now to organize this material and bring it into coordination with other branches of knowledge in such a way that we feel that we understand the resulting structure. This we may perhaps define as the problem of cosmogony in the broadest sense. In the working out of the problem we may perhaps recognize two main aspects. There is in the first place the problem of inferring from our observational material what the present complete structure of the universe is; this involves, for example, determining the nature of the inside of a star, and in general inferring the unobservable parts from what we observe. Then in the second place there is the problem of extrapolating our observations backward and forward in time in order that we may get some idea of where our universe came from and what is its future. This latter is by many regarded as the most interesting task of cosmogony. This extrapolation forward and backward should, if the present configuration is completely known, be capable of unique performance, so that we should be able to obtain a unique answer to our questions about past and future. But in view of the extreme incompleteness of our understanding of the present configuration, this ideal is very far from attainment. In fact, instead of making a straightforward extrapolation from the present configuration, the process is often reversed and inferential information about the present configuration obtained on the basis of what would be involved in the way of extrapolation. There are, in the first place, the data of geology controlling any extrapolation; it is obvious that our backward extrapolations must provide a long enough past for the demands of the geologist and any limitations which requirements of this nature impose may be accepted as perfectly legitimate. We may be grudging in our acceptance of this control, however, because we recognize that we ought to be able to reproduce the past of geology without aid from this adventitious course. Aside from this perfectly legitimate demand which we make on our extrapolation, we make other demands which we would find it harder to justify on any scientific ground. For example, we probably shall eventually reject any reconstruction of the past as highly "improbable" which represents all the matter of the universe as having originally constituted a single giant atom, in spite of Lemaître, and I am perfectly sure that any extrapolation into the future which predicted the destruction of the entire cosmos within 1,000 years would be at once rejected, although perhaps unconsciously, as being derogatory to human dignity.

In general the problem of cosmogony is so difficult that no sort of control or argument appears to be neglected that can have any bearing on the problem, even if the argument is as purely emotional as that just suggested.

We are now ready to consider the details of the attack on the problem of cosmogony, and it is natural to first set ourselves the problem of understanding how the individual units, the stars, are constructed. What we are given is the surface temperature, chemical composition, total size and total mass, and we are required to reconstruct the state of affairs at every interior point. At any interior point we must know the temperature, composition and pressure, and we must know how these quantities vary from point to point. The point to point variation is controlled by the differential equations of mechanics and thermodynamics, into which enter the parameters which determine the pertinent physical properties of the stellar matter, such as emissivity, absorption, etc. We assume that our knowledge of the nature of the material is sufficient to determine these parameters when temperature, composition and pressure are given, but it is only recently that enough data have been accumulated in the physical laboratory to give us the slightest confidence in our assumptions about these quantities. The problem in general features is not unlike other problems to which physics can give an exact solution, such, for example, as the problem of elasticity. In elasticity theory we are given a body of known physical properties subject to a given set of forces acting over its external surface, and perhaps other forces like those of gravitation acting on the material inside, and we are required to find the stress and strain at every interior point. It is possible to give a mathematical proof that a unique solution exists. Our physical intuition leads us to expect similarly a unique solution for a star, but it is still far from evident what the exact mathematical conditions are which would lead to such a unique solution. In fact the general problem of finding the appropriate mathematical method by which to attack this problem would seem not yet to be definitely settled. Certain plausible mathematical formulations have been rejected simply on the basis that in the solution they lead to infinities at the center. Now an infinity in a solution is no reason for rejecting an equation which leads to it. The validity of the equation is a matter which permits of direct test, and if under some conditions infinite solutions are demanded, the conclusion is that the physical assumptions which were at the basis of the equations have ceased to be valid, and must be replaced by others, the original equation still retaining its validity over the range within which it was established. The procedure by which the straightforward solution of the equation which naturally presents itself has been replaced is a complicated one of trial and error, starting with assumed conditions at the center and working out until we find conditions at the exterior as nearly as possible like those observed. Success has not been impressive and it is not certain that a single type of equation is adequate for the solution.

The mathematical difficulties in the way of the construction of a model of a star are therefore severe enough; the physical difficulties are not less formidable. The mathematical solutions, which have been obtained thus far, agree in assigning to the interior of the star perfectly scandalous temperatures and pressures—temperatures of the order of tens of millions of degrees, and pressures of the order of tens of millions of atmospheres. Such conditions are so tremendously beyond the range of anything that can be obtained in the laboratory that any extrapolation of properties observed in the laboratory must be viewed with extreme suspicion, even when this extrapolation is made with the help of the best theories that we have at present. Entirely unknown sorts of behavior of matter under these extreme conditions are to be expected. The recently discovered dense stars show definitely enough the possibility of matter existing in hitherto unknown dense forms, and it is not yet agreed whether we are to expect a core of such dense matter at the center of each star or not. The recent discoveries of the neutron and positive electron also tremendously affect the possibilities and there is the possibility of elements of very high atomic weights, not hitherto known.

Ignoring these difficulties, however, models of a sort have been constructed which have been successful in reproducing some of the outstanding observational regularities of the stars, such as the relation discovered by Eddington between mass and total brightness.

In spite of all the vagueness of our present formulations and our ignorance of the physical conditions inside the star, which we might be inclined to think would leave open sufficient possibilities to permit an eventual exact solution, every stellar model at once encounters one difficulty which peremptorily forces us to abandon our original program of completely reconstructing the star in terms of data of the laboratory. The difficulty, of course, is concerned with the radiation. The rate at which a star is losing energy by radiation is capable of measurement. (This involves the assumption that the radiation in every direction is the same as in the direction of the earth. Attempts have been made to postulate that radiation takes place only in the direction of bodies in position to receive the radiation, but this possible way out has encountered insuperable difficulties, such as that of accounting for the radiational equilibrium of the earth.) The total amount of energy radiated in geological time can therefore be calculated, and this turns out to be much greater than accounted for by any known source of radiational energy. It is not necessary here to assume a complete law of conservation of energy —the energy concept encounters logical and formal difficulties when we attempt to apply it to systems in which only uni-directional processes are taking place. All that is necessary is the observational fact that there is no known source of radiation which does not involve the exhaustion of its source; energy is radiated only at the expense of some sort of permanent change in its source. It is perhaps worth mentioning in passing that the times involved are so long that the direct observation of the cooling or other exhaustion of any celestial body in consequence of its radiation is hopelessly beyond us. Granting, however, that radiation means exhaustion celestially as well as terrestrially, an exploration of all known sources of energy discloses that they are inadequate. It seems unavoidable therefore to assume some unknown source. It happens that our present experience contains the suggestion of one possibility which, although not actually realized, does not demand a very revolting extrapolation of laboratory conditions. This is the transformation of matter into energy, first suggested by Einstein's relativity theory, in which it appeared that radiation of energy was accompanied by loss of mass of amount $m = E/c^2$. This equivalence of mass and energy has been established with high probability for the radioactive transformations. The largest effect of this kind to be expected cosmically is the change of mass accompanying the transformation of four hydrogens into one helium. This transformation perhaps provides an adequate source of energy, but the margin of safety is not large, and a number of cosmologists do not feel that this is the solution. They prefer to go further and find the source of energy in the complete annihilation of matter when electron combines with proton. This very probably provides an adequate source. But on the other hand, the process has never been observed and is purely inferential; the great argument is that it fits neatly into our mathematical formulation of relativity theory.

In any event the important feature for us is that we have unequivocally encountered a situation which shows that our original program is not capable of execution, but we must assume processes not directly given to us by laboratory experience. Having thus once let down the bars, a flood of possibilities descends upon us, and the question is, where are we going to stop? There are many other places where it would be plausible to look for unknown processes. What is the basis for assuming that the conservation of energy is sacrosanct? Why may we not simply postulate that energy is created in a star? Inside a star radiation is continually being emitted traveling a short distance and then being reabsorbed. Suppose that conservation fails by a small percentage amount at each process. One can get some idea of the relative number of total emission processes going on in the star compared with the number which are concerned in the net radiated energy by considering that in the sun the ordinary thermal content would supply the radiational energy for 15,000,000 years, and that a beam of light travels the solar radius in something of the order of 2 seconds. If conservation at each elementary quantum act of emission and reabsorption fails by an amount fantastically beyond the possibility of direct experimental verification, the total net radiation is adequately accounted for. Or again, how accurately is the inverse square law of gravitation checked by any direct observation under conditions approximating those in the interior of a star? What basis have we for thinking that gravitational screening may not be a property of matter with density 50,000 times that of water, when claims have been made that the effect has been detected under terrestrial conditions? What is the basis for thinking that the ordinary laws of electrodynamics retain their simple linear form when electron and proton are as close together as they must be or when we have as intense radiational fields as in the stars? Physicists are already openly discussing the necessity of modifying the accepted quantum laws for the nucleus. Why may not matter even be created inside the stars? The universe had to come from somewhere.

When one considers the criteria by which he attempts to judge the seriousness of these various possibilities I believe that it must be conceded that the whole matter is rather vague. Probably the broadest characterization of the criterion which we more or less unconsciously apply is that of simplicity, the same criterion which we use in other speculative work when the problem is undetermined. But simplicity has no absolute meaning; what may be simple from the point of view of a mathematical equation may be more complicated when the procedure is formulated in words or translated into physical operations. An example is the procedure for measuring the length of a moving object in relativity theory; the actual definition corresponds to simple equations, but is much more complicated when expressed in words than the naïve and rejected procedure of measuring the moving object by the application of meter sticks moving with the same velocity. By what right does the mathematical formulation acquire precedence? In this example the situation is completely determined and a decision may be made, but no such decision is possible in cosmogony.

In describing ordinary physical experience rough criteria of simplicity have stood the check of workability because it has been found possible to reproduce our physical experience in simple terms. Without such an experimental proof of the possibility of simplicity it would seem that there can be no logical reason for expecting simplicity in preference to complication. Now in the cosmic case the check against experience, in order to choose between rival theories, is not possible, each theory being constructed so as to be equally capable of dealing with the facts, and the criterion of simplicity loses objective probability. But other physical experience would suggest that in this realm of totally unknown conditions, pressures of 10^7 atmospheres and densities of 50,000, nature would be expected to become more complicated, and simplicity would be expected to fail. We might argue, therefore, that the more complicated of two rival theories would have the greater chance of being correct. But in the absence of specific indications of the direction which the complication should take, we must show no preference for one complicating hypothesis as distinguished from another, so that an attitude of perfect neutrality demands that we reject every complicating hypothesis that we can and thus revert to simplicity. In this domain, therefore, our expectation of simplicity in the physical phenomena fails us, whereas simplicity in our theories remains because it expresses most perfectly our complete ignorance.

It may happen that different models are equally capable of reproducing the present observational properties of the stars, but when extrapolated in time different pasts or futures may be demanded. Granted that the single condition is satisfied that a star like the sun has a tolerably constant past as far back as geological time, what further criterion in addition to those already discussed shall be applied in making our selection? One criterion of intrinsic probability is very definitely applied in practise, namely if any solution shows scattered throughout the universe stars in different stages of evolution, satisfaction is felt. Thus if my solution for a present red giant indicates a condition at some future time such as I now find in some white star, I am pleased, and feel that my solution has a better chance of being correct. That is, it seems probable to me that the stellar universe as at present observed contains stars in different stages of evolution. This involves the thesis that the stars did not all come into being at the same time, but successively. Why does this seem more plausible than the assumption that they all started together? I think examination will show that there is nothing very rigorous here, and that the argument is to some extent a "hunch" argument, resting partly on the feeling that in the nebulae we are observing localities in which stars are actually being born at the present time.

The problem of the structure of a star is the problem of the atom of astronomy. Besides this there is the problem of the aggregate of the stars, just as we have a kinetic theory of gases in addition to the problem of atomic structure. In kinetic theory the precise structure of the atom makes little difference as long as the atom has certain very general properties of elasticity, etc. In the cosmic case there is a closer connection between the problem of the structure of the unit and of the ensemble, for the life of the ensemble extrapolated backward must not be shorter than the life of the individual units. There is obviously no such corresponding condition in kinetic theory. For the present, however, we neglect this aspect of the problem, and confine our attention to the problem of finding the positions of the stars in past and future time, treating the stars as unalterable units.

The first impression on approaching this problem is, of course, one of overwhelming complexity;

mathematics has not been able to completely solve the problem of even three bodies moving under their mutual gravitation. Some sort of simplification is obviously necessary and we must be satisfied with only a rough answer to our problem. The first question is: what data are necessary in order to ensure a determinate answer? If the problem were one of ordinary mechanics, in which the mutual forces between the stars were known as soon as their mutual distances were known, it would be sufficient to give the present positions and velocities of all the stars. This we may hope to approximate observationally, although the velocities are determinable only very roughly. But the stellar problem is not a problem of ordinary mechanics, because the distances of separation of the stars are so great that the time of propagation of gravitation is important. The analogue of this problem is the retarded potential problem of electrodynamics. Here the solution is not determinate unless the initial positions and velocities of all the particles are given, and in addition the initial values of the electric and magnetic fields at every point of space. The analogue for the cosmic problem of this last requirement is a knowledge of the present gravitational field at every point of space. But the gravitational field throughout space is not observable, so that in principle the problem of extrapolating backward or forward in time is indeterminate, and the most that we can hope for, even with infinite mathematical skill, would be an approximate solution in which there is an indetermination which would be expected to grow in importance as the interval of time becomes longer. I do not know whether a quantitative discussion has been made of the importance of this neglected factor or not.

There are other mathematical difficulties in the case of even so comparatively simple a system as the solar system. Brown is authority for the statement that we can not be sure of gravitational stability for more than 10^8 years. This is much less than geological time, so that apparently the mathematical extrapolation runs into difficulties in times that are shorter than we know are necessary. One can never hope, therefore, to get a rigorous solution back to the time required. Another difficulty has been pointed out by Brown, who thinks that the equations of gravitational motion of so complicated a system may have such a high number of singularities that it is observationally impossible to supply the number of positions and velocities necessary to determine a solution.

There is another difficulty of a fundamental sort. The Heisenberg principle of indetermination does not permit of the simultaneous observations of position and velocity which are necessary for extrapolation, but there is a necessary reciprocal error in the observation of these two quantities, which means an error growing with time in any possible extrapolation. Over longer and longer intervals of time the details become more blurred, until the actual identity of the objects that we are talking about is lost, and we could not tell, for example, whether a star which we extrapolated to be in a certain position in 10^{50} years was Capella or Vega. Prediction does no good if we have no way of telling what object it is that we are talking about, so that we may say that it is meaningless to attempt to extrapolate time so far forward or backward. Or in other words, the concept of time itself fails if the extrapolation is too extensive. This of course all assumes the validity of the Heisenberg principle when applied to the motion of the stars. It is perhaps needless to say that there is not a scrap of experimental evidence for this, so that our application of the principle is nothing but an enormous extrapolation of a mathematically simple law, made in the same spirit as our assumption of a mathematically exact inverse square law or exact conservation of energy for individual quantum processes.

In spite of all these unavoidable vaguenesses in the extrapolations of positional astronomy, there are certain facts of observation which can not hide behind the possibilities left open in this way, but they indicate the need of some drastic rearrangements in our ordinary explanations, just as the radiational difficulty with the single star demanded the discovery of some new source of energy. The most striking of such phenomena is perhaps the shift in the relative angular position of the stars when their light passes close to the edge of the sun. The only solution proposed which has been at all well received is that of Einstein in his generalized theory of relativity. This has demanded a radical reconstruction of the four dimensional union of space and time with which special relativity theory was satisfied, and involves the idea of a curvature of space-time in the gravitational field. There is confirmatory evidence of this solution in the shift in the perihelion of Mercury and the displacement toward the red of lines radiated in an intense gravitational field, but these checks are not so striking as the other. In any event the entire scheme of explanation suffers from the logical difficulty that it is impossible to prove a curvature of space-time, which requires an infinite number of parameters for adequate specification, in terms of only three observational quantities. The fundamental assumption that space-time is curved can not be directly tested; for one thing, the space of astronomy is only optical, and the equivalence of optical and tactual space can never be adequately checked. The uniqueness of Einstein's solution can never be established; the argument for it, as in many other cases, can only be the argument from simplicity in the mathematical formulation.

The differential equations of general relativity theory are not sufficient to completely solve the problem of the entire cosmos, but integration constants appear for which we can offer no physical explanation, but which have to be accepted merely as brute facts. It is well known that entirely different behaviors are indicated in the stellar system at great distances accordingly as a positive or negative value is assumed for one of these constants, and that the observational material is not adequate to allow a choice. The expanding universe of Lemaître results from a particular choice of a constant of integration at a particular stage of the solution. It has been interesting in the last few years to follow the way in which opinions about the probable values of the constants have followed our increasing observational knowledge. We now have the experimental fact that the radiation emitted from the most distant objects is shifted toward the red by amounts indicating enormous velocities of recession if the ordinary Doppler explanation of the shift is accepted. But this property of radiation from distant objects can also be explained in terms of a proper space-time curvature, with the proper constant of integration. On what basis shall we choose one explanation in preference to the other? The preference at one time seemed to be in favor of a curvature, but at present it seems to be for a recession. The reversal of preference has been brought about by the discovery by Lemaître of a method of getting an expanding universe into a comparatively simple mathematical scheme. I believe that if a mathematician or astronomer were made to defend his present preference he could not do better than to urge that it seems *more probable* that the physical state of affairs should correspond to a mathematically simple scheme than to something more complex.

The same argument from feelings of probability

occurs in many other places in astronomy. It is justifiable when one is engaged in statistical studies, comparing one collection of objects from one part of the sky with another from another. But in strict logic probability considerations apply only to large numbers or when it is possible to repeat the experimental conditions a great many times. The idea of probability never applies to individual physical situations; probability considerations can not apply to a single throw of dice, for example. The stellar universe is all there is, and it makes its history only once. Probability considerations do not properly apply to it at all. It would be most difficult to analyze just what is involved logically in the frequent application of this sort of an argument to the cosmos. I suspect that at bottom the argument would be found to revert to the old argument from simplicity, and to those hazy arguments, popularly phrased in the language of probability theory but logically quite different, by which we determine our course of conduct when we are confronted with situations about which we are largely ignorant.

We have thus been driven in our positional astronomy to postulate new effects, not directly verifiable by observation. But are there not other unobserved and new effects which we would expect on general grounds? Must we not assume that there are places where electrons and protons come into being? What about radiation? Does it come back? Does it recombine to give proton and electron? What is the significance of the cosmic rays? May not all our physical laws be undergoing a course of evolution, with slowly changing values of all constants?

The difficulties which we have thus far discussed are to a greater or less extent concerned with the details of working out various specific aspects of our problem, but there are more fundamental difficulties, already hinted at. One may well question whether the very concepts in terms of which we do our thinking are adequate to the situation. We have already met an example that suggests the sort of failure that we may find in our concepts. The energy concept of thermodynamics is rigorously defined in terms of processes which involve bringing the system back to its initial configuration; this is obviously impossible when the system is the entire cosmos, so that in the strict sense of thermodynamics one can not talk about a conservation of the "energy" of the universe. In this particular case we have seen that the formal failure of the energy concept is not of much importance, because for our purposes we can get along with only a partial aspect of the energy concept, and it is possible to find an ideal meaning for this partial concept in its application to the entire universe. But it is not so evident that we would be similarly successful in side-stepping the difficulties of other concepts. Practically every one of our physical concepts demands the performance of an experiment, which in the first place can be indefinitely repeated in time, and which in the second place involves dividing the universe into two parts, one isolated from the rest, on which experiments are made by an external agency, whose actions are supposed arbitrary and unaffected by what occurs inside the isolated region. This procedure evidently breaks down when the subject is the entire universe. How, for example, shall we define the mass of the entire universe to the satisfaction of a critic who insists that the mass of the whole is not the sum of the masses of the parts, a fact which we ourselves very well recognize even in small parts of the universe when we make our measurements accurate enough.

There are particular difficulties with the concept of time in addition to the possible difficulties connected with the Heisenberg principle, already mentioned. The crude difficulties of the naïve time concept have been long felt. Such a difficulty has already appeared in a loose phrase purposely introduced earlier in this paper when it was asked "May not matter even be created inside the stars? The universe had to come from somewhere". We are here face to face with the age-old dilemma; we demand an antecedent for everything of our experience and again an antecedent for the antecedent and so on in never ending regression, and on the other hand we demand equally insistently something in the beginning to start things off. The only answer is the brutal and unsatisfactory one that the urge of our minds to act in this way must be resisted because it does not work; the origin of the urge is in limited experience, and we must recognize that such experience may land us in inconsistencies when pushed too far. The only precise way of dealing with the concept of time is the operational one to which all modern physics seems to be driving us, and which I have expounded in other places. What do I mean from this point of view by the future? In the strictest sense what I at the present, as I sit in this chair, mean by the future is nothing but the complex expectations which I can formulate to myself at the present, at which I arrive on the basis of all the regularities in nature which my past experience has disclosed to me. The operational meaning of the future, for me in the present, is the complex of those operations by which I deduce my expectations. But this severe meaning of the future will, I believe, be found to not quite correspond to what most people want it to mean. We can go part way toward meeting this instinctive feeling by admitting another operation to our armory, the operation of waiting. The operational meaning of saying that I shall have lunch at one o'clock is that if I perform the operation of waiting until one o'clock I shall have certain experiences. There are many difficulties with this operation of "waiting" and I feel that it is dangerous to admit it, but for the present purposes we may perhaps allow ourselves this liberality. The important immediate point for us is that none of us, I as I write, or you as you read, can possibly wait beyond the termination of our individual lives. Any possible meaning that the future can have for any individual must be sought in the things that can happen to him in his lifetime, or in an interval of not more than 200 years, a rather brief interval compared with astronomical times. Contemplation of this broadest possible meaning that we can give to the future will give, I believe, a rather different feeling about the significance of the predictions of astronomy. In physics the situation is qualitatively entirely different, for all the operations by which the fundamental concepts are defined and which are involved in the fundamental experiments are of such short duration that the "waiting" aspect hardly presents itself. However, the waiting aspect is always present to some extent, because operations are performed in time, and are composed of parts described in a prescribed order, so that on beginning a complicated operation one has to wait before one can perform the last part of it. Again, as so often before, we see that there are no hard and fast lines of demarcation between regions of validity of concepts.

With regard to past time, the operational meaning of the past is much more definite than that of the future, for there is no possibility of a questionable operation for the past corresponding to "waiting" for the future; I can never penetrate back into the past. The past for me, as I sit in my chair, means simply the aggregate of those reconstructions which I make on the basis of all the experience now at my command. It is evidently a most complicated thing, but is always subject to the limitations to which the reconstructions which I can make are subject. It means nothing to ask what was the past "actually", unaffected by the limitations of thought in reconstructing it. A proper realization of this again gives one a rather different feeling as to the significance of the extrapolations of cosmogony into the past.

Finally, I attempt to summarize the view to which this analysis leads us as to the nature of cosmogony. The essential limitations of the experimental material place cosmogony in a class by itself. It partakes as much as possible of the nature of the completely experimental subjects, physics and chemistry, but is compelled by necessity to introduce features relating to less sharply defined human activities verging into the artistic, the emotional and the metaphysical. The artistic instinct in the cosmologist finds expression in selecting those formulations or solutions, out of the many possible ones, which are most elegant or most simple. The emotional element is well illustrated by the attitude which various cosmologists take toward extrapolation into the indefinite past or future. There are diametrically opposite attitudes here. Thus to Tolman it is extremely repugnant to think of the universe being carried in time to such a configuration that extrapolation can be carried no further, which means either an act of creation at this epoch, or at least a fundamental change in the laws of nature. To Tolman the idea of a special situation presented by the problem of evolution which demands the assumption of new and unknown laws is so abhorrent as to make the whole picture almost unthinkable. This has driven him to hunt for oscillating solutions of the cosmic problem, which permit the universe to oscillate back and forth between extreme configurations, indefinitely repeated both in past and future, so that there is no limit in time either forward or backward. On the other hand, to a man like Eddington, the idea of a universe continually oscillating between extremes is irreconcilable with feelings of a purpose in stellar evolution. Eddington exclaims that he is an "evolutionist, not a multiplicationist". He prefers a solution in which a definite act of creation has to be assumed in the past, or at least some sort of catastrophe initiating the present régime, and perhaps a gradual decline to the "heat death" of Boltzmann.

The metaphysical element I feel to be active in the attitude of many cosmologists to mathematics. By metaphysical I mean the assumption of the "existence" of validities for which there can be no operational control, a statement which in itself is almost meaningless from the operational point of view, and in fact I personally have no feeling for this sort of thing, and can only use the term "metaphysical" in describing behavior which I observe in other human animals. At any rate, I should call metaphysical the conviction that the universe is run on exact mathematical principles, and its corollary that it is possible for human beings by a fortunate *tour de force* to formulate these principles. I believe that this attitude is back of the sentiment of many cosmologists toward Einstein's differential equations of generalized relativity theory—when, for example, I ask an eminent cosmologist in conversation why he does not give up the Einstein equations if they make him so much trouble, and he replies that such a thing is unthinkable, that these are the only things that we are really sure of.

I believe that there are dangers in any subject in which there is such an unavoidable mixture of purely "scientific" and "human" elements. It seems to me that there is particular danger of introducing actual inconsistencies into the structure if the metaphysical attitude with regard to mathematics is so far adopted as to obscure the perfectly legitimate use of mathematics in attaining simplicity of formulation. The dangers, I hope, may be minimized by discussions like this. But even a perfectly clear-eyed consciousness of the nature of cosmogony will still leave it a subject in which are inextricably mingled together the austere aspects of a purely scientific subject with the warmer and incalculable aspects of a "humanity". To many persons this will constitute an abiding source of fascination; it has at least added to the pleasure of this attempt at analysis.[1]

---

[1] After sending the manuscript of this article to press, I have read the inaugural lecture of Professor H. H. Plaskett, at Oxford University on April 28, 1933, entitled "The Place of Observation in Astronomy". There are many similarities between his points of view and those above.

16

EINSTEIN'S THEORIES AND THE OPERATIONAL POINT OF VIEW*

THIS EXPOSITION will endeavor to show that Einstein did not carry over into his general relativity theory the lessons and insights which he himself has taught us in his special theory.

Let us examine what Einstein did in his special theory. In the first place, he recognized that the meaning of a term is to be sought in the operations employed in making application of the term. If the term is one which is applicable to concrete physical situations, as "length" or "simultaneity," then the meaning is to be sought in the operations by which the length of concrete physical objects is determined, or in the operations by which one determines whether two concrete physical events are simultaneous or not. This is well brought out by the following quotation from Einstein himself in connection with a discussion of the simultaneity of two lightning strokes:

> The concept does not exist for the physicist until he has the possibility of discovering whether or not it is fulfilled in an actual case. We thus require a definition of simultaneity such that this definition supplies us with the means by which, in the present case, he can decide by experiment

*From Volume VII of the Library of Living Philosophers—Albert Einstein: Philosopher-Scientist, 1949.

whether both lightning strokes occurred simultaneously. As long as this requirement is not satisfied, I allow myself to be deceived as a physicist (and of course the same applies if I am not a physicist) when I imagine that I am able to attach a meaning to the statement of simultaneity.[1]

It is to be questioned whether this criterion of meaning by itself is very revolutionary. It is easy to imagine that even Sir Isaac Newton would have assented to it if he had been asked. But before Einstein people had not considered the matter to any great extent, and probably only seldom if ever consciously formulated or applied the criterion. Einstein's revolutionary contribution consisted in his self-conscious use of it in new situations and in the way in which he applied it. What Einstein did was to make a more detailed analysis of the physical operations used in the measurement of length and time than have ever been made before. In doing this he uncovered necessary details which are always involved in any measurement of length, but which had formerly been ignored simply because of their universality, and because no one had had the imagination to formulate them or to see that they might be significant. For example, Einstein's analysis brought to light that in measuring the length of moving objects manipulations with clocks as well as with meter sticks are involved. Before the analysis it had never occurred to anyone that the operations for measuring a moving object were not the

---

[1] From *Relativity*, 26, translated by Lawson, Henry Holt and Co. (1920).

same as those for measuring an object at rest, with the result that an "absolute" significance had been attributed to the concept of length. When Einstein's analysis also suggested that there are several conceivable procedures for measuring the length of a moving object, no one of which has any logical or even physical inevitability, the way was prepared for the recognition that the length of a moving object might not be the same as its length at rest, and that the precise way in which the length varies with the motion will be a function of the definition of the length of the moving object. Everyone now knows that the contraction of length of a moving object is embedded in the special theory of relativity, and that experimentally the contraction is found to exist, but that it is too small to be detectible under ordinary conditions and becomes important only at high velocities approaching the velocity of light.

The new vision given to physicists by Einstein through his special theory of relativity is the vision that the conventional operations of physics may involve details of which we are not ordinarily aware because of their apparent irrelevance or universality or minuteness, that when we extend our experience into new fields, as by going to very high velocities, we may expect new types of phenomena which from the point of view of the old may be paradoxical, and that the paradox may perhaps be resolved when we consider details in our operations which we had disregarded when dealing with ordinary phenomena. Einstein has conditioned us to regard it as a matter of the highest importance, when pushing into new ground, to acquire as vivid a consciousness as possible of all the details of our present operations and of the tacit assumptions back of them, and to anticipate that some of the factors which we have hitherto been able to disregard may prove to be the key to the new situation. Or, put negatively, we have come to see that it is not safe, when we penetrate into new ground, to disregard the effect of factors which could be disregarded in a narrower range of experience.

However, even when we have analyzed the operations which we now employ in as great detail as we are capable of, we can have no assurance that the particular details which our analysis may uncover will be pertinent to the particular new situation that confronts us. It would be difficult to set any limit to the details which more and more penetrating analysis can disclose. At least we must always anticipate the possibility of continually uncovering finer and finer details (or, from another point of view, presuppositions of increasingly great generality) as we push our analysis further. Whether the particular new details that our analysis discloses are pertinent in the new situation can be determined only by the test of effectiveness in application. Einstein's analysis of the operations of measuring length and time was by no means an exhaustive or unique analysis, any more than any analysis can be exhaustive or unique. Einstein's genius consisted, even more than in seeing that the measuring operations involve certain details that had hitherto been neglected as irrelevant, in picking out those particular details which in actual application proved to be the key to the new physical situations when we penetrate into the realm of hitherto unexperienced high velocities.

Now let us turn to the general theory and inquire what are the tacit assumptions in the operations required to give the general theory its meaning. Consider in the first place that part of the general theory embodied in the mathematical equations, such as the equation of light propagation,

$$ds^2 (\equiv \sum g_{mn} dx_m dx_n) = 0,$$

or the equation of motion of a particle,

$$\frac{d^2 x^\mu}{ds^2} + \Gamma^\mu_{\alpha\beta} \frac{dx^\alpha}{ds} \times \frac{dx^\beta}{ds} = 0.$$

Formally, the equations contain only co-ordinates and functions of the co-ordinates which can for the present be treated as given. But the co-ordinates are co-ordinates of something, and what it is that they are the co-ordinates of, or how we are to determine the co-ordinates in any concrete case, cannot be specified by the mathematical machinery of the equations alone, but must be known in other ways. What are the operations which one has to employ in applying the equations to any concrete physical situation? Evidently we must be able to determine the co-ordinates which correspond to the phenomenon under observation (such as propagation of a light-signal or motion of a mass particle) and this involves identifying the point at which the phenomenon occurs to the extent at least of being able to tag it with the coordinates. But how shall a point be identified? "Empty" space is amorphous and its "points" have no identity. Identifiability demands some physical substratum. That is, the framework in which the co-ordinates are determined must be a physical framework, and the specification of the framework involves a specification of at least some of its physical properties. In particular, if we use a framework which allows the conventional separation into space and time co-ordinates, then one specification of the framework is that the spatial co-ordinates shall be determined by "rigid" members, and the time co-ordinates by "clocks." Logically, we should be able to ascribe an independent meaning to "rigid" and to "clock," but as far as I know this has not been accomplished. In particular, the specification of what is meant by "clock" has given much difficulty, and at present "clock" seems to be circularly defined by implication as a physical apparatus so constructed that it functions in the way in which the theory of relativity says that a "clock" functions.

It would appear then that the complete operational specification of the framework still offers certain difficulties. Passing over the difficulties, what is the operational situation with regard to the phenomenon whose co-ordinates are to be determined in the framework? In the first place, the equations may refer to different kinds of events. What kind of event it is has to be specified by means not contained in the equations, and by means which are not usually made the subject of analysis. Consider, for example, the equation of light-propagation. The equation states that if the co-ordinates of a light-signal are determined physically, the equation will be satisfied when the co-ordinates are substituted into it. The implication is that the light-signal has identifiability and individuality, and that it can be followed observationally as it is propagated. Or whatever other equation we have to deal with or whatever other phenomenon, it would seem that as a very minimum a certain amount of individuality or identifiability in the phenomenon is demanded. This would seem to involve a certain amount of discreteness. But how much discreteness? Physical happenings never are mathematically sharp, but are always surrounded by an instrumental haze. How much haze is permissible is a question that seems not to have been discussed; it is quite conceivably a question that might become important when we enter fields remote from ordinary experience.

In general comment, Einstein seems to have concentrated his analytical attack almost exclusively on the co-ordinate system used in specifying physical events, and to have neglected the events themselves. In fact, the events are conventionally treated as primitive or unanalyzed and unanalyzable elements. Of course no theory can avoid ultimately its unanalyzed elements. The question can only be whether the analysis has been carried as far as the physical situation demands.

As far as the mathematical aspects of the general theory go, perhaps the most essential feature is the use of generalized co-ordinates. The arguments by which the equations are derived assert as a fundamental thesis that the frame of reference used in describing a phenomenon is a matter of indifference, and the possibility is contemplated of passing back and forth from one co-ordinate system to another, an enterprise for which the use of generalized co-ordinates is especially well adapted. This thesis is usually understood to have a physical content in addition to its purely formal content. From the purely formal point of view the content of the thesis is: given a certain physical phenomenon which is described in terms of a certain co-ordinate system, then it may equally well be described in terms of another co-ordinate system. This is to be done merely by translating the co-ordinates as measured in the first system into the corresponding co-ordinates in the second system, and this translation is to be made by applying certain purely formal procedures for correlating any set of co-ordinates in the first system with others in the second system. The operations for passing from the first to the second co-ordinate system are here purely paper and pencil operations, and are sterile with respect to any physical implications. From the point of view of the physicist they are trivial. Physical content is injected into the situation, however, by the supplementary thesis that the co-ordinates obtained by the paper and pencil operations are the co-ordinates that would have been obtained if the observer had originally measured the phenomenon in the second co-ordinate system, or, alternately, that they are the co-ordinates which would have been obtained by a second observer, observing the same phenomenon in the second co-ordinate frame. At any rate, the possibility is assumed of observing the same phenomenon or event[2] from two different frames of reference.

What does it mean to say that the same event has been observed in two frames of reference? The question hardly arises under ordinary conditions, when the two frames do not differ much from each other, and is, as far as I am aware, not raised by Einstein. That is, as we have already remarked, in Einstein's argument the event itself, which is the subject of the co-ordinate measurement, is not recognized as in need of analysis, but is treated as a primitive element. This may be entirely legitimate for present needs as long as we are concerned with only a single frame of reference, but it seems to me that the event, when regarded as something that can be equally viewed from two frames of reference, can by no means be treated as primitive or unanalyzable. If the two frames are allowed to vary without restriction, as they are in the general theory, the question of what it means to say that the same event has been

---

[2] I use *event* in the usual sense, and not in the technical sense of an aggregate of three space and one time co-ordinates.

observed in two frames of reference becomes far from academic. If, for example, the event whose coordinates are being determined is for the first observer the arrival of a train of radiation which he perceives as a flash of light in his eye or which he may register on a photographic plate, the second observer, moving with high relative velocity, may not be able to detect ocularly at all, but he perceives it as a sensation of warmth in his finger or registers it instrumentally on a bolometer. Unsophisticated procedure would not at first incline one to recognize these two experiences of the two observers, involving different sense organs or different instruments, as pertaining to the same phenomenon or event. The attribute of sameness can perhaps be recognized in the two experiences if the two observers are allowed to communicate with each other. If the first observer can say to the second observer, "Something just happened to me," and if the second can also make the same remark to the first, and if what happens to each observer is sufficiently discrete so that it does not overlap with other happenings, then we probably would be willing to say that both had observed the "same" event. But the "sameness" which can thereby be ascribed to the two experiences is obviously a sophisticated thing, involving considerations by no means simple, among which the ascription of a "sufficient" amount of discreteness to the signal would seem to be a very minimum.

Even more complexity is involved in the apparently necessary assumption that the two observers are able to communicate meanings to each other. This assumption appears, for example, when we talk about similarly constructed apparatus in the two systems, as two similar clocks. What are the operations by which observers in two different frames of reference communicate meanings with each other, and decide that their clocks are similar? A certain similarity in the observers themselves is necessary, but how much similarity? Even the inhabitants of this planet with different cultural backgrounds do not find it always easy to communicate. If the difference between the two frames is not excessive, it is possible to think of one of the observers as myself and the other as a vicarious edition of myself, who can step back and forth from one frame of reference to the other. But how shall we discover what are the relevant operational details which are involved in the possibility of thinking about two observers in this way? He would be rash indeed who would try to conceptualize what it means to communicate meanings with another observer moving with 99 per cent of the velocity of light, or living in the gravitational field occurring at the center of a giant star, or in a part of the stellar universe not yet explored by the solar system in its secular wanderings. Under such conditions we would do well to replace the "similar observers" and their biological connotations, with "physical observing apparatus." But what can we mean under these conditions by "similarity of two photographic plates," for example, which will not already assume a knowledge of the physical properties which it is the purpose of the analysis to deduce? We cannot, for example, adopt the easy answer of saying that we will manufacture the photographic plates both in the one frame of reference, and then transfer one of them bodily to the second frame, because this would assume that the process of transfer had introduced no essential changes in the properties of the plate, and we have no operational criterion for this.

In other words, when in our analysis of the physical operations involved in observing systems at high velocities or in intense gravitational fields, or in remote parts of the stellar universe, we neglect as irrelevant an analysis of the operations by which observations are transferred between different frames of reference, we are in effect saying that our understanding of the mechanism of transfer is so good that we are justified in anticipating that none of the details ordinarily neglected are pertinent. It seems to me that this point of view assumes an understanding of the details of the processes of communication between different observing systems to which no human being is as yet entitled.

There is another method of assigning a meaning to the "sameness" of the event which is the subject of observation in two frames of reference. If I could assume in the background a third observer, observing both the phenomenon itself and the two observers observing the phenomenon, then obviously a meaning could be assigned to the sameness of a phenomenon observed by the two observers whenever the third observer reports that the two observers are observing the same thing. It does indeed seem that such a conceptual observer in the background is implied in the argument of Einstein, for we have already seen that a meaning is assigned to the event in its own right apart from the frame of reference which yields the co-ordinates. This in itself amounts to the assumption of a certain amount of pre-Einsteinian "absoluteness" in the event. Operationally this "absoluteness" means merely that we are getting along without analyzing the details of what is involved when we say we can treat a thing in its own right independent of the frame of reference. In addition to the objection that the third observer in the background involves a preferred system of reference, there is the fundamental objection that even the third ghostly observer does not eliminate the necessity of assuming that two observers may observe the same event.

To what extent is it true that two observers may observe the same event? The assumption that this is possible is almost universal in modern science. It is often stated that science is by its very nature public, not private. This means, among other things, that the same phenomenon may be observed by different observers, and that when so observed their reports will be found to agree. What about the operational details? The complete situations are never exactly the same for the two observers for the reason, among others, that two observers never observe with the same beam of light. In neglecting the fact that the light-beams are different by which different observers observe, we are saying that this is irrelevant. Ordinary experience justifies us amply, but what assurance have we that we will continue to be justified when we push into new territory? Recognition of the discrete structure of light, a recognition which we owe in large part to Einstein's analysis of the photo-electric effect, would prepare us to anticipate failure at least when we push into the domain of the very small.

The question of the meaning of "sameness" in an event observed by different observers does not force itself prominently on the attention as general relativity theory is ordinarily expounded. The events tend to be replaced by "pointer readings," that is by the aggregate of the four numbers which are the co-ordinates of the event in the particular frame of reference. In fact, "event" has sometimes come to be used in the technical sense of the aggregate of these four numbers. The tendency is to fix the attention exclusively on the co-ordinates and the equations connecting them. But any such treatment can at best be only partial. It cannot offer even an adequate description of a physical situation, to say nothing of being able to establish correlations. For it obviously is impossible to reproduce the original physical situation, given only the co-ordinates (pointer readings) into which it is analyzed. We must know in addition what it is that the co-ordinates are of. Are they co-ordinates of an electron, or a proton, or a larger mass particle, or are they coordinates determined by the arrival of a photon?

In attempting to assess the importance of these considerations I think we have to keep distinctly in view whether the proposed application is to large or small scale phenomena. So far, the success of the general theory has been confined to large scale phenomena; attempts to extend the application to the small phenomena of the quantum domain have not been fruitful, in spite of the most serious efforts of physicists of the highest ability. From the large scale point of view and in the range of ordinary experience it certainly must be conceded by everyone that the assumption of the public nature of science and the possibility of observation of the same event by two observers from two frames of reference is a very close approximation. But even here we have seen that a certain amount of discreteness has to be presupposed. The term "object" or event implies a certain amount of differentiation from the matrix in which it is embedded, and therefore a boundary of the object or event. Even in the realm of ordinary experience instruments now in our possession are capable of showing that the boundaries of objects or events are not absolutely sharp, but there is always a haziness of outline. If this haziness were to become too great we would lose the identifiability of the object and the "sameness" of the event. If now we enter new realms of experience and attempt to foresee what would be found by observers moving with very high relative velocities, or in very intense gravitational fields, we must, by our general maxim, be prepared to find that the outlines of objects or events have become so blurred that we can no longer uniquely correlate readings made in one frame of reference with those made in another, and hence can no longer describe the events experienced in one frame of reference, as the "same" as those experienced in the other.

So much by way of general methodology. We may, however, play a hunch that these considerations are not as a matter of fact very important when it comes to large scale phenomena, and that we may neglect them. This is essentially what Einstein did in assuming the possibility of the observation of large scale events by two observers. The theory developed on this basis has been successful in embracing at least three types of large scale phenomena which could not be included in former theories. We must not conclude, however, that the success of the theory has been in *consequence* of the assumption of the possibility of two observers, that is, the assumption of the possibility of the description of the phenomenon in covariant form in generalized co-ordinates. The assumption of covariance is itself sterile in physical consequences, as was pointed out by Kretschmann[3] and admitted by Einstein. The physical content entered into the theory in other ways during the detailed working out, chiefly through the demand for mathematical simplicity.

---

[3] E. Kretschmann, *Annalen der Physik,* vol. 53, 575 (1917); A. Einstein, *Annalen der Physik,* vol. 55, 241 (1918).

This meant that the equations in generalized co-ordinates were taken as linear, of the second order, and that they reduce to the already familiar equations under proper limiting conditions. Among other things this sort of mathematical formulation involved the validity of the physical principle of superposition which states that two "causes" acting simultaneously produce the sum of their separate effects. I have discussed this matter more in detail in other places, especially in the chapter on "Relativity" in my book *The Nature of Physical Theory*, where most of the considerations presented here are also given.

The situation is entirely different, however, when we come to small scale events. We might perhaps make a fairly plausible argument for the thesis that the description of small scale situations can be adequately broken down into terms of pointer readings only. For although it is true that a specification of the pointer readings alone, without a specification of what the pointer readings are of, does not constitute adequate description for the reason that we cannot reproduce the primitive situation when given the pointer readings; nevertheless in the microscopic domain there are only a few distinct sorts of things to which pointer readings could refer, contrasted with the infinite variety of possible events on the large scale. Hence, if in addition to the pointer readings themselves we are told to what sort of elementary event the pointer readings refer, such as the motion of an electron or a proton or a photon, we believe, in our present state of physical knowledge, that we would be able uniquely to reproduce the primitive situation. It is probably considerations of this sort that are back of the contention of Eddington and others that the only important features in a physical situation are the pointer readings. This is also essentially the position of Einstein himself when he states that the *intersections* of the co-ordinate meshes are the only things with physical significance. But this thesis necessarily draws us into the microscopic domain, and in the microscopic domain we encounter phenomena diametrically contradictory to the spirit of the relativistic approach. The emission or reception of a photon cannot be observed by two observers or recorded in two frames of reference. The elementary processes or "objects" do not have individuality or identifiability, nor can they be repeated. The concept of "sameness" does not apply in the microscopic domain of quantum phenomena. It is natural to think that the failure of general relativity theory in the realm of the small is no accident, but is due to a fundamental contradiction between the presuppositions and attitudes of mind of the general theory and the actual construction of nature.

Two general aspects of the general theory of relativity may be recognized. Firstly, there is the mathematical edifice of the system of equations and the rules by which the symbols of the equations are to be correlated with the results of physical operations; and secondly, there is the attitude of mind, or what

I may call the philosophy, that leads to the arguments used in deriving the equations and to the expectation that the equations so derived will have physical validity. These two aspects are not uniquely connected; from a given mathematical edifice one cannot uniquely deduce the philosophy that led to the erection of the edifice, and even less can one infer from the success of the mathematics in reproducing certain aspects of experience that therefore the philosophy back of it was true. In this paper we are concerned with the philosophy of Einstein rather than with the equations which he deduced by the philosophy.

Although it is not possible to deduce uniquely from the equations what Einstein's philosophy is, we know pretty definitely what it is like from his writings. It seems to me that the things Einstein does and the way he talks about his theory are like the acts and words of a man who would say that there is a "reality" back of all our multifarious experience. Although explicit use of the world "reality" does not figure prominently, if at all, in Einstein's exposition, nevertheless without some such notion in the background it is difficult to understand such things as his continued insistence on the indifference of the language (co-ordinate system) in which a phenomenon is described. Again and again in Einstein's exposition appears his feeling for the importance of getting away from any special frame of reference, and his conviction that it *must* be possible to do this and that by so doing one may hope to arrive at something pretty fundamental. Something much akin to this is involved in the common thesis that science is by its very nature public, or universal, although such a thesis is much weaker than the thesis of an underlying reality. One may, if one chooses, make the public nature of science a matter of definition, but even so, one need not refrain from inquiring what the processes are by which the publicity is arrived at.

If one analyzes what one does when engaging in any scientific activity I think it will be recognized that the raw material of science is in the beginning private or individual before it becomes public or universal. The public "real" object, with its permanence and individuality, to which we correlate our private sensations, involves a tremendous amount of complex intermediate detail, as anyone might realize who has witnessed the struggles of an infant during its early months to acquire the concept of object. The concept of object thus arrived at is itself complex, and passes, one may guess, through a stage of private object before the concept of public object emerges. "Object" is palpably a construction, and as far as we know or can give meaning, is a construction only of the human nervous system. The apparent fact that different human beings can so universally agree and arrive at the concept of public object may excite our wonder, but it is not more wonderful than the fact that the human nervous system has the biological stability to reproduce itself over billions of examples and eons of time. The common sense notion of "object" with its reality and individuality apart from any frame of reference, is a concept of stark simplicity, from which all consciousness of the complexity of the processes by which it was engendered and maintained has been ruthlessly discarded. In other words, the common sense concept of object is a pre-Einsteinian concept, a carry-over from the days when we were not sophisticated enough to realize the complexities concealed in apparently simple situations, nor practiced enough in analysis to be able to bring these complexities into evidence.

If one examines the range of practical conditions within which the concept of "object" is known to be valid, it will appear that the range is exceedingly narrow. It occurs as far as we know only in connection with human nervous systems, which occur only in comparatively narrow temperature ranges, on the surface of a particular planet, in an approximately constant gravitational field of low intensity, in organisms that never have relative velocities of more than an infinitesimal fraction of the velocity of light, and which have not existed for an interval of time long enough for the planet on which they live to have moved through more than an infinitesimal fraction of the sidereal universe. Yet we are apparently so convinced of the necessity for the universal validity of this so complicated concept, checked under such a narrow range of conditions, as to use the assumption of its validity as a tool to determine the behavior under unknown conditions of such comparatively simple things as a light-ray in a gravitational field. Surely the plausible method of attack is to start with things which we feel we understand well and from them try to deduce the probable behavior of things we understand less. But who would maintain that we understand better the processes by which we arrive at the concept of an underlying reality than we understand the behavior of light in a gravitational field? This, however, is precisely what we have done in assuming to know that the terribly complex processes back of our mentation will not be modified in novel conditions, although at the same time we anticipate an effect of the gravitational field on light-beams. Surely the reason we have acted in this way has been lack of consideration. Once our eyes have been opened it seems to me that the tactics of our attack lose their plausibility.

Perhaps the most sweeping characterization of Einstein's attitude of mind with regard to the general theory is that he believes it possible to get away from the special point of view of the individual observer and sublimate it into something universal, "public," and "real." I on the other hand would take the position that a detailed analysis of everything that we do in physics discloses the universal impossibility of getting away from the individual starting-point. It is a matter of simple observation that the private comes before the public. For each one of us the very meaning of "public" is to be found in certain aspects of his "private." Not only is the starting-point in any scientific activity always private, but after it has emerged into the domain of the public, the story is not completed until we can return to the private from which we came. For the final test of scientific description or theory is that it enables us to reconstruct or to anticipate the immediate (private) situation. The concepts back of the first and second laws of thermodynamics, perhaps the most sweeping generalizations we have in physics, get their meaning from the possibility of recovering the starting-point. For neither energy nor entropy can be defined without reference to a standard state of the system to which we can always return by suitable manipulation.

In much the same way the fundamental measuring operations, without which even description of a physical system would not be possible, have to be defined by reference to some standard set of conditions. Consider, for example, the operation for determining "interval," which is perhaps the most characteristic concept of relativity theory. For the purposes of illustration consider this in the simplest case, when we determine the geometrical distance between two points at rest with respect to us. This is determined by the simple operation of laying a meter stick between the two points and taking the difference of the readings of the two points on the stick. If for some reason it is not convenient to make the observation by direct laying on of the meter stick, but if we know the Cartesian co-ordinates of the two points, then it is possible to calculate by a simple rule the results that we would have obtained with the meter stick. Or, if the physical situation becomes more complicated, and the two points are in motion with respect to our frame of reference, the operations for determining the length become more complicated, being now compounded of operations with meter sticks and clocks in a specified manner combined with computation in a specified manner according to mathematical formulas. The object of all the complicated procedure is to be able to get a numerical result which is the same as the result obtained in an original frame of reference in which the points are at rest. That is "interval" is an invariant, and the meaning of invariance is merely that it is always possible when measurements are made in strange and complicated systems of reference to return, by suitable calculation, to the results which would have been obtained with the original uniquely simple operation of reading the distance on a resting meter stick. All the complicated processes receive their meaning and significance from the fact that there is in the background a single definite procedure to which we can return, and from which *we do not want* permanently to get away. If one asks "why" it is that the interval is so fundamental for description, I think there is no answer. It is a brute fact that every individual observer finds that the interval as determined by him with meter sticks stationary with respect to him is especially adapted to the description of nature. The fact that nature itself provides this unique method of description would seem to rob the contention that all frames of reference are equally significant of some of its intuitive appeal.

Not only does nature provide us with a unique operation for measuring interval, but it also provides us with a unique frame of reference, namely a frame fixed with respect to the stellar universe, as was pointed out by Mach. Einstein, however, rejects this frame as having significance, because the ascription of significance to it would not be consistent with the "field" point of view. According to the field point of view local happenings are to be significantly correlated, not with distant happenings, but with happenings or conditions in the immediate vicinity, the aggregate of which constitute the "field." The advantage and necessity of the field point of view is usually considered to be that it avoids the difficulties of the old action-at-a-distance point of view. These difficulties are, I believe, generally recognized not to be of a strictly logical character, but to be connected with the difficulty of imagining any "mechanism" by which action at a distance occurs. I believe, however, that an analysis of the operations that are used in specifying what the field is will show that the conceptual dilemma has by no means been successfully met, but has merely been smothered in a mass of neglected operational detail. For the field at a point (considering the electrostatic field for simplicity) is determined by placing a charge at the point, measuring the force on the charge, and then proceeding to the limit by letting the charge become vanishingly small and calculating the limit of ratio of force to charge. The result is conceptualized as something characteristic of the point alone, from which any effect which the test charge may have exerted has disappeared with the vanishing of the charge. But this is plainly an improper conceptualization of this limiting process, because force as well as charge vanishes, and the indispensable rôle of the charge by no means disappears. I know of no means that has been proposed for giving operational meaning to the statement that a condition exists at a point of space independent of the presence at the point of something else, nor have I been able to think of any method by which such a meaning might be given. What one has done when he has shown how to obtain the force on a given distribution of charges in terms of the field, is at bottom nothing more than to find the force on a complicated distribution in terms of the forces on a simpler set of standard charges. It does not seem surprising that this should be feasible, nor would one anticipate that any very fundamental conclusions could be drawn about whatever mechanism there may be which determines the forces on the standard charges. The same considerations apply to dynamic as well as static conditions. One visualizes a "propagation" of a modification in the "field," but operationally one observes only the way in which a force which at one moment acts on a test-body acts a moment later on another test-body. One has in no wise exorcised the mystery of the successive appearance of a force at successive test-bodies by the invention of the field.

It seems to me that the broadest and least restrictive base that can be imagined for the attack on the problem of understanding nature is correlation between the parts. For the broadest attack, we must set up no thesis as to what sort of correlations we will accept as significant, but any universally observed correlation must be given potential significance. Nature presents us with a unique frame of reference; the meaning of "unique" implies a correlation with our measuring operations. Furthermore, this unique frame has a correlation with ordinary mechanical phenomena (Foucault pendulum). When Einstein refuses to accept this frame as having significance, but on the contrary sets up the thesis that it is not possible in the nature of things that there should be a unique frame, I think he is being influenced by the special and, to my mind, erroneous considerations back of the field concept in a way opposed to the spirit of his own general approach.

It has already been intimated that unique frames of reference or preferred starting-points have some of the attributes of the "absolute." It might appear therefore that to recognize their existence is a throwback to the Newtonian point of view. I think any misgivings on this score will vanish, however, when it is appreciated that operationally the preferred starting-point is different for each individual observer. That this is true is a matter of simple observation, whether or not we like it. There is here nothing of the old Newtonian absolute, metaphysically existing in its own right, the same for all observers. One can see that a complete working out of the implications of each observer having his own unique frame of reference is a matter of the very widest philosophical import, but it is not necessary for present purposes to go into it further here.

In Einstein's argument another type of consideration plays an important part. A distinction is made between the general "laws" of nature and phenomena which are special, local, and adventitious. The velocity of light or the gravitational constant are taken as manifestations of general laws, while the acceleration of gravity at the surface of the earth would be an example of the second sort of thing. The distinction is made fundamental, because it is the general laws that are required to be capable of covariant formulation. I believe, however, that analysis will show that there is no way by which the concept of "general law" can be made operationally sharp. If, when we have telescopes a million times more powerful than any at present, we find that there is reason to think that the gravitational constant varies in different parts of space, and that its value in any particular region cannot be correlated with anything observable, any more than the actual size of the earth can at present be correlated with anything observable, I think we would not maintain that the gravitational constant is connected with some universal law. The point is that the meaning of the concept of general law becomes operationally hazy as we extend our measurements or our thinking toward domains as yet unexplored. It would seem that a sound scientific methodology would not allow us to use as a tool for stupendous extrapolations any concepts which have the slightest recognizable amount of haziness. Such an extrapolation should not be made until we have at least some basis for estimating the order of magnitude of the haze and its probable effect on such an extrapolation. It is difficult for me to imagine a way of doing this that would not involve some prior knowledge of the region into which we are trying to penetrate.

In summary, the obvious structure of experience is based on the individual and particular. Our fundamental operations of description and measurement do not get away from it. We find it present in the structure of the universe in a unique frame of reference when we go to the very large; and when we go to the very small we find it in the impossibility of public knowledge or observation in the quantum domain. The indictment that this article would bring against Einstein is therefore the following: That in his conviction of the possibility of getting away from any special co-ordinate system, in his conviction of the fruitfulness of so doing, and in his treatment of the event as something primitive and unanalyzed, he has carried into general relativity theory precisely that uncritical, pre-Einsteinian point of view which he has so convincingly shown us, in his special theory, conceals the possibility of disaster.

17

*IMPERTINENT REFLECTIONS ON HISTORY OF SCIENCE**

HISTORY OF SCIENCE is a many-sided subject, permitting approach from the point of view of various human interests, and presenting a wide variety of problems, many of them paradoxical and perhaps not capable of satisfactory solution. In the following it will probably seem to the reader a number of times that I am talking at cross purposes. Anything that I can say is of necessity limited by my background as a physicist.

History of Science is a particular branch of history and is subject to its general limitations. All history is concerned with the past, and therefore subject to whatever limitations may be imposed by the nature of the past itself. What sort of limitations are thus imposed? This may strike you as a philosophical matter in which the physicist must be incompetent, but one of the tasks of the physicist is to reconstruct the past of his systems as well as to predict their future, so that he has had to give some thought to the matter. It is usual, I think, to conceive of the past in common-sense terms as something that "really exists" and which has as much

*From Philosophy of Science, 17, 63-73, 1950.

objective validity as the world which we now see about us. It is a corollary of this general point of view that the past can be analyzed into events with individuality and identifiability, and that it makes sense to ask whether any event, of any conceivable fineness of detail, actually occurred in the past or not. For example, it would make sense to ask whether Montezuma had a nightmare at 2:15 of the morning of the fifteenth day before the landing of Cortez.

It seems to me that neither the general point of view nor its corollary can be maintained. The thesis that the past has an objectively real existence is devastatingly shattered by the consideration that there is no way whatever by which it can be proved that the entire universe was not created five minutes ago. For if at the moment of creation five minutes ago all the fossil records and all the imprints of memory in the minds of men had been created as they were at that moment, there would be no way of distinguishing one situation from the other. In the absence of the possibility of implementing any distinction between the two situations the distinction itself loses meaning. With regard to the corollary that assigns meaning to an indefinite fineness of detail in the past, it is perhaps possible to maintain this position with regard to any single specific detail. It is, for example, conceivable that at some time in the future a record of the minutiae of the court life of the Aztecs might be discovered which would permit an answer to our question about

Montezuma. But although any specific detail in the past can be treated in this way, it is impossible so to treat simultaneously all the possible details of the past, for a multiplicity in the record would be demanded that would bankrupt the resources of the present world to store it. The only way by which meaning can be given to indefinite detail in the past is by the postulate that the construction of the world is such as to permit the recovery of the past in indefinite detail from the present, as was possible, for example, to the mechanistic God of Laplace. Such a state of affairs would prevail if the causality principle were of unlimited applicability. But the tenability of this view about the construction of the world has been destroyed with quantum mechanics and the Indetermination Principle of Heisenberg. The best opinion at the present is that the world is so constructed that the present cannot be determined or described as would be required to permit the indefinitely detailed reconstruction of a past. The best that can be done is to make a reconstruction which becomes more and more nebulous as we recede further. It is therefore in principle impossible to assign the same fineness of detail to the world in the past as to the world in the present, and it is therefore meaningless to assign "reality" to fine detail of past events. The principle of causality becomes more and more nebulous as we recede into the past; it becomes more and more impossible to reconstruct causal chains in the past, and the principle of causality itself gradually loses meaning as something applicable to the past.

The inescapable conclusion from all this, it seems to me, is that the only meaning which the past has is to be found in the present. Any records on which we base our reconstructions are records which exist now, and our reconstructions are reconstructions which we make now. Even the reconstructions of past historians stored in the books in our libraries are merely dead marks on paper until they are made to come to life by acceptance and incorporation into our own present intellectual activities.

To me, standing on the outside, it seems that much of history is not written with an adequate appreciation that the past has meaning only in terms of the present. The impartial recovery of the past, uncontaminated by the influence of the present, is held up as a professional ideal, and a criterion of technical competence is the degree to which this ideal is reached. The ideal is, I believe, impossible of attainment, and cannot even be formulated without involvement with meaningless verbalisms.

The meticulous reader will doubtless before this have cast the reproach of inconsistent, if not meaningless, verbalisms on my own exposition of my own position. For instance, we have spoken of the writing of history as involving a reconstruction of the past, the obvious implication in the word "reconstruction" being that the past is something that can be reconstructed. To this I shall have to plead guilty, and can offer as my only justification that the language does not exist which is consistent with the structure of the world as analysis discloses it. Limited as we are to a language inherited from an uncritical past, we can talk together only by the exercise of mutual good will.

The reader may well be impatient with me not only because he finds my language infested with the same verbalisms which I have been deploring, but also because the point which I have been making may seem to him trivial. Here again I must admit an element of justice in the criticism. For I think that the processes by which we try to "reconstruct" the past and the result of our reconstruction will neither be very much altered by what we have been saying; in fact, I do not see how we could do much differently. But I think there will be a real difference in our appraisal of the significance of what we have done, and so a reaction on certain aspects of the "philosophy" of history. There may well be a change in our attitude toward what constitutes the "best" reconstruction of the past. I think that, for instance, the "post hoc, propter hoc" method of writing history, or any method into which the personal prejudices of the historian have been allowed to intrude, will continue to be regarded as bad methods, but the reasons why they are bad methods will probably have to be restated. However, these are questions for professional argument into which I am not competent to intrude.

With these generalities, perhaps glittering, we

may turn to consider the special features presented by history of science. In discussing the situation we cannot well avoid asking in the first place what is our purpose in cultivating history of science. There are a number of purposes, all of them good, and all of them valid for one person or another. The historian of science may have an intrinsic interest in his subject apart from any connotations which it may have for other fields. He may enjoy for its own sake the discovery of hitherto unknown or unvalued sources of information and the solution of the puzzle of piecing together from the fragments the most plausible reconstruction. I imagine that every professional historian of science is appealed to in greater or less degree by this sort of motive. To the extent that he is actuated by this motive he is in much the same position as the artist, and his activities are to be justified by the same considerations and limited by esthetic criteria similar to those of the artist. There can be no quarrel with this attitude, but I cannot help wondering whether in practice devotion to this idea will not falter a little under the realization that the past is an aspect of the present. In any event, we need not consider this attitude further here, since it is sufficient unto itself.

Next after history of science for its own sake we may perhaps put history of science for its cultural values. This aspect is becoming increasingly important. Science plays a constantly increasing role in our civilization, so that a man with no scientific understanding or aptitude is increasingly becoming a social parasite. Not only are the processes and results of science penetrating ever further into our daily lives, but the conversation and writing of the members of a modern community is increasingly concerned with scientific matters, so that a man is coming to feel less and less at home in a modern community without some understanding of the scientific background. The increasing trend in this direction is witnessed by the prominent part played by scientific survey courses in our modern courses in general education. It is felt by many university authorities that a man cannot function in a modern society without some understanding of the broad scientific principles at the back of many recent developments, whether or not the particular concern of the man in his future career will be with scientific matters. It is furthermore felt in many informed quarters that this understanding of fundamental principles can best be imparted by the historical method.

I think it must be at once conceded that any method of imparting a true picture of what science involves cannot avoid a very strong historical component. For science itself is the activity of scientists; it has been said that science is "sciencing." Scientists themselves think and talk about their science in terms of their own activities or that of their fellows. The layman who would understand the scientist must know what these activities are of which the scientist talks and which constitute the living science of the present. In other words, contemporary science and contemporary history of science are almost indistinguishable. The time span to be understood in "contemporary" cannot be set at less than the memory span of any living scientist. The "present" for the historian covers a finite duration no less than for the psychologist, and the limits between present and past are not sharp. By pushing into the past by memory chains of overlapping generations of scientists we can connect with any distant epoch and lend support to the thesis that the science of the present is a compound of all the ingredients of the past and can therefore be understood only in terms of its history.

These considerations naturally introduce what to many appear the chief purpose and function of a study of the history of science, namely to instill an understanding of science itself. This view may appear natural enough, but a different point of view may be defended with considerably more justification than would be possible in other fields of history. I think it will be generally conceded that an adequate understanding of contemporary politics, for example, is impossible without an understanding of political history. A reason for this is that the political actions of any individual in the present are to a large extent conditioned by his historical antecedents. The intransigeance of the Irish in Eire is largely a consequence of what happened to their grandfathers. This sort of thing is true to a much smaller extent in science. Many maintain that the science of the present is a self-contained objective thing, existing in its own right, independent of how it got here. What it is can be determined by taking the consensus of contemporary scientists, and in fact it is sometimes defined as this consensus. The proof of this pudding is claimed to be in the eating. In particular, this point of view may be made the basis of a method of teaching. During the war the "objective" method of teaching science was much exploited because of the speed with which results could be obtained. Technical schools today often employ an objective method, in which the scientific "facts" are taught, with no heed to the historical development or any recognition that great names are associated with science. This sort of thing is nothing new. The possibility of it was inherent in the philosophy of Plato, and was to a high degree attained in the impersonal detachment and perfection of the propositions of Euclid. In recent times it has been to a particular degree the ideal of French science, with its cold lucidity, its suppression of all evidence of the scaffolding by which the scientific edifice was erected, and its implications of timeless validity.

There is no denying that it is possible to treat science in this way, and that certain limited objectives may be attained with a high efficiency. But it seems to me to overlook certain essential features of the situation, and therefore to make impossible an understanding of what science actually is. For it seems to me that the one most important thing to realize about science is that it is a human activity, and this can only mean the activity of individuals.

The objective public science of consensus obviously originated in the brains of individuals. The scientific stage at any epoch is largely occupied with the process by which science progresses from private to public. If science is taught with a large admixture of history this point of view will automatically be stressed. In so doing a purpose will be served that is increasingly important in our present day, namely to impart an adequate appreciation of the fundamental conditions under which science flourishes. One of these conditions is obviously complete freedom for the individual scientist at the initiating level. An appreciation of this by the man in the street who supports the programs of taxation may well be decisive for survival in a world in which the totalitarian ideal of science for the service of the state finds increasing support.

Not only is science initiated on the private level, but it returns to the private level for its consummation. No scientific journal will accept a paper for publication unless it is so written that the qualified reader can verify for himself the statements made in it. No scientific proof has validity unless it clicks for the individual reader.

A due appreciation, imparted by the use of the historical method, that science is initiated at the individual level and returns to it, may perhaps have some effect as an antidote to some of the unfortunate consequences of the present tendency to large-scale mass production in science itself, particularly in modern physics with its enormous instruments.

These instruments must, of necessity, be served by teams of physicists, and the young physicist in particular is naturally being indoctrinated with the virtue of cultivating those traits which make for efficient functioning in teams. This is doubtless necessary, but at the same time it carries obvious dangers to the development of powers of individual initiative in the majority of the individuals who compose the teams. A properly handled use of the historical method may help to minimize this danger.

We seem driven, in order to acquire a complete picture of the scientific scene and in order to be able to push on to the source of scientific action, to go back to the individual scientist. If we do this, we cannot avoid eventually considering the motives of the individual. This may well be an unwelcome conclusion, for it seems to negative the impersonal ideal so often held for science and the scientist. It does not, however, represent anything new in the history of science as it has often been written, for a portrayal of the motives of scientists has, I think, been rightly regarded as of concern to the historian. There is, however, one recent example of what I regard as so flagrant an abuse of this concern that I would like to consider it further.

This has to do with the popular modern movement to describe all science in terms of and as the result of economic pressures. The movement has had a particular vogue in England, although there are plenty of adherents in this country. This is a question on which no dogmatic or sweeping position can be maintained. It cannot be denied that many of the problems with which scientists have been concerned have risen from industrial or economic situations, and that the opportunities for scientific progress are enormously enhanced because our culture is so largely industrial and mechanical. But the thesis is usually pushed further, and it is claimed that the individual scientist is motivated in making his discoveries by the economic pressures exerted by industry. For instance, it is maintained that Kelvin was driven to formulate the laws of thermodynamics by the insistence of industry for a better steam engine, and it is claimed that Boyle was inspired to discover the laws of gases in order to predict the behavior of cannon. This might be of only academic concern were it not that the conclusion is drawn that science is indissolubly tied up with the society in which it finds itself, with the consequences that science owes this society certain duties and society has certain rights with respect to science.

Before we can decide whether science is the creature of economic pressures, we would like to be able to answer such questions, for instance, as: "Is it true as a matter of fact that the motive that stimulated Boyle to a study of the laws of gases was the desire to understand better and to improve the operation of cannon?" We regard it as beside the point to be shown that it *might* have been his motive. But unfortunately the phraseology of our question presupposes a structure of the world which is contrary to fact, and the question slithers toward the meaningless. For no detail of the past can be fully reconstructed, and I suspect motives least of all. It is difficult enough to discover the motives of our contemporaries, with whom we have the advantage of being able to put direct questions or to observe facial expressions. If my neighbor sets himself wilfully to conceal his true motives from me it is so difficult for me to devise a method for discovering them that the very concept "true motives of my neighbor" is almost meaningless. With respect to the past we are immeasurably worse off, for we are reduced to the haphazard procedure of finding some written record, either the man's own writings or something someone else may have said about him. This written record usually does not exist, and the historian is driven to reconstruct a plausible set of motives. And unless the historian is of the highest integrity he is only too likely to reconstruct motives so as to support his own preconceptions.

It seems to me that the only possible method of dealing with this situation must be built around our recognition that the past is of necessity an aspect of the present. If we find that in the present the motives of scientists are not exclusively economic and utilitarian, then, in the absence of any drastic change in the characteristics of our culture or of the individuals who compose it as we recede into the past, I think the only position we can take is that in the past the motives of scientists were pretty much as they are today. What do scientists now active say about the motives which make them go? The question is very closely related to the question as to whether there is a valid distinction between pure and applied science. This question has been much discussed lately; there are many who maintain that there is no valid distinction, and it must be admitted that it is easy to set up examples in which the distinction is difficult to draw. But the fact that there are nebulous borderline cases is not unique to this situation, for no verbal distinction is ever sharp. Furthermore, I do not believe that this consideration is important, for I believe that inquiry will show that in practice there is a distinction easily enough recognized to make it profitable to maintain it. What we need to find out here is comparatively simple. Is it true that at least some scientists are primarily motivated by scientific curiosity and the desire for understanding when they tackle a scientific problem, and are not particularly concerned with any further use, utilitarian or not, which they or anyone else may make of the understanding when acquired? It is not pertinent to find that there are many scientists, particularly those employed in industry, who find it difficult to answer this question or to tell what is their most impelling motive. If there are some scientists who are sure that their most impelling motive is the acquiring of understanding, then those scientists, when acting in response to this motive, are engaged in what I call pure science. I believe it to be merely a matter of observation that there are such men (I am sure that I am one of them), and that therefore pure science corresponds to something real, and that the economic motive is not always uppermost or even visible.

The application to our present question is immediate. If there were pure scientists in the past as well as in the present, as we must assume in the absence of any drastic change in human nature, then present day science has not been exclusively fashioned by economic or social pressures. My reasons for thinking that this aspect of science is important would take us beyond the range of our present topic. In any event it behooves society to recognize this aspect of science in any control measures which it may seek to impose.

One generally accepted virtue of the historical method in teaching science is that the logical connection of the different developments becomes easier to see, the implication being that in the historical developments the steps have been taken in the logical order. In any particular case this may as a matter of fact be true, but there is no necessity for it, because there are plenty of cases where progress has been made in an illogical order. The various steps in the development of science do not necessarily form a linear sequence, each step following logically from the preceding after the fashion of the sequence of theorems in Euclid's geometry. This being the case it is necessary to determine by some ulterior criterion whether the course of historical development has as a matter of fact been logical in any special case. In many cases it will prove there is no unique logical course, or even indeed no logical course at all. In any event, knowledge of the historical course is not necessary to find what the logical course is, so that if the primary interest is to determine the logical sequence, historical considerations might as well be discarded from the beginning. As far as logical development goes, historical knowledge can at most play little more than the role of a mnemonic device, to make easier the logical reconstruction.

Instead of using the historical approach to show the logical order of scientific ideas, I think the impartial historian will be compelled to invert the process by showing how seldom the course of scientific development has been the logical course. Logic is, after all, a human enterprise, and to assume that it has controlled the development of science is to assume a dominance of the human will in its reactions to the external world which is not usually justified by the event. Much more often the course of development is determined by factors which are quite adventitious as far as any connection goes with immediate human purpose. For example, anyone who has worked in the laboratory knows how greatly what he may do is circumscribed by the instruments at his command. In the solution of his problems the scientist is always pushing against the limitations of instrumental technique, and often is estopped from doing what he would like because the requisite instrument does not exist. Sometimes he is able to devise a special instrument which will serve, but more often the development of the suitable instrument, when it does come, proves to have involved fields of science so remote from that in which the problem arose that a superhuman ability would have been demanded to foresee the way in which the instrument could have been constructed. Many instruments are developed, not in response to the explicit need for them, but as an incidental result of an entirely unrelated development. The inverse method of progress is common in science, that is, the method of first finding the answer, and then finding what the problem is to which it is the answer. A recent and dramatic example is the enormous surge forward in all sorts of instrumentation which has followed the development of the vacuum tube, which in turn was made possible by a clearer understanding of the nature of electrons. Many times in the past the problem of, for example, amplifying small mechanical vibrations had presented itself. It would have required superhuman foresight in the day before electrons were known to see that the answer to the problem would be found in the realm of electrical phenomenon, and that the most rewarding line of attack on the problem would have been to drop entirely, for the time being, concern with mechanics at all, and to turn instead to a miscellaneous investigation of electricity.

The insight that the progress of science is often illogical is perhaps more important to the scientist himself than to the layman, and constitutes one of the reasons why the scientist is concerned with his history. This suggests that perhaps one of the most important fields of service of history of science is to the scientist. He has always been concerned to a certain extent with history, because scientific ethics and tradition demand that he know the literature of any particular research in which he is engaged and that he give due credit to his predecessors. Whatever concern the scientist has already had with history must often have disclosed to him the illogical progress of science in the errors of the past and the retraced steps. What perhaps the scientist does not see so readily is that this implies the existence of mistaken points of view in the science of the present and the necessity of presently retracing steps from positions now regarded as secure. A history of science properly written could make us see which of our present positions are weakly held, perhaps because our supporting positions had been inadequately consolidated, but this demands a critical capacity and technical competence on the part of the historian which is seldom found. As an example of what I have in mind I cite O'Rahilly's book on Electromagnetics. In spite of many and obvious defects, I regard it as a remarkable achievement in painting a picture showing how the flood of factual discoveries hurried the physicist into adopting theoretical points of view before their necessity or inevitability was established.

The adventitious as distinguished from the logical element in the development of science appears not only in the exigencies of instrumentation, but also in the occasion which calls the attention of the scientist to an unsolved problem. This may be an accident of his daily life, a journey or a chance remark by a fellow-scientist, or the insistence of his wife that he do something for the baby, or some social or economic need, or even nothing more than a good night's sleep. That these factors play a role is obvious enough to the creative scientist as he contemplates his own present activity. They are not so obvious to his nonscientific fellow. Neither are they so obvious from a study of the historical record, because a detail in the keeping of the record is demanded which is seldom found and which to most persons would appear irrelevant and which would certainly be boring. Here then is one of the weak spots in the use of the historical method, which can be avoided only by self-conscious effort and then only under special and favorable circumstances.

When it comes to the processes by which the solutions of problems are actually obtained, the adventitious element becomes so strong that even the creative scientist himself is usually at a loss to know by just what process he arrived at a solution. The process is to a high degree personal, and every scientist must by trial and error find the method which has most probability of success for him. Even after he has found it, it is not certain to what extent his formulation has predictive value for the solution of the next problem, instead of being merely a description of common features in past situations. Scientists have in the past been interested in their own psychology sufficiently to sometimes attempt a formulation of the conditions under which they are most likely to find the solutions of their scientific problems, and the communication of these formulations may well be one of the important functions of the historical approach. Unless the actual formulation is extant, however, I think this is one of the most dangerous of all situations in which to attempt a reconstruction in the light of inherent probability.

The point of view which sees a close connection between a logical development and the actual historical course is a specialized form of one ideal for the writing of history which is not uncommon. This is to present the chain of historical events as a causal sequence, in which every event followed inevitably from the events which preceded it. This point of view derives great satisfaction from talking about the "laws" of history. It involves an ideal which I believe is fantastically impossible of attainment and which furthermore is fallacious, even if we neglect the necessary blurring of detail in the events of the past and the implications of the Heisenberg principle. For consider what the historian must do in order to realize his purpose. Suppose he has stationed himself at some given epoch in history and is endeavoring to show that what followed that epoch was a necessary consequence of the events which had preceded it. In proving the inevitability of subsequent events the historian must, of course, not beg the question by using his knowledge of what these subsequent events were. This makes the problem of the historian the same as the problem of any of us at the present moment who tries to predict the future. I think none of us has the hardihood to claim success in prediction, and the historian may profit by our example.

There are other reasons why the scientist often has a particular interest in history of science. There is a large personal element here. He feels a personal kinship with anyone working on the same problems and has an intrinsic interest in anything that he does. In particular he wants to know how his fellow in the past went to work to solve his problems. To a certain degree this is because he thinks that in this way he may get some light on how to solve his own present problems. Partly, however, it is for the pure intellectual stimulus that comes from trying to invent a way in which he himself might have set about to solve the problem, and then comparing it with the way which his fellow actually adopted. But this demands a detailed knowledge of the intellectual processes of the scientist in the past which we have seen is most difficult of all to obtain. This would suggest that the historian of science most effective for this purpose is himself a creative scientist.

I would now like to make some remarks that apply to the study of history in general as well as to the history of science. It seems to me that there is a very real danger in a too assiduous devotion to the historical point of view, and that attention to a mass of detail may obscure more vital matters. There are a few essential points of view that are easily imparted by the historical method, such as that science is a human activity and therefore an activity of individuals; that science flourishes only when the conditions allow the individual scientist to find his most effective conditions for productivity; that the actual development of science has seldom followed the logical order and that many errors have been made and many steps had to be retraced; that the accidental plays an important role and that the course of scientific development is unpredictable. All these essential insights can be given by the historical method, but a few well chosen examples will suffice and detail does not need to be elaborated. But a more important vision is not so easy to impart by the historical method, namely that the potentialities for future progress are infinitely great compared with our progress to date and that the methods by which these potentialities will be realized may well be so revolutionary that too great a familiarity with our present methods may be a handicap. The historical method does not easily lend itself to a realization of limitations arising from universal characteristics of the human race, which have always been determinative in all past history, and which must be transcended if our potentialities are to be realized. It seems to me more important to know where we are than to know how we got here, and more important to know where we might go if we properly direct our steps than to know where we will go if we continue in our present path. The historical method must be used with discretion if these more important objectives are to be reached.

The upshot of all this scepticism and criticism is my conviction that the most profitable sort of history of science, at least for the scientist himself and perhaps for others, is contemporary history. This implies that the historian can make his most important contribution by seeing to it that the significant features of current progress are recorded during the lifetime of the actual participants before the essential personal elements are lost. This will involve not only scanning contemporary literature, both the ephemeral literature in the newspapers and the more permanent literature in the professional journals, but intimate personal contact with the scientists themselves, attendance at scientific meetings and prodding of the individual scientists by correspondence or personal interview to disclose the more personal aspects which a false scientific modesty often inclines him to believe are irrelevant. This is going to demand a high degree of technical competence on the part of the historian himself, the acquiring of which will put serious demands on his abilities and demand long preparation. For this reason it seems to me that perhaps it will prove that the historians of science best able to serve this purpose will be scientists themselves who in their later years and out of the fullness of their experience are moved, because of an intrinsic interest, to set down their reminiscences. I believe, further, that an informed and intelligent recording of contemporary scientific history will be of value not only for the scientist himself, but will also have cultural and educational value for the layman.

18

THE STRUGGLE FOR INTELLECTUAL INTEGRITY*

I

THE AUGUST 1933 NUMBER of *Harper's Magazine* contains two important articles dealing with current social changes: one by James Truslow Adams on the Crisis in Morals, and one by T. L. Harris on the changing attitude of the younger generation, particularly that in the colleges, toward religion. Both of these are matters of large social import, and correct thinking about them is essential. Both articles left me profoundly dissatisfied, and with the feeling that both authors had missed a vital and fundamental feature, peculiarly characteristic of our evolving culture, common to both situations. Let us first discuss the changing attitude toward religion, where the nature of the situation is a little plainer than with regard to morals.

The decay among the younger generation in the colleges of the hold hitherto exercised by the conventional forms of Protestant faith is recognized by Mr. Harris to be a complex phenomenon; but apparently in his mind the situation is to be mainly

*From Harper's Magazine, Dec. 1933.

understood in terms of the forces which have already been active in the past. In the tendency of some of the younger men to revert to the forms of Catholicism Mr. Harris sees only another swing of the pendulum marking off another of the never-ending repetitions of past history.

But there is another element in the situation which Mr. Harris as well as many other writers has failed to appreciate at its true value. It is surprising with what complete unanimity all inquirers with professional religious training have failed to put their finger on what must seem to be the gist of the situation to many who have gone through the actual experience of losing the religion with which they were brought up. The hold of religion on such persons has failed because they have come to feel that many of the teachings of the conventional religion of their childhood or even of the present time simply are not "true", to express it very crudely. Of course this description is patently applicable to the religion of fifty years ago, which was entangled with a false cosmology. This mistake was obvious enough, and no modern apologist for religion would admit for a minute any necessary connection between religion and opinions about demonstrable historical fact; but much the same sort of thing remains, although in a somewhat subtler form. Thus, both the Protestant and Catholic churches take a definite attitude on many social questions, such as marriage and divorce, birth control, prohibition, war and peace, and education, and often justify their attitudes by special pleading not untinged by a certain amount of sheer rationalizing. These social questions are doubtless of enormous and hitherto baffling complexity, but it can hardly be doubted that they will eventually succumb to rational attack, and that a rationally satisfying answer is some day possible. There is no reason to think that the answer which religion now claims to find to these questions by mystical means will eventually prove any more correct than the answer which it has already found by mystical means to the question of what happened in the year 4004 B.C. The result is that acceptance of any of the traditional or conventional religions seems to many incompatible with plain decent intellectual honesty.

It is not pertinent to say that this view of the nature of religion is superficial, and that it is possible to analyze out of that complex welter of emotions, urges, and sensations which has conventionally become associated with religion a pure residuum, non-rational, dealing with the emotions and aspirations of man, which is the essence of religion. Irrespective of whether such an analysis has yet been made or is possible, the fact is that many individuals in the community feel that acceptance of a conventional religious faith or participation in any of the recognized religious forms could not be for them reconcilable with intellectual honesty. That this is not an unfair description of the actual situation in the community, I think anyone may verify by inquiry among his friends. This, I believe not to be properly appreciated by Mr. Harris or by any other inquirer with professional theological training who has sought to explain the recent decay of formal religion.

Furthermore, the question, which is at least debatable, of whether the feeling is justified that a religious life, conventional or possibly even unconventional, is incompatible with intellectual honesty, is of comparative unimportance; the important matter is the mere existence in the community of a demand for intellectual integrity widespread enough to modify, perhaps decisively, an important social institution. The growth of this demand to a magnitude great enough to be socially significant I believe to be a recent development, which distinguishes this era from any that has preceded it, which constitutes something novel in the present situation, and which contains the implication that this may not be just another swing of the pendulum, but that we may be on the point of breaking through into new ground.

II

The reasons for the appearance in the community of the motive of intellectual honesty are doubtless complex. In the first place a certain amount of intellectual power is necessary; animals and morons are incapable of intellectual honesty, and doubtless an appreciable proportion of our own modern community is incapable of the self-conscious practice of intellectual honesty on the highest level. In fact, I believe that no individual can ever attain to what he feels to be his own potentialities in this respect. Not only is intellectual power necessary, but example and practice are also necessary and powerful aids; it is not always easy to see all the implications, to detect all the inconsistencies in a mental attitude, or to realize where rationalizing has crept into an argument. Furthermore, the opportunity for the practice of intellectual honesty demands that the community as a whole be so far from the struggle for bare subsistence that an appreciable fraction of its people may be primarily engaged in intellectual pursuits. Society has only recently reached such a condition on any considerable scale. In such a modern society the activity which *par excellence* demands and exemplifies intellectual honesty is the scientific, and I believe that the most potent immediate cause for the increase of intellectual honesty in the community is the recent growing prevalence of scientific disciplines in education, the popular dissemination of the results of scientific inquiry, and the presence in the community of a body of men actually engaged in scientific work. This is not to deny that intellectual workers in fields other than the scientific need or possess the quality of intellectual honesty; but in scientific activity the necessity for continual checking against the inexorable facts of experience is so insistent, and the penalties for allowing the slightest element of rationalizing to creep in are so immediate, that it is obvious to the dullest that a high degree of intellectual honesty is the price of even a mediocre degree of success.

Once the scientific worker has started living the life of intellectual honesty, perhaps in no other spirit than as the condition of success in a field which has aroused his interest, he finds growing within him the realization that he is in possession of something much more than merely a tool by which he may get right answers. The ideal of intellectual honesty comes to make a strong emotional appeal; he finds something fine in the selflessness involved in rigorously carrying through a train of thought careless of the personal implications; he feels a traitor to something deep within him if he refuses to follow out logical implications because he sees that they are going to be unpleasant; and he exults that he belongs to a race which is capable of such emotions. Intellectual honesty appears to such a worker as the last flowering of the genius of humanity, the culmination of a long cultural history, and the one thing that differentiates man most notably from his biological companions. The discovery that the human animal is so constituted that it responds emotionally to the practice of intellectual honesty is just as great a discovery as that other great discovery of the human race about itself, that it responds emotionally to music.

It would be ludicrous to maintain that life on such heights as these has suddenly become common in these last years or that in certain sections of the community intellectual honesty is not apparently decreasing. In fact, it could not be maintained that more than a small fraction have really caught the vision; but it does seem to me that enough have caught it to be appreciably effective, and that a new leaven is working in society. The feeling is certainly becoming common that man would be a traitor to himself if he refused to follow his mind wherever it leads him. To convince oneself of this consider the suggestion often made—that since much of our recent economic trouble is doubtless to be ascribed to the fact that invention and scientific discovery have come too rapidly to be assimilated, we should suspend scientific inquiry until human institutions have caught up. Although this suggestion may be seriously entertained by some, I believe that general inquiry will disclose that for the most part such a suggestion is instinctively repudiated as impossible; we feel that we cannot accept the imposition of limitations to mental inquiry; that we must carry on no matter where it leads.

What now will be the effect of suddenly letting loose in a civilization such as ours an appreciable amount of intellectual honesty? One cannot answer this question without first appreciating what an utterly inchoate mess our society is, judged by any rational standards. Social institutions have a history as long as that of mankind itself and have evolved with it. They contain the reminiscences of the great episodes through which the human race, or parts of it, has passed. They have been subject to no conscious or rational control; one can be sure only that an existing social custom is not so bad that the possessor of it has already been eliminated in the struggle for existence. One aspect of human evolution is the growth of the capability for rational thought and action, and one aspect of this growth in turn has been the demand for some explanation in rationalistic terms of the phenomena which human beings see about them, including the phenomena of man himself. A dog is content to turn around three times before lying down; but a man would have to invent an explanation of it. These explanations are often fantastic and rationalistic in the highest degree. There is not a single human social institution which has not originated in hit or miss fashion, but, nevertheless, every one of these institutions is justified by some rationalizing argument as the best possible, and. what is worse, the community demands the acceptance of these arguments as a precondition of happy social life.

III

What will the man do in whom has been suddenly born an appreciation and capacity for intellectual honesty, with its disregard of ulterior consequences, when confronted with our social institutions and the demand to accept them and to live with them? The first and inevitable reaction will obviously be a complete repudiation in his own mind of the bunk that he is asked to accept. So much he must do, though it slay him. But he must also continue to live in society as he finds it, and he must try to work out for himself some code of conduct which he can pursue without intellectual stultification. He finds the problem difficult; he does not even feel certain that the problem of how a rational being may live rationally in surroundings which are often willfully irrational has any solution. His doubts and uncertainties are reflected in his relations with others. In bringing up his children he finds himself incapable of forcing upon them the positive sanctions for conduct which psychologically are so necessary in the young, and because he knows of no other substitute, can offer them only the negative substitute of example and precept in intellectual integrity. If he is a novelist or a playwright, who has filled an important part in maintaining the moral consciousness and tone of the community, he finds that conviction has gone from him, and he falls back on the practice of his art for its own sake. If he is an editor, the political institutions of his time no longer appear as divinely ordained, and his editorials degenerate to destructive criticism. The mass of the people who are not fortunate enough to have time to spare from earning their livelihood for much intellectual activity, or to whom by temperament and capacity the ideals of intellectual honesty do not appeal, and who have, therefore, been accustomed to accept without question their codes of conduct from other members of the community, are left without the authoritative guidance to which they have become accustomed, and the aggressive, unthinking element in the community becomes ascendant. From the point of view of an external observer the whole community is drifting and floundering morally.

I believe that in a setting of social institutions like ours it is inevitable that we should pass through an epoch like this, and I believe that we are in such an epoch now. This it seems to me is the most lastingly significant factor in the explanation of the crisis in morals of which James Truslow Adams writes. The decay of morals according to my point of view is only superficial and apparent. It may be quite true that the actual number of disinterested deeds performed in the community, which may be taken as a rough measure of its degree of moral elevation, may be declining, while at the same time those fundamental characteristics of the human race which in the proper setting make disinterested actions possible, and which measure potential morality, may be growing in strength. In fact, in a community and under conditions like ours, a decline in apparent morality would be the necessary prerequisite to a general advance. Whether as a matter of actual fact this is the correct explanation of the phenomenon which Adams deplores would be almost impossible to decide certainly, as is every other question dealing with the actual motives back of large-scale social conduct; but it must be an important element in the situation, and for the present at least I see no reason why one should despair of humanity on this account.

It thus appears fairly evident that the incidence

upon the human race of a passion for the practice of intellectual honesty must at first be entirely negative and destructive in its social results. To go farther, it is not self-evident that a race of individuals who so order their lives as to bear thoroughgoing rational scrutiny would necessarily be capable of ultimately surviving as a race. A simple example will disclose the possibilities. Death, from the point of view of any individual free from mysticism, can be no calamity; for death itself is not experienced, but it is only the preliminaries of death which are experienced and to be dreaded. If I should be completely annihilated in the next minute with no preliminary warning, it would be a matter of complete indifference to me. Suppose now that some improved method of suicide were invented by which the cessation of life could be made instantaneous and with no perceptible physical preliminaries. A completely rational conduct of one's affairs would then demand that if ever one found oneself in such a situation that the probable future held more pain than pleasure, one should immediately find the way out by suicide. There are few people indeed who at one time or another do not encounter such moments, so that in a society constituted like this all those capable of rational action might automatically be eliminated, and society would drop back again to its old irrational, unthinking level, to work back slowly again to the capabilities of rational action and then to drop back abruptly again. The only thing that would save the thinking elements in the community in such conditions is the non-rational factors in each individual which determine whether a given future, including in the future the preparations for the act of suicide, is contemplated with pleasure or pain. Whether the non-rational elements making for the preservation of the rational individual would at first prove strong enough must be decided by the event; it is probable, however, that a rational individual would eventually be bred up with the suitable combination of non-rational elements.

Even if the rational individual is not singled out for such drastic special attack as in our imaginary example, it seems to me, nevertheless, that the period of instability inseparable in a society constituted like ours from the first incidence of a widespread capacity for intellectually honest action is a period of particular danger to just that part of the community which has attained the capability for honest action, and that it is not at all inconceivable that just this part should be eliminated, leaving society to repeat, like Sisyphus, the old climb up the heights of intellectual achievement. The essential tragedy of Germany at the present moment is that it is eliminating this class of the community, proving traitor to the crowning capabilities of humanity, and dropping back to former levels. The human race as a whole cannot win through this period of instability and come out on the far side with permanent advance except by the self-conscious exercise of the utmost intelligence of which it is capable. Few, I think, would question that under the proper conditions the human intellect is capable of designing a rational society capable of self-preservation; but whether in the present setting the human intellect is powerful enough to grapple with the enormous complexities of the situation is not self-evident. At any rate, there is obviously no possible course for us except to carry on.

IV

In our impatience it may seem as though nothing constructive were happening to carry us beyond the purely destructive first stages. I believe, however, that such a pessimistic attitude overlooks the enormous complication of the problem, and underestimates the tremendous amount of preliminary work that must be done. It does seem to me that it is already possible to descry the beginnings of the next advance. Such an advance must be based on a preliminary analysis and an adequate awareness of the nature of the problem and the situation; I believe that the materials for this better understanding of the nature of the problem are already in our hands and are beginning to be used.

The nature of the very complex social problem has certain very close similarities to the problem presented by recent developments in physics, and becomes more understandable in terms of a realization of just what it is that has happened in physics. Physics has in the first place gone through a period of enormous extension of its store of experimental knowledge; it then discovered that its traditional concepts were not capable of dealing with the new situations, and that such apparently fundamental forms of thought as space, time, causality, and identity were not capable of application to the new phenomena. It then had to devise new ways of thinking about the situation, and in doing this it has had to examine to a certain extent into the nature of human thinking itself. It has come to see that thinking is merely a form of human activity, performed with the brain, subject to the limitations of its evolution and its organ of production, and with no assurance whatever that an intellectual process has validity outside the range in which its validity has already been checked by experience. The parallelism between this course of development in physics and recent social developments is obvious. We have in the first place rapidly changing conditions and new social experiences to correspond to the new observational material of physics. The most completely new of these is perhaps the situation presented by the extraordinarily rapid development of labor-saving machinery; it is now possible to produce enough for the needs of every one in the United States with only four hours' (let us say) labor per day on the part of everyone. But the ability of man to work eight hours without hardship has not been diminished, and the tendency of every employer to expect his individual employees to give him the eight hours which they can without hardship is not altered, nor the desire of every employer to push his own production to capacity. The result is an *impasse* which can be broken only by purposeful external control, and to which the traditional social ideas are not applicable, in the same way that the traditional concepts of physics were not applicable to its new experimental situations. And just round the corner there is the obvious possibility of a few simple biological discoveries which will be even more devastatingly revolutionary. We are coming to see as a matter of course that social ideals evolved in old situations should not be expected to be applicable to such entirely novel conditions.

Besides the absolutely new situation, presented by the development of labor-saving devices, so many things have been happening in the last few years that each individual has in his own experience a wealth and variety of observational material absolutely without precedent in the experience of any single individual in past history. Consider what has happened in the last twenty years; the World War with the unwilling entry into it at last of the United States, the peace and the failure of Wilsonian idealism, the League of Nations, the economic aftermath of the War, boom, depression, the return of economic nationalism, Mussolini, Russia, Germany and Hitler, Japan and Manchuria, Gandhi in India, the loosening of the British Empire, world congresses for peace and economics, woman suffrage, the rise and fall of prohibition, and the voluntary economic revolution in the United States. The observation of all this cannot help being most educational in showing how society actually functions in various situations, and it must have as important an effect on social thinking as the discovery of new physical phenomena has had on the thinking of physicists.

One most important conviction, gradually spreading, which results from all this new observational material, is that planned and managed societies are possible, that man may to a certain extent control his own future. If present attempts fail it will be for reasons which can be determined and probably avoided, and we may hope for better success on the next attempt.

There is another result of all this new social experience which seems to me most important in determining the eventual attitude of man toward his own social institutions, but which has not been much emphasized because it is not of great immediate importance. This is the growing appreciation of the realistic nature of social conventions and institutions as opposed to the traditional idealistic point of view, which is perhaps best exemplified in the disappearing notions of abstract justice and abstract rights, and of the nature of law, with which legal practice and theory are still encumbered. Here again the parallelism with the developments in physics is most illuminating. Probably the greatest contribution made by Einstein in his theory of relativity was his insistence on the realistic nature of the concepts of physics; the true significance of a physical concept is not to be found in what we say about it or even in what we think about it, but rather in what we do with it.

Making the social application, there is evidently something the matter with current idealistic philosophies of the nature of law, for example, when so many of the respectable members of the community have simply ignored the prohibition law. How will history describe these people—as malicious law breakers, traitors to society, or as heroes, who by remaining true to their inner lights have compelled a return to realities? Must I wait for the verdict of history before it can be determined whether my present social action is right or wrong? There is also something illuminating in the way in which theories of the nature and the proper function of the Constitution of the United States were brushed aside by many people in their efforts to get an amendment into the Constitution restricting child labor. It was felt that the matter was of extreme importance and that it should be put into the Constitution because there seemed to be no other feasible way of bringing it to pass, although fortunately another way has now been found. The point is that people asked: "What difference does it make whether this is theoretically a proper subject for constitutional amendment or not? If the Constitution is once amended in this way then in fact it becomes the sort of thing that can be thus amended, all idealistic theories of its nature to the contrary notwithstanding". Such realistic thinking obviously has its great dangers—it is the sort of thinking that every hold-up man uses—but intellectual honesty seems to demand it. It is evident that with regard to these questions we are still in the preliminary destructive stage, where the mutual inconsistencies of different lines of social thought stare us in the face, and that we have not yet found how to synthesize the antagonistic elements. The situation is exactly parallel to that in physics, which for a number of years after the discovery of the disconcerting new phenomena was in a phase, to quote Sir William Bragg, where it had to use the corpuscular theory on Mondays, Wednesdays, and Fridays, and the wave theory on Tuesdays, Thursdays, and Saturdays.

Physics is now making its synthesis, and we may hope that society will eventually be as successful. But the social problem is infinitely more complex than the physical problem, and infinitely more dangerous because of the necessary period of instability which must precede the initiation of the new regime. There is need for the most strenuous efforts and the greatest haste. It is easy to see that in spite of the greatest haste of which we are capable, this revolution cannot be completed in the lifetime of any of us, but must involve the training of the coming generations. It would be impossible here to attempt to go into details of the various methods by which such a preparation of our children may be accomplished. Probably everyone connected with any important institution will think of ways in which his institution may be instrumental. I myself am associated with university life, and it is easy for me to envisage here a field of new usefulness in the community for the university. Its function may be twofold. In the first place it can enhance the general apreciation of the human worth of a rationally ordered life, controlled emotionally by the passion for intellectual honesty, by increasing the numbers of its graduates who live such a life in the community. In the second place, by creating and developing new lines of inquiry, it may provide the material, at present non-existent, which the individual will find more and more necessary in the pursuit of such a life. No one who has not thought about it can realize how pathetically deficient we are at present in even the preliminary data which are necessary before a start can be made in living a rationally ordered life. The development of new philosophies, new psychologies, and new biologies is necessary.

For the present we may allow ourselves to take a certain amount of comfort in the belief that the human race has in it the possibilities of creating for itself a rationally satisfying life. Real discouragement need not be faced unless it should prove, after full self-consciousness of the situation has been awakened and time has been allowed for the terribly complex adjustments, that we are incapable of creating the opportunities that we need.

19

SOCIETY AND THE INTELLIGENT PHYSICIST*

A PHYSICIST CANNOT spend his life in the laboratory constantly striving to get the right answer, checking every idea against the inexorable requirement that it shall work, without something happening to his general outlook. Some of the points of view that he thus acquires react on his social impulses and behavior and on his understanding of what social conduct involves. We shall consider some of these here.

I think that the physicist comes to appreciate more vividly than anything else that the game of getting the right answer is a hard game, and that if he is going to be successful he must exert to the utmost all the intelligence he possesses. The only thing in his control by which he may command the situations which confront him is his intelligence, and even this is often enough not sufficient. When he is not successful he knows the reason is that he has not been intelligent enough, and he strives to realize his potentialities for greater intelligence.

*From The American Physics Teacher, 7, 109, 1939. Given at the eighth annual meeting of the American Association of Physics Teachers, in Washington, December 1938.

Furthermore, he comes to appreciate that the *utmost* exercise of intelligence means the *free* use of intelligence; he must be willing to follow *any* lead that he can see, undeterred by any inhibition, whether it arises from laziness or other unfortunate personal characteristics, or intellectual tradition or the social conventions of his epoch. In fact, intelligence and *free* intelligence come to be synonymous to him. It becomes inconceivable that anyone should consent to conduct his thinking under demonstrable restrictions, once these restrictions had been recognized, any more than as an experimenter he would consent to use only a restricted experimental technic. He finds often enough, as his experience grows, that as a matter of fact he has been operating under hampering restrictions, of which he had not been previously conscious. He also finds, if he wants to be confident of the foundations on which he builds intelligent action, that these foundations must have passed his own scrutiny. He honors no statement or procedure that does not offer at least the possibility of being checked by himself, and when he accepts authority, as he often must, it is merely in the spirit of saving himself time. He finds it difficult to avoid ascribing to results thus accepted on authority a somewhat smaller degree of probability than he does to results checked by himself.

The physicist presently becomes aware that merely good intentions or trying as hard as he can are not adequate to secure intelligent action, but that there is a technic of being intelligent which itself can be acquired only by the exercise of intelligence. The realization that there is a technic of being intelligent and that this technic can be acquired only by seriously taking thought unto oneself has been slowly dawning on the physicist since perhaps the beginning of the century. As everyone knows, the dawning of this realization has been accelerated by the discovery of many unsuspected phenomena in the realm of very small things that could not be fitted into the edifice of knowledge without important modifications in ways of looking at things which hitherto had proved good enough.

The physicist has thus come to be conscious of the existence of his intellectual tools, and has discovered that these tools have properties which he had not suspected. He observes that his own intellectual tools were acquired in school mostly by imitating the use of these tools by other people. He saw that these tools were used in certain kinds of situations in order to achieve certain purposes. He observed the success of others in using the tools to attain their purpose, and he presently verified by experience that he too could use the tools with success in similar situations. There thus arose a feeling of what his tools were good for, which was a compound of the opinion of others and the opinion of himself derived from successful use; but there was no serious attempt at analysis as to whether these assumptions were really valid, or what might be their range of validity if their validity was not universal. But presently, after much experience, analysis of what he did in using his tools disclosed that often his tacit assumptions as to their validity were not quite right. He came to see, for instance, that the complete sharpness and certainty which tradition ascribes to the conclusions of mathematics and logic were ultimately illusory. He found that he could always carry his analysis back to the point where certainty vanishes, for the reason that he always has to assure himself that he is correctly performing his own mental operations, if for no other reason. The need for continually checking his own procedures is perhaps something carried over from the laboratory by the physicist, and appears not to be felt so vividly by the mathematician or the logician. Mental processes not being absolutely sharp, it follows that our mental success can be only an approximate success, just as any measurement or adaptation of the laboratory is approximate. Partly, but not entirely, because of this lack of sharpness, it comes about that we often try to give meanings that cannot be given and to do things that cannot be done. We invent all sorts of absolutes and abstract existences, and find that we are mistaken about what we can do with them. The physicist discovers that he is a welter of urges which have only a historical or perhaps physiological significance, and he feels under no compulsion to honor them in his endeavor to get the right answer. For example, we discover that there are unsuspected infelicities in the way we have to deal with time. It was a shock to most physicists, and other people too, to discover that the time of experience does not have the property of absolute simultaneity that we had thought. Or we think it means something to talk about the "reality" of the past, and are helpless when we discover that there is no way of proving that the entire universe was not created five minutes ago. Or when it comes to a showdown, that is, application to concrete instances, we discover that we cannot mean by truth what we had thought we mean or what we want to mean. Or the idea of causality, which has been considered by many to be so fundamental that thinking could not be done without it, proves not to be applicable in the way we had thought in the realm of very small things now becoming accessible to experiment. Or there is a new and striking example: At temperatures close to absolute zero, liquid helium has readily measurable properties, such as fluidity, which at present can be treated only with that form of quantum theory which denies the property of individuality to the atoms. It is hard to think of anything more paradoxical than a particle to which the idea of individuality does not apply.

Out of all this experience one conclusion emerges perhaps more clearly than others; namely, there is no inherent presumption that ways of handling things or ways of thinking which have grown up to meet a certain range of experience and which have proved their validity within that range will continue to be valid when the range is extended. As a matter of fact, the range is continually being extended by the discovery of new experimental phenomena, made possible by the development of new experimental technics for controlling higher temperatures or higher voltages or higher vacuums, for example, or by greater precision of measurement. An example of this that even yet has not got itself completely assimilated into everyday thought is the new properties of matter moving with speeds which approach the speed of light. Because of all this the physicist has come to *expect* that he will have to change his way of thinking about things when his range is very much increased.

In analyzing what has happened when he has had to revise his concepts to meet new ranges of experience, he has been struck by the fact that different operations which gave the same result in the original range no longer give the same result when the range is extended. For example, the length of a moving streetcar is the same whether it is measured by taking an instantaneous photograph of it and properly measuring the photograph, or by boarding the car with a meter stick and measuring the length with the meter stick in quite the conventional way while it is in motion. But there is every reason to think that if the same two operations were performed on some object moving with a speed approaching that of light the results would be different. The physicist recognizes here an important characteristic of his thinking; namely, the impulse to simplify procedures by giving the same name ("length" in this example) to recognizably different operations when these different operations lead to the same result. But he also recognizes that there is concealed here a grave potential danger in assuming that the equivalence of these two operations will continue to hold when the range of experience is extended. One may describe the situation in language suggested by quantum theory: Our ordinary concepts are multiply degenerate in the range of ordinary experience, and this degeneracy is revealed by separation into different levels when the range of experience broadens.

With all this experience, merely hinted at above, it is natural that the physicist should presently begin to wonder what the applications are to his social relations. For one of the impulses that he has acquired from his physical experience is to treat things as a piece; and since the problem which confronts him in many social situations is at bottom no different from that which confronts him in the laboratory, namely, to get the right answer, he wonders whether some of the lessons of his physical experience will not carry over into the social domain. He is the more inclined to make this application because he has found that the sorts of consideration which are becoming necessary for his understanding of physics are edging over, more and more, in directions pointing toward the problems of everyday life. For example, in understanding quantum theory he has to analyze what he means by the act of observation, or whether it is possible, and what it means, to divide the universe into an observer and the observed—considerations that get much closer to what he has, perhaps, called "philosophy" than he had at one time supposed.

This attempt of the physicist to enter the field of social thinking is very modest and unpretentious, and does not involve the assumptions that people are sometimes inclined to suppose and that lead them to view this attempt with something approaching resentment. There is not involved here any thesis that the methods of quantitative measurement of physics are applicable to the "social sciences", nor is there any thesis that "science" is competent to decide between values. All that the physicist wants in his modest way is that his actions as a social being be intelligent. He has seen things go wrong so often when intelligence was not exerted, and his drive to intelligence acquired in his laboratory is so powerful, that he insists on the exercise of intelligence in his social activities as no less essential than any of the many other things without which social existence would not be tolerable.

The preliminary to the exercise of social intelligence is the same as the preliminary to every exercise of intelligence in the laboratory; namely, searching analysis to discover everything that can be seen in the situation, and then, after everything has been dragged out into the light of day with no reservations whatever, discussion of what course of action is best fitted to produce the desired result. The desired result may perhaps be dictated solely by considerations of value; these may not be argued, but can only be accepted by intelligence as one of the conditions of the problem set for it to solve.

It is something of a shock to the enthusiastic and unsophisticated physicist who thus rushes to the social attack to discover how very often the practices and demands of society are positively inimical to the exercise of intelligence. Most people do not like to think beyond a certain point; the primary demand is not for the most effective social action, but merely for one that is acceptable, and if conventions which secure sufficiently acceptable action are already in force, any attempt to make inquiries which might lead to modification of that action is likely to be received with impatience, to say the least. The individual, after sufficient experience, comes to see this and learns to suppress the impulse to follow certain lines of argument or inquiry which he sees will not be well received by his fellows. It does not take the child long to learn that he cannot say, when his Sunday School teacher calmly assumes that of course he will want to be good, "But you cannot *make* me want to be good", and he keeps his mouth shut. Everyone knows that harmonious living together requires the exercise of good will, and good will is often incompatible with following every argument to its logical conclusion. If any proof is needed of this it will be afforded presently by the way you will find yourselves reacting to various things that I shall say. Although the result of such exercise of good will is a society in which open friction has disappeared, nevertheless the method by which this desirable result is attained too often involves an element of intellectual surrender on the part of the individual which discourages future impulses toward intelligence in his social relations, and which, under proper conditions, may be fraught with sinister potentialities.

The physicist sees that not only are there unusually great opportunities for the suppression of intelligence in social thinking but that the need for intelligent thinking is even greater than in physics, because there is much greater chance that those requirements which he has found the technic of straight thinking demands will not be met. He sees this when he reflects on the way in which he acquired the concepts he uses in his own social thinking. These concepts, even more than those of physics, he usually acquired imitatively from his fellows while he was still too young to subject them to any critical analysis, and while he was still under the immediate necessity of finding some solution of the problem of the adaptations demanded by daily life. It was almost inevitable that he should merely assume that the ordinary social concepts could be used for the purposes for which he saw his fellows using them. But presently he comes to suspect that his fellows have never critically examined the concepts any more than he himself has but that they too acquired them when they were too young to reflect, and have been satisfied if they were decently effective in doing what was wanted of them. Although his fellows assume an unlimited validity for their social concepts, he becomes actively skeptical toward this assumption when he observes that other peoples with different backgrounds of tradition and different present purposes may not recognize the validity of these ideas at all, as the Japanese and the Germans apparently do not recognize the validity of moral ideas which an uncritical outlook insists are universal. He sees in all this an exemplification of what his physical experience has taught him; namely, ideas are to be suspected and reexamined when the domain of application is extended beyond that in which they arose. In one very important respect he recognizes that the present epoch differs from former epochs in that the enormous increase of invention, bringing peoples nearer together and increasing their command over forces more advantageous to man, effectively provides just that extension in the domain of application of social concepts which he is prepared to expect would demand fundamental revision.

He is struck by the fact that, on the social level, the handling of language requires much greater caution and conceals much greater dangers than on the level of physics. On the social level, language plays a deliberately dual role: it is not only a rational tool adapted to describe and analyze factual situations, but it is also used to affect and control the actions of people. There is no necessary connection between these two functions of language, particularly since most people are not by instinct notoriously rational and do not demand a rational appeal to be stirred to action. Hence in many cases the presumption is that if language is adapted to one role it will not be adapted to the other. The distinction between these two roles is, however, almost always overlooked; and the general feeling seems to be that all and any language, except such as is obviously and intentionally poetic or esthetic, must be applicable on the factual plane. Whence arise great confusions, supernaturalisms and mysticisms of various kinds. The number of cases proves to be distressingly great in which our verbalisms never get down to the factual plane at all, in spite of the fact that we want them to and think they do. So we have open verbal chains, the meaning of one verbalism being expressed in terms of another verbalism, with never emergence into something that we do or that happens to us. This cancerous tissue of open verbal chains infests much of our social thinking.

Social thinking particularly exploits the intellectual device of giving the same name to recognizably different things when these things are equivalent in the limited range of use which is of most importance to us. In this way a great simplification of thought is often accomplished; to bring about a simplification in this way may constitute an intellectual invention of the first rank. But there is also danger in this exercise of intellectual invention, as already suggested, because we are likely to be caught unaware when an extension of experience dissolves the equivalence of the different things which we had fused under a single name. The only defense is an analysis that recovers and emphasizes the complexities of the original situation, instead of discarding them.

The supreme social invention, I think, is to be found right here in a very broad type of situation in which we use a single name and ignore differences that are patent on consideration. Perhaps the earliest social lesson I learned was to say that my playmate was another person just like me, with feelings just like mine, which, therefore, were entitled to equal respect. What does it mean to say that the feelings of my fellow are the same as my own? How can I assure myself that his sensations in the presence of a hot object are the same as mine, and how can I be sure that a hot object does not feel to him as a cold object feels to me, and vice versa? Neither he nor I can find words to describe our feelings to the other which are of the slightest help. I can propose various tests, such as that he put up his right hand when he feels a hot object, and his left hand when he feels a cold one; but this avails only to show that he knows when he is in the presence of a hot object as distinguished from a cold one, and has no relevance to the question of what his feelings really are. After we have played with this situation long enough we come to see that we cannot possibly make our statement that his feeling of hot is the same as mine mean what we wanted it to. The statement is meaningless in the desired sense, and there is no way of getting the desired sense into it. My feeling of hot has a different meaning from my fellow's feeling of hot because what I do to decide whether I have the feeling of hot is different from what I do to decide whether my fellow has the feeling of hot. Anyone who reacts to this situation by saying that we cannot *prove* that his feeling of hot is the same as mine, but that all we can have is a greater or less degree of probability, has entirely missed the point. It does not make sense to think of his feeling and my feeling in terms such that this desired property of "sameness" is applicable. The only meaning which we can give to the statement that his feeling is the same as mine is that, in similar situations, his verbalizations and other reactions are the same as mine.

The social advantage of this invention of saying that my fellow has feelings exactly like mine are so obvious that it is hardly necessary to elaborate them. Because of it the actions of my fellows take on a certain measure of understandability and predictability. I can foresee what will please or displease them, and I can therefore influence their actions to a certain extent, so that I can plan my future with a certain amount of assurance; and, if I desire it, I can even attain to a certain degree of smooth cooperation with my fellows. This invention is the necessary background of the golden rule. Yet, in spite of the indispensability of the invention, I believe that its misuse is at the root of the most serious of our social difficulties and maladjustments. Its misuse consists in forgetting that it has a strictly limited field of applicability and of meaning. For it is evident enough that there is another side to all this.

REFLECTIONS OF A PHYSICIST

I am separated from my fellows by an impassable chasm, a chasm so impassable that even meanings cannot be the same on both sides of it, in spite of my passionate desire. My pain and your pain, my pleasure and your pleasure, my thoughts and your thoughts, my death and your death, are irreconcilably different and can be made to fuse only by ignoring the obvious. Yet most of the conventions of society and of language itself are erected on a purposeful disregard of the difference. In fact, so deeply is the assumption of the equivalence of me and thee woven into the texture of language that, if my fellow does not see the difference for himself, it is almost impossible to make him see it, as I have found by many vain attempts.

The reason that the consequences of disregarding the difference between me and thee are important is that I see, and I presume that you see also, that the difference between me and my fellows is the most outstanding feature in my whole landscape. Society, by ignoring it and suppressing, even forcibly, the impulse of the individual to say what he sees, thus comes to be founded on a falsehood to which the individual must adapt himself as well as he can. For the child knows and continues to know, although he soon finds that he had better not say it out loud, that no one can get inside him and make him want to be good. I know that my thoughts are my own and that there is no way by which you can discover what my thoughts really are: in fact, you cannot make my "real thoughts" even mean what you would like. I know that the most cogent argument of mathematics or logic, although it come to me with the authority of the world's greatest masters, is powerless to touch me until something clicks inside me. I know that the most high-minded moral motives leave me cold and uncooperative until I have accepted as my own the purposes back of the system of morals. I know that it is in my power to accept or reject any and every expectation and demand of society, and that furthermore, as a matter of fact, I do thus accept or reject many of the expectations of society. I know that often my immediate personal interests, and also my long range interests as far as I can see, are opposed to the interests of society. I know that often enough my purposes and ideals are not the same as those of my fellows, so that what seems good to me may not seem good to them. I know that any action of mine which is free and well considered—that is, intelligent—is dictated by what seems good to *me*, and if the action is one which is also to the advantage of society, it is because I have accepted the view of society. I can see these things and say these things, whether or not the things which seem good to me are socially good. I know that society can secure my *free* action only by making that action seem good to me, and that otherwise society can modify my action only by compelling me by the exercise or the threat of superior physical force. I know all these things are true of myself, and, in accordance with my social maxim that I can understand you in the light of my understanding of myself, my actions toward you must be guided by the conviction that you find them true for yourself also. Yet society does not recognize this in its appeal to me, but tries to get hold of me by absolutes and supernaturals and verbalisms.

When I analyze the method by which my fellows appeal to me to get me to act in a way that is socially acceptable, what do I find? Ideals of service and unselfishness are held up to me. Why should society expect that it can get hold of me by talking about the virtue of service and unselfishness if it should happen that the purposes and consequences of unselfish action do not seem good to me? It appears that the reason it is expected that I will respond to ideals of service and unselfishness is not that such ideals are harmonious with my nature and therefore good to me, but that it is my "duty" to accept such ideals. This "duty" is conceived as something eternal in the nature of things, completely external to my own poor self, in virtue of which I am under a compulsion to act as I "ought". It has been remarked before this by more than one cynical observer that it is a rather surprising coincidence, to say the least, that in so many cases what is thus specified to be my duty turns out to be for the ordinary material advantage of the average member of society, or of that class of society which has the power. The intelligent but unsocial individual sees the irrationality of all this, and the intensity of his scorn of society is doubled because society appears to him not only dishonest but stupid. Why should society be so calm in its assumption that I am like the average of my fellows, or that what is good for it will also seem good to me? Even if my fellows are all honest in contending that what seems good to them is also good for society, society cannot get inside me to know what really seems good to me; even if I say what seems good to me, they cannot be sure that I am not lying for fear of social pressure. I think my fellows would not so easily say that I am like the average of all of them if it were not for our fundamental invention of saying that your feelings are the same as my feelings.

I think that society, before it can become a fit abode for intelligent beings, has got to recognize that the individual will freely act in a socially acceptable way only if such action seems good to that individual. The only way it can alter the free acts of the individual, if it should be necessary to alter them for the advantage of society, is to modify by example or some other form of education what the individual accepts as his good. Since "society" means you and me, this means that I, in my capacity as a member of society, will not allow myself to appeal to my neighbor by some mystical argument which analysis proves to be for my own disguised advantage rather than his. I think that examination will show that this requirement would wipe out a surprisingly large fraction of the conventional ethical arguments.

The importance of clearly seeing that the intelligent individual will freely act only in the way which seems good to him should be particularly evident at the present time. If society were composed exclusively of members so constituted that what every individual accepted as his good was also for the good of the others, there would be no problem; I would not have to say the things I have just said, and you would not be saying to yourselves, "If I had as mean and unsocial a disposition as that fellow I would be jolly careful to keep it to myself". But it is obvious enough, particularly at the present, that not every man is by nature a social animal. If he is also intelligent he will act in an unsocial way if he has opportunity, and it is just silly to think that he can be got hold of by being shown the unsocial consequences of his actions. Hitler is *right* and intelligent in persecuting the Jews if the exaltation of the German race is for him a good; or he is right in exposing the world to the danger of war if war is for him a good, and the rest of us who sputter at him have just failed to be intelligent in expecting him to act according to a code that is for our advantage and against his. Hitler is right in despising the intelligence of people who expect him to be guided by motives which he hasn't got. One element of our failure to be intelligent in this situation consists in our mistaken appraisal of the factual situation. It was inconceivable to us that human beings should exist whose good differs by so much from what we conceive to be the normal as does Hitler's. It should now be obvious to all of civilization that human beings may be expected to appear every now and then whose good, either because of their nature or because of an unusual combination of circumstances to which they have been exposed, it matters not which, may diverge by any amount whatever from the norm. An intelligent society has got to be constructed on a recognition of this possibility.

The means that society must be prepared to take when this possibility is adequately recognized are connected with another of those inescapable properties of the world in which we live which is so obvious that it need only be said to command assent; namely, I am powerless in the face of overwhelming physical force. There is no argument with an exploding bomb. Furthermore, I often experience such overwhelming physical force in the concerted action of my fellows, and conversely, I see that sometimes I can so maneuver as to procure the application of an overwhelming physical force to my neighbor and thus secure from him the action which I desire. The recognition of all this is merely a recognition of the factual nature of my environment. I must count on my intelligent neighbor seeing all this; and if the exercise of force seems to him a good in itself, or if the exercise of force seems to him a lesser evil to be overbalanced by some greater good, then I must also count on his using force against me in his attempt to procure his ends. In reply to his action I have the choice of yielding without a struggle, or of attempting to meet his force by superior force of my own. There are people to whom the exercise of force against their neighbor, under any circumstances, is so repugnant that they would rather be exterminated than oppose force with force. Most people, however, do not seem to be constituted in this way. Although the exercise of force is intrinsically repugnant to them and, up to a certain point, they will yield or compromise to avoid the necessity for exerting force, nevertheless, beyond a certain point incompatibilities become too great, and they will fight. Sometimes people appear to find it necessary to justify their willingness to use force when incompatibilities become too great. It seems to me that no apology should be necessary, but willingness to use force beyond a certain point constitutes nothing more than clear-eyed recognition of the nature of the world about us. There is no more reason why I should hesitate to recognize this natural "law" any more than any other natural law, such as that I must keep my head above water if I wish to live. The physicist, particularly, who has spent his life adapting himself to the world about him, will, I think, have little inclination to apologize when he accepts the naturally imposed necessity to use force to secure desired results in certain situations.

Society in its relation to the individual is almost always, by virtue of its enormous superiority of numbers, in a position to exert, when it chooses, such overwhelming force that the individual can only yield. This possibility is always in the background, and constitutes an essential element in the relation of the individual to society. An honest analysis of the situation demands that this be said out loud with frankness. But society is composed of you and me, and in its actions will reflect to a certain degree what seems good to you and me. If most of us dislike to use force, as seems to be the case, we expect that society will use force against the individual only as the last resort, when incompatibilities become so extreme that they can be handled in no other way. Such a society will first make every attempt to bring the individual to adopt freely a socially acceptable line of conduct.

If you and I are intelligent, we will want to have society a fit abode for intelligent beings, which means that, below the point at which we have to apply force, we will appeal to our fellow as an intelligent being, and will try to bring him to adopt freely, *because all things considered, it seems good to him,* that line of conduct which is also to the advantage of you and me. How great a modification this means in conventional social practice is evident enough. It will be a slow and difficult process that can be accomplished only by a long campaign of education extending over generations. The problem is to present to the individual all the relations and consequences of his actions, allowing the vision of *all* the consequences to modify his drives and what seems good to him, until in the end his drives are self-consciously stabilized in perfect accord with whatever his own nature may be. If, when his drives have been educated and stabilized, they are still antisocial, we must be prepared to restrain him by force. There is obviously a great gamble in such a program; you and I are gambling that the majority of our fellows are so constituted that when their drives have been educated a harmonious society is possible. Although we must always expect that there will be a certain number whose educated drives may be antisocial to any degree, we are gambling that there will not be so many of them that the rest of us cannot restrain them by force. That is, we are gambling that the human animal is so constituted that the race as a whole is capable of building up an intelligent society. I think many people are afraid to make this gamble—fear is back of a great deal of social conservatism. The more courageous course appeals to me; if man is not the kind of animal that can create for himself an intelligent society, I would rather not have any society at all.

Although Hitler may be right in following his own drives in the face of the abhorrence of a large part of his fellows, he is dead wrong if he thinks that an intelligent society can be created by suppressing the individual and turning the world into a human ant heap. An intelligent society has got to start with the individual and end with the individual. Nothing else makes sense.

20

SCIENCE, AND ITS CHANGING SOCIAL ENVIRONMENT*

THE FIRST PART of this address dealt with recent work of the author in extending the pressure range attainable in the laboratory. The subject has been similarly treated in the third volume of Science in Progress, published by the Society of Sigma Xi.

And now I will turn from these technical matters, with which I have been personally concerned, to matters of more immediate and vital interest to all of us. In the present world struggle physics has come to occupy a position in the very front line. A large part of the body of physicists has been asked to divert its activities from accustomed channels, and all of us who have been able have rejoiced that the opportunity has been offered and that we can be of service. Because of the obvious importance of the service that physics is rendering, many physicists are anticipating, after the war, a permanent increase of the appreciation of the public for physics, and a

*From Science, 97, 147, 1943. Part of the retiring presidential address to the American Physical Society, given at Columbia University, January 23, 1943.

great increase in the attractiveness of physics as a profession for our abler young men.

There are however, other aspects of this rosy future to which I wish to direct your attention. Because of the heavy social impact of the products and techniques resulting from scientific investigation, there is a growing tendency in many quarters to maintain that science, and this of course includes physics, is the servant of society and that all scientific activities should be under complete supervision and control by society or the state. This point of view is finding advocates among scientists themselves. It seems to be growing in favor in some quarters in this country, but not yet to the same extent as in Russia, where it is widely accepted, judging by various mass proclamations of Russian scientists published in our press, or in England, where there is an aggressive and articulate group with a similar attitude—the book by Bernal entitled "The Social Function of Science" comes to mind. Indicative of the feeling in some quarters in this country, there is an article in a recent number of the *Popular Science Monthly* which is an extreme example of this point of view. I believe that there is a probability that after the war this feeling will be intensified in proportion to the very success that physicists may have in helping to win the war.

Closely connected with the thesis that scientific activity is a social function is the growing impulse to hold the scientist personally responsible for all the consequences of his discoveries. In all this there is a good deal with which one may sympathize, but I believe that nevertheless an unqualified and unreserved acceptance of the current popular views about the social position of science will result in a false placing of emphasis which in the long run will be harmful both to scientists in their profession, including physicists, and to society as a whole.

The issue is confused by the looseness with which the word "science" is used. Popular usage lumps under the single word "science" all the technological activities of engineering and industrial development, together with those of so-called "pure science". It would clarify matters to reserve the word science for "pure" science. Because a single word is used, there is an impulse to assess a blanket responsibility and to set up blanket controls. Superposed on the confusion arising from verbal looseness there is another less innocent factor. It seems to me that there is often just plain resentment that changes in accustomed routine are so often the outcome of investigations in pure science. Large numbers of the genus homo do not like to be shaken out of an accustomed routine. It is this resentment more than anything else which I believe leads to fastening of "responsibility" on pure scientists. In extreme cases this has even led to the demand for a compulsory moratorium on all scientific investigation.

I think there has been a tendency for scientists in general and physicists in particular to acquiesce too meekly in the implication of social responsibility for their discoveries. The conjuring up of "responsibility" is often only the device of a lazy man to get some one else to do for him something of vital concern to him which he should be doing himself, and scientists in their naiveté have not seen this.

Let us imagine what acceptance of the thesis of responsibility would involve. Perhaps the most fundamental of all the conditions for success in scientific discovery is complete freedom. If the scientist were required to make only those discoveries which could not wilfully be perverted to harmful uses, he would almost certainly feel himself so restricted that he would make no discoveries at all. Furthermore, it is impossible for a physicist or any one else limited by human fallibility to foresee all the consequences of a discovery, much less, to balance all the good consequences against all the bad consequences. Responsibility does not exist when there is no mechanism by which the responsibility can be determined. Neither is there any mechanism by which the physicist can control such consequences of his discoveries as he can foresee. It is society as a whole that is in a position to provide the mechanism of control rather than the individual discoverer, so that it is therefore the responsibility of society to see that discoveries in pure science are properly exploited, not the responsibility of the discoverer. When a physicist makes a new discovery and imparts it to society, he is presenting society with an opportunity, and this opportunity implies responsibility on the part of society.

Society already has available a mechanism of at

least partial control in a control of patents and production. Whether an entirely adequate control can be exercised in a frame work of a society broken up into separate nationalities as at present may not be easy to decide; certainly the decision and the resultant action is out of the province of the individual scientist.

What is it that makes the "pure" physicist go, when he is on the trail of some new idea in his laboratory? The answer is, of course, complex, but I believe that through all the multifariousness runs one simple guiding thread, the craving for understanding. To the extent that the guiding motif of an enterprise is the craving for understanding, to that extent the enterprise may be said to be purely scientific, as distinguished from technological, or utilitarian, or artistic, or political, or what not. The craving for understanding reaches its greatest poignancy only in a few cases, but all of us who are engaged in pure research have it to a certain extent, and it is the vital part of what makes us go. It is not a matter to be argued about, as to whether such a craving has economic or other justification; it is only to be accepted as a fundamental fact about human beings that some of them have developed to a high degree the passion for understanding and a delight in the corresponding activities, just as others have a strongly developed sense of beauty or of conduct. If society is ever going to become anything more than a vicious merry-go-round of circular activity, if ever there are ends in themselves or goods in themselves, then surely the gratification of the craving for understanding is one of them.

To those who have a passion for understanding society will not be a satisfactory place unless it affords opportunity for the acquiring of understanding, so that to the extent to which the function of society is to make life satisfactory for its members, and it seems to me that this is pretty nearly the whole function of society, one of its responsibilities is the making and providing of adequate scientific opportunity. Society is the servant of science even more and in a more fundamental sense than is science the servant of society. Any control which society exerts over science and invention must be subject to this condition.

Physicists are, I think, even if they give intellectual assent, inclined to be too diffident to insist on all the implications of this conclusion. Many of us find it uncongenial to thrust ourselves forward and to insist on the service owed us by society, particularly at the present. We have a feeling that we should not confuse the issue of winning the war by insisting on matters of obvious personal concern at a time when the very existence of the society to which we are accustomed is threatened. I would urge that on the contrary now is the time more than ever to insist that society must conform to the pattern of service to science. What are we fighting for anyway? After we have scavenged the world of the blight of totalitarianism, what are our long-range objectives? Have we nothing eventually in view more admirable than the abolition of want and the securing of comfort for everyone, ends which at present bulk so large in our programs? Will we be permanently satisfied with these, or will something more be necessary to give dignity and worth to human activity?

In urging the claims of science and scientists on society we may fortify ourselves by reflecting that we are not urging society to give without return. The exercise of the mind and the acquiring of understanding is after all not an ignoble human activity. In more idealistic phraseology it is sometimes described as the pursuit of truth. One might even argue that it is the one human activity which distinguishes us most from the brutes; certainly it is the one in which there is the greatest room for future development and in which we have most failed up to now to realize our full potentialities. In the long run society is a better place for every one when there is intellectual freedom and encouragement and flourishing activity in pure science. It does not put much of a strain on other social mechanisms to have scientific activity going on, nor are we an obtrusive class. We work hard and like it; the pursuit of personal comfort or even happiness is not a particularly compelling motive with us; there is a certain disinterested impersonality in our striving which has on occasion been commended. We do not ask for much in comparison with what we give: freedom and leisure to do our work and decent security for the future.

Many of us already have been more or less fortunate in these respects, and some of us already have been living under conditions which approach the millennium according to our simple standards. But it seems to me that the prospect is becoming less bright. Not many people like to use their minds, and there is always some spontaneous hostility of those who do not like to think toward those who do. For years before the war there were signs of a growing anti-intellectual sentiment, which I believe is now becoming visibly intensified with the passions and emotions always associated with war. It seems to me that scientists are curiously obtuse as to the social conditions which make possible their existence as a class. It is by no means a certainty that society will so evolve that the individual will be allowed to engage in independent intellectual activity. The danger of such an evolution increases with the growing command by society of techniques assuring a satisfactory degree of common ease and comfort. Society may well come to feel that the scientist has not enough more to give it in the way of material benefits to justify keeping him. If society is ever going to become a place in which intellectual activity is encouraged and intellectual ability prized, those of us who like to think have got to fight for it. If we do not take action in our own behalf, no one else will do it for us. And we must do it now because social institutions are changing so rapidly that after the war it may be too late. Judging by the one criterion of greatest significance in this country, economic position, there is no doubt that the changes now taking place are leading to a worsening of the position of those who like to think as contrasted with those who do not. When we contemplate all the pressure groups insistent only on their own advantage, we need not be diffident in striving for an even greater recognition than in the past of the social importance of intellectual activity, and of the importance of stimulating such ability by commensurate rewards.

A distorted conception of democracy is forming under stress of the war, a conception which urges the equal right of every one to share the goods of society irrespective of what he gives back to society. The conception of democracy which was implicit in the old fashion "American ideal" seems to me more admirable. According to this conception democracy meant equal opportunity for ability, no matter how humble its origin, to rise to its natural level. So far as capitalism was discussed at all, it was justified, at least in theory and in spite of its defects, because it incidentally provided a machinery by which special service received special reward. It was not considered that a society was either ignoble or undemocratic that gave special reward for special service. Nor was the individual who consented to receive special reward for special service considered to have debased himself. It was felt that society need not grudge to act to its own advantage because it was also for the advantage of the individual; society did not resent the individual of exceptional abilities but took pride in him. It seems to me that a certain crabbed and ungenerous spirit of envy and resentment against unusual ability is growing; this is underlined by recent events. To me there is something dead wrong with a social philosophy that attempts to set *any* upper limit to the value of the contribution which a man of unusual ability can make to his society, particularly in time of war. In the name of democracy our ideals are becoming less democratic. A partial explanation is doubtless to be found in industrial and capitalistic abuses. But an explanation does not constitute a justification.

We, who are perhaps more vitally concerned than any other group, have thus far failed to take steps to ensure that the economically altered society of the future shall retain those essential features that once inspired our democratic vision. Our conviction has not been strong enough that a society is a good society in which intellectual ability is prized and rewarded. We are passively accepting a change in the economic system by which the relative position of all intellectual workers, including the scientist, is being definitely debased, and in which assurances and commitments made by society in the past are being needlessly scrapped. This applies with particular force to the private universities and to the workers in them. We are not fighting against these things ourselves, and we in the universities are not insisting that our university and educational administrators fight for them for us.

What are we going to do about it? In the first

place, we are not going on strike, but those of us who are in the position will continue to work as hard as we can to develop all the devices in the power of our ingenuity or to make what other special contributions we can to destroy totalitarianism and all that it implies. Neither, I think, will scientists attempt to organize themselves into a pressure group to try to mold society to their pattern. Even if it were not ludicrous for so small a minority to think of making such an attempt, we would find such an attempt distasteful at a time when so many of our young men are being called on to make extreme sacrifices. And even if not distasteful, who could find time to devote to such an attempt when we are all so busy with immediate things? But it would be stupid not to take time to at least see what the situation is, and once having seen it, it will be possible to do many things incidentally without slackening in our other efforts. Merely by letting it be known that we are aware of the situation we may accomplish something. From the long range point of view our job is primarily one of education. We should avail ourselves of every opportunity and even go out of our way to make opportunity to let our conviction be known that a society is in the long run the best society in which those who have the ability are given every opportunity and inducement to practice the pursuit of truth and of understanding. We must hold up intellectual power and accomplishment to the admiration and emulation of our young and stimulate their pleasure in intellectual activity. Our educational programs must be revised if necessary to give this emphasis. We must teach our young a social philosophy which recognizes that society is a means and not an end, and we must give them a technique by which they can discover those ends which they can accept with intellectual integrity as making society worth while. If we do not do these things, we are in danger of finding when this struggle is over that we have been fighting for a lifeless husk; if we do them we will be playing our part in molding a public opinion which will create the society of our vision.

21

SCIENTISTS AND SOCIAL RESPONSIBILITY*

THE TOPIC PROPOSED for this symposium, "How far can scientific method determine the ends for which scientific discoveries are used?" is obviously of much generality and also, I am told, of an intentional vagueness. The general background of the topic is plain enough; the topic has evidently been suggested by the present atmosphere through which society is looking at science, inspired by the preponderating role of invention and the applications of scientific discoveries in the late war, culminating in the atomic bomb. Not only is the general public becoming increasingly conscious of the impact of science on the whole social structure, but the scientist has himself in the interval since Hiroshima displayed a noteworthy concern with the social effects of his discoveries. This has resulted in the formation of societies of scientists dedicated to controlling as far as possible some of the aspects of scientific discoveries. There is growing up among scientists a more or less articulate philosophy of what the relation should be between science and society as a

*From The Scientific Monthly 45, 148, 1947. Given at a symposium at the annual meeting in Boston, Dec. 1946 of the A.A.A.S. in a joint session of section K and L and the American Philosophical Association.

whole. It seems to me that it is a matter of the greatest importance what this philosophy is, and that it may well be determinative of the future course of civilization.

There are, I think, unfortunate features in the present trend of this philosophy, and I should like to devote part of this discussion to them. This will involve giving a rather broad and liberal interpretation to our topic. I would in any event be constrained to place a liberal interpretation on it, because it is my feeling that the "scientific method", in the narrow sense in which scientific method is often understood, does not have a very immediate application to determining the ends for which scientific discoveries are used. I like to say that there is no scientific method as such, but rather only the free and utmost use of intelligence. In certain fields of application, such as the so-called natural sciences, the free and utmost use of intelligence particularizes itself into what is popularly called the scientific method. From this point of view I should like to rephrase the topic for discussion to read "What is the most intelligent way of dealing with the uses of scientific discoveries?" A discussion from this broad point of view will necessarily involve aspects of social philosophy, and in particular the philosophy of the relations of science to society.

The detailed discussion might well start with such questions as: How far is it desirable that scientific discoveries be controlled? or, What "ought" to be the attitude of the scientist toward his own discoveries? No discussion along these lines will get very far before the word "responsibility" occurs. Let us examine the implications of this word. It is frequently stated that science is responsible for the uses made of scientific discoveries. This is obviously a highly abstract statement. The meaning must be that *scientists* are responsible for the uses made of scientific discoveries. But even this is so general as to have little meaning. Does it mean that scientists as a group are responsible? But what is responsibility that it can pertain to a group? Here we begin to encounter shades of meaning and ambiguities in the word responsibility itself. A few people apparently use the word in a purely factual sense with no further connotations. From this point of view it can certainly be said that scientists are "responsible" for the uses made of scientific discoveries, for the simple reason that the discoveries cannot be used until after the discoveries are made, and the discoveries are undeniably made by scientists. Responsibility in this sense merely denotes a link in the causal chain. But I believe that this colorless and factual use of the word is comparatively rare. The more conventional usage implies a moral obligation and involves a moral condemnation if the obligation is not met. To say that "scientists are responsible for the uses made of scientific discoveries" implies, according to what I believe is the usual usage, that each and every scientist has a moral obligation to see to it that the uses society makes of scientific discoveries are beneficent. This is getting pretty near home. It means that *I* have a moral obligation, and that if I do not meet the obligation I shall be deemed culpable by society and may justifiably be disciplined. The discipline that would be imposed is the natural and obvious one, namely, loss of scientific freedom. This is, I think, the temper of an important part of society today, and the attitude seems to be growing. Furthermore, it is an attitude in which a number of scientists, particularly those of the younger generation, are showing a tendency to concur. Any such concurrence arises, I believe, from a failure to realize the larger implications and involves an essentially short-range philosophy of the relation of the individual to society.

I think it is obvious that the thesis that the scientist is responsible for the uses made of his discoveries must involve the assumption that there is something special and exceptional in the situation. For certainly in more common situations individual responsibility is not considered to extend to all the consequences that may be initiated by the act of the individual. The miner of iron ore is not expected to see to it that none of the scrap iron which may eventually result from his labors is sold to the Japanese to be used against his country. Such an extension of responsibility would be absurd because of the impracticality of it, and in particular would make impossible that specialization and division of labor that is one of the foundation stones of our modern industrial civilization. Furthermore, it is obvious that if such detailed and individual responsibility were imposed a certain ideal of society implicit in the thinking of many of us would have to be abandoned. The society of this idealized vision is a society so constructed that every individual in it may be allowed to strive to choose for his lifework what he can do best. Unfortunately, society is still tragically far from this ideal for the average man, but our departure from the ideal arises, not from failure of good intentions, but from the practical difficulty that we have not yet found a mechanism that makes this possible. However, many individual scientists, so far as they have been allowed to follow the driving force of their inner scientific compulsion, have come pretty close to this ideal. From the point of view of society, the justification for the favored position of the scientist is that the scientist cannot make his contribution unless he is free, and that the value of his contribution is worth the price society pays for it. The demand that the individual scientist be responsible for the uses made by society of his discoveries would constitute a repudiation of this ideal. For if I personally had to see to it that only beneficent uses were made of my discoveries, I should have to spend my life oscillating between some kind of a forecasting bureau, to find what might be the uses made of my discoveries, and lobbying in Washington to procure the passage of special legislation to control the uses. In neither of these activities do I have any competence, so that my life would be embittered and my scientific productivity cease.

 The thesis of the responsibility of the individual

scientist therefore involves a repudiation of the general ideals of the specialization and division of labor, and the ideal of, as far as possible, each man to his best. This repudiation can be justified only by some special feature, and the only justification that I can see which is to be taken with any seriousness is the thesis that scientists are in some special way qualified to foresee the uses society will make of their discoveries, and to direct and control these uses. This thesis does indeed seem to be tacit in much of the popular discussion. The question now is whether this thesis is true, and, if so, whether it constitutes justification for the imposition of responsibility. As a physicist with pride in my profession, I would naturally be loath to admit that a physicist could not do a better job than outsiders in controlling the uses made of discoveries in physics, but nevertheless I think an inspection of such activities of physicists as their attempts during the last year to get through Congress a bill establishing the National Science Foundation would show that the batting average of even the physicist would presumably be so low as to make it unprofitable for society to support him in the role of prophet and administrator. For of course society must recognize that if it imposes responsibility on a man it must be prepared to support him in the exercise of that responsibility.

Leaving further elaboration of this question to the tender mercies of others, I now address myself to the question of whether, even granted that scientists are specially qualified to foresee, direct, and control the uses made of their discoveries, society should therefore hold them responsible for the uses made of their discoveries? I think that the temper of the times is such that many people would answer this question with an unqualified yes. Such an answer implies a social philosophy that has been growing rapidly in this country, namely, that the community has a right to exact disproportionate service from special ability. It is epitomized in the Marxian epigram "From each according to his ability, to each according to his need". Three stages of evolution can be recognized in the present philosophy of the relation of the individual to society. The first granted the right of the bright people to exploit the stupid ones; the second recognized the right of everyone to receive from society a reward proportional to his contribution to society; and the third and present stage recognizes the right of the stupid people to exploit the bright ones. It is perhaps obvious that my sympathies are with the second, or the median, of these three philosophies. The third philosophy, insofar as it involves anything beyond the more or less disguised willingness of the majority to use naked force, is based on a metaphysical concept of society as some superthing, transcending the individuals who compose it. This, to my way of thinking, does not make sense. Society is composed of you and me; society does not have an individuality of its own, but is the aggregate of what concerns you and me. The function of society is expressible in terms of its relations to the individuals who compose it, and any justification for the acts made by its members is to be found only in the effects of these acts on the members of society as individuals.

It seems to me that the thesis of the right of society to exact disproportionate service from special ability can be analyzed very simply. If society exacts disproportionate service, this means that certain individuals in society acting in their collective capacity, are willing to exact disproportionate service from other individuals. But I, as an individual, would certainly not presume to think of demanding that my neighbor give me special service merely because nature had endowed him to do the job better than I could do it myself. The sort of thing I am unwilling to do in my individual capacity I am also unwilling to do in my capacity as a member of a group. Furthermore, it seems to me only decent and self-respecting for me to do my best to see to it that the group to which I belong does not act in a way in which I as an individual would not be willing to act. If every member of society applied to his social acts the same criteria of decency and self-respect that he applies to his individual acts, the problem of exaction by society of disproportionate service from special ability would not arise.

The assumption of the right of society to impose a responsibility on the scientist which he does not desire obviously involves acceptance of the third philosophy, that is, the right of the stupid to exploit the bright. There are, I believe, specific objections to the application of this philosophy in the present situation, apart from the general considerations just mentioned. It is not necessary. Society can deal with the issues raised by scientific discoveries by other methods than by forcing the scientist to do something uncongenial, something for which he is often not fitted. The course of action that can accomplish this seems to me the only self-respecting one. The applications made of scientific discoveries are very seldom made by scientists themselves, but are usually made by the industrialists. It is the manufacture and sale of the invention that should be controlled rather than the act of inventing. This could surely be accomplished by specific action rather than by throwing out baby and bath together. One can think of revisions in the patent laws, for instance, that would be pertinent. Or society can control the situation by other means already in its possession. If it had not wanted to construct an atomic bomb, it need not have signed the check for the two billion dollars which alone made it possible. Without this essential contribution from society the atomic bomb would have remained an interesting blueprint in the laboratory.

Why is it that there is such popular clamor for dealing with this situation by the tremendously clumsy and backhanded method of imposing responsibility on the individual scientist, a method which involves the sacrifice of fundamental principles and the development of social mechanisms of more than doubtful practicality? I suspect the clamor arises from the unconscious operation of very human motives. The cry of responsibility is often no more than the cry of a lazy man to get someone else to do for him what he ought to do for himself. There may perhaps be a small element of despair in the clamor. It is obvious that if society would only abolish war, 99 per cent of the need for the control of scientific discoveries would vanish. Furthermore, it is obvious enough that the abolition of war is the business of everyone. The difficulties of doing this, however, appear to have become so enormous that the average man may well despair of being able to accomplish it himself. Into this situation comes the vision that if only some *deus ex machina* would stop scientific discoveries from being put to bad uses we could all be at peace in our minds. Whereupon the human race, with its capacity for wishful thinking and rationalization, needs only this hint to invent the legend of the responsibility of the scientists for the uses society makes of their discoveries. Let society deal with this situation by the means already in its hands, means by which it deals with similar situations. If it truly believes that the peculiar qualifications necessary to deal with the misuse of scientific discovery are to be found among the scientists, which I, for one, very much doubt, then let it create mechanisms and make opportunities by which those scientists who can do this sort of work well will be attracted to this field, rather than to insist on its right to the indiscriminate concern of all scientists with this problem. And let the scientists, for their part, take a long-range point of view and not accept the careless imposition of responsibility, an acceptance which to my mind smacks too much of **appeasement** and lack of self-respect.

I believe it to be of particular importance that the scientist have an articulate and adequate social philosophy, even more important than that the average man should have such a philosophy. For there are certain aspects of the relation between science and society that the scientist can appreciate better than anyone else, and if he does not insist on this significance no one else will, with the result that the relation of science to society will become warped, to the detriment of everyone.

The social philosophy which seems to be spontaneously growing up among some of our scientists is, I believe, a short-range and inadequate philosophy. It is well known that the scientists who have shown the most articulate concern with the social implications of the atomic bomb are young. The philosophy that is coming into being betrays this. It is a youthful philosophy, enthusiastic, idealistic, and colored by eagerness for self-sacrifice. It glories in accepting the responsibility of science to society and refuses to countenance any concern of the scientist with his own interests, even if it can be demonstrated that these interests are also the interests of everyone. Such a philosophy is unmindful of long-range considerations and blind to the existence of other scales of values than those of the philosophers themselves.

What are the characteristics of an adequate social philosophy? It seems to me that first and foremost this should be a "maximum-minimum" philosophy. That is, society should be so constructed as to allow the maximum number of its members to lead a good life, while at the same time the minimum of dictation and interference should be imposed on any individual in determining what shall for him constitute a good life. The most outstanding characteristic of such a society is its tolerance. What would be a good life for one man would not be a good life for another. It is, I think, with regard to this minimum requirement that actual societies are most likely to fail. No society dedicated to a special thesis satisfies this requirement. A totalitarian society, such as that of Russia, in which a man may anticipate happiness if he thinks as the majority, but in which he may expect to be liquidated if he opposes it, is obviously not such a society. Neither is the conventional Christian society, with its thesis that the good life is the one devoted to the service of a man's fellows, and with the correlative assumption of the right of the community to impose this ideal on the individual. Both these types of society are too narrow. The broadly tolerant society, committed to no special thesis as to what constitutes the good life, is evidently a late product in the evolutionary chain. When the struggle for survival is too intense, tolerance may well be a luxury society cannot afford. But as the struggle for survival ceases to dominate the social pattern, an increasing amount of tolerance becomes practical, until in the end the attainment of the maximum of tolerance may well become the dominating ideal. This, it seems to me, is the sort of society we should strive for; it also seems to me that in this country today a high degree of realization of such a society is possible.

WHAT is the relation of the scientist to such a society? It seems to me that he occupies a position of high strategic importance, a position impossible of attainment for the man who has not directly experienced the significant factors basic to this type of society. The conception of what constitutes the good life does not present itself as a primitive datum in consciousness, but is a product of cultivation and education. Furthermore, various ideals of the good life are possible, competitive with one another and to a certain extent mutually exclusive. The ideals that come to prevail will to a large extent depend on the self-conscious activities of those most concerned. It may even be that the ideals will have to be fought for. What constitutes the good life for the scientist does not at once appeal to the majority as constituting the good life. Nay, more than this, without education the majority cannot be trusted to see that it is to the advantage of the community as a whole that the scientist be allowed to lead his good life. With education, however, I believe that this can be accomplished, and that the scientist is strategically situated to impart this education. It is, of course, easy for anyone to see that the material benefits we now enjoy would not have been possible without scientific activity and to see that for this reason science should be supported. What I have in mind, however, is something less material. I think the scientist, in endeavoring to impart the vision of what this is, would do well not to take a too narrow view. The scientific life, which for him is a good life, is a special kind of a more general life which is also a good life, namely, the life of the intellect.

I think the scientist's most important educative task is to get the average man to feel that the life of the intellect not only is a good life for those who actively lead it, but that it is also good for society as a whole that the intellectual life should be made possible for those capable of it, and that it should be prized and rewarded by the entire community. It is perhaps a gamble that society as a whole can be made to feel this. But I believe it is a gamble to which the scientific man is committed. If the human race is such a sort of creature that it cannot be made to feel that intellectual activity and satisfaction of the craving for understanding are goods in themselves, then we might as well shut up shop here and now, and those of us who are made that way henceforth get the intellectual satisfactions necessary to us as best we can, surreptitiously and in spite of our fellows. Example itself can be educative. Appreciation of the element of high adventure in achieving understanding of the ways of nature should not be difficult to impart. In other fields human beings do this. There must be widespread sympathy with, and understanding of the mountain climber who, when asked why he had to climb mountains, replied, "Because the mountain is there". I believe that most men similarly can be made to feel the challenge of an external world not understood and can be made to see that the scientist has to understand nature "because nature is there". The challenge to the understanding of nature is a challenge to the utmost capacity in us. In accepting the challenge, man can dare to accept no handicaps. That is the reason that scientific freedom is essential and that artificial limitations of tools or subject matter are unthinkable. The average man, I believe, can be made to see that scientific freedom is merely freedom to be intelligent, and that the need for this freedom is born with us, and that we will practice it in the inmost recesses of our thoughts no matter what the external constraints. And I believe also that the average man can be made to see that the imposition of restraints on the freedom to be intelligent betrays fear of the unknown and of himself, and that he can be made to feel that this fear is an ignoble thing. My gamble is that the human race, once it has caught the vision, will not be willing to yield to fear of the consequences of its own intelligence.

It may appear that we have been straying rather far from our ostensible topic. I think, however, that from the broad point of view we have not. What we have been saying amounts to saying that the most intelligent way of dealing with the problems arising from scientific discoveries is to create an appropriate society. This society will be a society that recognizes that the only rational basis for its functions is to be sought in its relations to the individuals of which it is composed; a society in which the individual in his capacity as a member of society will have the integrity not to stoop to actions he would not permit himself as an individual; a society broadly tolerant and one which recognizes intellectual achievement as one of the chief glories of man; a society imaginative enough to see the high adventure in winning an understanding of the natural world about us, and a society which esteems the fear of its own intellect an ignoble thing. In a society so constituted I venture to think the problems created by scientific discoveries will pretty much solve themselves.

22

SCIENCE AND FREEDOM REFLECTIONS OF A PHYSICIST*

THIS WILL NOT attempt to reproduce exactly what I said at the dinner on January 11, 1947, but I shall avail myself of the suggestion of Dr. Sarton to make a partly imaginary speech, composed of parts of what I actually said, and of what, in the light of afterthought, I wish I had said. I shall not attempt to reproduce a number of the more or less personal and informal details, but shall confine myself to matters of more general interest.

Of all the conditions of my work which in retrospect appears most important, and of which at the time also I was keenly conscious, freedom of investigation is outstanding. There has never been any suggestion from any outside source as to the nature of my investigations. Even in the early days, when I sought and obtained the maximum relief from teaching and administrative duties for the ostensible purpose of more complete devotion to my research, no attempt was made by the University authorities to impose as a condition that I continue to devote

*From Isis 37, 128, 1947. This essentially reproduces part of the remarks made at a dinner given at the Harvard Club of Boston on Jan. 11, 1947 by the Dean of the Faculty of Arts and Sciences of Harvard University in recognition of the award of the Nobel Prize in physics in December 1946.

myself to high pressure investigation or even to investigation itself. The apparent attitude of the authorities was that if you are going to gamble that you have found a good man, a gamble without strings attached is the most likely to succeed. Any consistency which my experimental program may have shown has been a consistency imposed entirely from within; this I believe to be the proper source of consistency. In spite of the fact that I have in the main followed one guiding experimental idea, I have nevertheless at all times felt free to pursue other lines of interest, whether experiment, or theory, or fundamental criticism.

Another outstanding characteristic of my work has been the smallness of its scale. Not only is the apparatus itself small, in fact becoming smaller the higher the pressure, because of inherent physical limitations on strength, but I have never had more than two or three students at a time or a couple of assistants. The result has been that I have been able at all times to maintain the closest contact with the details of the work, and also have been able to conserve the requisite amount of leisure. Both of these features have been of the highest importance. In advancing into new territory, as in this high pressure work, the necessity is continuous for the development of new methods and new ideas. For me, at least, new ideas germinate only in an atmosphere of leisure. I have to immerse myself in a problem and then let it gestate in my brain, without the distraction of other interests, if I am to expect the solution to come sauntering into my mind when I wake up two or three mornings later. In this process manual cooperation plays a great part. Adjoining my laboratory is my machine shop; in fact, it is an integral part of the laboratory to which I can repair and stimulate inspiration by working out half-formed ideas with my own hands. Not only do I have enough leisure so that I can work in the shop with my own hands on occasion, but I am also able to carry through my own experiment, including making all the readings, myself. I find this necessary if I am to have confidence in the results of some method not hitherto tried. There are too many pitfalls of unanticipated sources of error, which often require ingenuity for their elimination, and which may take much time to discover if one is only watching from the side lines. I have been able to make it an invariable practise to stay with each new method long enough to get material for a complete paper, before turning the method over to an assistant for more or less routine application to a large number of substances. Not only this, but even when an assistant makes the experiment and the readings, I have always made the computations and written the paper myself. This gives me a confidence in the results not possible when working on a larger scale. Another great advantage of working on a small scale is that one gives no hostages to one's own past. If I wake up in the morning with a new idea, the utilization of which involves scrapping elaborate preparations already made, I am free to scrap what I have done and start off on the new and better line. This would not be possible without crippling loss of morale if one were working on a large scale with a complex organization under one.

Another characteristic of the field in which I have been working is that it is not a particularly popular field, so that there have been comparatively few workers in it and correspondingly little competition. This has both advantages and disadvantages. It is an advantage that one can do his work with no sense of hurry, so that there is little temptation to make premature announcements, and should questions arise one can take the time to repeat the experiment or make other modifications that will clear up the matter. Also, the order in which the problems are attacked can be the order of greatest scientific economy, rather than the order of a competitive politics. On the other hand, the principal disadvantage, obvious enough to everyone, is that the investigator loses the stimulation of conversation with his colleagues on mutual problems. Just how important this stimulus is will depend in considerable measure on the individual investigator; some may find it well nigh indispensable, whereas others may be much less dependent on it. I myself have been able to get along to a considerable measure without it. Even at scientific meetings, which every physicist seems to have to attend at intervals for rehabilitation of his inner man, the stimulus which I have received has not been detailed and specific, but rather general, in suggestions of trends and areas of coming interest.

It has, I think, been a happy circumstance that my field, although obviously narrow in the sense that pressure is a highly specialized physical parameter, nevertheless from another point of view has been exceedingly broad. For the general problem has been no less than to determine the effect of pressure on all physical properties, and it therefore covers the entire reach of physical phenomena with the exception of such things as vacuum tube phenomena.

Mention of the stimulus of conversation with one's colleagues naturally prompts one to consider the increasing trend during the last few years to large-scale cooperative enterprises among physicists. The reasons for this are obvious in the enormously increasing size and expense of the apparatus necessary for modern physical research, such as the cyclotrons and the piles of nuclear physics. Although we may recognize that such instruments are necessary, we may nevertheless deplore some of the consequences. Up to now ideas have been in such a rapid state of flux that the instrument itself has been continually evolving, with the result that most physicists in this field have been spending an increasingly large fraction of their time on the purely engineering job of the design and construction of new and better instruments, and correspondingly an increasingly small proportion of time on the calculation of results and rumination on their significance. The competition in this field is intense; rivalry between different groups at different universities can offer little opportunity for leisure or the scholarly digestion of results before publication. Within the last year there has been one glaring example of hasty publication of a spectacular result of such presumptive importance as to start a rush of other investigators into the field, only later to be withdrawn as erroneous because of inadequate consideration of factors which obviously were crying for evaluation in the beginning. Not only is there haste because of competition, but there is haste because of financial considerations. The apparatus is so expensive that consideration of the overhead demands that the apparatus be kept in operation for twenty-four hours a day, and this is not conducive to a feeling of leisure. Each of the teams which is the slave of one of these instruments has to be driven by some one at the head who has the ideas. There is danger here that all the rest of the team will pick the brains of one man, with an ultimate decrease in the number of physicists in the community capable of independent and critical thought. Still worse, the physicist who should be directing his team by his creative ideas is likely to be so swamped by the administrative details of the large enterprise under him that he is overwhelmed and his purely scientific activity destroyed. This is well known to have happened, at least temporarily, in the case of one of the the new mammoth calculating machines, machines whose ostensible purpose is to free the scientist from drudgery and make possible the creative use of his time. Doubtless some physicists have the natural knack of being able to work together harmoniously and perhaps even efficiently in teams, and perhaps others can acquire it, but I believe there are many who are permanently unfitted for effective cooperation in this way, and it will be a major loss if they are not able to find a niche in which they may function.

During the war practically all the physicists in this country were diverted to war work of one sort or another, and a large part of them were engaged in large-scale enterprises which involved team work developed to its maximum efficiency, with the consequent and necessary submergence of the individual. The older men, who had previously worked on their own problems in their own laboratories, put up with this as a patriotic necessity, to be tolerated only while they must, and to be escaped from as soon as decent. But the younger men, who had been drawn into the maelstrom before starting work for their Ph.D. degree, had never experienced independent work and did not know what it is like. Some of these younger men will continue in government work; others who return to academic circles will there join in the teams serving the mammoth instruments. The result is that a generation of physicists is growing up who have never exercised any particular degree of individual initiative, who have had no opportunity to experience its satisfactions or its possibilities, and who regard cooperative work in large teams as the normal thing. It is a natural corollary for them to feel that the objectives of these large teams must be something of large social significance.

The temper of the rising generation is recognizably different from that of the older. I may mention one example with which I have had personal acquaintance. The Association of Cambridge Scientists was one of many similar associations formed soon after the dropping of the atomic bomb on Hiroshima to consider all the implications of the situation thus created. In the early days of the Association the May-Johnson bill was a matter of much concern. With regard to this there was in the ranks of the Association a cleavage of attitude almost exclusively along lines of age. The older men were troubled and concerned by the threats to scientific freedom contained in the bill, whereas the younger men were not at all concerned about this, but took the opposite view that it was on the whole a rather base and self-indulgent thing for the individual not to be willing to sacrifice his scientific freedom on the altar of the good of society. The young men, never having experienced scientific freedom, did and could not see that the question of self-indulgence does not enter at all into the situation, but the existence of science itself, which I think all conceded to be a social good, is impossible without scientific freedom.

The increasing amount of administrative work falling on some of the scientists composing the large teams has a parallel in the ever increasing amount of routine administrative work expected from the members of a University faculty. As I look back on the forty years of my work there can be no question but that the fraction of the time of the average faculty member spent in routine of administrative or other sorts has increased unconscionably. There seems to be a natural law operating here; the larger an institution becomes, the more cumbersome and less efficient it becomes. One might think that when the institution becomes ten times as large it would have ten times as much business and ten times as many people to do it, so that each individual would need to give only the same amount of time. But it does not work this way; it is more like the development of a telephone exchange, which when it increases by a factor of n has to provide for the handling of factorial n as many combinations. Each new functionary in a University has to justify himself, which he does by exacting attention from every member of the faculty. When, for example, the office of archivist is created, *every* member of the faculty is asked to provide material for the archives. Ten times as many officials tend to demand ten times as much attention from *each* member of the faculty. In a recent number of the *Scientific Monthly* there was an amusing and satirical article depicting the eventual extinction of the human race by suffocation in its own intellectual effluvia. It is well known that every large library tends to increase in size geometrically with the simple arithmetical passage of time. Why this should have to be true does not seem to have been explained, but it is an undoubted description of the observed behavior of the human animal. Unless some way can be discovered of breaking the cycle, the logical final result is catastrophic. In the past the cycle has been broken by wars and the collapse of civilizations. In the hoped-for brighter future in which war has been eliminated, some specific means will have to be devised to cope with the situation. The satirical article portrayed the consequences of the inability of the human race to devise an adequate means. It is no less a problem to devise a means by which the time of the members of university faculties may be saved for creative effort. Otherwise creative science will be driven to other asylums, if indeed it is not destroyed.

As I look to the future I am therefore troubled by two misgivings: that there will be less and less place for the small individual experimenter, and that the time of all of us will be increasingly commandeered by administrative mechanical details. In view of these misgivings I cannot help wondering as I look back on the past whether, if I were to start over again now, I could or would be able to do again what I have done.

23

*THE STRATEGY OF THE SOCIAL SCIENCES**

I AM SURE, despite President Conant's introduction, that you are still wondering why a physicist should be asked to speak on this subject and on this platform. I entirely share with you that wonder. When your Chairman, Mr. McCann, asked me to speak I told him a multitude of reasons why I thought I was not qualified on this subject, and was amazed and chagrined, after I finished, to find that I had completely failed. He said "That makes you all the better candidate". I am sure, in spite of this, that you must not expect too much from what any physicist can do. There may be certain broad points of view which experience in physics may have to contribute, but no one realizes better than I that the details of physics are in many respects entirely different from those of the social sciences, and that the problems in the social sciences are enormously more complicated. I think that no one can speak with more diffidence on this subject than I, and I hope you will take anything I say as entirely personal, and perhaps not sound and perhaps not justified. I

*Remarks made at the meeting of the Graduate Forum of Harvard University on April 20, 1948, here reproduced as taken down on the wire recorder, with emendations of English.

441

can only give you some general impressions which I get from standing on the outside, and make, perhaps, certain observations, but I certainly shall not presume to indicate any line of strategy for the social scientists themselves. All I can do is to present my observations and then let the social scientists themselves indicate what strategy had best be pursued in view of these facts.

The first observation I want to venture from the outside is the difference in general atmosphere between the physical and the social disciplines. It seems to me that in the social sciences there is lacking, to such a large extent as to make a difference in the general atmosphere, that disinterested point of view which in the physical sciences we associate with so called pure science as distinguished from applied science. There has been much discussion as to the difference between pure and applied science, and some people even do not recognize a difference at all. I think that although for some purposes it may be a mistake to try to make the distinction, nevertheless one who has worked in the subject can recognize differences which, for some purposes at least, it is profitable to emphasize. A pure scientist is primarily interested in understanding phenomena which confront him, without any regard for their practical application. I realize that even the pure scientist has a mixture of attitudes; but in as far as he is a "pure" scientist there is a large component of sheer intellectual curiosity. Standing on the outside, and I may be entirely wrong in this, it seems to me that the social sciences do not include very many men who have this disinterested attitude. The reason is easy enough to see. All the social sciences have practical applications, and the need of solving the problems of the present is so desperate that it is almost inevitable that the demand for immediate application should obscure purely intellectual interest. That seems to me a statement of fact.

What you can do about it I do not know, but I think it must be recognized as one of the handicaps that social scientists have to struggle against. I think it is a fact of human nature, proved by experience, that for the long view the best way to get things done, the surest way to make progress into new domains, is to start from the point of view of purely intellectual curiosity without immediate regard for practical application. Seldom in history is it that a successful solution of a complicated problem has come by direct frontal attack. The other things came first, and the solution which was eventually found came more or less incidentally.

I think the whole history of modern technology is an example. For instance, look at what the steam engine has done—it has completely revolutionized our economy, incidentally abolishing the need for slavery. If at the time of the Greeks one had set himself the problem of finding how to eliminate slavery and the answer had been that independent sources of power must be developed, you cannot conceive that the solution would have been found by directly attacking the problem of how to generate power. It had to come after a long time and rather incidentally as the outgrowth of long development in pure physics. Even mathematics, as well as physics, is full of situations in which the direct attack cannot be made. It is only after matters have reached a rather advanced stage that one can expect to get a solution by direct attack. In fact in mathematics the inverse method is a recognized method of solving problems. In many situations you find the solution and then you set yourself the problem of finding the problem this is the solution of. This is a well known method and has yielded many solutions, but obviously it is not a very good method of getting the solution of any given specific problem. From the outside it looks to me as though the social scientists were too concerned with the practical results and too impatient to be willing to let their subject go through a long preliminary stage of development like that of the physical sciences for the last 200 years, without any immediate reward in the way of practical results, or any immediate vision of what the practical results would be. In the social sciences you are flustered all the time with the immediacy and the urgency of the problem.

Before we go further, I suppose a few definitions are in order. What do we really understand by the physical and the social sciences? In the first place I do not think it is particularly profitable to argue whether the word science is properly applied or not, and President Conant has suggested that this is to a large extent a matter of words. What I understand by the physical and the social sciences is simply this: the domain of the physical sciences is the domain in which we are concerned with inanimate phenomena and the social sciences is that domain in which we are concerned with phenomena in which human beings play an integral part. This is obviously an enormous domain and includes both human beings individually and human beings in combination. Of course it is human beings in combination that most concern us and make it most difficult. It might appear that human beings individually should be relegated to biology and psychology, but it seems to me that an understanding of the basic human unit must be fundamental to any proper social science. Both of these domains, that is, the domains of inanimate and of human phenomena, have certain features in common which make it perhaps profitable to try to apply to the social sciences certain lessons which we have learned from the physical sciences.

One feature that is common to both these domains is that they are both intellectual enterprises in which the primary object, as I see it, must be to acquire understanding. The *control* which comes as a result of understanding is, as I have suggested, something less immediate. I think that from this point of view at least the subject and the problems of social science can be just as truly designated by "science" as the subject and the problems of physical science. Whether the methods are worthy of that designation is another matter, which I think is not so important to settle.

In domains in which we want primarily to acquire understanding any questions and answers which we can give have certain characteristics. For instance, the primary question is "Is it true?" Any statement of which it makes sense to ask "Is it true?" or "Is it correct?" implies that there is a recognized method for answering that question. In my understanding "social science" is a science in so far as methods exist for answering the question "Is it true?" in that domain.

It is perfectly obvious that certain things do not apply in social science which apply in physical science, and for that reason many people have been unwilling to use the word science in the social domain. The most obvious of these are the controlled experiment and the use of mathematics. The controlled experiment is the one thing that is responsible for the modern development of physical science. It constitutes a new technique. It enables us to isolate factors and analyze one by one the effect of the different components into which a situation can be split up. And of course the application of mathematics is characteristic of physical sciences, and that again is something which has made the advance of the physical sciences so rapid.

In spite of the fact that obviously neither of these things apply to nearly as great a degree in the social sciences, I think that we have here a distinction in degree and not necessarily in kind. It seems to me that a fundamental characteristic of both these domains is the necessity for some sort of *analysis*. In the physical sciences we can analyze into components which are capable of measurement. Measurement is simply a means of describing by numbers, and the fact that we can describe by numbers in the physical sciences is what it is that makes it possible to apply mathematics.

Description in terms of numbers is not so easy in most of the situations in the social sciences. But nevertheless I think you must have description and I think you must have analysis before you can begin to treat social phenomena in a scientific spirit. Analysis means the ability to separate into component parts. If the component parts can be physically isolated, we are in a position to make a controlled experiment. Now you usually cannot isolate the parts physically in the social sciences and therefore you seldom can make a controlled experiment. But not all the physical sciences can isolate the parts either; astronomy cannot and geology cannot. But nevertheless we can have quantitative theories in both of these; these theories may involve systems of equations which can be solved mathematically, in spite of the fact that we cannot set up the physical situation which corresponds to any single one of the equations.

Something of the same sort should be possible in the social sciences. But before you can do that you have to have the ability to analyze and describe significantly. What I mean by significant description is the picking out of features from a situation in terms of which you can reproduce the situation and around which you can build a theory. Significant description and theory go hand in hand; you cannot have one without the other, and they are a mutual growth. To me, standing on the outside, it seems that the social sciences have not got very far in the ability to make significant description. It appears to me that the social scientist is not yet able to pick out the significant things in a large complex and then analyze the effect of each one of these significant factors. An obvious example of significant description and analysis in the physical sciences is the isolation of those particular aspects of a situation which are connected by the laws of mechanics. The analogue of this does not yet appear, I think, in the social sciences.

I think until you have as much as this you are not going to get very far ahead or make very rapid progress. This is in spite of the fact that the subject is obviously so terribly important. For the mere importance of a subject does not warrant the expectation that results can be obtained. This applies no matter how hard you work or how many people are working. I was present at an informal gathering recently at which a number of economists and other social scientists betrayed a point of view which struck me as rather naive, if you will pardon me for saying so. Some physical scientists were also present, and the social scientists turned to them and implored them to please direct some of the good young men who were getting doctor's degrees from the physical sciences into the social sciences. "You are taking all the good men. Why don't you turn some of the good men over to us?" I think that betrayed an ignorance of the way things happen in science. People do not go into a subject merely because it is important. They do not go into a subject until a method of attack is obvious—until someone has got hold of the end of a string which you can pull out and which is evidently going to lead somewhere. Just conviction of importance is not going to make any young man with intelligence or ambition go into a subject unless he sees far enough ahead to be convinced that he is going to get somewhere. Standing on the outside, I do not yet see that assurance sufficiently in the social sciences.

I have indicated that this is a long range problem. It may be thousands of years before you get anywhere. It was 2,000 years before physics got anywhere. I do not know why you expect to get ahead so fast.

The ultimate problem in the social sciences is similar to that in the physical sciences but is infinitely more complex. The ultimate problem is the problem of understanding the functioning of the elementary units of which the systems are built up. The elementary units in the physical sciences are particles. There are only a few kinds of them. It took us a long time to find some of the laws and we haven't got the laws for some of the elementary particles yet. The elementary units in the social sciences are men, and the corresponding ultimate problem is to understand the individual human being. We see how infinitely more complex the social problem is. This is not only because man is built up of so many atoms, that is, physical particles, but for another reason which may in principle make a fundamental difficulty. This it seems to me is the fact that the behavior of a man is not determined by the present state of the man but is determined by his entire past history. For present purposes we may say that a particle is described by its position and velocity and the forces acting on it at this present moment. A man, unless we literally take him apart into his component atoms, is described by everything that has happened to him since he was born. It is not certain that as a matter of principle you can ever analyze, even conceptually, things like a man into ultimate elementary components.

The principal problem in understanding the actions of men is to understand how they think—how their minds work. We are perhaps beginning to get some understanding of this and we appreciate more than formerly the part our mental tools play and the part that verbal structures play and to what a great extent man has built his own verbal and mental structures. But this means that there are great essential limitations on what men can do with their minds, and this I think we do not yet adequately appreciate.

Finally, what makes it most difficult of all is the

problem you discussed at your last meeting, that is, the problem of values. Values, I suppose, are essentially non-rational. People look at these things in an entirely different way than they do the problems of the intellect. Mankind is apparently divided into two groups, and to explore how great is the chasm between these two groups is perhaps the first task for the social scientist, because the answer is usually assumed. The usual assumption is that human beings are eventually all alike in at least the respect that they can come to agreement—that there are certain public matters on which all can agree. To what extent this assumption is true has never been subject to adequate factual examination. I think you must answer that question before you know how far ahead you can expect to go with the social sciences. It may be that there are two irreconcilable groups of people—the people who like to make things rational and the people who prefer to have feelings. Most of the questions associated with values are emotional questions—connected with feelings—and people regard it as a vested right in these matters to have their own private reactions. If a man has a belief about a matter he thinks that is enough. "This is my own private belief. I do not have to justify it. You have to respect it". As long as this attitude is common it is certainly going to be extraordinarily difficult to put the social sciences on a broad rational basis. It may be that we will not have a true social science until eventually mankind has educated itself to be more rational.

24

SCIENCE, MATERIALISM AND THE HUMAN SPIRIT*

THE CONNOTATION of this juxtaposition of words, with their background of usage in our modern society, is not, I think, altogether a pleasant one. In certain circles, at least, science is regarded as devoid of emotional elements, coldly logical and completely materialistic, while materialism is a term of opprobrium for a brand of philosophy which sees nothing beyond the world of the senses and is callously indifferent to the higher things of the spirit. Since science is coming to play such a large role in modern life, it is important to examine the justification for this widespread feeling that science is in some way inimical to a realization by man of the highest within him.

Such an examination demands in the first place a clear understanding of the meaning of the terms science and materialism. "Human spirit" might perhaps be thought to be most in need of definition, but I think a certain vagueness is tolerable here. We can get along with the negative qualification that I shall not use "human spirit" with any extranatural connotation, and in particular do not imply the existence of a soul in the sense of the theologian

---
*From the Convocation Commemorative Volume issued by The Technology Press, commemorative of the inauguration of President James B. Killian at Massachusetts Institute of Technology, 1949.

or make any commitments with regard to a future life. But "science" requires clarification because we shall be concerned with a wider range of human activity than is often covered by the accepted usage of "scientific." This is often restricted to imply the physical and biological sciences, whereas we shall want to cover psychology and the social sciences. More generally, I shall want to cover in this discussion all those activities to which the word "intelligent" is applicable, regarding science as only a special case of the exercise of intelligence in special fields. Some may want to use intelligence with a wider connotation than I shall employ here; my use of it in the sense that intelligence becomes identical with science in certain fields sufficiently indicates the sort of restriction I have in mind. Perhaps it would be better to qualify it by saying "natural intelligence." Some people, for example, might say that conscience as the voice of God is a form of intelligence; it is usage like this that I am trying to avoid.

Turning now to "materialism" this has had a special implication in traditional usage, and originally was associated with a mechanical theory of the construction of the universe. At one time materialism involved a very special mechanical hypothesis, namely that the universe could be explained in terms of the actions on each other of particles endowed with mass and exerting forces on each other which were knowable and which presumably in the last analysis could be reduced to inverse square forces. This special thesis was abandoned when the significance of the electromagnetic field equation was properly appreciated, and was presently replaced by the less restrictive thesis that the explanation of the universe could be reduced to the action on each other of particles and their fields of force. Even this more general picture is now superseded with the advent of the Heisenberg principle of indetermination and other more recent developments, so that I doubt whether a physicist today would know whether the epithet "materialistic" was properly applicable to his subject or not. We might therefore, if we were captious, take the position that materialism is a dead issue and refuse to discuss our proposed topic. But it seems to me that there was indeed a point of view underlying the old science-materialism dualism which survives and inspires present-day science, and it is to this transformed older idea in its present dress that I would like to direct your attention.

It seems to be that what survives from the old point of view is the resolve by scientists and by many other people of intelligence to carry through to the utmost the program of dealing with the universe by the methods of intelligence alone, without resorting to methods which might be roughly described as mystical or supernatural. I think it will be agreed that scientists as scientists are committed to carrying through such a program. I propose as the question for our examination to find what the implications and the reactions of such a commitment by the scientist are on the human spirit. Is the human spirit restricted by such a commitment, and if so are the restrictions onerous or degrading? I shall discuss this under two headings: In the first place, what are the demands made on the human spirit in accepting such a commitment, and in the second place, what are the reactions on the human spirit from carrying through the commitment to the extent which present-day science has carried it?

Acceptance of the commitment to exclusive use of the methods of intelligence is itself an act of intelligence. For we are not here concerned with the acceptance of arbitrary limitations for their own sake, as when one composes a crossword puzzle on a pattern of his own creation. We accept the commitment to the use of the methods of intelligence because that seems to us from all the evidence at present in hand to be the only method which has any prospect of successfully accomplishing the purpose of the scientist, which may be broadly described as understanding. The judgment that this is the only method has come from a detailed examination of all the evidence in that spirit of impersonal detachment which is usually described as "scientific." This is not the place for argument as to the validity of the conclusion, but for our present purposes we take this conclusion as given. In reaching this conclusion we have not allowed ourselves to be influenced by what it might be pleasant to believe, but have subjected ourselves voluntarily to a single supreme control, the control of agreements with the facts. In the face of a fact there is only one possible conveniences. I believe, however, that the refusal of the scientist to follow the mystic, and his resolution to submit himself to the discipline of the actual, is founded on something much deeper than considerations of convenience, and involves emotional components and value judgments which touch the human spirit. The scientist finds something abhorrent and unclean in a willingness to live in a constructed world. For this feeling no completely rational justification is possible. Although no rational justification can be found, it is nevertheless possible to analyze out several components which make more understandable the willingness of the man of science to submit himself to this discipline.

There is in the first place the intellectual challenge of the problem of adapting oneself to the external world and finding the explanation of it. This problem is enormously more difficult than the problem of constructing a world in which one may live by oneself. The joy which every true scientist feels in accepting the challenge of difficulty is, I think, not without spiritual elements. Then there is the consciousness of integrity which is the gift of the intellectual honesty that dares to discover the correct answer irrespective of personal discomfort. This consciousness of integrity abides with the scientist and is, I think, one of his most precious compensations. Finally, by voluntarily making himself the complete slave of the fact, the scientist has at the same stroke won complete freedom for himself in all other respects. For if the fact is to be supreme, a psychological device which makes it easier to carry through a program of action without continually reminding oneself that the program was adopted only because it was the program which seemed to have the greatest probability of success, or even indeed because it was the only program which was at all possible in the circumstances. It seems to require an unusual fortitude to be able to carry through a program in the clear-eyed recognition that we are doing it because some action is necessary and there is nothing else to do, without help from the belief that we shall be successful. Many of the situations of daily life are of this character, and faith has survival value in enabling us to carry on. But this need not restrain us from analyzing what faith involves or from realizing that faith is not for the scientist when he is pushing his analysis as far as possible and making his analysis as articulate as possible. Neither do I think that when he has made the analysis he will feel a sense of spiritual loss in his inability to perform acts of faith in the conventional sense, but will rather have a feeling of spiritual attainment in that he has made a step forward in his adjustment to things as they are.

The resolution to accept the fact as the supreme arbiter is not necessary. We might prefer, as does the mystic, to live in the world of fact only in so far as we are compelled by physical necessity, and to live as much as possible in a world of our own free construction. It is true that the mystic, in so doing, runs the risk of encountering certain practical inconveniences. I believe, however, that the refusal of the scientist to follow the mystic, and his resolution to submit himself to the discipline of the actual, is founded on something much deeper than considerations of convenience, and involves emotional components and value judgments which touch the human spirit. The scientist finds something abhorrent and unclean in a willingness to live in a constructed world. For this feeling no completely rational justification is possible. Although no rational justification can be found, it is nevertheless possible to analyze out several components which make more understandable the willingness of the man of science to submit himself to this discipline.

There is in the first place the intellectual challenge of the problem of adapting oneself to the external world and finding the explanation of it. This problem is enormously more difficult than the problem of constructing a world in which one may live by oneself. The joy which every true scientist feels in accepting the challenge of difficulty is, I think, not without spiritual elements. Then there is the consciousness of integrity which is the gift of the intellectual honesty that dares to discover the correct answer irrespective of personal discomfort. This consciousness of integrity abides with the scientist and is, I think, one of his most precious compensations. Finally, by voluntarily making himself the complete slave of the fact, the scientist has at the same stroke won complete freedom for himself in all other respects. For if the fact is to be supreme, course of action for the scientist, namely acceptance, no matter how much the fact may be at variance with his anticipations, and no matter what havoc it may wreak on his carefully thought out theories. In the face of the fact, the scientist has a humility almost religious.

The commitment of the scientist to the program of intelligence does not involve a blind commitment to a special "belief" about the structure of the universe, nor does it constitute an act of "faith" on his part, although it is often stated that the scientist, as well as the mystic, cannot get along without his articles of faith, in this case faith in the existence of uniform laws in nature. It seems to me that for the scientist faith can be no virtue, because it is inconsistent with the resolution to accept the fact as supreme. If it is accepted that the object of the scientist is to discover the laws of nature, as is often stated, it is perhaps justifiable to claim that the scientist, by the very form of this formulation, proclaims his belief that there are laws of nature before they have been established, and that this belief without adequate evidence is by definition an act of faith. But the scientist cannot commit himself in advance of the evidence even to the thesis that nature has laws. A more careful formulation of an objective of science is that it is to discover in nature those regularities which exist, with certainly no commitment as to how far these regularities will be found to extend.

It seems to me that the exercise of faith is mostly

restricted by such a commitment, and if so are the restrictions onerous or degrading? I shall discuss this under two headings: In the first place, what are the demands made on the human spirit in accepting such a commitment, and in the second place, what are the reactions on the human spirit from carrying through the commitment to the extent which present-day science has carried it?

Acceptance of the commitment to exclusive use of the methods of intelligence is itself an act of intelligence. For we are not here concerned with the acceptance of arbitrary limitations for their own sake, as when one composes a crossword puzzle on a pattern of his own creation. We accept the commitment to the use of the methods of intelligence because that seems to us from all the evidence at present in hand to be the only method which has any prospect of successfully accomplishing the purpose of the scientist, which may be broadly described as understanding. The judgment that this is the only method has come from a detailed examination of all the evidence in that spirit of impersonal detachment which is usually described as "scientific." This is not the place for argument as to the validity of the conclusion, but for our present purposes we take this conclusion as given. In reaching this conclusion we have not allowed ourselves to be influenced by what it might be pleasant to believe, but have subjected ourselves voluntarily to a single supreme control, the control of agreements with the facts. In the face of a fact there is only one possible there must be no limitations on the methods by which facts are discovered, but there must be complete freedom, unfettered by extraneous considerations of any sort. There are here obviously two freedoms, an inner freedom and an outer freedom. Maximum efficiency in the output of the scientist demands that he have as much outer freedom as possible. This outer freedom comes from society; it may involve financial support and support by public opinion, or it may be denied by political compulsion. But however society may be able to control the outer freedom of the scientist, it is powerless to touch the inner freedom of his thoughts. Once he has seen the vision, the consciousness of inner freedom abides with him, a companion of the consciousness of integrity, and is no less his solace and his strength. For him, the words of the scripture take on vital meaning: "The truth shall make you free."

Having examined some of the spiritual implications of the commitment of the scientist to his program, we turn to a consideration of some of the consequences of the new insights which have been acquired in carrying out the program thus far. I believe that the most important aspects of these new insights are connected with a realization of man's true intellectual position in the world, and it is to these that I shall confine my attention.

One of the new insights is a growing realization of the importance of semantics to our whole intellectual enterprise. The origin of this realization was in the experience of physics with the theory of relativity, but the full sweep of the implications is, I believe, not realized even yet. The paradoxes of relativity theory were found to be associated with imprecisions in the meanings of such common-sense words as mass and length and time. The tacit assumption of common sense that the intuitive uncritical meaning of these terms was adequate for describing nature was refuted by the discovery of unexpected experimental facts. When the meaning of such a term as length, for example, was made by Einstein precise enough to deal with the physical situation, it was found that the meaning was not unique, but multiple, and not consistent with a common-sense treatment. The physical world proves too complex to be dealt with by common sense. We are coming to see that the situation is similar in a much wider setting, as indeed it would be a miracle if it were not, considering the uncritical and haphazard way in which the whole apparatus of common-sense thinking has evolved. We see that many of the misunderstandings and failures of every-day human relations are to be laid to imprecisions in meanings. This is particularly true in the field of abstractions and of religion. For instance, the single concept of "truth" is not precise enough to do the work that we want to do with it. We have to recognize that there are different sorts of truths, such as theological truth and scientific truth, just as relativity theory forces us to recognize that optical length is not the same as tactual length. The experience of physics gives a vision of the possibility of eventually so clarifying meanings that all misunderstandings which arise from that source shall disappear as a cause of friction between men. But the task is obviously one of enormous difficulty and constitutes a challenge to the spirit of man. I believe that we have the techniques in hand for solving this problem, and that with adequate intellectual morale we shall find how to emancipate ourselves from the trammels of common sense and more effectively realize our potentialities.

A second vision which I believe is even more important than that of the role of semantics is given by a realization of the implications of the discovery of unsuspected physical structures in the direction of the very small and in the direction of the very large. In the direction of the very small, we enter a world in which the very concepts of identity and of recurrence are not applicable. Thought demands its permanent objects and its consciousness of recurrent situations; how shall we think about a world that has not these intellectual necessities? In the direction of the very large, more and more structure is being discovered by the astronomer, so that we have no right to maintain that the universe is not open. But the most sweeping generalizations that we have, energy and entropy, find their meaning only in terms of closed systems. How shall we think about a truly open system? And in general, what meaning can we give to our most fundamental concepts, such as existence itself, in realms in which the necessary processes of thought fail?

The new vision that results from an apprehension of the significance of this is a vision of man isolated on an island of phenomena between the very large and the very small, which he cannot transcend because of the nature of thought and meaning themselves. It is an evident corollary that if man is to integrate himself, he must discover his springs of action within himself. This is a task which man has been effectively shirking since the beginning of conscious thought in his endeavor to find the solution by the invention of essences and cosmic purposes and absolutes. The acceptance by man of his essential intellectual limitation and isolation, which make meaningless his absolutes, will confer upon him a freedom similar to the freedom of the scientist in accepting the fact as his supreme arbiter. For it will free him of the consequences of attempting to do with his mind things which cannot be done because of the nature of thought itself, attempts which have cluttered his entire intellectual history.

There will emerge the vision that man is standing on the very threshold of his potential development, and that this can be attained only by breaking drastically with the past. It seems to me that education can have no more important function than to impart this vision. The challenge to the human spirit of a vision like this is too obvious to need elaboration; what the eventual unfolding of the spirit may bring, no man may venture to predict.

25

*THE DISCOVERY OF SCIENCE**

THE HUMAN RACE is at present in the process of finding out something new about itself. The process of discovery has been extending over the last few hundred years and is not yet complete. The discovery has two aspects. In the first place we have discovered that the human animal is capable of engaging in scientific activity, in making scientific discoveries, and making scientific theories to help understand these discoveries. That is, the human animal is capable of "doing" science. In the second place, we have discovered that this scientific activity has emotional involvements and, in particular, is capable of giving a special satisfaction to those who engage in it.

This is not the first time that the human race has discovered that it has unsuspected characteristics, characteristics produced only incidentally in the course of evolution and by no means necessary for survival. A very early discovery must have been that words can be used for pleasure only, apart from their use in communicating factual information, and the art of poetry has been with us ever since. Perhaps a somewhat later discovery was that the human animal responds emotionally to music. We

*From Harvard Alumni Bulletin, November 8, 1952.

can imagine that music, at least in its instrumental modes, was discovered after poetry, because the fashioning of musical instruments demands a fairly highly developed craftsmanship. The reason that science has appeared on the human scene so much later than poetry or music is that much more elaborate preparation is necessary for it. Science is not possible without a background of an enormous amount of factual information or without the development of technical tools of research.

The human race has by now pretty well found what values to attach to poetry and music and has found how to live with its poets and musicians. I have no doubt, however, that among the early cavemen there were some who groused at the late hours of a too popular bard and perhaps even subjected him to mayhem. The human race, on the other hand, has not yet found how to adapt itself to all the implications in its newly-discovered capacity for science, although adaptation is urgent because the impact of science on the life of everyone is incomparably more formidable than was ever the impact of poetry or music.

There are pleasant and unpleasant aspects of this impact. The pleasant aspects may be typified by the multifarious new amenities of daily life, such as the telephone or the automobile or modern medicine, all of which are an outgrowth of previous scientific activity and would not have been possible without it. The unpleasant aspects may perhaps be typified by the atomic bomb. The impact of the bomb has been so tremendous that at present the unpleasant results of science seem to be uppermost in the minds of many people, and there appears to be an increasing mood of animosity toward science and scientists. Furthermore, the reaction against science is overshooting its mark and is resulting in a general mood of anti-intellectualism and intellectual defeatism. Many people despair of the ability of the human intelligence to grapple with its problems and are grasping at any straw that offers. It is therefore of the greatest importance that the true nature and implications of science be understood. There are implications not only for the more material circumstances of our existence, but also for those more intangible aspects which may be conveniently lumped under considerations of value. It is with these latter that we shall concern ourselves.

What are the drives that make the scientist go, and what are the values implied in these drives? We must also ask what are the values which society must prize if science is to flourish, for the attitude of society does determine to a large extent whether science will flourish or whether it will be driven underground and eventually extirpated. It is to be said in the first place that the question of values is not very consciously present to the scientist himself as he engages in his scientific activities, nor is he conscious of his drives. These have to be inferred by a disinterested spectator from the sidelines, or even by the scientist himself as he thinks over his day in his armchair at night. It seems to me that what the scientist does is perhaps best characterized by saying that he has set himself a problem, and that his values are more or less incidentally involved in its solution—it is the problem that bulks important for the scientist. The problem of the scientist is, as I see it, to find out as much as he can of the world about him, and having found what the facts are, to reduce them to the best sort of understanding that he can.

This characterization of the scientist is obviously not inclusive. It would be difficult to make an inclusive characterization, but, with the exercise of a little good will, I think it will prove adequate for our purposes. There is no compulsion on any individual or even on society as a whole to accept the problem of the scientist, and in fact a large part of the human race feels no compulsion and recognizes no intrinsic interest in the solution of the problem. That the scientist does accept this problem involves what may be called, I suppose, his system of values.

Given then the problem of the scientist—to find out as much as he can and to understand as much as he can about the world around him—it is evident that the fact occupies a position of fundamental importance. The facts must be correctly reported in all pertinent detail, and no theory can endure which is at variance with any single fact. The discipline of the fact, to which the scientist must submit himself, is a discipline of complete rigor, incomparably more rigorous than the discipline of any medieval monk. Acceptance of this discipline demands the suppression of some favorite human frailties, particularly those dealing with enhancement of the ego. We have to mistrust the reliability of our senses, and be willing to submit any report to constant cross-checking and verification. We must similarly submit the results of our reasoning processes to continual questioning and checking. All this is to say nothing of the crasser vices of intellectual conduct, such as wishful thinking or the seeking of personal advantage.

There is, it seems to me, an emotional component in the acceptance by the scientist of the discipline of the fact, just as there was doubtless an emotional component in the acceptance by the medieval monk of his discipline. The emotional factor is not to be dismissed with the observation that acceptance of the discipline of the fact is a necessary precondition to the solution of his problem by the scientist.

Many people, perhaps most, do not regard the discipline of the fact as something to be accepted, but rather as something to be avoided as far as possible. Such people would be willing to live in a world of their own construction, and I can see no reason why they should not if they can find how to get away with it. Acceptance of the fact is, however, so deeply ingrained in the scientist that he finds something unclean in the thought of living in a world of his own construction.

The scientist, having made himself the complete slave of the fact, has at the same stroke won complete freedom in every other respect, for no prohibition or inhibition can be recognized which militates in any way against the recognition of any fact. In designing his experiment or formulating his theory no holds are barred for the scientist—his limitations are set by his own capacities and such limitations are not felt as limitations of freedom. The consciousness of freedom is, I think, always present to the scientist and is itself one of his values.

To the scientist there is no argument about this matter—he feels an inner freedom of which no external social compulsion can deprive him, although he always recognizes that social compulsion can drive him underground. This sense of freedom is, of course, not peculiar to the scientist, but all of us have it to a greater or less degree. I hope I have not misinterpreted the anthropologist in my opinion that the concern of the individual with his own freedom appears comparatively late in social evolution. The scientist's especial feeling of the necessity of freedom and his exultation in it would appear to be consistent with his late appearance on the evolutionary scene. Incidentally, it seems to me that the ideology of communism, in ignoring and suppressing the sense of freedom of the individual, is attempting to live in a world constructed contrary to nature, a course which it seems to me must eventually react unfavorably on the effectiveness of at least its scientific activities.

The problem which the scientist has set himself is not an easy one, and in the challenge offered by the overcoming of difficulty is to be found one of the values of science. Of course every discipline has its own difficulties and the challenge of difficulty can always be found. We can all appreciate the reaction of the mountain climber who has to climb the mountain simply because the mountain is there. In science, however, the challenge of difficulty is particularly insistent and in fact the limits which most hamper the scientist are limits set by difficulties which he has not yet found how to surmount. The scope of his problem is enormous and is taking him further afield than he had ever suspected when he embarked. He is finding, for example, that an essential part of his problem is to understand the nature of his intellectual tools, an understanding which the race has not yet achieved, in spite of long concern with it. The highest capacities of the mind are demanded.

Added to the challenge of difficulty is the challenge of the unknown, which has always appealed to men in all conditions. The scientist gets no less a thrill out of penetrating into a previously unknown domain of knowledge than does the explorer in finding landscapes previously unseen by man. This element of adventure is always present to some degree in every activity of the scientist, because he is almost entirely occupied with finding facts or inventing theories which are new—the scientist does not go over ground already known. Just as the average human being can take vicarious pleasure in the discoveries of the explorer, so he can take a vicarious pleasure in the discoveries of the scientist—once discovered, they are a part of the heritage of the race which cannot be taken from it.

All these drives and values thus far discussed play their part in making the scientist go, but I think the most powerful is still to be mentioned. The scientist would not concern himself with a problem to which the fact is so basic if he did not feel a certain congeniality in the presence of the fact. The scientist likes facts, particularly new ones, and he wants to find what they are. Or, differently expressed, one of the most important drives of the scientist is curiosity. He wants to know just for the sake of knowing, and he also wants to understand just for the sake of understanding. These two drives can hardly be separated, for usually knowledge is a prerequisite to understanding. Although the driving curiosity of the scientist is often recognized as one of his most important characteristics, I think that nevertheless the full implications are not usually appreciated.

Many people have claimed that there is a basic incompatibility between scientist and non-scientist, and there have been many attempts to diagnose and formulate the differences. Thus, it is said that science is materialistic and incompatible with the things of the spirit or with religion, or that science is hard, unemotional, literal, and incapable of poetic feeling. I think that most of these formulations are beside the mark and can be refuted. Much scientific work is highly imaginative, and the scientist often stands in wonder before the beauties he finds or constructs. At the same time I think that in rejecting the unsound formulations we may minimize what seems to me the incontrovertible, very real difference between scientist and non-scientist. This has got to be squarely faced and analyzed as best we can and not shrugged aside by arguments which to me smack too much of appeasement. I think there can be no question of the existence of an incompatibility or of the reality of the dislike which many people feel toward the scientist. It seems to me that the incompatibility and dislike are tied in pretty closely with the insatiable and universal curiosity of the scientist of which we were speaking a moment ago. The scientist *wants* to know and to discover, even if what he finds is disagreeable.

I think the great majority of people, on the other hand, would rather not know the disagreeable things, a frame of mind expressed in the popular saying "what you don't know can't hurt you." With a frame of mind like this it is only natural to feel resentment against anyone who forces one to think of disagreeable matters and therefore presumably to do something about them. This is understandable enough and is perhaps unavoidable, but I think the resentment overshoots its mark and the scientist is often charged with creating the disagreeable situation which he uncovers.

The atomic bomb is a dramatic example; it is very common for the scientist to be charged with the whole responsibility for the situation created by the bomb, and I have no doubt that most people wish that the scientist never had discovered that the bomb is possible. Many even think that the scientist should not have allowed nature to be so constructed that the bomb is possible. To which, I imagine, the scientist would retort that it is not the knowledge that atom bombs can be produced that is making the trouble, but rather it is that men are willing to produce them. If one does not want atom bombs, the way to deal with the situation is not to make them. I believe the scientist would add that it is not he who is making them but society—at least it is society that is footing the bill, including two billion dollars for the first one.

Even in a case as extreme as this, I think the scientist would maintain that knowledge in and of itself is wholly good, and that there should be and are methods of dealing with misuses of knowledge by the ruffian or the bully other than by suppressing the knowledge. It looks to the scientist as though a large part of society in its present temper is willing to deal with the situation by suppressing the scientist because it is easier to suppress the scientist than to suppress the ruffian and the bully.

To the scientist this fear of knowledge displayed by a part of society appears wholly contemptible, and acceptance of the proposal advocated by many that a moratorium should be declared on science to be wholly unthinkable. Here is what seems to me the fundamental incompatibility that has got to be squarely faced, an incompatibility perhaps more deep seated than the incompatibilities between the common man and the poet or the musician with which the race has long since found how to deal. Scientists are human beings, and the potentiality for science is not the least precious of the great heritages of the human race. What do you propose to do with your heritage?

26

*THE TASK BEFORE US**

IT IS ONLY FAIR that I should acquaint you with some of the personal background of this talk. The immediate incentive came from Professor Northrop's talk last month, which to those who heard it was a stimulating and for me, at least, a provocative experience. He painted a vivid picture of the roots of our democracy in the philosophy of the founding fathers, a philosophy based on scientific views of nature stemming from Galileo and Newton. Professor Northrop illuminated his thesis by the observation that the moral awakening of Thomas Jefferson followed on his study of mathematics, with its revelation of absolute certainty and rigor based on eternal truths. He closed his talk with the intimation that we have been straying from the vision of the founding fathers, and his very last sentence was that the founding fathers were *men,* and men of high intelligence at that. As I listened I could not help wondering whether the philosophy of the founding fathers, if they were living today, would not be altered by the revolutions in scientific thinking of this century. In particular, how would Thomas Jefferson have reacted to the apparently irreconcilable schism between mathematicians as to the foundations of

*From Proc. Amer. Acad. Arts and Sciences, 83, 97-112, 1954.

mathematics. Would he have reacted like Bertrand Russell, who in his early days set himself the goal of absolute rigor and certainty, and who has ended by declaring that the only certainty in this world is uncertainty? What sort of democracy would have been created by founding fathers who had taken to heart the lessons of relativity and quantum theory? I think the presumption is that it would at least have been different from what we have. If it would have been different, why should we not now be discussing how it would have been different? But a re-examination of fundamentals is distasteful to many, perhaps particularly in the context of present world affairs. It seems to me that from the long-range point of view it may turn out that the most serious scar left by our encounters with Nazism and Communism will have been inflicted by our defense of our democracy as a finished institution. We have forgotten to regard it as a growing thing, evolving to meet our evolving conceptions of ourselves and our place in nature.

Professor Northrop's talk only accentuated in me an intellectual malaise which has many other sources. A growing anti-intellectualism is in the air, the manifestations of which on the political stage are too clearly before us to require further comment. Anti-intellectualism may be only one symptom of something more deep-seated. I must confess that the recent change of emphasis at my own University introduced by the new administration gives me misgivings in this direction. The emphasis is on a return to humanistic attitudes which we are forgetting in the hurly-burly of our technology, but without, as far as I can see, any notable revitalization of these humanities themselves in the light of our recent intellectual experiences. It seems to me that in this cry for a "return" there is grave danger that we shall turn our backs on a job which not only is not finished but which is hardly begun. This job is to assimilate into our whole intellectual outlook, and in particular into our relation to social problems, the lessons implicit in scientific experience. What these lessons are in detail or how they may modify our social structures is not yet evident; only is it evident that we are standing on the threshold of outlooks so revolutionary that when the revolution has been accomplished most of man's intellectual, as distinguished from his esthetic, history will be obsolete. If only a glimpse were caught of this situation, I think the importance of getting on with the problem thus presented would so overwhelm us that the possibility of any sort of "return" simply would not occur to us.

A theme such as this is one for the tongues and minds of angels; you may well ask by what right have I the temerity to undertake it? But I think the question of right does not bother me as much as another question, the question of profitableness. Will a talk on this theme do any good? One is, I think, justified in serious misgivings on this score. I was much taken aback recently by the remark of one of my scientific colleagues that people in general are fed up with being told what a mess the human race has got itself into and with any sort of destructive criticism. The widespread revolt against "positivism" is part of the same pattern. Somewhat in the same vein was a talk before this Academy a number of years ago by the son of a very eminent philosopher. He described the intellectual confusion in the younger generation in England after the first World War, who had lost all sense of purpose and direction, and he placed the blame squarely on the older generation, who he said had failed the younger generation in not giving them the certainties they needed. This attitude is, I think, pretty widespread. As if a man can have certainty because he needs it, or as if the older generation can produce a certainty for their children which the human race in all its experience has not yet achieved!

This audience may perhaps be willing to take it as a compliment that in spite of all these misgivings I have nevertheless been willing to take the gamble that the loftiness of the theme might justify me in imposing on your time. I was encouraged to take this gamble by the remarks of President Land at the end of the last session, who said that a speaker for the next session had not yet been engaged and asked for suggestions. To which I responded by unblushingly suggesting myself. I am at any rate most grateful that you were willing to give me the opportunity.

I propose now in the first part of this talk to consider some of the changes in intellectual attitude forced on us by recent scientific experiences. The full effect of these changes on our attitude toward society will doubtless require considerable time to become manifest, and some of you may feel that the whole thing is too long-range and indirect to be of immediate concern. In the second part of the talk, however, I hope to present other sorts of considerations of more concrete and immediate application.

There has been extensive popular discussion of the lessons of both relativity theory and quantum theory, and such notions as the shortening of a meter stick when set in motion or the Heisenberg principle which states that a particle cannot simultaneously have both position and momentum are fairly well known. But it is not these narrow technical matters which are of significance for us, but broader points of view, points of view to which we would be equally forced whether a meter stick shortened or lengthened when set in motion. What appears to me to be one of the most important of these, so important that I would regard its possession as a necessary mark of a liberally educated man, is a vital realization that our thinking and our intellectual processes in general cannot be taken for granted. When we think, we use intellectual tools; and these tools have properties and have their limitations. We usually take our concepts for granted, not realizing that their use grew over many generations, generations which never were very conscious of what was happening but were satisfied if the new concepts served the purposes of the moment. In particular, recent experience shows that when we push the application of many of these concepts into new fields, limitations appear which we could not have anticipated from anything in our former more limited common-sense experience. In fact, we have now come to *expect* that a concept inherited from our ancestors will not be applicable when pushed into fields hitherto unentered. Thus it is that our common-sense notions of simultaneity failed in new regions of extraordinarily high velocities, or our everyday notions of the permanence and identity of objects failed in the submicroscopic domain. Analogy should lead us to see that the presumption is that such social concepts as human rights or duties or responsibilities will have to be modified when the environment in which they arose is altered, as it now is, by technological advances that bring all men all over the world into immediate mutual relations.

It does not need a very extensive acquaintance with the new physics to draw the sort of lesson that we have just emphasized: relativity and quantum theory would suffice. These are parts of physics which have already become "classical" in the sense that there is practical unanimity in their acceptance, and there is an impressive record of success in applying the ideas in concrete situations. But there are other parts of physics in which the physicist himself is not yet clear as to the ultimate outcome and which are still controversial. Without waiting for the final solutions, I think we may draw even more important conclusions from the fields yet unconsolidated than from those which we have already mastered. It is perhaps not a common idea that there are still regions in which the scientist is groping his way and knows that he has not yet found the answers. Failure to realize this is, I think, one of the reasons back of the impatience of so many people with the scientific point of view, and back of the urge to return to a more humanistic outlook.

We have already mentioned one of the still unsolved problems in the inability of mathematicians to agree on the logical foundations of mathematics, particularly on the nature of infinity and mathematical "existence." Another unsolved problem with even farther reaching implications is the problem of the "observer" in quantum physics. We find that we can always push our analysis to the point where the measuring instrument has to be considered as part of the system, and the interaction of the measuring instrument with the rest of the system essentially modifies the results. This sort of thing can be handled satisfactorily enough by the Heisenberg principle of indetermination. But the question which has not yet been satisfactorily answered is how to handle the observer that uses the measuring instrument. May perhaps the observer be handled as a sort of super-measuring instrument? But if I can replace the observing you by an instrument, how then shall I handle the observing me which observes you, and which is always in the background and has never been got rid of? The dilemma with which we are faced is that in order to think about a system or situation we apparently always have to imagine ourselves as an observer standing on the outside, whereas when we try to do it, we find that we always end inside the system we try to stay outside of. The problem is important for our general point of view because the problem of understanding how I function as an observer or a measuring instrument is part of the wider problem of understanding myself. This problem has been recognized for a long time as one of the fundamental ones. It was Socrates who said, "Know thyself." I can hardly expect to construct a satisfactory society unless I understand my fellow man, and how shall I understand my fellow man if I do not understand myself? I think recent experience is beginning to throw new light on this age-old problem of knowing thyself; we are beginning to see that it is a very special kind of problem and that perhaps it does not admit the sort of solution we had anticipated.

There is a recent technical achievement in logic which I find tremendously suggestive in this respect. Some of you may be familiar with Gödel's theorem. Gödel was able to prove that it is not possible to prove that a logical system does not contain concealed self-contradictions or inconsistencies by the use of any theorem which can itself be derived from the basic postulates of the system in question. In other words, no system can ever prove itself free from contradiction. If you want to prove freedom from contradiction you have to go outside the system to do it, which implies using theorems for which there is no proof in the original context. The enunciation of this theorem by Gödel created no less than a furor among the logicians, and the buzzing has not yet died down. For this theorem at one stroke stultified the attempts of some of the ablest mathematicians. It showed that attempts are forever futile such as those of Hilbert, for example, who sought to prove by the principles of arithmetic that arithmetic contains no concealed contradictions which some day may be discovered and bring down the whole intellectual edifice in ruins. One can perhaps prove that arithmetic contains no self-contradiction, but in order to prove it one must go outside arithmetic. If then one tries to prove that the system in which it was proved that arithmetic has no contradictions itself has no contradictions, one must now go outside the super-arithmetical system. The regress has no end. But actually there is an end. For at any epoch the system containing all men and their activities is an upper limit which may not be exceeded. Logical certainty is unobtainable, and in hoping for it we are deceived by a mirage of our own creation.

It is tempting to generalize Gödel's theorem to situations wider than those presented by formal logic. A logical system attempting to prove that it itself is free from contradiction is a special case of a system dealing with itself. We are tempted to try the generalization: "Whenever a system attempts to deal with itself by including itself as a special case among others, it will be found that special awkwardnesses and infelicities, if not downright impossibilities, are encountered." The "Know thyself" of Socrates presents a special case of a system dealing with itself. I rather suspect that Socrates bit off more than can be chewed. The pressing problem for us becomes "what sort of self-knowledge is the best that we can hope to acquire?"

A possible line of attack on this problem is through a better understanding of the nature and functioning of the brains that do our thinking. Much attention is now being given to this problem; many papers are being written on models which imitate one or another of the aspects of the brain, and there was, for example, a symposium at Christmas time in the house of this Academy on the question as to what extent the brain may be regarded as a machine. All the recent interest and activity with cybernetics points in the same direction. Parts of cybernetics deal with highly technical problems of communication theory as needed, for example by the telephone engineers, but back of it all there is a growing concern with the basic problem of what sort of a thing the brain is. This, I think, can only result in a better understanding of the whole situation. One of the results which is beginning to emerge is a realization of the extent to which our conscious activities have to be selected from the overwhelming number of potentialities. Ever since Freud, people have known that large parts of the activities of the brain never get into consciousness. It is only recently, however, that calculations have been made of the numerical possibilities of our conscious awareness. The figures that one gets are no less than stunning. It is known that the neurones in the brain serve in some way as basic elements in brain processes, and it is known that the brain contains something of the order of ten billion neurones. Let us suppose for the argument that different states of consciousness correspond to different ways of connecting the neurones together. Furthermore, suppose that recognizably different states of consciousness cannot follow each other more rapidly than one hundred per second, much too generous an estimate. Then it may be calculated that in a lifetime of one hundred years a man will be able to have about three hundred billion different conscious experiences. But the total number of conscious experiences with which his mental machinery is capable of providing him is so great that the number of lifetimes of one hundred years required to experience them all is a billion times the total number of electrons in the entire universe. It follows that the pictures which our perceptions are capable of giving us must be inconceivably abridged and conventionalized. Yet with such an instrument we have set ourselves the goal of knowing ourselves and our neighbor and the incomparably more complex external world, which we have clothed with the concept of a reality independent of the brain that conceives it. I cannot help feeling that it will have a pretty sobering effect when the significance of this simple calculation gets under our skins. I think a certain decent humility is inevitable. The problem for us becomes not to find the absolute truth but to find how to do the best we can with what we have.

So much for the lesson of cybernetics. Another recent development I find equally suggestive, this time a development in psychology. There has been much discussion in the popular press recently of the inquiries into the nature of perception initiated at Hanover by Dr. Adelbert Ames, Jr., and now taken over and extended by a group in the Department of Psychology of Princeton University, headed by Professor Cantril. Their analysis of perceptions is made by a systematic exploitation of illusions of various sorts. What the psychologist will get out of this is a better understanding of the nature of the process by which perceptions are formed. It is already apparent that the process is a complicated one which involves not only the object that is being perceived but the condition of the perceiving subject. By suitably changing the immediate past experience of the perceiving subject his perception of the object may be made to vary. There is evidently a rich field of investigation for the psychologist here in finding how the perceptions depend on the experience of the subject. For me, however, the most significant aspect of this new approach is the simple realization that it forces upon us that all our conscious thinking is done in terms of perceptions. Naked sense impressions simply do not occur, and the traditional analysis of our conscious experience into naked sensations as building blocks is palpably bad description. Perceptions we have always had with us, but they are so ubiquitous that we have not been aware of their presence. The stock question of classical epistemology has been "How is it that our perceptions are able to give us true pictures of the real external world existing out there in three dimensional space?" But what is this real world itself except a reflection of our perceptions? What sort of "reality" do our perceptions have? Under what conditions do perceptions occur? It is a matter of observation that perception occurs only in the presence of a nervous system.

We cast the world into the mold of our perceptions. The fact that the world I construct is so much like the world you construct is evidence of the similarity of our nervous systems, something which any physiologist could demonstrate for you more directly. We all of us perceive the world in terms of space and time. As interesting question is how inevitably we are forced to this perception by the common properties of our nervous systems, or to what extent it is adventitious, depending on universal features in early experience and in particular on necessities incident to the use of language. This question is possibly capable of some sort of experimental attack, but I think in any event we are here perilously close to the verge of meaning, itself. Some answer may eventually be found to the meaningful aspects of the question. In the meantime, we cannot help wondering whether perceiving the world in terms of space and time is a good way to perceive it.

You may think that we already have the answer to this question, because we already know that common-sense notions of space and time have failed in the microscopic domain of quantum phenomena. But the quantum situation is not quite the same as that which we now consider. In the quantum domain we are beyond the reach of direct perception and the "space" and "time" of this domain are constructions made and extrapolated by us. We have had to ask whether these extrapolated constructions are useful, and our answer has been that there is a point beyond which they lose their usefulness. But what we are now asking is whether in the domain of ordinary experience the mold of space and time into which perception pours our world is a good mold. There can be no question but that it is a good mold for the business of everyday life, but I begin to have my doubts when I consider the apparently endless structural detail on a continually increasing scale which the astronomers are discovering, or reflect on the significance of the continuous creation of matter which many of them are finding acceptable.

These considerations are to some extent all matters of detail. Out of all the detail emerges the one stark fact that we can never get away from ourselves. Yet apparently this is the one thing that the human race feels it has to do. The philosopher with his eternal principles and truths, the man in the street with his real external world demonstrated with a kick, the mystic with his transcendental visions, and the scientist Einstein with his general theory of relativity, are all equally engaged in the search for an absolute by which they may get away from themselves. Yet the kick of the man in the street is a kick activated and apprehended by his nervous system, and the vision of the mystic would be no vision without his nervous system. Wherever we go we find *ourselves;* an observation which has the profundity of tautology, a tautology which reduces the age-long quest of the human race for standards and springs of action outside itself to the ultimate futility, the futility of meaninglessness. What sort of peace we shall eventually make with this insight I do not know, nor do I know how the founding fathers would have acted if they had been confronted, as are we, with the necessity of finding acceptable terms for a temporary armistice until the terms of a final peace can be hammered out. But it seems inconceivable that the precise form of such of their concepts as human rights, or the dignity of the individual, or freedom or justice, so confidently enumerated in our Declaration of Independence, would have come through unscathed, for they are all tainted with the odor of the absolute.

We cannot have the founding fathers back to reconstruct our foundations for us, but we must do for ourselves the task which we may wish they might have done for us. This task is to find the present status, in the light of all the insights now available to us, of such fundamental concepts as human rights and freedom and equality and duty and justice, and in the light of these insights to strengthen if possible, or to revise if necessary, the conceptual foundation of our social and political system. This task it seems to me is a long-range one, and will demand too drastic changes in habits of thought to be accomplished in a single generation. Accomplishment of the task will demand a long campaign of education and the slow development of new intellectual techniques by a process involving much trial and error. It seems to me that the most important vision an educator can have today is the vision that this is the task of the education of the future.

Let us now turn from these abstract and somewhat academic considerations to more concrete aspects of the situation in which present-day society finds itself. These are aspects connected with the increased scale on which society now functions. A simple increase of scale may amount in practice to just as radical an alteration of fundamental conditions, and may impose as great a strain on the validity of our habits as an alteration in more patent characteristics, such, for example, as a change from a democratic to a dictatorial form of society. You remember that it was a change in scale that brought about the conceptual revolution of special relativity theory, in this case the extension of laboratory experience to velocities of a new scale of magnitude. There are several directions in which the scale of modern life has drastically altered. There is the scale of communication, by which knowledge of events may be communicated to the entire earth with the speed of light; there is the scale of transportation by which persons and goods may be transported with the speed of sound to any part of the earth; and there is the increase in size of the communities committed to the democratic process, notably our own country. In a large community the individual comes to be so remote from the details of the social machinery that he loses his sense of connection and responsibility. Furthermore, in a large community the social machinery loses the capacity to function in ways in which it could in small communities, with the result that what may have been social virtues in a small community become virtues no longer and must be replaced by new virtues.

The weapon with which we shall try to analyze the present situation is a detailed analysis of the processes which occur in a democratic society. But before doing this I shall digress long enough to remark that this weapon of detailed analysis of process is an exceedingly potent weapon and capable of the widest application. It seems to me that it is a realization of the importance of the awareness of process which is perhaps the most sweeping characterization of the new critical outlook on the nature of concepts and thinking. It was an awareness of the processes by which time is measured that led to Einstein's special relativity theory. It was the experiencing of the logical process by which certainty is to be sought that led Bertrand Russell to renounce the goal of certainty. It is by following through the details of what we do, that we have arrived at the insight that we can never get away from ourselves and that there are some things that we cannot do with our minds.

An insight which we achieve at once by an analysis of process is the insight that society is the sum of its individuals, in the sense that if the behavior of all the component individuals is specified, there is nothing more required to specify the society which these individuals constitute. In other words, a state or a society involves no super-thing in addition to its component individuals. The contrary view has been widely held and has played no little part in political developments; a striking example was the German attitude toward the State at the beginning of the first World War. Most people, I find, accept the view that its individuals compose society, when they see what the issues are. The issue can be made clearer by imagining what would be implied if there were some super-thing beyond its individuals in society. Imagine two societies, in each of which the behavior of every individual was exactly the same in all respects as the behavior of a corresponding individual in the other society, but one society was endowed with this hypothetical super-thing and the other lacked it. Then, unless one were informed, there is no way by which it can be told which of the two societies has this super-thing. The only function of a thing of this sort is to be talked about, and my own feeling is that even this deference should not be granted it. I have, however, met a few people who still want their super-thing in spite of all argument; if there are such in the present audience I cannot hope to touch them by what I am about to say.

Although most people will grant when they think about it that there is no mystical super-thing about society, nevertheless their actions are often the same as if they did believe in such a thing. "Government" is the name they give to this imaginary entity. The average citizen thinks that government can in some magic way procure for him any conceivable good. A society such as ours has become so large that the details of the process by which the government functions do not force themselves on the attention, with the result that the fundamental role of the individual is forgotten. In his happy conviction that the government can do anything, the average citizen does not bother to think where the things are coming from that he so easily demands. But things have to come from somewhere, and in a society they often have to come from other individuals. This I think was what Professor Northrop had in mind when he said that a society must have its roots in nature. There is a conservation law in society no less than in physics, and the things which people acquire have to come from somewhere.

If society is composed of its individuals it follows that my relations to society are a resultant of my relations to all the individuals who compose it, and that the roots of any rules which I may adopt to regulate my relations to society are to be found in the rules by which I regulate my relations to the component individuals. We will pursue some of the consequences of this presently.

Another insight which the consciousness of process gives is that always in the background of the relations of the individual to society is the potentiality of overwhelming force. Obviously, in an orderly society, laws require for their effectiveness the possibility of enforcement of some kind, but even in an anarchistic society at any moment ten men can band together and enforce their will on any individual. Conversely, any individual in society can, by banding with other individuals, enforce his will on any other individual or indeed on a band of other individuals weaker than his own. In a society administered by a dictator with a strong police system there is not much opportunity for the exercise of this sort of forceful compulsion by the average citizen, but in a modern democracy every citizen has the power through his vote to exert force on his fellow citizen. Modern democracies have reached such a scale, our own in particular, that the sense of force is not very vividly before the individual when he goes to the polls, but it is always there in the background, and in the aggregate it is the force exerted by individuals and the groups into which they band that runs the country. This is all too evident in the functioning of the various pressure groups which have sprung up. But every pressure group is composed of individuals, and the total force which the group exerts is the result of the behavior of its individuals.

A new social problem arises; what should be the

ethics which control the exercise of force by the individual in his role as a member of society? This problem is essentially new in its emphasis if not in its logic. Christian ethics was addressed in the large to the downtrodden members of a society ruled from above, to whom the suggestion that the average man could exert a directive force on large social movements would have appeared farcical. Greek ethics developed in city states so small that the effect of the vote of the individual on the well-being of other individuals was evident even to the unimaginative.

If our analysis of society into an aggregate of individuals is valid I think it is evident that the basis for the ethics of the unavoidable exercise of power by the individual in his capacity as a member of society is to be found in the ethics which govern the exercise of power by one individual on another. In particular, how shall I govern my imposition of force on my neighbor? Now I, and I think most decent people also, find it distasteful to exercise force on my neighbors; and we therefore endeavor to so direct our lives that any necessary such exercise of force will be reduced to a minimum. What sort of rules will conduce to this end? It is at once evident, I think, that some rules will not conduce to this end. My greater need is not a self-respecting or feasible basis of my relation to my neighbor. This is so clearly recognized between individuals that it is just as distasteful for a decent man to demand the other's property or services because he has the greater need as it would be for him to exercise physical force to compel the other to do his will. If I may not base my demand on my neighbor on my greater need, on what may I base it with self-respect? The answer is obvious. I may make demands on my neighbor if these demands are based on services which I have rendered him. Conversely, I will gladly recognize demands which my neighbor may make on me if these demands are based on services which he has rendered me. The beauty of this reciprocal relationship is that each party gains by the transaction, exchanging something he values less for something he values more. What now will be the result of an extension of this attitude between individuals to the attitude of the individual to society in the aggregate? It will mean, first, that the individual will *not be willing* to accept from society benefits for which he does not make a return. And, secondly, when all individuals in society have this attitude the net result will be that society will not exact from any individual anything for which society cannot make return to the individual. I can see no good reason why the relations between society and individual should not be based on the same considerations of exchange and mutual advantage as the relations between individuals. Many people will perhaps be loath to accept such an ideal because it seems to offer little place for the warm personal feelings which inspire their private charities to the unfortunate. I think, however, that in any event ordinary plain humanity will compel us to honor certain minimum claims of the unfortunate on the community whether or not any return is made. But except for this, it seems to me that the basis of the relationship must be the impersonal one of exchange and mutual advantage when we operate on as large a scale as in present-day society—a community of one hundred and fifty million people in our own country and the much greater community of the free world. In fact, it is obvious by now that part of the difficulty which we are finding in dealing with the rest of the free world is just the unwillingness of a self-respecting man to accept favors for which he can make no return or for which he is allowed to make no return.

The alternative to an ideal for the relation between society and individual based on mutual advantage and service is a relation based on relative need. This, it seems to me, leads directly to the welfare state with all its unlovely implications, as we can see by looking at England, where equal hardship for everyone is treated as an end in itself, whether or not the hardship of the individual bears any relation to the functioning of the community, and where envy of one's fellow receives official sanction as a basis for legislation. A society such as this can function only if it tolerates what seems to me the most obnoxious of all forms of do-goodism, namely the willingness of Paul to compel Peter to give Peter's goods to John if Paul decides that John needs them more than Peter.

Applied to our own society perhaps the most immediate consequence of acceptance of a mutual relationship based on mutual advantage would be a revision of the philosophy underlying our system of taxation, a philosophy which at present is to tax so as to evoke the minimum squawking from the whole community as measured at the polls. In a country with such an ideal I do not think we would have such spectacles as the recent pronouncement from Washington that although a certain tax is a bad tax we must keep it because we need the money.

A society in which the relations between society and individual are based on mutual advantage will be a society in which emphasis is placed on unfamiliar virtues. I will mention two of these. The first and absolutely fundamental virtue is the repugnance of the individual to exercise force against his neighbor for his own advantage. It may be that this virtue runs so counter to intrinsic drives in the human animal that there is no chance that society will ever accept such an ideal. For the masterful men, to whom the past progress of the race has been in large part due, have not been notable for their unwillingness to exert force on their fellows. Even the most necessary of human relationships, that of parent to child or of teacher to pupil, demand for their effective exercise some, perhaps slight, element of satisfaction in the consciousness of power, although we usually disguise it as a beneficent exercise. Education will certainly be necessary for the acceptance of this virtue, but it seems not an impossible goal. You may perhaps think that it was this that the Scriptures had in mind in saying that the meek shall inherit the earth. I think not, however, for the obverse of the virtue of being unwilling to force one's neighbor to act to one's own advantage is the virtue of an aggressive determination to resist encroachment by one's neighbor. This is a rather paradoxical combination; perhaps it is so rare for that reason.

The second great virtue will be the imagination that can sense the significance of the simple underlying processes and relationships that are so easily lost to sight under the ever-increasing complexities of modern life. It is not easy to keep the underlying complexities in view, and it will require high intelligence, intelligence fortified with education. Perhaps this is merely another way of saying that the great second virtue will be intelligence. This is not a new virtue; you remember that Professor Northrop told us that the founding fathers were men of intelligence.

27

"MANIFESTO" BY A PHYSICIST*

MANY SCIENTISTS MUST have been profoundly disturbed by the revelations of recent events as to what the implications of the totalitarian philosophy of the state really are. There would seem not to be room on the same planet for totalitarian states and states in which freedom of the individual is recognized. Many scientists must have been moved to try to find something to do about it. In my own case this urge to find something to do has resulted in the decision to close my laboratory to visits from citizens of totalitarian states. I have had the following statement printed, which I hand to any prospective visitor who may present himself.

Statement

"I have decided from now on not to show my apparatus or discuss my experiments with the citizens of any totalitarian state. A citizen of such a state is no longer a free individual, but he may be compelled to engage in any activity whatever to advance the purposes of that state. The purposes of

*From Science 89, 179, 1939 (February 24).

the totalitarian states have shown themselves to be in irreconcilable conflict with the purposes of free states. In particular, the totalitarian states do not recognize that the free cultivation of scientific knowledge for its own sake is a worthy end of human endeavor, but have commandeered the scientific activities of their citizens to serve their own purposes. These states have thus annulled the grounds which formerly justified and made a pleasure of the free sharing of scientific knowledge between individuals of different countries. A self-respecting recognition of this altered situation demands that this practice be stopped. Cessation of scientific intercourse with the totalitarian states serves the double purpose of making more difficult the misuse of scientific information by these states, and of giving the individual opportunity to express his abhorrence of their practices.

This statement is made entirely in my individual capacity and has no connection whatever with any policy of the University."

Science has been rightly recognized as probably the one human activity which knows no nationalisms; for this reason it has been a potent factor making for universal civilization. Action such as this is therefore to be deeply deplored and to be undertaken only after the gravest consideration. But it seems to me that the possibility of an idealistic conception of the present function of science has been already destroyed, and the stark issues of self-survival are being forced upon us. Perhaps the only hope in the present situation is to make the citizens of the totalitarian states realize as vividly and as speedily as possible how the philosophy of their states impresses and affects the rest of the world. Such a realization can be brought about by the spontaneous action of the individual citizens of the non-totalitarian states perhaps even more effectively than by their governments. Here I think is one of the few conceivable situations in which the popular conception of the social "responsibility" of "science" can touch at all closely the individual scientist.

28

A CHALLENGE TO PHYSICISTS*

THAT PHYSICISTS ARE making an important technical contribution in the present crisis is readily conceded; I believe it is in their power however, if they will only seize the opportunity, to make another contribution which ultimately may prove even more important.

From a long-range point of view the deepest issues of the present crisis are intellectual. The failure of this country up to the present has been primarily an intellectual failure—intellectual sloth, lack of imagination, and wishful thinking. The crisis of a totalitarian victory is, from the perspective of ten thousand years, an intellectual crisis. The day when the human race may evolve into a race capable of the intellectual mastery of its fate will be immeasurably postponed by such a victory. The fundamental thesis of the totalitarian philosophy is an intellectual monstrosity; to maintain that the individual is subordinate to the state simply does not make sense, and it is an intellectual affront to be asked to accept it. The only society which can suc-

*From Journal of Applied Physics, 13, 209, 1942. Written at the request of the editor.

cessfully maintain such a thesis is a society intellectually half slave and half free, a society in which compartments of intellectual activity are forever closed to scrutiny by edict. More than this, the totalitarian philosophy is actively anti-intellectual, even anti-intelligent. The totalitarians do not like to have people use their minds, and are committed to produce a society in which it will be impossible.

There is no minimizing the enormous difficulty and complexity of the task of acquiring intellectual mastery of our fate. In fact, to many people the difficulties are so patent that they have no confidence that a solution is possible. There are disturbing signs everywhere, here as well as in the totalitarian countries, of an anti-intellectual movement. There is no will to intellectual survival; there is intellectual defeatism and intellectual appeasement. Even without a totalitarian victory there is danger that Hitler may have done a permanent disservice to the race if the present intellectual defeatism, for which he is largely responsible, persists.

The race will not save itself until it achieves intellectual morale. Perhaps the two chief components of intellectual morale are intellectual integrity and a fierce conviction that man *can* become the master of his fate. The physicist is peculiarly likely to possess the two components of intellectual morale. A lifetime in the laboratory, struggling to make things work, has shown the inexorable need of intellectual integrity. And as a participant in the one most successful intellectual enterprise of the human race to date, that is, the technological mastery of nature to the extent achieved by modern physics, he is in a peculiar position to have won the conviction that not only is there no substitute for using one's mind, but that the problems which confront us are soluble and soluble by us. If physicists will only make others see their own wider vision, their ultimate influence will far transcend that of any possible technological contribution.

29

SCIENTIFIC FREEDOM AND NATIONAL PLANNING*

I HAVE TO BEGIN by pointing out the unavoidable limitations of anything that I am in a position to say. I have had no part in attempting to draw up any of the programs proposed to meet the so-desperate immediate situation. I have never been invited to appear before a Congressional hearing and have never been consulted by the government with regard to any of these problems. With regard to my own experimental work I am in the fortunate position of not needing a cent of government money and of not having received any. In view of all this and also in view of the extreme difficulty of the questions brought up by the new situations, of which no one could be more conscious than myself, I shall have to warn you that anything that I can say runs the risk of being both unpertinent and impertinent. I can see no way of avoiding this risk, however, and I shall have to take it.

All that I can hope to do is to present to you certain considerations which have struck me as a

*Here printed for the first time. Read at a Symposium on American Public Policy on Science, held at the New School, New York, December 7, 1947.

more or less detached outside observer. I have read the five volumes of the Steelman Report with more or less care, and I have talked with many of my colleagues and with many other people, some of them pretty close to the focus of things. I have received some rather definite impressions, which I would like to present for what they are worth.

The first broad impression is that practically all the considerations receiving popular attention at the present time—considerations such as are presented in the Steelman Report or in the discussions in such journals as Science or the Bulletin of the Atomic Scientists—are short range considerations. The important questions which now concern us obviously have both short- and long-range aspects. I think it fair to say that up to the present it is short range aspects which have almost completely dominated our discussions. Under the circumstances this is entirely understandable, because immediate national survival may be involved in some of the short range questions pressing for solution. But nevertheless, after the immediate emergency has been surmounted, if indeed it is surmounted, I think that you will find that long range questions remain to be answered, and that some of these are also questions of national survival. These long range questions cannot be answered by impromptu consideration when the moment is upon us, but they demand long range consideration, and that means consideration now. I think our entire national history, particularly the history of the last war, makes it only too evident that a besetting national weakness has been our habit of trying to settle fundamental questions when the emergency is upon us. It is true that in the last war we did show a marvelous ability to rise to the immediate situation, but there were other aspects which are not so pleasant in retrospect and which would have left a better taste in our mouths if we had made a long range ideological preparation. In my opinion one of the less satisfactory of our activities was the way in which the draft was handled. It was handled in such a way that we now find ourselves confronted with such a shortage of scientists that it may prove crippling. This situation was anticipated by many at the time and many abortive attempts were made to rectify the matter. The reason that those in authority allowed matters to take their course, in spite of the crisis which they could see approaching, was that in their opinion it would have so offended the democratic ideals of the general community to modify the terms of the draft in the direction of the exemption of scientists that the community would not have stood for it. But if this situation could have been seen coming far enough ahead, the democratic ideals of the community could have been modified by education sufficiently to permit action which was so obviously to the ultimate advantage of the entire community. Other instances of the same sort of thing could be given.

Somewhere and somehow it should be the business of someone to be concerned with such long range matters. I am assuming that this organization is one which may properly concern itself with such questions.

These long range questions cannot be answered without consideration of the entire social background and the fundamental social philosophy of our country. Temperamentally the people of our country find uncongenial the discussion of long range questions or even planning for the future of the sort contemplated in the Steelman reports. We must, I think, recognize this as a source of weakness, particularly in the present cold war with Russia, which has its roots in a conflict of ideologies. We do not find consideration of ideologies congenial, whereas our opponents revel in this sort of thing, and are prepared for the present conflict by argument and ideological discussion extending through the last fifty or one hundred years. In order to cope with them I fear we will have to bring ourselves to do things uncongenial to us.

Among the fundamental long range questions of which there seem to me to be no adequate discussion is: how to reconcile our present ostensible ideal of a free science with a science which is at the same time the servant of the state. It is no answer to say, as one might be tempted to, that science is not the servant of the state, because it is obvious to everyone that if the emergency became too serious science would be impressed again into the service of the state as it was in the last war. But how far should we go in this direction now, when there is possibility of war but no certainty, while we are trying to save all those values, including a free science, which make life worth living, and which ultimately are the justification of any war we might fight? I have seen no adequate discusssion of this matter. But obviously considerations of this sort color the entire Steelman Report, which throughout shows a consciousness of the existence of these two entirely incompatible requirements, but without the formulation of any principle by which the dilemma may be resolved. Even if war should come, there should be some preliminary discusssion of how we may best preserve the maximum of scientific and intellectual freedom compatible with survival.

The crisis which will force this sort of consideration upon us may be nearer than is realized in view of certain developments in Russia of which no one in this country apparently has any knowledge. The British are, however, aware of it, as shown by two quotations which I shall read from Nature, the British scientific weekly. The first is from the issue of September 6, 1947. "The new law on disclosure of State secrets published in Moscow on June 11 is a portent which may more than outweigh movements among scientific workers themselves, such as...... The new Russian law classifies, among other subjects, as secret and not to be disclosed under penalties up to twenty years imprisonment, 'information constituting State secrets concerning industry as a whole and individual branches of it, agriculture, trade, and transport', and 'discoveries, inventions, technical improvements, research and experimental work in all branches of science, technology and national economy'". The second is from the issue of November 15. "Whether even in the field of science these relations of trust and understanding can be established in the face of restrictions on movement and such restraints of communication of scientific and technical information as those of the new Russian law on disclosure of State secrets, may be doubtful". It seems to me that the situation is weighted with the most serious possibilities. In the face of a situation like this, one of the objectives outlined in Part I of the Steelman Report becomes impossibly naive, namely that we should support a revival of the laboratories and the scientific work of Europe on the understanding that information so obtained shall be made free and available to everyone.

I think that long-range considerations demand more discussion of the reasons why national planning and encouragement of science are necessary at all. The reason given in the Steelman Report is that encouragement of science is necessary to maintain that continual expansion of our national economy which is essential to our way of life. What is involved in such a thesis and where does it lead us? Do we want to be committed to such an economy that we are compelled to be always ahead of the whole world? It seems to me that this is one of the things contributing to our present difficulties. We are already so far ahead with our labor-saving devices that we can produce more than we use, while at the same time our economy demands that we keep on producing more than we can use. This demands that we export the surplus. Obviously there would be no demand for this surplus if other nations were as advanced as we, so that in order to keep ourselves going we have to continually remain in a position of superiority to other nations. A result of this is that other nations find themselves in the position of being continually less and less able to repay us for what we force them to take. The situation is self-defeating, and furthermore is a potent source of feelings of bitterness toward us by the other nations. We have the tiger by the tail and do not know how to let go.

It seems to me that there should be some examination of the tacit assumption of the necessity for maximum efficiency in our science. We may be willing to grant that science may be made more efficient by the sort of planning that is outlined in the Reports, but why should we want the maximum efficiency if that means that we are getting ourselves into the position of having to support the entire world and making it impossible for them to support themselves or to repay us? It seems to me that a little less efficiency is indicated. Once we had made up our minds to put up with a little less efficiency, many of the problems raised by planning would solve themselves.

There are certain other aspects of the contemplated government support of science which I would now like to consider. To me one of the most significant things is the attitude of the scientists themselves. I have talked wih many of them and have not found a single one who is happy about it. They may accept it, but with misgivings and nostalgia for the days when it was not necessary. They regard it as necessary partly because of the international situation and partly because of the changes within science itself. Here things have become so large and expensive, particularly in the field of physics, that the necessary instruments cannot be financed by our privately endowed universities. Of course a large part of the reason for this is the change in our whole economic set-up, which is making impossible the private accumulation of large wealth. The scientists are unhappy and disturbed both from long- and short-range considerations. From the short-range point of view they are disturbed because they know how unpleasant dealings with the government can be; they know how complicated government action can be and how tied up with red tape. I still have vivid recollections of my endeavors to collect seven dollars of travel money. This sort of thing is perhaps particularly uncongenial to the scientist, with his habit of direct dealing.

From the long-range point of view the scientist has a deep mistrust of this continual drift of all the resources of the country into the hands of the government. It is an irreversible process, with everything eventually getting down to the dead level of government management—a sort of second law of social dynamics. In this connection I venture to quote from Professor Rabi, who is in the audience this afternoon. If I had known that he was to be here, I would not have undertaken to give this talk at all, because he is so much better qualified than I. At one of the centennial meetings in Princeton in September, 1946, Dr. Rabi made the following statement, which I quote from the book *Physical Science and Human Values* recently issued by the Princeton University Press. "If it was decided to control universities and university research, there could be no better way to do this than the way it is being done now". That is, if the government set out to eventually control the universities it would start gradually, getting them at first to accept support under conditions which were perfectly innocuous. Presently the universities will get so used to accepting government support that they become dependent on it, and then other sources of support will dry up and then there will be some accidental change in the community set-up or something more deliberate and sinister which will modify the conditions of government support and the universities will have to accept or perish.

It seems to me that these possibilities constitute a very real source of apprehension. It is obvious that it is not in the realm of the inconceivable that some of these sources of apprehension might be removed. Many people with whom I have talked have remarked how fine it would be if the government would only give money in support of the universities without any strings attached, just as a private individual now can give money to the universities. But, of course, everyone wistfully added, it is hopeless to expect such an idealistic solution. The reason that it appears hopeless is that such a thing would be contrary to the governmental process and to the theory of government in this country. It seems to me that this is evidence of something pretty deep-seatedly wrong. Here is something which all admit would be to the advantage of the whole country, but we are estopped because of our theory of government. Is it not time to begin a long range reexamination of the presuppositions of our government?

A striking example of the wide-spread prevalence of this feeling, not only among scientists but among everybody else, is afforded by the President's veto of the National Science Foundation bill. I read about this in the newspapers when the veto was announced, and my first reaction was that the reasons given by the President for the veto were a manifestation of extraordinary naivete on his part. It seemed to me perfectly obvious that one of the objects of the bill was to get control of these matters out of the hands of the President and into civilian hands, and here was the President saying that he had to veto the bill because the bill was trying to accomplish just what everyone was agreed ought to be accomplished. But it turned out that it was I that was naive and not the President. For the minute it was pointed out that to have taken these things out of the hands of the President and given them to civilians would have violated our theory of government, all agreed that nothing else could have been done, and took their scoldings and agreed to be good boys in the future.

It seems to me that it is at least unimaginative to be willing to be balked by things like this in this new atomic age, when we are discussing such things as the necessity of sacrificing our national sovereignty and inventing new machinery such as United Nations and perhaps world government. Is it not at least arguable that in situations of such novelty the foundations of our own government should be re-scrutinized to see what revision is demanded there? Yet throughout the whole Steelman report runs the tacit thesis that operation out of the frame work of our present theories and practices is impossible and inconceivable. The scientist is continually being exhorted to learn to operate within the democratic process, as if there were any such a thing as "a" democratic process. In one place in the report there is a statement that an obviously desirable method of dealing with the employment of scientists by the government is impossible because it would violate government personnel policies which had been sanctioned by long use, and which rest on the theory that in a democratic government the government is a single employer and as such must deal with all its employees in the same way.

Whatever our underlying philosophy of government it seems to me fair to say that it has never been adequately scrutinized and is one into which, in its present form, we have drifted. We have drifted into a sentimental democracy, in which everyone is considered to be as good as everybody else, no matter what his native ability or his contribution to the community. While Russia is drifting away from the sentimental equalitarianism of Marx, we are drifting toward it, as expressed in the celebrated aphorism, "To every man according to his need, and from every man according to his ability". It seems to me that if it is to the obvious advantage of the entire community to give special treatment to special groups, such as the scientists, it is absurd to be shackled by such a theory of government that this is impossible. It seems to me that this could be handled without imperiling any of our fundamental democratic ideals, which I am convinced all of us would insist on retaining even at the expense of certain disadvantages. By removing all individual considerations from the relation between the government and the scientist and putting it on an entirely impersonal basis, it seems to me that we would be adequately safe-guarding the foundations of democracy and at the same time giving it sufficient flexibility to meet obvious social needs.

30

SENTIMENTAL DEMOCRACY AND THE FORGOTTEN PHYSICIST*

IN THE ECONOMIC reshuffling which has been taking place in this country during the last fifteen years the relative economic position in society of the physicist has very materially worsened. In fact, for many physicists, particularly in the upper age groups, not only their relative position but their absolute position has worsened. For in many universities the rate of salary increase has not kept pace with the increase of differential taxation, so that the take home pay of these physicists in dollars is actually less now than it was fifteen years ago. What this means with our depreciated dollar is all too evident. Physicists are not alone in a debasement of their relative position, but the same is true more or less of all whose livelihood depends in one way or another on mental ability above the average. It is not from a desire to flatter my audience that I make no apology for including the physicist among those with more than average mental ability, but it seems to me that this is merely a statement of fact.

*After dinner speech made at the annual meeting of the American Physical Society in January 1949. The speech is here reproduced substantially as read, except for the addition of the second paragraph. Printed here for the first time.

DEMOCRACY AND THE FORGOTTEN PHYSICIST

For instance, no teacher of physics can have any doubt of it who has seen the difficulty of the average student in assimilating the concepts of physics, or who has seen the woefully small number who manage to eventually emerge with a Ph.D. degree. This wide spread relative debasement in the community of the intellectually gifted and the exaltation of the intellectually mediocre is the consequence of many motives held by many people, motives at the worst sinister and discreditable, and at the best accidental, incidental, and thoughtless. I like to think that on the whole the reasons have been accidental, incidental and thoughtless, so that the mentally gifted and the physicist in particular may more properly feel that he has been forgotten rather than deliberately abused.

I know that there are many in this audience who will deprecate the theme that I have chosen to discuss, and they will particularly deprecate my concern with the economic position of the physicist in society. They would like to remain on a higher plane where financial returns are ignored, and where the physicist finds his rewards and satisfactions in the consciousness of service to the community and the gratification of his passionate quest for understanding of the operation of the natural world about him. I can appreciate and sympathize with this point of view, and I remember that in my youth my only demand was that I be given the opportunity to push my research and the dollars could take care of themselves. However admirable this may be, I think it is a point of view that cannot long be maintained, and that eventually the disinterested life of the scientist becomes impossible in a society in which his position does not have adequate financial recognition. It is inevitable in human nature that when the financial position deteriorates, that admiration and respect which alone can give the physicist influence in the community deteriorate also. It seems to me that one of the most obvious and sinister of the social changes of the last fifteen years is just such a deterioration of the admiration and respect with which the community holds the man of unusual intellectual ability.

What now are some of the reasons for this abasement of ability in favor of mediocrity, an abasement which even the mediocre must be able to see will have disastrous long range consequences? Different sorts of reason apply at different social levels—the reasons which appealed to President Roosevelt were not the same as the reasons which appealed to the coal miner or to John L. Lewis. I would like to consider, not the reasons which have driven the mediocre to seek exaltation, which are obvious enough, but the reasons which have appealed to the superior to justify acquiescence in their own abasement. For I think that there can be no doubt that there has been such acquiescence, and that this acquiescence has played an important part in making possible the economic reshuffling. It was notorious ten years ago that a large part of communist strength and sympathy in this country was to be found among the so-called intellectuals. I must confess that I have witnessed almost with consternation the complacency with which many of my fellow physicists and other colleagues on the University faculty have accepted the debasement which is on its way to overwhelm them. Such complacency and acquiescence might conceivably be due to bad conscience. Doubtless a large part of the attitude of the English aristocracy in accepting with so little protest the leveling down of their class was a result of bad conscience. But I think that in this country bad conscience now hardly enters the picture at all, whatever may have been the case in the past, but that something else is responsible. This I think is a combination of factors that together could be found in no other country. First of these is an easy going tolerant good nature which condones our neighbor's peccadilloes and makes us unwilling to hurt his feelings or to see him uncomfortable. This characteristic in general makes for harmonious living together, but when practised uncritically may on occasion lead to less happy results. A paradoxical accompaniment of this characteristic is a willingness to force on one's neighbor one's own private conception of the good or of what is good for the neighbor, whether or not the neighbor has a similar conception of the good or wants to do what may be good for him. Paternalism in government springs from this trait. Such a conception of what is permissible for a man to do to his neighbor seems to me curiously out of place in a democracy, which should be founded on a jealous respect by every individual in it for the personality of his fellow individuals. Finally, and not least important, there is a doctrinaire attitude toward the fundamental philosophy of democracy which springs directly from its roots in the French Sentimentalists who so influenced our founding fathers. This doctrine glorifies the common man simply because he is a common man. This attitude toward the common man, combined with our fatal good nature and acceptance of paternalism, are together changing our democracy into a type of thing for which it seems to me the most fitting adjective is sentimental.

To me the glorification of the common man and the interest in him merely because he is common is one of the hardest things to understand about this country, for there is no gainsaying that common man is also mediocre man. I had supposed that the most important thing for the long range progress of a society was the way it treats its exceptional men, and I can understand a passionate admiration of supreme ability. It is easy for me to understand how mediocre man can fight for his own exaltation at the expense of his superior fellow, and I can understand how in the past he has been to a certain extent justified in his fight by the abuses of economic power by those who possessed it. But it seems to me that the evils of this situation have by now been obviously over corrected, and I can understand how the superior man can continue to welcome the triumph of mediocrity only by supposing him the victim of a short sighted sentimentalism. Is mediocrity really admirable, or can you admire the sort of thing mediocrity is on its way to turning this country into now that it has received the green light? Is it admirable for a man to be willing to be guaranteed a minimum wage whether or not he is capable of earning it? Is it admirable for a labor union to compel its ablest members to limit their output to that of the poorest, thus essentially making a public enemy out of the exceptional man? Is it admirable for a man to be willing to sponge on his neighbors to compensate him for deficiencies in the abilities with which nature furnished him? The slogan "To everyone according to his need, from everyone according to his abilities", when associated with the Marxist social philosophy, is not usually regarded in this country as admirable or consistent with self respect, but this is exactly what is involved in the philosophy which justifies our graded income tax. If the mediocre man had imagination, how would he expect the superior man to react to the claim of mediocrity that it has a right to exact from superiority more than its proportionate contribution, or how would the superior man react to this claim if he had guts and self respect? The economic philosophy which has seriously supported the proposition that no individual should be allowed to keep more than $25,000 a year for his services, to me constitutes as keen an affront to my self respect as ever a militant suffragette smarted under, denied the right to vote simply because of her sex. Whichever way you look at this proposition it is equally bad. The thesis either has to be that no individual is able to make a contribution to the community worth more than $25,000 a year, whereas I know that no limit can be put on the value of the contribution that unsusual ability is able to make. Or else the community has to declare that it will not pay more than $25,000 for any contribution, no matter how much more it may be worth, and this bespeaks a churlishness and jealousy toward the fortunate individual possessing exceptional ability which makes me blush to be in any way a partner to such an enterprise.

What is to be done about all this? In the first place, the man of exceptional ability, including the physicist as a special case, must learn how to discard his sentimentality and his false modesty, and be willing to urge more articulately the worth of his contribution to society. The physicist must acquire a greater class consciousness. In this he may fortify himself with the reflection that the structure of our government was built on the assumption that each class in the country would act in its own interest. For if the high minded classes deferentially leave the pushing of their own interests to the low minded classes, and if the low minded classes do not hesitate to push their own interests to the exclusion of all others, how shall we avoid precisely that deterioration to the standards set by the lowest which we are now witnessing?

In the second place, the situation demands the development of a new system of ethics, namely an ethics which shall specifically apply to the behavior of any individual in his capacity as a member of a pressure group able to impose its will by brute force on a minority. Situations in the past have not been numerous in which emphasis on this aspect of the behavior of the individual was important, so that none of the great traditional systems of ethics has paid much attention to it, but the situation is obviously now changing and a new situation has arisen. Perhaps Christianity with its golden rule comes as close as any to meeting the need, but obviously even here the emphasis given to this problem leaves much to be desired. Every individual must be made to feel how unlovely it is for him in his capacity as a member of a pressure group to act toward his neighbor in a way which he would reject in his capacity as an individual. Few in this country could bring themselves to directly take money away from their neighbor merely because they thought they needed it more than he, but few would hesitate to take it from him by taxation under the same conditions.

Finally, I think that the situation demands that all men, exceptional and common alike, return to a conception of the proper functions of government a little closer to that with which we started in this country. This was a minimum conception of government, in which the individual was to be given impersonally the maximum freedom consistent with equal freedom for his fellows, and in which every individual could freely find the level to which his abilities and his contribution to society entitled him. This is becoming replaced by a maximum conception of government, in which a sentimental equalitarianism is imposed by force on everyone in the name of democracy, and in which envy masquerades as justice. It is doubtful whether our founding fathers in their wisdom saw all the consequences of the minimum as opposed to the maximum conception of government, but certain of the consequences in fact are now becoming apparent. The minimum concept avoids as far as possible the consequences of a tendency to which all human group activities are subject to a certain degree. In the field of economics the tendency is formulated in Gresham's law, to the effect that bad money will always drive out good. Correspondingly, in any large scale activity involving the interplay of many people, standards tend to become debased to the level of the lowest. This is obviously what is happening in our society. The exceptional man prefers freedom to security: the mediocre man prefers security to freedom—security at the expense of freedom is what we are getting. The exceptional man finds his highest values in the satisfaction of the creative impulse, while the highest good of the mediocre is creature comfort—we are getting a society in which the supreme good, to which the government should bend all its efforts, is raising the standard of living. From this point of view, the advantages of a minimum government are obvious; the less the government controls, the fewer the things subject to this debasing action, whereas in a country in which the government controls everything, everything is debased.

It would be naive and fatuous to suppose that any efforts of ours can have much effect in reversing the trend to ever wider government control in this country. However, by well directed effort we may perhaps be able to do something to minimize what seems to me its most sinister consequence, namely the submergence of the exceptional individual in a sea of mediocrity, a submergence in the long run equally harmful to exceptional and mediocre alike.

31

THE PROSPECT FOR INTELLIGENCE*

OUR WIDESPREAD DISCUSSIONS of public affairs are evidence that the present crisis in world affairs is stimulating an enormous amount of thinking. Why is it that we find ourselves in our present difficulties? What sort of world would we like to make evolve out of the present if we could have our say? What can we do to further the development of the sort of world we would like? It is a safe guess that everyone who has been thinking about these problems is doing his best to make his thinking intelligent. He recognizes that without the addition of intelligence to the highest motives and the greatest amount of good will, such motives and good will can be of little avail. I venture to surmise that anyone who has thought about these problems, if he is honest as well as intelligent, has been presently baffled by a sense of his own intellectual inadequacy. He may even have come to feel that satisfactory solution of our problems may be beyond our present intellectual capacities. Pointing in the same direction is the often expressed misgiving that our technological

*From the Yale Review, 34, 444, 1945.

advances have outrun our intellectual capacity to adjust ourselves to them or to profit by them.

In spite, however, of this general recognition of the necessity for the maximum of intelligence and of our present comparative intellectual inadequacy, there has been almost no recognition of even the existence of the background problem. I mean the problem of formulating the general conditions that favor the development of the greatest intelligence of which we are capable, and of finding what we may do to secure the existence of these conditions. This, from the long-range point of view of the human race as a whole, seems to me by far the most important problem to be considered in the present crisis. It is much more important, both for our own and other countries, than the economic or political problems that dominate our discussions of the coming peace.

That our own present intellectual inadequacy is widespread must be obvious enough to anyone, no matter how patriotic, who considers the many unsatisfactory reactions of the country to the war emergency. What I have in mind is not the many inevitable failures of co-ordination or even the gross inconsistencies which are to be expected when so much had to be done by so many in so short a time, but something more deep-seated. An example of this has been the popular reaction to the draft. The logical situation here is intrinsically difficult. There is a palpable contradiction between the ideals of democracy and the necessities of total war which never forced itself on our consideration before wars became total—while they could be fought with volunteers. An intellectually satisfying reconciliation of the fundamental democratic principle that the individual is of paramount importance with the physical necessity that some individuals should die in order that other individuals may flourish is exceedingly difficult. If ever such a reconciliation has been achieved it has not been formulated so as to percolate down into popular consciousness or acceptance.

The result is that the popular reaction has been a reaction of frustration, primarily emotional rather than intelligent, like that of a rat in a maze, wilfully confronted with an impossible problem. The emotional solution unconsciously accepted by the majority is that all must suffer an equal amount of inconvenience, whether or not there is any connection between the inconvenience and the necessities of war. Perhaps the most striking consequence has been the widespread feeling that no able-bodied young man should be spared from sharing with his neighbor the hazards of combat duty, and that it is in some way contemptible if a specially qualified young man is willing to render service enormously more valuable to the country from some protected niche in a research laboratory. The impression conveyed by our general reaction to the draft is of mass bad conscience. It arises from our realization that we have not adequately thought through the problem and are demanding sacrifices of our young men incompatible with principles which on other occasions we have professed to accept. Added to this there is the glaring inconsistency that those deferred by industry are allowed to make more money than ever before and to strike for still more. The situation has been simply too difficult for our minds to deal with. One thing, however, has been obvious; we were not intelligent enough to start thinking soon enough. It takes time to think out these things. When the emergency is upon us it is humanly impossible to think fast enough to piece together all the elements in the intellectual jig-saw puzzle, and we have to extemporize as best we can.

Our intellectual inadequacy as a country was shown by our whole attitude in the face of the growing inevitability of the approaching conflict. We met the crisis with intellectual sloth, lack of imagination, and wishful thinking. We lacked sufficient intellectual morale to be able to bring ourselves to the purely negative task of doing something disagreeable in order to prevent something more disagreeable from happening to us. We demanded, and continue to demand, almost as a right, something more positive and dramatic to force us to action. In fact, our inability as a group to respond to the stimulus of a negative necessity was so obvious to the outsider that Hitler could esteem us incapable of responding to the intellectual stimulus in time; otherwise it is doubtful whether he would have risked war.

If the need for greater intellectual power has been

only too plain in our conduct of affairs to date, it is still more painfully obvious when we contemplate the requirements for the future. To solve the problem of creating conditions under which the peoples of the earth with their diverse ideologies can live together with the maximum of compatibility will demand a self-conscious analysis of the presuppositions of our own social thinking possible only to a high order of intellectual power. We seldom realize to what extent all our thinking is colored by our tacitly accepted values or by our cultural background. As a group we ostensibly accept ideals of unselfishness, of service, of Christianity, and of duty to purposes transcending the human race. Our social institutions recognize the worth of the individual and the validity of the individual conscience, and the right of the individual, on occasion, to act in response to a higher obligation than that towards the state—which we regard as the servant rather than the master. None of these presuppositions is necessary to valid thinking, nor are the values implicit in our ideology universally accepted. Other peoples have them in a different degree, have them not at all, or even have diametrically opposed points of view. Our thinking has got to be broad enough to embrace these multifarious points of view, and this is hard. Nothing is more difficult than to divest oneself of the hitherto scarcely conscious part of one's mental machinery.

It is evident, I think, that the greater the emotional diversity in the conditions that have to be met, the greater the certainty that they can be met only on the intellectual level. It is, perhaps, easy to misunderstand the role of intelligence in dealing with emotional situations involving values. Depreciation of the attempt to run one's life on an exclusively logical and rational basis is popular and common, and lends itself to easy caricature. The mistake is to assume that such an ordering of one's life is intelligent. The role of intelligence in questions of value is primarily a neutral one—that of a tool by which values may be effectively realized. It is true that intelligence also has a role to play in the education which is back of the system of values. The values which one accepts may be altered by a visualization of all the consequences, and this act of vision requires intelligence. But except for this, intelligence accepts the values without question, as one of the conditions of the problem, and applies itself to the task of realizing these values as effectively as possible. By its neutrality, intelligence acquires universality; it is the one common denominator of mankind, independent of creed or culture, spanning the hemispheres and the centuries.

Certain measures could be adopted now to increase the adequacy of our intellectual response. By awakening public interest in the fundamental problems of government and society and by stimulating discussion of broad underlying principles, it should be possible at least to mitigate the impact of another emergency like the present by a certain degree of ideological preparedness. Or, going further, it is possible to envisage something much more elaborate and effective, if it could only be carried through in sufficient detail.

Social thinking suffers from a patent disadvantage as compared with scientific thinking. Much of the effectiveness of our scientific thinking rests on the work of our predecessors, on whose shoulders we stand and whose results we accept as valid without independent check by ourselves. Even Sir Isaac Newton would not have got far if he had had to start by inventing the multiplication table. The situation is by no means so favorable for social thinking. Many of the fundamental issues have never been thought through, much less discussed, accepted, and recorded. For example, to what extent are democratic principles reconcilable with the existence of total war, and what is the least harmful way of making those sacrifices of principle which may be necessary? Or, to what extent are the commonly accepted ideals of democracy reconcilable with the enormous differences of native ability between individuals? One can imagine much more elaborate and systematic attempts than in the past to anticipate all possible eventualities and thus avoid the necessity for the extemporized measures of the present. This would involve the analysis of many different sorts of situation, actual or hypothetical. The analyses must be discussed, and accepted or rejected by those competent. Then the results must be recorded, together with the steps leading up to them, in such a way that they shall be accessible for future consultation and permit intelligent acceptance or rejection by the future analyst, exactly as the results of scientific investigations are now recorded. Libraries might be filled with the results; the mere designing of an adequate system of reference would be a formidable task. The enterprise would take time, and it might well require generations before the full effect could be felt. To be of value, many of the situations dealt with would be so widely at variance with those now encountered that little likelihood would appear that they would ever be realized. One of the reasons for our present difficulties is that we were not imaginative enough to see that present conditions could conceivably be realized. In short, the enterprise, on an enormously greater scale, would do for society what the Prussian general staff does when it plans for war.

By methods like these, or by others which we cannot consider here, it would certainly be possible to effect an improvement in the over-all intellectual effectiveness of each one of us, and this in spite of the fact, often quoted as a justification for intellectual pessimism and defeatism, that there has been no apparent increase in our physiological capacity for intelligence since the time of Neanderthal man. What we are concerned with here is effective as distinguished from physiological or intrinsic intelligence.

We may, therefore, assume that there is need for greater intelligence in order to cope with our social problems, and that it is possible to increase our intellectual power by appropriate methods. Let us now set ourselves the problem of appraising the probability that conditions favorable to the enhancement of intelligence will, as a matter of fact, get themselves established in future human history, so that the race will ultimately transcend its present intellectual stature and make itself the intellectual master of its fate. We may approach this problem in a more or less academic manner, for the needed reforms are too time-consuming to offer the slightest prospect that we shall be able to develop an improved intelligence in time to meet the immediate requirements of the present emergency. We can, however, justify ourselves with the consideration that our conclusions may have value from the long-range point of view. They may indicate the intermediate steps that society will have to take before reaching the final goal, and these intermediate steps can be provided for in what we do now.

In the first place, it would seem doubtful whether any attempt to prepare ourselves exhaustively, like a Prussian general staff, for all possible eventualities, has much prospect of being seriously made on a sufficiently grand scale, although partial and more systematic preparations than any at present may well be made. Such an enterprise smells too much of pedantry and interferes too much with the pleasant business of living to be acceptable to ordinary human nature. Most of us would, I suspect, prefer to take our chances of peace in our time and consign our children to the devil or piously hope that they may pull through by the old method of trial and error. Only more attractive and also more powerful methods of attack have, I believe, much prospect of being actually employed. There may well be a number of such methods; many psychologists could doubtless outline changes in education which, if allowed to have full scope over several generations, would result in a notable enhancement of general intelligence. I cannot attempt here, nor am I qualified, to discuss all the possibilities. There is, however, one aspect of the situation with, I believe, truly revolutionary possibilities to which I may direct attention.

The race has already gone through a period of intellectual enhancement similar in kind, although not in magnitude, to that which we envisage for the future—the period of the development of science since Galileo and Newton. I am not one of those who hold that there is a scientific method as such. The scientific method, as far as it is a method, is nothing more than doing one's damnedest with one's mind, no holds barred. What primarily distinguishes science from other intellectual enterprises in which the right answer has to be obtained is not the method but the subject matter. The development of modern science I believe to have been primarily a development of effective intelligence. Because it was an intellectual development it has significance for any attempt to appraise the possibility of further intellectual developments in the future.

Certain of the lessons from the development of modern science are obvious enough. Science has made a step-by-step progress, starting with a patient analysis of the complex situations of experience into as simple components as possible, acquiring mastery of these simple components, and then applying the results of the accumulated experience to more complex situations until we have the irresistible and accelerated progress of the present. This is obvious and trite enough. Other aspects of the development of science are, however, of more significance for us. Two epochs may be distinguished. The first runs from Galileo and Newton to the first part of the present century. The influence of this epoch on our intellectual outlook in other fields has by now sufficiently run its course so that its significance can be appraised with a certain degree of finality. The second epoch begins with this century, with the revolutions in scientific thinking involved in relativity theory and quantum mechanics. It is still too early to assess precisely what will be its ultimate effect on thinking in other fields, but it is not too early to see that the impact will be the most momentous that has yet occurred to human thought.

The first scientific epoch was initiated by what was in essence a new trick of intellectual technique —the controlled experiment. This is now accepted so much as a matter of course that it requires a forceful act of imagination to recover the point of view of the early days. In those days nature was hopelessly complex, for it had not yet been envisaged that laws of mechanics and chemistry even existed. It was, therefore, not at all obvious that it was possible artificially to create simple situations which would be significant because they repeated themselves in more complex situations. In fact, it was not obvious what constituted simplicity in a situation. Long practice is back of the intuitive recognition that it is a simple and repeatable experiment to time the fall of a lead weight, but that it is not simple or repeatable to time the fall of a feather. The final result of decades of trial and failure, cogitation and instruction, was the development of a new tool for use by intelligence, which alone has made possible present science and technology.

The first scientific epoch has a double significance for our purposes. In the first place, factual discoveries about the actual constitution of the world, possible only after the technique of controlled experiment had been established, have fundamentally altered the conceptual foundations of our thinking. The most striking examples of this are the conviction of the universal sway of natural law—a result primarily of Newton's formulation of the law of universal gravitation, and the realization of man's place in the hierarchy of nature which followed the acceptance of the fact of biological evolution. The second point is that a realization of the significance of the first scientific epoch gives a vision of the importance of finding the intellectual technique adapted to the subject matter and of the spectacular advances which may be expected once the technique has been found. Nearly the whole domain of physical phenomena has fallen into our hands in the few hundreds years since the invention of the controlled experiment, after thousands of years of blindness to even the conceivability of mastery of this domain.

In one important respect, the influence of the first scientific epoch on our social thinking is not yet exhausted. The controlled experiment is a device of intelligence that is applicable almost exclusively in the scientific field. Not only are the problems which so press for solution in the present crisis incomparably more complex, but their nature is such that they are not easily attacked by the controlled experiment. We can repeat human situations only to a limited extent, and human beings would not often be willing to be the subject of experiments in which situations are so simplified that the zest might be taken out of living. About the best we can do at present is to study the reports of the anthropologist as to human behavior under a considerable diversity of conditions, but not, unfortunately, a controlled diversity. However, there is one recent development that has some of the implications of the controlled experiment, and may ultimately prove to be in certain respects a substitute for it. This is the growing consciousness that various sorts of "planning" are possible in the direction of our affairs. Forty years ago not much was heard about planning, and there was a certain fatalism in the popular attitude towards large-scale social phenomena. We now hear a great deal of talk about it, and this denotes a fundamental change of attitude. We would not be planning if we did not think that planning would do some good; that is, we have acquired the vision that large-scale social movements are susceptible of conscious direction by us. This vision constitutes a new intellectual tool, which will more and more affect all that we do in this field as the vision spreads until it is finally accepted and used in the thinking of everyone. It is to be recognized, however, that there are preliminary problems to be solved, such as reconciling the demands of effective centrally controlled planning with those of individual freedom.

The second scientific epoch also has a twofold aspect. There is, in the first place, the discovery of the astonishing wealth of structure in the microscopic domain, beyond the limits which the scientists of one hundred years ago sought to impose, by their very definition of the atom, on the possible existence of mechanism. On the other hand, there are the recent discoveries in astronomy of the unsuspected reach of the universe in the direction of the very large. Together, these two extensions of our knowledge of the physical universe cannot but revise any conception we may have of man's significance. However, the second aspect of the modern epoch in science is, I believe, of incomparably greater significance. The new facts have proved to be so deeply at variance with what had been conceived to be the possible order of nature that the physicist has had to dig down into an analysis of the fundamental tenets of his thinking, and has had to revise his entire conceptual structure. He has come out with what amounts to a new intellectual technique of analysis, of great power and unexpectedly wide range of applicability. The new technique is applicable to all questions of meaning. When applied to the new discoveries of the structure of the universe at the upper and lower bounds it gives a picture of man isolated, in a sense different from the old theological sense, in an oasis of phenomena which he never will be able to transcend because beyond its bounds the operations are impossible which are necessary to give meaning to his thought. It is true that the possibility has been not infrequently adumbrated in the past that man's potentialities may be intrinsically limited by the very nature of thought, but the physical documentation of this thesis presents, I believe, a radically new outlook. The full impact of this new outlook will, I believe, ultimately be more devastating than was ever the impact of evolution. We may also anticipate that the impact will be more emancipating, because we shall know when to give up striving to do with our minds things which are intrinsically impossible.

The potentialities of the new technique when applied to domains outside the present application of science may be glimpsed by contemplating the confusion which now reigns. To take only a single example, it is no less than an intellectual scandal that much of philosophy in its present form, particularly the parts dealing with theology and metaphysics, exists today. After thousands of years of discussion, philosophers still argue the same old questions, without even being able to agree as to whether agreement should be possible. No one who has even that minimum of confidence in the potentialities of the human intellect necessary for the humblest intellectual enterprise can admit for a moment that this is a necessary or a permanent state of affairs. The fundamental difficulty in the philosophical situation seems to be that of meaning; seldom do two philosophers use the same terms with the same meaning. At present the technique of analysis of meanings is not sufficiently powerful—in a field where so many shades of meaning are possible and where so much depends on individual experience—to permit the analysis even of what it is that we disagree about.

The invention of language is often proclaimed as the one most characteristic thing that sets man apart from the brutes, but the invention is proving to have unsuspected sources of bedevilment. It is becoming evident to an increasing number of people that an important part of our difficulties in analyzing and conveying meaning is of verbal origin. Other lines of attack in addition to that implemented by modern science are being directed at overcoming our verbal difficulties; semantics is appearing as an independent logical discipline. Popular consciousness of the situation is increasing; there is popular discussion of semantics, and there are popular books on the dangers inherent in language. It is only just coming to be realized that language has different functions and is used on different levels, The amount of lost motion in our social contacts because of failure to realize this is appalling. The implication in language as used always seems to be that it is on the factual level, whereas analysis of meanings discloses that in social situations the factual use is probably the least frequent of all. The speaker himself usually does not understand on what level he is talking, and what he says is for that reason often inconsistent with what he does. Whence arise the appearances of dishonesty, the misunderstandings and recriminations. How much would be left of any political speech if the language were rigorously kept to the factual level? Imagine the speaker being required to label the levels of his discourse, as: "Now I am talking on the factual level; now I am talking on the emotional level; now I am talking on the propaganda level". What will happen when every listener labels the levels for himself?

One important field for verbal analysis is the field of religion, particularly important at the present time when in many quarters there is a powerful emotional drive for a "return to religion" as offering the only possible solution of our problems. Analysis will show, I believe, that the level of most of the language of religion is so far from that of the ordinary workaday world that one would be almost justified in recognizing a special religious level of language. Yet the implications when we hear the language in action are that it is on the factual level, with the result that the true object and legitimate claims of religion are misunderstood, and the endeavor is made to use the religious guide for conduct in spheres into which we would never attempt to push it if we were able to make a more adequate analysis. This may lead to disaster in the present situation when we are dealing with peoples with such a wide diversity of religious idealism.

When the technique of verbal analysis has been worked out and the mastery of it has become widespread through education, it is not too optimistic to anticipate a time when we shall be able to eliminate all human difficulties which arise from imperfect communication of meaning. We shall be able to analyze out the purely emotional part of our reactions to situations which at present we attempt to meet by purely verbal rationalizations. Having made the analysis, we shall be able to understand better the nature of whatever antipathies and differences of taste still survive, and shall be better able to make intelligent provision for meeting them. It takes little imagination to see what the impact of a clarification like this must be on our present racial, political, and religious difficulties. We may also anticipate far-reaching effects in other fields where the difficulties are primarily due not to an unconfessed emotionalism but to the intrinsic difficulty of the factual situation, as in economics. The general increase of intellectual effectiveness inevitable when such tools of analysis are mastered justifies us in expecting that we shall presently be able to introduce an order into the present chaos of economic phenomena analogous to the order which the organic and biological chemists have introduced into the once hopeless complexity of the phenomena of fermentation.

It would be overoptimistic to think that the new techniques of analysis will produce even in this country spectacular changes in our time. Changes of fundamental habits of thought are involved, and habits of thought, in order to be used spontaneously and at their maximum effectiveness, can be acquired only in youth as part of elementary education. The most effective method of elementary education is that of imitation of the teacher; the teacher himself, therefore, must have been educated. The complete process will be one of successive approximation, each successive generation getting closer to the goal.

The possibilities are limitless, and the technical means for realizing them are already in our grasp. Will the human race take this road that lies open to it? I believe there is a fighting chance, but only in a democracy. For, in the first place, this is an enterprise that will require co-operation from a number of people. It will not be sufficient for a few supermen to see the light, but the new knowledge must be diffused until it sufficiently colors the thinking of the entire community. The amount of preparatory work is so great that it will be possible only by the co-operation of large numbers; no single human brain would be able to make combinations of its cells fast enough to cover the subject. Such large numbers of participants can be found only in a country in which education is widespread—a condition which is satisfied by the democracies. But another matter is more important than mere numbers. The sort of analysis that we contemplate is impossible without complete intellectual freedom; no line of inquiry must be omitted, no matter what the consequences; and the results of any such inquiry must be made available to the public. It does not need to be elaborated that such a program would be impossible in a country with a totalitarian ideology. Whether it would be possible even in a democracy like ours is open to discussion. Such activities might not be proscribed by the central government, except perhaps in time of war, but any widespread action does get rather effectively limited by public opinion. It is by no means obvious that public opinion in this country is today liberal enough to stand for, much less support, such a program of ruthless analysis.

There are disquieting evidences that the line of future development of democracy in this country may be increasingly inimical to the unlimited development of intelligence. The majority appear not to enjoy using their minds or to be inclined to put themselves out in order that others may. As technological improvement advances, as the standard of living rises, and as increasing numbers acquire a degree of leisure, there is an increasing tendency for the effective level of intellectual ideals and attainment to become that of the mass average.

The extent to which the majority will force their ideals and tastes on the intellectual minority will depend largely on the philosophy of democracy which comes to prevail. This philosophy is at present too little concerned with what the norms of conduct of a majority should be. At present any individual is only too likely to be willing in his capacity as a member of a majority to force demands on the minority which in his capacity as an individual he would think indecent to attempt to exact from any other individual. It seems to me that democracy will never attain its ultimate object, namely, to secure for each person the maximum opportunity to realize his own needs compatible with the needs of his neighbors, until each individual in it is unwilling to act as a member of a majority in a way in which he would not act as an individual.

An illustration of the feeling of the majority that they have a right to force on the minority action to the advantage of the majority is afforded by the recently proposed Kilgore bill (s. 702) for the mobilization and control of all scientific activity in the country, not only as a war measure but as a matter of permanent policy. This bill would subject all scientific activity in this country, whether technological research in industry or "pure" research in private universities to a governmental control effectively totalitarian. The argument for it is obvious, because it would certainly be pleasant for the majority if they could have all the scientists of the country working for them on any problem which might appear important. Such a proposal is in a way flattering to the scientist, because it reveals a high opinion of the benefits which science can bestow, but it does not flatter the intelligence of scientists, and it is a flagrant violation of the spirit of the principle proposed above. It would presently defeat itself because of rebellion among the scientists, if for no other reason, because no minority will long suffer the consciousness of being exploited as a class.

There is another tendency in our democracy unfavorable to the development of intelligence, namely, the growth of the idea that a man's relations to his society should be determined by his rights and not by his services. On the one hand, there has been the ideal that all a man should demand is a fair field and no favor, so that he can count on rising to the level to which his abilities and his attainments entitle him. On the other hand, there is the ideal, growing in favor at present, that a man has a right to a comfortable living in virtue of his mere existence and without regard to any return he may make to society, with the corollaries that the majority have a right to commandeer unusual ability and exact special service from it, and that no man may receive more than a fixed maximum reward. Apart from all other considerations—and it is possible to advance arguments for both ideals—it seems to me there can be no question which ideal is more stimulating to the development of intelligence, or more acceptable to plain self-respect.

Assuming that our democracy evades these pitfalls and adopts a philosophy permitting a line of evolution favorable to the development of intelligence, this will, nevertheless, not be the actual line of development unless it is consciously directed. The direction can be given only by those who appreciate the enormous possibilities, who realize the difficulties, and who earnestly desire the final result, that is, only by the intelligentsia themselves. This word—intelligentsia—has obnoxious connotations of smugness and the ivory tower, but there seems no other; I shall use it to denote those who like to use their minds better than anything else they can do.

This development must be directed by the intelligentsia themselves because there is no one else capable of directing it. The intelligentsia will have to grow, however, before they can acquit themselves of this task. At present they have too little vision of the possibilities. They see intelligence too much as an individual matter, limited by the structure of the individual brain, and too little as a co-operative enterprise, partially conditioned by the social environment, and capable of indefinite expansion. They are too little conscious of the techniques of thinking, and they do not sufficiently realize the limitations imposed by the unconscious presuppositions of past history. They are too complacent in their acceptance of the best thinking of the past as setting the standards of possible achievement. They see too little that the diversity of human outlook, as exemplified in philosophies and religions, can be disentangled, at least to the extent of formulating and analyzing the nature of our differences.

There is a fundamental weakness in democracy which may well prove the undoing of us all, which I believe can be met only by a self-conscious and concerted attack by the intelligentsia, who are in the best position to appreciate the magnitude of the danger. This has to do with the attitude of the community towards unusual ability, already touched on in connection with the draft. It is easy in a democracy to take the position that all are of equal value and therefore all must receive equal treatment, irrespective of natural gifts, for is it a man's fault if he is not as bright as his neighbor, or does a man enjoy being stupid? A philosophy of democracy like this is blind to the very undemocratic distribution of talents by nature; the chances of indefinite survival are poor for any democracy founded on so flagrant a violation as this of a natural limitation. The fallacy in the philosophy of the sacredness of mediocrity is obvious enough: from the long-range point of view it is important for *everyone* that unusual ability, so long as it is accompanied by social responsibility, be cherished, encouraged, stimulated, and given any special treatment necessary to induce it to produce to capacity. The intelligentsia are in the best position to urge this point of view, because they know best how rare true ability is, and how important for progress. Yet the intelligentsia have shown a curious slowness in coming to this point, or at any rate have not been able to bring themselves to push the matter. The reason is human and understandable enough, for it is the intelligentsia who possess the ability they are lauding and who will receive any special privileges that may result from it. It is distasteful to a man—the more so, the more sensitive he is—to urge his fellows to grant special service to himself, no matter how justifiable the grounds. But here is no place for false modesty; the intelligentsia must have a more militant conviction of their own worth, and if they can think of no more tactful way of doing it must be able to say bluntly: "We have special abilities which make us of special importance to the community, and we demand that we be given suitable opportunity to use our abilities and that we be rewarded according to what we produce".

Up to now our intelligentsia have not been able to do this. There is one significant example before us at the present moment. Our scientific leaders who have been directing the war research of the country have not been able to withstand the pressure, exerted presumably by the military, to treat all young men between the ages of 18 and 26 on an equal footing, regardless of proved or potential unusual ability. Here was a unique opportunity to get the country to accept the principle that unusual ability is of prime importance and must be accorded special treatment. This thesis could have been urged with special force, because it would have been obvious that the scientific leaders who might have urged it were in a position to gain nothing by it personally. It is most to be regretted that the opportunity was missed. If our intelligentsia cannot see their own interests or bring themselves to urge their own cause, not only will it be worse for everyone but they themselves will disappear.

However, the fundamental requirement, without which all these others will be in vain, is intellectual morale. Without the fierce conviction that we can solve our problems or the will to push through the solution in spite of difficulties, we shall fail. Intellectual morale at present is low; there is widespread intellectual defeatism and appeasement. It will take effort to get started on the way out, but once started, progress will be accelerated. Never in past history have conditions been so favorable, for never has the leaven of the scientific temper been so widely diffused, nor has obvious necessity provided so powerful a stimulus. On the other hand, it may be that this is the last chance that will be offered to humanity. It will not be long now before the entire world becomes of one piece, with all parts so interlocked that independent action by the parts may become impossible, frozen in the pattern which happens to prevail at the moment of union. The present fluidity and mobility may never return. It is getting late and we must hurry.

32

*NEW VISTAS FOR INTELLIGENCE**

WE ARE ALL agreed that the invention of the atomic bomb has presented us with problems which must be solved within the next few decades if the survival of civilization is to be more than a matter of good luck. Nevertheless, in spite of the urgency of these problems, I venture to invite your attention to certain longer range considerations which are equally fundamental and which have an equal claim to the attention of some of us now, for the solution of the longer range difficulties requires a longer period of preparation and must also be initiated in the present. It seems to me evident enough that many of our present social difficulties have their origin in our previous failure to begin thinking about the problems far enough ahead.

The opening of the atomic age may well mark the end of the first chapter of the physical sciences and our partial mastery of our physical environment. It is conventional to ascribe this mastery to the development of scientific method, and there has been much discussion of what the essence of the

*From Physical Science and Human Values. Princeton University Press, 1947. Given at the Princeton Bicentennial Conference, September, 1946.

scientific method is. It appears to me, however, that it is easy to take too narrow a view in this matter. I like to say that there is no scientific method as such, but that the most vital feature of the scientist's procedure has been merely to do his utmost with his mind, *no holds barred*. This means in particular that no special privileges are accorded to authority or to tradition, that personal prejudices and predilections are carefully guarded against, that one makes continued check to assure oneself that one is not making mistakes, and that any line of inquiry will be followed that appears at all promising. All of these rules are applicable to any situation in which one has to obtain the right answer and all of them are only manifestations of intelligence. The so-called scientific method is merely a special case of the method of intelligence, and any apparently unique characteristics are to be explained by the nature of the subject matter rather than ascribed to the nature of the method itself. For example, the universal and profitable use of mathematics in the physical sciences is a consequence of the possibility of using a system of precise numerical measurements in describing the systems which are the subject matter of physical science. The subject matter of other disciplines is not so often adapted to description in numerical terms, so that mathematics plays a smaller role in such disciplines.

The second chapter in the application of intelligence may well deal with the application of intelligence to the problems of human relationships.

There are many people, perhaps the majority, who are convinced that these problems cannot be solved by intelligence. Their attitudes may range from the downright belligerency of those who maintain that the only solution is to be found by some supernatural method to the apathetic despair of those who plead that intelligence has never got us anywhere in the past. I shall not attempt to argue with either of these groups, but I address myself without apology to that minority who have the intellectual morale to believe that a serious application of intelligence to the solution of social problems is worth attempting. I shall pause only long enough to remark that I would challenge the validity of the evidence on which the bellicose base their confidence in the efficacy of supernatural methods, and to point out to the apathetic despairers that the method of intelligence has never had a fair trial.

If we grant that science is merely a special case of the application of intelligence, we may reasonably anticipate that our experience with scientific problems can suggest profitable lines for the attack by intelligence on the infinitely more complex and difficult problems of human relationships. Let us consider some of the suggestions from this experience.

Perhaps most important of all, we have acquired by this experience some insight into the nature of the process of intelligence itself. The revisions of scientific concepts made necessary during this century by relativity theory and quantum mechanics have shown that a certain self-conscious sophistication is necessary about being intelligent. Intelligence has its techniques, and we must be intelligent about being intelligent.

In popular estimate, perhaps the most important characteristic of science is its impersonality or "objectivity". The necessity for impersonality arises not from prejudice against people as such but because of the irrelevance of personal reactions to the commonest enterprises of science, which are concerned mainly with our external environment. In addition there is the consideration that our emotions are too likely to distort our report of factual situations. The "objectivity" of science is usually considered to be a guarantee of its truth. There is much of importance in this point of view to which we might devote our discussion with profit. The connotation here is often that science is objective because it is "public", independent of the idiosyncracies of any particular individual. This aspect of the use of intelligence which constitutes science must not be pushed too far, however, nor allowed to obscure the essential role played by the individual in scientific activity. Science is not truly objective unless it recognizes its own subjective or individual aspects. For example, scientific proof, or the conviction of truth or correctness, is something which each individual has to experience for himself. A proof vicariously accepted is dead. This is generally recognized. No editor of a reputable scientific journal will accept an article unless it is so presented that the reader may repeat the experiment and check the conclusions for himself.

The participation of the individual is necessary in every process of intelligence, not merely in the processes of science. Intelligence can be given a meaning only in terms of the individual. It seems to me that this has a far-reaching significance not usually appreciated, for I believe that here is to be found perhaps the most compelling justification for democracy. Intelligence is based on the individual. An authoritarian society in which the individual is suppressed cannot, by the nature of intelligence, be characterized by *general* intelligence.

There is another and much wider sense in which an objective science must recognize subjective aspects. However objective a science may be, it is still subjective from the point of view of the human race as a whole. Every activity of science and intelligence is a human activity, which necessarily involves the cooperation of the human nervous system. This characteristic of all that we do is so universal that it is not usual for us to recognize its existence. Even worse, we may deny its existence and elaborate its denial into a scheme of philosophy. There is a tendency to do this even in physics. As an example, I mention the philosophy of general relativity theory as distinguished from its mathematical formulation which (it seems to me) is based on an attempt to transcend the inescapable human reference point. Or, in another direction, there is perhaps danger that the spectacular success of the theoretical physicist in contributing to the atomic bomb will make him forget the limitations of the processes which he has used and give him so much confidence that he may even feel that experimental check has become superfluous.

From the wider point of view, the history of most philosophy and religion and much of politics has been the history of an attempt to repudiate the inescapability of the human reference point by the erection of absolutes and transcendentals. Our whole social structure has been built on the widespread acceptance of such absolutes and transcendentals. The intellectual basis for this acceptance goes back far into the past and acquired perhaps its most self-conscious expression with the Greek philosophers. The urge to invent absolutes seems to be an artifact of the human intellectual structure. It doubtless has its pragmatic justification and at a certain stage of evolution may have been as necessary for survival as that other indispensable invention, the external world. But whatever the origin or the pragmatic justification for this urge, there are aspects of it which will not survive intelligent scrutiny, and once the scrutiny is made and doubt begins to spread, the foundations of our social structure begin to crumble. This very process is going on at present. To put it crudely, men no longer believe in hell, and without the belief they will not respond to the same arguments to action which were potent while they believed. This decay of vividness of the old absolutes and transcendentals has been mainly an intellectual affair, due to a growing recognition that the absolutes simply are not "true". The movement has been gaining momentum for perhaps several hundred years, at first underground and only now breaking into the open and threatening social revolution. This is truly a chain reaction; what initiated the reaction would be difficult to say, perhaps the Protestant Reformation or the formulation of positivistic philosophies. The relative time scale of the explosion may not be so different from that of the atomic bomb when the different size of the fundamental units is considered, a human being and a lifetime corresponding to an atom and the duration of an excited state.

One consequence of this chain reaction is of special importance in present society and may be at the bottom of the growing tendency to fascist ideals all over the world. The old philosophical arguments for the necessity of the freedom of the individual rested importantly on the nature of God and other absolutes. If the thesis is to be now maintained new arguments must be found; they may well be based on the relation of the individual to intelligence.

Until now repudiation of the old absolutes and transcendentals has been almost entirely of a negative character. They are no longer accepted, and people are no longer moved by motives which presume their acceptance; but the repudiation is a repudiation in a vacuum, for there are no new motives to take the place of the old ones and no new insights to take the place of the ones we thought we had. Our first task is to convert this repudiation into something more positive and constructive. This reconstruction is the task before us now. It will be a long slow process to which we must devote nothing less than our maximum intellectual capacity.

Such a reconstruction may well begin with an attempt to acquire understanding of the immediate situation by painstaking analysis, without any definite visualization of all the steps by which this analysis may prepare for the final solution. We might perhaps begin by asking what was the precise meaning of the absolutes and transcendentals by which we formerly sought to guide our conduct. In searching for these meanings we may take over the technique by which modern physics discovered the meaning of its concepts.

This technique is to examine exactly what we do when we apply a concept in any concrete situation. For example, an examination of the concept of simultaneity by Einstein by an analysis of the process used to determine whether two events are simultaneous showed the concept to be relative in nature instead of absolute as had been uncritically supposed before the analysis was made. Such a method of analysis will show the predominantly verbal character of most of our absolutes. For instance, analysis will often disclose that we can check in only one way on the propriety of using in a complex situation some word with an absolute connotation—to wit, asking our colleagues whether they would use the same word. There is usually no other method which

I alone could apply in a laboratory remote from any social contact. Furthermore, the situation itself to which the word is applied is only too often a purely verbal situation, arising because my colleagues and I would use the same language. Consistent analysis by this method will disclose the exceedingly complex nature of the verbal structure which human beings have erected. Man has always been the builder, not only of pyramids and Chinese walls, but of intellectual and verbal systems as well. These come to absorb his complete attention; within them he may live an entirely self-contained existence, forgetful of the natural world about him and content with the companionship of his fellows. It seems to me that no education should be considered complete until a vivid consciousness has been acquired of this situation. How seldom is this recognized as one of the ends of education!

The analysis of meanings should be extended to all the important terms of daily life. Because there is such a large verbal element in these terms, it will be found that people with different linguistic backgrounds give different meanings to ostensibly the same words. All students of language recognize that it is very seldom that an abstract word in one language has an exact equivalent in another. To attempt to clarify this situation by getting more precise correspondence in different languages may well lead to the next step in the systematic development of a program of intelligence.

This next step might be to find how far the common assumption is justified that men are fundamentally alike intellectually and can come to agreement. This has never been established by direct experiment, but is nevertheless basic to all social thinking. To what extent are different people capable of responding in the same way to the same situation? After a certain age do people lose their ability to make certain intellectual discriminations as they lose the ability to make certain speech sounds? It is obvious that people of different backgrounds will at first almost certainly respond differently to many situations. But to what extent is this incidental? To what extent may people of different cultural backgrounds be made to see each others' points of view and make the same responses? The answer is not at all obvious, because there are certainly intellectual differences and limitations which are deep-seated and real. For example, it is probable that only a small fraction of the human race is intellectually capable of reacting to the subtleties of logic of the *Principia Mathematica*, and it may well be that there are analogous intrinsic differences in other lines of intellectual activity. It is important to know what the limitations are and at what level it is safe to set the minimum that may be presupposed in social institutions.

I think we have been too complacent in the past in assuming that our diversities of opinion are not of fundamental significance. Diversities are symptomatic of something, and we do not know what. It is time that we analyzed our disagreements and found their significance. Have we a right to our bland assumption that the human race is intellectually all alike, or may there be truly irreconcilable points of view? It is a crying disgrace that after twenty-five hundred years of philosophy the philosophers cannot agree in their description of what it is that they disagree about. I think our campaign of intellectual rehabilitation might well begin by collecting small groups of about five people, with different intellectual interests, and shutting them up until they emerged with statements as to what they could agree on in matters of ordinary social concern. In cases of disagreement they would be required to find the focus of disagreement, and agree in their formulation of the nature of the disagreement.

A prerequisite to the functioning of such groups would be a declaration of freedom from mental reservations by all the members. There must obviously be willingness to ask any question whatever with regard to any topic and to answer that question as honestly and completely as intellectually possible to the individual. That is, no holds are barred. A claim that certain types of topics must be exempt from analysis would automatically disqualify the maker of such a claim from participation, and at the same time would afford a pretty clear presumption as to the character of any opinions which he might hold on such topics.

The group having been properly constituted, its deliberations might well begin by assuring themselves that all are really using language in the same sense. The very minimum of agreement that should be exacted is agreement on description of what happens or of what is done when social situations are verbalized. Physical science could not have started before physical situations could be significantly described in such terms that they could be reproduced. Social science might well set for itself the same prerequisite of significant description. I believe that it is not now known to what extent significant description of social or economic phenomena is even possible. Significant description in the physical sciences is closely correlated with successful prediction. How few social or economic situations there are in which prediction is at present possible! An example of the present confusion is the recent break in the stock market—there were as many attempts at significant description of what caused the break as there were commentators. Although we may never achieve sufficient mastery to predict in social or economic situations as we do in physical situations, I believe that we have the right to demand that we be able to predict at least the words which we use to *describe* such situations.

The ultimate result of such a campaign of analysis would be the removal of misunderstandings as to meanings from the causes of human disagreements. I think that most of us would admit that plain misunderstanding of meaning is one of the most common and potent causes of conflict, and that with its removal our problems would be far on their way to solution.

The people who would be excluded from such a clarification of meanings would be those who have disqualified themselves from making the analysis by their claim that certain holds are barred. It may be that right here will be found an unreconcilable cleavage between human beings, namely between those who bar no holds and those who bar some. If so, this method of attack will at least bring the situation out into the open where it can be better dealt with. The greatest difficulty here is that those who bar certain holds do not like to admit it openly. Part of the problem before us is to generate such a climate of public opinion that those who bar certain holds will feel themselves under pressure to admit it openly. They would certainly also try to justify themselves, and this would be all to the good in the way of clarification.

When the misunderstandings which arise from ambiguous meanings have been removed as a source of human friction, the next task for intelligence is an analysis of the implications and presuppositions of various social systems, in particular the social systems of the present. One of the lessons made vivid by the war was that in this country there is almost no self-conscious recognition of the necessary conditions of existence of a democracy like that of our ostensible ideal. There is great haziness in our ideas of the relation of the individual to his fellows. What are the minimum codes of conduct, which if universally accepted, would lead to a stable society in which conditions of living would be sufficiently tolerable? No systematic discussion is given of this question. The solution is usually attempted by some method more specialized than the minimum, as, for example, by exhorting everyone to live with complete unselfishness, putting the good of the whole in all cases unquestioningly above his own good. Universal acceptance of this exhortation would doubtless lead to a society appearing harmonious to a visitor from Mars. It is, however, a lazy man's solution, which begs the main questions at issue. Such a lazy man's solution is likely to conceal a metaphysical conception of society, ascribing to it an existence of its own apart from the individuals who compose it, and ascribing a meaning to the good of this superthing. Such a view of the nature of society as a whole may be eliminated by an analysis of what one would have to do to prove the existence of such a superthing. The solution and the justification must be found in the individuals.

The importance of finding a minimum solution is obvious, for any solution more specialized than the minimum involves the imposition by force of the views of certain pressure groups of individuals on other groups of individuals incapable of exerting as strong a pressure. Since a pressure group is itself composed of individuals and functions only through the functioning of its members, the discussion will involve norms of conduct and the ethics of the behavior of individuals in their capacity as members of groups. It seems to me that it is perhaps here that our general social consciousness is in its most primitive state of development. It is seldom indeed that an individual realizes that when he functions as a member of a pressure group his conduct demands special scrutiny, but he is nearly always willing to accept blithely the maximum that the group can obtain by the exercise of naked brute force.

Any discussion of the conditions basic to living together in society will lead inevitably to considerations of norms of conduct, ethics, purposes, and values. Now these are precisely topics which the popular view holds are outside the scope of the methods of science. In so far as the methods of science are methods of intelligence, a corollary would be that questions of value are also not to be answered by the general processes of intelligence. There is a sense in which this contention may be maintained, for the task of intelligence may be regarded as merely to find methods of realizing the values which are presented to it from some external source. This view, while perhaps justified from the point of view of a narrow methodology, certainly overlooks features in the total situations in which values present themselves. For values are not static, but are subject to evolution and to education. The value which we ascribe to a course of action depends on the consequences of the action, and a more vivid realization of the consequences may lead to an alteration in the value ascribed to it. But a vivid appraisal of consequences demands intelligence. Rather than admit impotence in the field of values, it seems to me that just here is one of the most important arenas for the exercise of intelligence, in purging and educating our values.

It will perhaps be not too difficult for anyone to yield formal assent to the justifiability of much of what I have been saying. It will not, however, be easy for him to have a living quickening sense of all that is involved, of the shortness of the path that the human race has trod already, of the magnitude of the reformations necessary, and of the enormous potentialities in the future. Practically all conventional human thinking which deals with abstractions is cluttered with the debris from the past of absolutes and realities and essences. These abstractions are ingrained in all conventional thinking about human institutions, and all must be revised. It seems to me that no scheme of education is adequate to our modern needs which does not instill as its most important ingredient a realization of this situation. I for one am not willing to admit that a man has been liberally educated for a free society who has not learned to view instinctively the doings of men against the background of the potentialities of the future rather than of the incoherencies of the past.

REFLECTIONS OF A PHYSICIST

Note 1

The article "Some General Principles of Operational Analysis" was one of the articles in a "Symposium on Operationism" conducted under the auspices of the Psychological Review and published in the September 1945 issue. The contributors to the symposium were Professors E. G. Boring, P. W. Bridgman, Herbert Feigl, Harold Israel, Carroll C. Pratt and B. F. Skinner. The symposium was initiated at the suggestion of E. G. Boring, who submitted a list of eleven questions to guide the discussion. Each contributor first prepared a discussion of the questions; these were circulated among the other contributors, who then prepared such further comment or rebuttal as he desired, which was published as Rejoinders and Second Thoughts.

A brief summary of the questions follows:
1. What is the purpose of operational definitions?
2. If a construct is defined by two independent operations should it be said that there are really two constructs?
3. Are hypothetical operations at present physically impossible of scientific use?
4. Is *experience* a proper subject for operational definition?
5. Are there scientifically good and bad operations?
6. Is operationism more than a renewed and refined emphasis upon the experimental method?
7. Must operationists in psychology relegate theorizing of all sorts to the limbo of metaphysics?
8. Is it adequate to say "Intelligence is what the intelligence test tests?"
9. Are *all* scientifically legitimate definitions operational in character?
10. What is a definition, operational or otherwise?
11. What class or classes of operations may be properly used in definitions?

ACKNOWLEDGMENT

is gratefully made to the publishers and editors of the following journals for their kind cooperation in permitting the republication of the indicated material. *Operational Analysis; Science: Public or Private?* is published through the courtesy of PHILOSOPHY OF SCIENCE (Vols. 5 & 7); *Freedom and the Individual* is from: FREEDOM: ITS MEANING, edited by Ruth Nanda Anshen, 1940, and is published by courtesy of the publishers, Harcourt Brace and Company, Inc.; *Some General Principles of Operational Analysis* is published through courtesy of the PSYCHOLOGICAL REVIEW; *The New Vision of Science; The Struggle for Intellectual Integrity* through the courtesy of HARPER'S MAGAZINE; *Permanent Elements in the Flux of Present-day Physics; The Recent Change of Attitude Toward the Law of Cause and Effect; Science and its Changing Social Environment; Manifesto by a Physicist* through the courtesy of SCIENCE; *The Time Scale: The Concept of Time; On the Nature and Limitations of Cosmical Inquiries; Scientists and Social Responsibility* through the courtesy of SCIENTIFIC MONTHLY; *Society and the Intelligent Physicist* through the courtesy of the AMERICAN

ACKNOWLEDGMENT

Physics Teacher; *A Challenge to Physicists* through the courtesy of the Journal of Applied Physics; *The Prospect for Intelligence* through the courtesy of the Yale Review; *Statistical Mechanics and the Second Law of Thermodynamics* through the courtesy of the Bulletin of the American Mathematical Society; *New Vistas for Intelligence* is from Physical Science and Human Values, published 1947 by Princeton University Press; *Science and Freedom* through the courtesy of Isis, quarterly journal of the History of Science Society, copyright by the History of Science Society. *On "Scientific Method"* is published through the courtesy of The Teaching Scientist; *Some Implications of Recent Points of View in Physics* through the courtesy of Revue Internationale de Philosophie; *The Operational Aspect of Meaning* through the courtesy of Synthese; *Science and Common Sense* and *Remarks on the Present State of Operationalism* through the courtesy of Scientific Monthly; *Einstein's Theories and the Operational Point of View* is from Volume VII of the Library of Living Philosophers, "Albert Einstein: Philosopher-Scientist" and is published through the courtesy of the Library of Living Philosophers; *Impertinent Reflections on History of Science* through the courtesy of the History of Science Society and Philosophy of Science; *Science, Materialism and the Human Spirit* through the courtesy of the Massachusetts Institute of Technology and the Wiley Bul-

ACKNOWLEDGMENT

LETIN; *The Discovery of Science* through courtesy of the HARVARD ALUMNI BULLETIN; and *The Task Before Us* through the courtesy of the American Academy of Arts and Sciences.

INDEX

Adams, 361, 370
Ames, 147, 151, 484
Bentley, 127
Berkeley, 185
Bernal, 404
Birge, 205
Birkhoff, 161
Bohr, 143, 191, 270
Boltzmann, 307
Boyle, 349
Bragg, 378
Brown, 297
Cantor, 101-03
Cantril, 147, 484
Clausius, 236
Compton, 173-75
Conant, 441, 444
Cortez, 339
Davisson, 177
Dewey, 60-61, 127
Dirac, 191, 270
Doppler, 283, 300
Dunsany, 228
Eddington, 237, 246-54, 278, 289, 307, 326
Edison, 167

Einstein, 84-85, 91, 93, 98, 111-12, 126, 127, 135ff., 143, 176, 195, 254, 269-70, 278, 290, 298-99, 307-37, 376, 460, 486, 489, 560
Euclid, 124, 202, 346, 352
Feigl, 131
Frank, 157
Freud, 482
Galileo, 473, 535, 536
Gandhi, 375
Germer, 177
Gibbs, 236
Gödel, 146-47, 480-81
Harris, 361-64
Heisenberg, 175-77, 179, 183, 191, 195-96, 198-200, 220-23, 226, 270, 274, 297-98, 303, 340, 357, 454, 477, 479
Hempel, 165
Hilbert, 481
Hitler, 375, 398, 402, 502, 529
Jakobson, 119
James, 259n
Jeans, 105, 278

INDEX

Jefferson, 473
Jordan, 191
Kant, 143
Kelvin, 236, 349
Kretschmann, 324
Lameere, 84
Land, 476
Langer, 149
Laplace, 340
Lemaître, 278, 285, 300
Lewis, C. I., 84
Lewis, G. N., 237, 246, 251-52
Lewis, John L., 518
Lindsay, 1, 15, 165-66
Mach, 333
Marx, 421, 515, 521
Milne, 278
Montezuma, 339-40
Mussolini, 375
Newton, 93, 133, 150, 168-69, 173, 187, 310, 473, 532, 535-37
Northrop, 473-74, 491, 497
Northrup, viii

O'Rahilly, 355
Planck, 220
Plato, 100-02, 157, 346
Plaskett, 308n
Poincaré, 195-96, 262, 274
Pratt, 32
Rabi, 512
Roosevelt, 518
Russell, 100, 255, 474, 489
Sarton, 431
Schilpp, 112
Schrödinger, 191
Sellars, 131
Shapley, 161
Skinner, 38
Socrates, 480, 482
Tarski, 54, 131-32
Tolman, 278, 306-07
Watson, 245
Weyl, 191
Wiener, 144
Zeno, 101
Zipf, 120